# PERGAMON INTERNATIONAL LIBRARY
## of Science, Technology, Engineering and Social Studies

*The 1000-volume original paperback library in aid of education,
industrial training and the enjoyment of leisure*

Publisher: Robert Maxwell, M.C.

*CLASSROOM MANAGEMENT*
*The Successful Use of Behavior Modification*

2nd Edition

(PGPS-27)

———— Publisher's Notice to Educators ————

### THE PERGAMON TEXTBOOK
### INSPECTION COPY SERVICE

An inspection copy of any book published in the Pergamon
International Library will gladly be sent without obligation for
consideration for course adoption or recommendation. Copies may
be retained for a period of 60 days from receipt and returned if not
suitable. When a particular title is adopted or recommended for
adoption for class use and the recommendation results in a sale of
12 or more copies, the inspection copy may be retained with our
compliments. If after examination the lecturer decides that the
book is not suitable for adoption but would like to retain it for his
personal library, then our Educators' Discount of 10% is allowed on
the invoiced price. The Publishers will be pleased to receive
suggestions for revised editions and new titles to be published in this
important International Library.

# PERGAMON GENERAL PSYCHOLOGY SERIES

*Editor:* Arnold P. Goldstein, *Syracuse University*
Leonard Krasner, *SUNY, Stony Brook*

---

## TITLES IN THE PERGAMON GENERAL PSYCHOLOGY SERIES
### (Added Titles in Back of Volume)

The terms of our inspection copy service apply to all the above books. A complete catalogue of all books in the Pergamon International Library is available on request.

The Publisher will be pleased to receive suggestions for revised editions and new titles.

# CLASSROOM MANAGEMENT
## The Successful Use of Behavior Modification

2nd Edition

K. Daniel O'Leary and Susan G. O'Leary
*State University of New York*
*Stony Brook, New York*

PERGAMON PRESS INC.
New York/Toronto/Oxford/Sydney/Frankfurt/Paris

*Pergamon Press Offices:*

U.S.A.              Pergamon Press Inc., Maxwell House, Fairview Park,
                    Elmsford, New York 10523, U.S.A.

U.K.                Pergamon Press Ltd., Headington Hill Hall, Oxford OX3,
                    OBW, England

CANADA              Pergamon of Canada, Ltd., 207 Queen's Quay West,
                    Toronto 1, Canada

AUSTRALIA           Pergamon Press (Aust) Pty. Ltd., 19a Boundary Street,
                    Rushcutters Bay, N.S.W. 2011, Australia

FRANCE              Pergamon Press SARL, 24 rue des Ecoles,
                    75240 Paris, Cedex 05, France

WEST GERMANY        Pergamon Press GmbH, 6242 Kronberg/Taunus,
                    Frankfurt-am-Main, West Germany

**Library of Congress Cataloging in Publication Data**

O'Leary, K      Daniel              comp.
    Classroom management.

(Pergamon general psychology series ; 27)
Includes bibliographies.
    1. Classroom management--Addresses, essays,
lectures. I. O'Leary, Susan G.  II. Title.
LB3011.04   1976      371.1'02      76-41004
ISBN 0-08-021396-0
ISBN 0-08-021395-2 pbk.
            —

Printed in the United States of America

To our parents,
    William and Ramona Gilbert
    Keith and Alma O'Leary
and our children,
    Michael and Kathryn.

# Contents

# Contributors

Teodoro Ayllon, Ph.D.
Department of Psychology
Georgia State University
Atlanta, Georgia 30303

Jon S. Bailey, Ph.D.
Department of Psychology
Florida State University
Tallahassee, Florida 32306

Wesley C. Becker, Ph.D.
Department of Special Education
University of Oregon
Eugene, Oregon 97405

Ronald G. Bittle, Ph.D.
Behavior Research Laboratory
Anna State Hospital
Anna, Illinois 62906

Philip H. Bornstein, Ph.D.
Department of Psychology
University of Montana
Missoula, Montana 59801

David R. Brown, Ph.D.
Flowing Wells Public School System
Tucson, Arizona 85712

Sandra Burke
Department of Psychology
Georgia State University
Atlanta, Georgia 30303

Jeane Crowder, Ph.D.
Juniper Gardens Children's Project
University of Kansas
Lawrence, Kansas 66045

Michelle Dolnick
216-42 68th Avenue
Bayside, New York 11364

Ronald S. Drabman, Ph.D.
Department of Psychiatry and Human
  Behavior
University of Mississippi Medical
  Center
Jackson, Mississippi 39216

Paul S. Graubard, Ed. D.
P. O. Box 634
Lenox, Massachusetts 01240

Ronald W. Henderson, Ph.D.
Department of Educational Psychology
University of Arizona
Tucson, Arizona 85721

Marsha Ironsmith
Department of Psychology
State University of New York
Stony Brook, New York 11794

Brian A. Iwata, Ph.D.
Department of Psychology
Western Michigan University
Kalamazoo, Michigan 49008

Fredric H. Jones, Ph.D.
Department of Psychiatry
University of Rochester School
   of Medicine and Dentistry
Rochester, New York 14642

Ruth E. Kass
Institute for the Development of
   Human Resources
Random House, Inc.
New York, New York

Kenneth F. Kaufman, Ph.D.
Behavior Management Unit
Sagamore Children's Center
Melville, New York 11746

Frank D. Kirby, Ph.D.
Coswell Center
Kinston, North Carolina 28501

Patricia J. Krantz, Ph.D.
Princeton Child Development
   Institute
Princeton, New Jersey 08540

B.B. Lahey, Ph.D.
Department of Psychology
University of Georgia
Athens, Georgia 30601

Dale Layman, Ph.D.
Department of Special Education
University of Illinois
   Chicago Circle
Chicago, Illinois 60680

James D. Long, Ph.D.
Department of Psychology
Appalachian State University
Boone, North Carolina 28607

Charles H. Madsen, Ph.D.
Department of Psychology
Florida State University
Tallahassee, Florida 32306

Margaret C. McNees
Nashville, Tennessee   37200

M. Patrick McNees, Ph.D.
Luton Community Mental
   Health Center
Nashville, Tennessee 37200

M.B. Miller, Ph.D.
Department of Special Education
Ferkauf Graduate School
Yeshiva University
New York, New York 10003

Wm. H. Miller, Ph.D.
Department of Psychiatry
UCLA
Los Angeles, California 90007

Rudolf H. Moos, Ph.D.
Stanford University School of
   Medicine
Stanford, California 94305

Betty Morris
C.P.I.C. School
Birmingham Board of Education
Birmingham, Alabama 35202

Robert D. O'Connor, Ph.D.
Center for Studies of Social
   Behavior
Oklahoma City, Oklahoma 73112

K. Daniel O'Leary, Ph.D.
Department of Psychology
State University of New York
Stony Brook, New York 11794

William E. Pelham, Ph.D.
Department of Psychology
Washington State University
Pullman, Washington  99163

Gloria H. Price, Ph.D.
Division of Psychology
Department of Texas Health
   Science Center
Dallas, Texas 75235

Randal P. Quevillon
Department of Psychology
University of Montana
Missoula, Montana 59801

Daniel Reschly, Ph.D.
Psychology Department
Iowa State University
Ames, Iowa 50011

Todd R. Risley, Ph.D.
Department of Human Development
University of Kansas
Lawrence, Kansas 66045

Arthur Robin, Ph.D.
Department of Psychology
University of Maryland at
   Baltimore County
Baltimore, Maryland 21200

Alan Rosenbaum
Department of Psychology
State University of New York
Stony Brook, New York 11794

Harry Rosenberg, Ph.D.
Department of Special Education
Visalia Schools
Visalia, California 93277

Marlene Schneider
Point of Woods Laboratory School
Department of Psychology
Stony Brook, New York 11794

Frank Shields
Department of Psychology
Humboldt State College
Arcata, California 95521

Robert W. Solomon
Department of Psychology
The University of Tennessee
Knoxville, Tennessee 37916

Rosemary A. Swanson
Department of Educational
   Psychology
University of Arizona
Tucson, Arizona 85721

Don R. Thomas, Ph.D.
Minnesota Learning Center
Brainerd, Minnesota 56401

Edison J. Trickett, Ph.D.
Department of Psychology
Yale University
New Haven, Conneticut 06510

Hillary Turkewitz
Department of Psychology
State University of New York
Stony Brook, New York 11794

Robert G. Wahler, Ph.D.
Department of Psychology
The University of Tennessee
Knoxville, Tennessee 37916

Howard Wasserman, Ph.D.
Egg Harbor Township School
   District
Egg Harbor City, New Jersey 08215

Robert L. Williams, Ph.D.
Department of Educational
   Psychology
University of Tennessee
Knoxville, Tennessee 37916

Jerry W. Willis, Ph.D.
Department of Psychology
University of Western Ontario
Ontario, Canada

Barry J. Zimmerman, Ph.D.
Department of Psychology
City University of New York
New York, New York

# *Preface*

Behavior modification is a term now heard in almost all schools and clinics. In the past year, articles about behavior modification have appeared in the major educational journal, *Today's Education,* the major psychiatric journal, *Archives of General Psychiatry,* and the major psychological journal, *The American Psychologist.* In brief, behavior modification is essentially a "household word" among professionals who deal with children's problems. Like most household words, it triggers many different attitudes and feelings that range from complete rejection of behavior modification as an educational change method to total embracement of behavior modification as an intervention model. It is the purpose of this book to enable teachers to evaluate the utility of a behavior modification approach, both as a model for understanding behavior change and as a set of procedures for altering classroom behavior. Although many teachers, psychologists, and psychiatrists may be reluctant to accept totally all of the basic assumptions of behavior modification, it is hoped that many of the procedures can be utilized by people irrespective of their basic views of the teaching process. This book presents both principles and data which we feel provide some clear solutions to the problems which teachers face daily.

The purposes of this book are to:

1. Supply the reader with a set of principles about changing behavior and to place those principles within the historical context of the development of treatment of children.

2. Present research evidence documenting the efficacy of such procedures in the classroom.
3. Discuss how teachers can implement such procedures for both preventing problems and for dealing with existing problems.

A criterion for selection of all articles was that they involve implementation of behavior modification procedures in classroom or small group settings (e.g., a tutorial session). It is hoped that the articles chosen will have immediate relevance for the day-to-day classroom teaching of academic and social skills.

This volume is intended for undergraduate students in education and psychology, for teachers who are currently in the field, and for clinical, educational, and school psychologists who consult with teachers about educational problems. The book contains explanations of basic terminology; it introduces the reader to the field of behavior modification with children in some detail; comments are made about each article in the book, and the concluding chapter discusses the implementation of the procedures illustrated throughout the book. Consequently, the book could stand alone as an advanced undergraduate text. It might also be used, however, with basic experimental texts utilizing an operant learning framework since it well exemplifies many of the operant principles. Because of the emphasis on application of behavioral principles, we hope young teachers will find that this book serves as a guide for developing their repertoire of classroom skills. As importantly, we hope that the evidence and conceptual framework presented will be strong enough to change the behavior of the teachers and psychologists who have already been trained by mentors who had a different conception from the one here presented.

References used either in the first chapter, the commentaries, or the last chapter appear in the Reference section at the end of the book. References for each article reprinted in the book appear directly at the end of each article.

Our most heartfelt thanks goes to Mrs. Ruth Shepard, our administrative assistant, who edited, reedited, and typed all sections of this book and who discussed all reprinted articles with us. Drs. Kenneth Kaufman and Carol Whitehurst provided us with helpful evaluation based on their use of the first edition of *Classroom Management* which aided in this revision. Sharon Foster read many of the articles and provided very valuable feedback on associated commentaries. Rolf Haugan of Pergamon Press was a friendly, encouraging editor who always kept us abreast of evaluations and reactions to the original *Classroom Management.* The authors are indebted to a continuing association with the Middle Country School District in Centereach, N.Y., and the Three Village School District of Stony Brook, N.Y., for their cooperation in many joint efforts that served as the basis for a number of the observations made herein. Finally, we wish to thank the authors of the studies included in this book for their permission to reprint their work.

# 1
## Behavior Modification with Children

### WHAT IS "GOOD" AND DESIRED BEHAVIOR

Classroom behaviors that are labeled "good" in one culture may be labeled "bad" in another. Further, within a culture, teachers in one century may have called some behaviors, such as whispering to a neighbor, "bad," whereas teachers in another century may have encouraged such task-related whispering. In the 1880s, children in New York City schools were punished for staring at visitors who came into the room, for having dirty hands, and for moving after the bell rang for silence (Ravitch, 1974). Presently, in many New York schools, movement within and between classrooms is encouraged. Even within a school today, the same behavior may be viewed as desirable by one teacher and undesirable by another (Silberman, 1970).

Ullmann and Krasner (1975) argues that the labels such as "sick," "crazy," and "abnormal" are social evaluations. They noted that even a physiological anomaly such as an epileptic trance is called abnormal by some but an indication of special knowledge by others. Swearing, hitting others, destruction of property, and very extreme withdrawal are viewed as "bad" by most teachers. Beyond these obvious extremes of aggression and withdrawal, however, there may be no behaviors that are universally labeled "bad." The classroom behaviors deemed "good" and desirable are probably even more difficult to define. With the exception of some agreement regarding

1

achievement in the three Rs, educators in different decades in the 20th century have given markedly different emphases to emotional development, vocational and preprofessional training, and mental skill training in the classics such as Latin and Greek. Given that there are no absolute standards for normal and abnormal behavior or appropriate and inappropriate classroom behavior, let us itemize some of the conditions under which a teacher will label certain classroom behaviors "good."

1.  The behavior requires minimal effort for the teacher, e.g., the student works very well independently.
2.  The behavior is viewed positively by the school staff, e.g., the student is especially creative as exemplified by a special art project or painting that could be hung in the hall.
3.  The behavior is viewed positively by most people in the community, e.g., in some communities, having children busily working in the halls and having children moving freely from one classroom to another is seen as very desirable, while in other communities having children hard at work in rows of desks is responded to positively.
4.  The behavior is seen as a necessary step in achieving a predetermined academic goal as defined by state educational standards, e.g., progress in multiplication is seen as a necessary step in achieving the goal of long division.
5.  The behavior makes the classroom atmosphere positive, e.g., students interact well with one another at appropriate times.

Perhaps because the issue of which behaviors are "good" is so complicated, teachers tend to focus on undesirable behaviors. The present authors have found that when teachers are asked to identify classroom behaviors they wish to change, approximately 80% of the teachers choose a "bad" behavior to decrease in frequency. This tendency to focus on "getting rid of the worm in the apple" is not immutable, but it has a long history.

## THE DEVELOPMENT OF TREATMENT PROCEDURES FOR CHILDREN

### Historical Introduction

Children have always had behavioral or emotional problems, but until the early part of the 20th century their problems were not considered worthy of any special attention. According to Despert (1965), the term "emotional disturbances" was not applied specifically to children until Sullivan used it in 1932. Despert noted that children with problem behaviors which are now called neurotic or psychotic were "variously labeled through the ages as possessed, wicked, guilty, insubordinate, incorrigible, unstable, maladjusted and problem children, roughly in that order" (p. 38). As one can see from such labels, there has been a fortunate change in attitude toward children's problems. However, this change in attitude has come slowly.

In the third century B.C., newborn children were examined by a council of elders to see if they were fit to live in the military state of Sparta. If they were too weak, they were left in the woods to die. This practice of abandoning physically unfit children or children with behavioral problems declined across the ages, but other forms of infanticide or infant killing continued as a widespread practice even in the 17th and 18th centuries. In ancient Rome, children were treated as little more than animals. According to Roman Law as outlined in the Twelve Tables, children could be sold; the law specified that the buyer could make extensive use of physical and intellectual potentials of the child. Imprisonment of children with behavior problems was frequent in London in the 1800s, and child employment was extensively abused in the United States until the child labor laws were passed in 1916. Even in 1975, more children died from child abuse than from any of the most heralded childhood diseases such as polio, smallpox, and diphtheria. In fact, nationwide child abuse has caused more fatalities per year among children than auto accidents, leukemia, cystic fibrosis, and muscular dystrophy combined (Early, 1974). Abused children are not victims of a single brutal day of beatings; they are usually abused day after day because they don't eat properly, because they talk back, and because they frustrate parents in numerous ways. In brief, it is unfortunate that the current most frequent killer of children is a condition which gradually develops and which usually can be prevented. Despite this present unfortunate state of affairs regarding child abuse, let us examine the gradual development of positive conceptions and attitudes regarding the treatment of children's psychological and educational problems.

Some landmarks in the history of thought regarding the treatment of children's psychological problems are found in the works of Freud, Healy, Kanner, Meyer, and Witmer. Though G. Stanley Hall is regarded as the pioneer in child psychology because of his historic work on the "content of children's minds" in 1883, psychological treatment of children did not begin until the turn of the century, and child psychiatry did not begin until the 1930s. In sum, prior to the late 19th century there was little compassion for children's problems, and as we shall see, treatment for children was not generally available until the 1930s.

The first psychological clinic in the United States was established by Leightner Witmer at the University of Pennsylvania in 1896. Witmer's clinic treated children who had learning difficulties and what were then referred to as "moral defects" (Reisman, 1966). Once a diagnosis was made, treatment consisted of retraining to alleviate the particular defect. Witmer was pragmatic in his outlook, and his assessments involved both a physical and a mental examination which included anthropometric measures, eye tests, and measures of reaction time. In his opinion, many social and academic difficulties were a function of undetected physical problems such as hearing loss and poor vision. Witmer pioneered the practices of collaborating with other disciplines such as social work, neurology, and education, but the teacher was always central in his collaborative efforts. His feeling that the teacher should be aware of many facets of the child's life is reflected in the following statement (Witmer, 1911):

> There is a body of knowledge dealing with the out-of-school life of the child, with the child's father and mother, the food that he eats, the room in which he sleeps, his play, his life on the street, which is no less important to the teacher than a knowledge of special methods of instruction. (p. 270)

Using a very different but equally influential approach to treatment, Sigmund Freud applied psychoanalytic techniques to a child's problem in the frequently cited case of Little Hans in 1909. A Viennese physician who was a follower of Freud kept detailed anecdotal records concerning his 4-year-old child's fear of going out of doors. The child purportedly was afraid to go outdoors because he feared that he would be bitten by horses. The child's father took Hans to see Freud once, and the remainder of the therapy or analysis was executed by the father who corresponded with Freud and who later interpreted the fear to the child. In brief, the child's fear was interpreted by Freud as a fear of his father. The child was particularly bothered by horses that "wore things in front of their eyes and had black things around their mouths." Freud felt that the description of the horses resembled the child's father because his father wore glasses (the things in front of the horses' eyes) and his father had a mustache (the black things around his mouth). Through a series of discussions with the child, the father tried to give the child "insight" so that the child would see that his fear was really of the father and not of the horses. Freud was convinced that the treatment was successful when he was unexpectedly visited by a tall, sturdy, 14-year-old lad who presented himself with the words: "Ich bin der Klein Hans" (I am Little Hans). The case of Little Hans is significant since it is the first published account of a child analysis and since it was the first opportunity Freud had to verify his theories of infantile sexuality (Jones, 1955).[1]

During the period of the establishment of the Witmer clinic and the first child analyses made by Freud, another significant pioneering effort was begun with a psychiatric study of childhood disturbances at the Healy School in Chicago. In the early 1900s, delinquent behavior was assumed to be almost solely due to organic deficiencies, e.g., "bad heredity, enlarged tonsils, inflamed adenoids, uncorrected refractive errors, impacted teeth, cigarette smoking, intracranial pressure, systematic absorption of toxins from focal infections, phimosis (need for circumcision), and feeblemindedness" (Reisman, 1966). Fortunately, some people were disturbed by the fact that courts imposed penalties based solely on a physical exam, and they prompted an investigation into the causes of delinquency. William Healy established the Juvenile Psychopathic Institute in 1909. This institute was particularly significant because its researchers placed a much needed emphasis on environmental factors related to delinquency, such as neighborhoods, peers, school milieu, and general living conditions. Unlike the present behavior modification conceptualization of delinquency, however, Healy and his associates placed strong emphasis on unconscious motivation as a critical factor in delinquency.

In 1912, the Boston Psychopathic Hospital was the first mental hospital in the United States to establish an outpatient clinic which accepted children as patients. A year later the Phipps Psychiatric Clinic in Baltimore was opened under the direction of Adolph Meyer, and this clinic also accepted children as outpatients. Psychological clinics and clinical psychology courses at universities began to emerge rapidly during the first and second decade of the 20th century—with Clark, Iowa, Minnesota, and Washington being among the first to

---

[1]Wolpe and Rachman (1960) presented a detailed critique of this classic case which seriously questioned whether the case verified any of Freud's theories.

follow Pennsylvania's lead. Interestingly, these clinics generally operated on the assumption that they were dealing with people who had *learning problems*—not people who were physically sick or mentally ill. For example, Meyer (whose views served as the basis for the practices of many of the first child guidance clinics) felt that "mental" disorders were generally maladjustments of personality and behavior rather than diseases of the nervous system. As Meyer (1908) noted, "The concrete conduct and behavior is the main thing deranged in our patients . . . the mental facts we speak of are not mere thoughts but actual attitudes, affects, volitions and activities and possible disorders of discrimination." Meyer, like many psychologists today, felt that parents had to be involved in child treatment, and he proposed a rather straightforward approach to such treatment. He saw psychotherapy as the "regulation of action," and like current behavior modifiers, he felt that changing overt behavior was the backbone of treatment programs for children.

By the early 1920s there were a number of psychoeducational approaches to child treatment. Such approaches did not offer very comprehensive treatment or explanatory systems, and consequently, no single psychoeducational treatment approach was adopted by the majority of psychologists or psychiatrists. Psychoanalysis, on the other hand, offered a comprehensive explanatory system for both normal and abnormal behavior and was adopted by the majority of practitioners. It explained behaviors such as dreams and slips of the tongue which previously were a mystery to most people. In addition, psychoanalysis had the blessings of G. Stanley Hall, one of the most prestigious psychologists of the early 1900s, who invited Freud to attend the 20th anniversary of Clark University in 1909 (Jones, 1955). Despite many early schisms among followers of Freud concerning the ubiquitousness of sexual aspects of the problems and neuroses of clients, psychoanalysis began to pervade the conceptualizations of both normal personality development and clinical treatment. This psychoanalytic domination of the mental health field continued, and even at present, the preponderance of psychiatrists and psychologists regard the psychoanalytic notions or derivations thereof as their basis for treatment.

*Psychoanalytic Psychotherapy with Children*

In order to appreciate the intellectual climate in which behavior modification developed, let us now turn to discussion of the psychoanalytic or disease model approach to the treatment of children. The psychoanalytic approach to child treatment, sometimes referred to as the disease model, has the following assumptions:

1. Problem behaviors are symptoms of an underlying cause.
2. Therapy should consist primarily of allowing the child to express his emotions.
3. A good relationship is a prime requisite for successful therapy, and the relationship between the therapist and the child is seen as the critical element in bringing about change in the child's behavior.

As Helen Witmer (1946) noted:

> child guidance clinics have as patients children who display a wide variety of behavior and personality disorders. The *symptoms*[2] that cause the parents concern are of many types: aggressive, uncontrollable behavior; nervousness, sensitivity, fears, excessive shyness, and other difficulties in relating to people; various kinds of school maladjustment; physical disorders without discoverable organic bases; delinquencies of various kinds; marked peculiarities of behavior and personality. ... It is a fundamental tenet of dynamic psychiatry that these maladjustments in behavior and personality are but symptoms of some underlying disturbance ... [which] 'give no more specific information about the individual than would the terms fever or cough  if they were similarly applied. ...' 'psychic life is governed by psychic laws and follows its own course and rules,' and it is psychic life which must be studied if one is to discover what the behavior symptoms represent. Accordingly, in order to show to what kinds of problems child guidance is addressed, it is necessary to use a classification that is based on the nature of the disorder rather than on its symptoms.* (pp. 16-17)

Ullmann and Krasner (1969) described the disease model of treatment as one in which "the individual's behavior is considered peculiar, abnormal, or diseased because of some underlying cause, usually physical in nature." As germs produce symptoms, people's inner problems produce abnormal behavior, and in order to alleviate or change the abnormal behavior one must find its cause. With adults, the search for such causes proceeds by having the client talk, free associate, and describe his dreams. However, since communica-

---

[2] Italics ours.

*Reprinted with permission of the Commonwealth Fund and Harvard University Press, from Helen Witmer (Ed.), *Psychiatric interviews with children.* Harvard University Press, Cambridge, Mass., 1946.

tion with children is difficult through the normal verbal means employed by therapists who are treating adults, expression of problems is thought to be encouraged by allowing a child to play with dolls and toys in the therapist's office. The therapist usually takes a warm, passive, or permissive role after establishing the setting with materials that are appropriate to the child's problem.

As Bakwin and Bakwin (1967) noted, "cars, soldiers, and electrical equipment could be useful for children preoccupied with problems of aggression or sexual excitement whereas a toy baby carriage, baby dolls, and the like, could be used with problems relating to the birth of a sibling or sibling rivalry." It is assumed that children will dramatize their own problems by their placement of the toys in the room and by their activity with them. It is also assumed that a child will release his emotions through catharsis or expression of feelings, and "as the bad feelings go out, the good feelings will sprout." The words and actions of the child during the play are "considered equivalent to the chain of free association" (A. Freud, 1964) which can later be interpreted by the therapist. Such interpretation may involve certain feelings that the child has toward the therapist or toward his parents. Presumably through expression of feeling, there is a dissolution of some of the restraints or bottled-up feelings which the child has. Psychoanalysis of children's problems also proceeds in an educative sense by "exercising outward influence by modifying the relations with those who are bringing up the child, creating new impressions, and revising the demands made upon the child by the outside world" (A. Freud, 1964).

The importance of the conceptualization of disorders and its ramifications for treatment is reflected in the following statements of Helen Witmer (1946) regarding the significance of the therapeutic relationship in child psychotherapy:

> Dynamic psychiatry regards disorders of personality as disorders of personal relations; that is, as evidence of the difficulty the individual encountered in maintaining a feeling of security with the human beings who are emotionally important to him. It is highly logical, then, that chief reliance for therapy should be placed on the development of a satisfactory relationship between psychiatrist and patient and that numerous ways should be devised to use that relationship for therapeutic ends. (p. 34)

Unfortunately, the relationship between the therapist and the child has been so stressed that traditional therapists rarely make contacts with or visit the child's school (Berkowitz, 1968).

The conclusions generally made from evaluative research concerning the effectiveness of traditional psychotherapy offer little hope for teachers or parents. Levitt (1957, 1963) has been unable to detect any significant influence of psychotherapy with children. Levitt (1957) reviewed articles involving the results of psychotherapy between 1929 and 1955. Almost 8,000 child patients were included in the survey. Comparing treated children with defectors (i.e., those who had been accepted for treatment but who never began treatment), Levitt found that both treated and non-treated children improved at approximately equal rates. While such research may have some shortcomings (Subotnik, 1972), the continued failure to find any consistent improvement or more than a small improvement in children resulting from traditional psychotherapy should alert one to alternative methods of dealing with human problems. The treatment being evaluated by Levitt (1957) was largely psychodynamic psychotherapy. As mentioned earlier, in such therapy the relationship between the therapist and the child is crucial. That is, the therapist is advised to establish a warm relationship with a child in order that the child can regain a sense of his own worth. In addition, there is often an emphasis on the release of emotion in the therapy session which is usually held in the therapist's office or in an adjoining playroom. The release of emotions through catharsis or expression of feelings is seen as a method of draining off bad emotional feelings. In almost all psychoanalytically oriented child therapy, an attempt is made to give the child some insight into his problem by interpreting events, feelings, or the fantasy life of the child. Such interpretation might involve discussing with the child certain feelings he has toward the therapist or his parents.

The Levitt research is one of the few attempts to critically evaluate the effects of psychotherapy with children, and despite his failure to find any evidence for the effectiveness of psychotherapy, he was quick to warn that his research does not prove that psychotherapy with children is futile. Large-scale evaluations like Levitt's are plagued with partial answers. However, considering the thousands of children involved in the Levitt studies, the large number of clinics and therapists, and the wide variety of children's problems, Levitt's failure to find any evidence that psychotherapy is effective should make our search for alternative treatment methods more urgent.

Partly associated with the psychoanalytic tradition was the development of various personality assessment batteries. These batteries consist of projective tests such as the Rorschach or Thematic Apperception Test (TAT). The Rorschach and the TAT consist of ambiguous ink blots and semi-ambiguous scenes. The child is instructed to tell a story about what he sees in the pictures. It is assumed that the child will *project* his personality in such a test since the vagueness of the ink blots or scenes will necessitate some elaboration which is presumably a function of one's personality. Evaluative research suggests that such tests are practically a waste of time for planning a treatment program for an individual (O'Leary, 1972). Although there are some projective tests which do differentiate "normal" children from children with many behavioral problems, they are often not sensitive enough to differentiate "normal" children from those children usually referred to child clinics, and even if they did, one could probably make such distinctions more rapidly without such tests.

In sum, while many teachers may feel that referral to a psychologist for personality testing may be valuable, the tests themselves appear to contribute very little, if anything, in formulating a treatment plan for a child. On the other hand, there are a number of checklists which differentiate an average child from one with behavioral problems and which focus on classroom behaviors. The checklists alert one to particular problems which might have been missed in an interview with a teacher. Such checklists will be discussed in the last chapter of this book.

### Behavior Modification with Children

In 1913, John B. Watson made a sharp break with the psychological and psychoanalytic conceptions of his time when he published a treatise, *Psychology as a behaviorist views it.* Reacting to what he felt was a psychology of little practical significance, Watson argued that the concept of consciousness and the method of introspection should be the domain of philosophers. He claimed that psychology is a purely objective experimental branch of natural science whose goal is the prediction and control of behavior.

The time seems to have come when psychology must discard all reference to consciousness; when it need no longer delude itself into thinking that it is making mental states the object of observation. We have become so enmeshed in speculative questions concerning the elements of mind, the nature of conscious content ... that I, as an experimental student feel that something is wrong with our premises and the types of problems which develop from them ... I believe we can write a psychology ... and ... never use the terms consciousness, mental states, mind, content, introspectively verifiable, imagery and the like. ... Certain stimuli lead the organisms to make the responses. In a system of psychology completely worked out, given the response the stimuli can be predicted, given the stimuli the response can be predicted.* (pp. 163-167)

Within such a framework, Watson and Rayner (1920) published a study which reported how a child could acquire fearful behavior through classical conditioning. Watson and Rayner chose a healthy, 11-month-old infant who did not display any unusual fearful behavior. When a white rat was presented to Albert, he reached for it. When he touched the rat, a loud noise was made, and Albert started to cry. After a number of soundings of the noise as Albert touched the rat, he became fearful not only of the rat but also of other furry objects. Thus, by pairing a neutral stimulus such as a white rat to which the child did not respond fearfully with a stimulus such as a loud noise which did elicit a fearful response, the neutral stimulus acquired fear-evoking properties. In short Watson and Rayner reported that they had demonstrated one method of learning a fearful response.[3]

In 1924, Jones continued work with fears but in this case with their elimination. In a now classic study, Peter, a boy who was fearful of a white rabbit, was placed in a room with the rabbit that was some distance from him. The treatment proceeded as follows:

Peter was seated in a high chair and given food which he liked. The experimenter brought the rabbit in a wire cage as close as she could without arousing a response which would interfere with the eating. Through the presence of the pleasant stimulus (food) whenever the rabbit was shown, the fear was eliminated gradually in favor of a positive response. (Jones, 1924)

*Reprinted with permission of the American Psychological Association, Inc., from J.B. Watson's "Psychology as a behaviorist views it," in *Psychological Review,* 1913, 20, 158-177. Copyright © 1913 by the American Psychological Association, Inc.

[3] English (1929) followed the Watson & Rayner (1920) paradigm and failed to replicate the establishment of a conditioned fear response in a 14-month-old child when a large metal bar was struck as a wooden duck was lowered near the child. Bregman (1934) also failed to develop a conditioned response in infants of 8-16 months, and she concluded that conditioning could not be accepted as the explanation for the changes in emotional behavior of a young infant.

Occasionally the experimenter also had children participate in the treatment to help with the "unconditioning." Such children were selected because of their fearless attitude toward the rabbit and because of their generally satisfactory adjustments. The modeling of the fearless behavior and the association of the originally feared rabbit with a pleasant stimulus, food, presumably accounted for the reduction of Peter's fear. Most importantly, Jones felt that not only had one method of the acquisition of a normal fear been demonstrated but also the deconditioning of that fear.

In 1938, Mowrer and Mowrer devised an apparatus for the treatment of enuresis (bed wetting) which they viewed as a case of simple habit deficiency. The apparatus consists of a liquid-sensitive pad which is placed on the child's bed. When the child begins to urinate, a bell rings. The bell is loud enough to wake the child and his parents, and the parent takes the child to the bathroom to urinate in the toilet. The apparatus is then reset before the child returns to bed. Mowrer and Mowrer advocate the use of the pad and bell device until the child is dry for seven consecutive nights followed by seven additional dry nights with increased fluid intake before retiring. In the original 1938 study by the Mowrers, all 30 children who were treated by this method reached the criterion of 14 consecutive dry nights within 2 months after commencement of treatment.

Despite the successes of Watson and Rayner (1920) and the Mowrers (1938), behaviorally-oriented treatment procedures had little prominence until the 1960s, probably because the popular psychoanalytic conceptualization of abnormal behavior was almost antithetical to the use of such treatment. The conditioning principles like those of Watson and Mowrer were seen as mechanistic and as oversimplified models for the procedures that most therapists felt necessary for treatment of the total individual, i.e., his attitudes, habits, thoughts, and feelings. Furthermore, most of the basic principles of conditioning had been demonstrated with animals or rats, and practitioners saw conditioning therapy as synonymous with rat therapy and thus inadequate for solving problems of human concern. A critique of psychoanalytic procedures and a reconceptualization of learning principles with implications for many human problems was made by Skinner in 1953 in his book *Science and human behavior*. This book was a major impetus for a drastic reconceptualization of procedures for changing behavior in schools, hospitals, and outpatient facilities. In discussing psychotherapy, Skinner had the following to say:

The field of psychotherapy is rich in explanatory fictions. Behavior itself has not been accepted as subject matter in its own right, but only as an indication of *something wrong somewhere else*. The task of therapy is said to be to remedy an inner illness of which the behavioral manifestations are merely "symptoms" ... the condition to be corrected is called "neurotic," and the thing to be attacked by psychotherapy is then identified as a "neurosis." The term no longer carries its original implication of a derangement of the nervous system, but it is nevertheless an unfortunate example of an explanatory fiction. It has encouraged the therapist to avoid specifying the behavior to be corrected or showing why it is disadvantageous or dangerous. By suggesting a single cause for multiple disorders it has implied a uniformity which is not to be found in the data. Above all, it has encouraged the belief that psychotherapy consists of removing inner causes of mental illness, as the surgeon removes an inflammed appendix or cancerous growth or as indigestible food is purged from the body. ... It is not an inner cause of behavior but the behavior itself which—in the medical analogy of catharsis—must be "got out of the system."

In emphasizing "neurotic" behavior itself rather than any inner condition said to explain it, it may be argued that we are committing the unforgivable sin of "treating the symptom rather than the cause." This expression is often applied to attempts to remove objectionable features of behavior without attention to causal factors—for example, "curing" stammering by a course of vocal exercises, ["curing"] faulty posture by the application of shoulder braces, or ["curing"] thumb-sucking by coating the thumb with a bitter substance. Such therapy appears to disregard the underlying disorder of which these characteristics of behavior are symptoms. ... [However], by accounting for a given example of disadvantageous behavior in terms of a personal history and by altering or supplementing that history as a form of therapy, we are considering the very variables to which the traditional theorist must ultimately turn for an explanation of his supposed inner causes.* (pp. 373-379)

While the reconceptualization of behavior change and therapy was very important, the "proof of the pudding" rests in its product— that is, does such a reconceptualization lead to significant behavior

*Reprinted with permission of the Macmillan Company, from B.F. Skinner's *Science and human behavior*. Copyright © 1953 by Macmillan, New York.

change? In 1956, Azrin and Lindsley taught cooperative behavior to children 7-12 years of age through the use of learning principles. They placed two children on either side of a table and demonstrated that cooperative behavior—defined as simultaneous placement of two metal pins in matching stimulus holes—could be developed, eliminated, and re-established without the use of specific instructions. Gewirtz and Baer (1958) investigated how depriving or satiating a child with adult attention affects adults' later reinforcing power. They found that when a child was deprived of adult attention by being left alone in an experimental room for 20 minutes, the adult's reinforcing power was greater than if the adult had interacted with the child in a friendly manner for 30 minutes. The assessment of the adult's reinforcing power was made by analyzing to what extent the adults could change the frequency with which the child dropped marbles into different holes.

In 1959, Williams reported that the tantrums of a 21-month-old child could be eliminated by ignoring or extinguishing the undesirable behavior. The child had developed tantrums after a long illness and would scream for as much as two hours when the parents left his bedroom. It was assumed that the parents had been reinforcing the tantrum behavior by attending to it (i.e., by remaining in the room when the child cried). After a medical examination which determined that there was no physical problem, the parents were told to put the child to bed in a "leisurely and relaxed" fashion, to close the door, and not to re-enter the room. The first night the child cried for 45 minutes, but by the tenth occasion the child no longer whimpered or fussed when the parents left the room. In short, the removal of the reinforcement for tantrum-like behavior led to the elimination of the tantrum behavior. The authors reported no unfortunate side-effects resulting from their treatment, and at three years of age, the child was reported to be a "friendly, expressive, outgoing child."

A number of applications of behavioral procedures which have direct relevance to classroom management were made in a nursery school at the University of Washington in the early 1960s. Regressed crawling, isolate behavior, and noncooperative behavior were significantly altered by changing the behavior of the teachers. A study illustrating the type of behavioral changes they obtained was conducted by Harris, Johnston, Kelley, and Wolf (1964). They reported that Dee, a three-and-a-half-year-old child, showed "unusually strong withdrawal behavior." More specifically, they observed a great deal of crawling around the classroom which persisted after the first week of nursery school. The usual teacher attempts (being warm and solicitous) to change Dee's behavior were unsuccessful. The teachers made a conservative estimate that Dee spent at least 75% of her time in a crawling position (when she was expected to be on her feet). The teachers were told to ignore her crawling behavior and to give her attention for standing or for approximations to standing, e.g., rising partially to her feet when she put her coat on a hook. Within a week after the change in the teacher's behavior, Dee's behavior was "indistinguishable" from that of the rest of the children, i.e., she was standing as frequently as all the other children. In order to be certain that the change in the teachers' behavior was related to the change in the child's behavior, the teachers were then asked to give attention to Dee whenever she was crawling and to withhold attention when she was standing. By the end of two days, Dee was spending nearly 82% of her time off-feet—she behaved just as she had earlier. The teachers were again told to ignore crawling and to attend to Dee when she was standing. Within several days Dee was standing as frequently as the rest of her classmates. This study, as well as many others conducted at the University of Washington preschool, clearly demonstrated the potential of the systematic application of learning principles to changing the behavior of children in a classroom.

Also in the early 1960s, Bandura and his associates conducted a series of experiments with modeling procedures. In some now classic studies, Bandura and his associates were able to demonstrate that simply having a child view a film of a child behaving aggressively was related to the subsequent aggressive behavior of the child who watched the film. More specifically, children who watched cartoons, adults, or peers behave aggressively on film displayed more aggressive behavior when subsequently placed in a playroom with a variety of toys than did children who observed non-aggressive films or no films at all (Bandura & Walters, 1963). The results of such studies cast serious doubt on the catharsis hypothesis and its application to psychotherapy and behavioral change procedures. That is, instead of decreasing aggressive behavior by a venting or drainage of aggressive feelings, viewing aggressive models appeared to increase aggressive behavior (Bandura, Ross, & Ross, 1963).

The more deviant behaviors of autistic children were also modified through the systematic application of behavioral procedures by Ferster and Lovaas. An autistic child usually displays very severe forms of social withdrawal, some gross motoric abnormalities, a parrot-like speech pattern called echolalia, eating disturbances, and an intense desire for sameness (Bakwin & Bakwin, 1967). Ferster and DeMyer (1962) conducted an analysis of the behavioral repertoires of three autistic children. They demonstrated that these autistic children could learn to obtain tokens or coins by pressing a lever in a token dispensing machine and then later to insert the tokens or coins into other machines or reinforcing devices, such as a T.V., a 35mm viewer, or a record player. In addition, Ferster and DeMyer were able to develop more complex behavioral repertoires, such as coin saving and simple discrimination learning. Most importantly, these investigators showed that the same learning principles which had proven effective in changing the behavior of animals and young normal children operated quite efficiently in changing the behavior of a child with a very unusual behavior pattern. Lovaas (1967) and his colleagues showed that by applying learning procedures for long periods of time (months or several years), the behavior of autistic children could be changed very dramatically. Self-destructive behavior could be eliminated; speech, self-help skills, and even reading, writing and arithmetic skills could be taught to these autistic children. Lovaas' work was exceptional in that he demonstrated not only that the behavior of autistic children could be changed but that the procedures could be taught to parents and university undergraduates who, in turn, could execute a continuing "treatment" program for the children.

Since the early 1960s, the application of learning principles to changing the social and academic behavior of children and adolescents has developed at an extremely rapid pace. Laboratories investigating the application of behavioral principles to children's problems now exist in almost every state. In addition to the changes in a host of classroom behaviors which will be documented later in this book, numerous other childhood problems have been cured or ameliorated with behavior therapy procedures. Enuresis or bedwetting has been repeatedly cured (Azrin, Sneed, & Foxx, 1974; Baller, 1975; Lovibond, 1964). Delinquency rates have been reduced (Alexander & Parsons, 1973; Schwitzgebel, 1964; Trotter, 1973). Children with autism and childhood schizophrenia, very serious disorders characterized by social withdrawal and speech disorders, have evidenced marked improvement when behavioral treatment programs were instituted (Lovaas, Koegel, Simmons, & Long, 1973). Retarded children have gained bowel and bladder control, have acquired proper eating and dressing habits, and have improved in their speech (Azrin & Foxx, 1971; Spradlin & Girardeau, 1966). Finally, fears of hospitals, buses, and dentists have been reduced by the application of behavioral principles (Lazarus & Rachman, 1967; Melamed & Siegel, 1975; Obler & Terwilliger, 1970).

In sum, the results of a decade or so of research have documented the effectiveness of the behavior modification approach in a wide variety of settings with very diverse child populations. As will be evidenced by the readings in this book, the behavior of children in classroom settings has been repeatedly altered by a variety of different procedures used by a number of investigators. In contrast to a host of other approaches applied to educational problems, most of the behavioral principles which appear in this book were first documented in laboratory settings, and thus there is evidence from both basic and applied research of the efficacy of such principles. Before analyzing the articles which apply such principles, however, let us look more closely at the conceptualizations which have guided the researchers and practitioners working in the behavior modification area.

## CHARACTERISTICS OF BEHAVIOR MODIFICATION WITH CHILDREN

### Focus on Observable Behavior

Behavior modification is a process in which some observable behavior is changed by the systematic application of techniques that are based on learning theory and experimental research. The rationale for insisting that the behavior selected for modification be observable is based on the assertion that the behavior modifier should be able to evaluate the effectiveness of his techniques, and that when the behavior to be modified is not observable or susceptible to evaluation in a manner such that more than one person would agree to the frequency, rate, intensity, duration, or pattern of behavior, evaluations become mush less stringent. For example, while one might wish to evaluate the "mood" or emotional state of a depressed child, it is quite difficult to teach two people to evaluate mood in exactly the same manner. On the other hand, it is relatively easy to teach observers to record the frequency with which the child talks to others, smiles, or gets out of his chair. These behaviors are often critical in helping one arrive at a conclusion about the degree of a child's depression.

The types of behaviors that have been evaluated in the behavior modification area range from precise and easily defined behaviors such as correct answers on a spelling test to broader and more conceptual categories such as information seeking (Krumboltz & Thoresen, 1964), and creative behavior (Reese & Parnes, 1970). The behaviors may be verbal (talking out of turn) or motor (out of seat behavior) or a combination of verbal and motor behavior (throwing a temper tantrum). On the other hand, the behaviors may be internal or "inside the organism" yet made observable through various recording procedures. For example, one might record heart beat, blood pressure, or galvanic skin response. This emphasis on overt behavior means that one does not concern himself with intrapsychic conflicts (e.g., conflicts between the id and superego or between sexual and appetitive desires and the conscience). Similarly, a behavior therapist does not treat the child with play therapy to increase his self-concept. Rather than treating the child with play therapy, the behavior modifier feels teaching the child new social or academic skills which will lead to more positive reactions from his environment may have the additional benefit of having the child think better of himself. That is, the child will acquire what many people term a better "self-concept" or greater "ego strength" as a consequence of learning new academic or social skills.

While it would be folly to say that no aspect of a person's behavior is controlled by unobservable factors, the behavior modifier generally assumes that a great deal of a child's behavior is controlled by observable antecedent and consequent events occurring in the external environment. That is, events which precede behaviors and events which follow behaviors are of utmost importance in determining the frequency of these behaviors. This emphasis on overt or observable factors which control a behavior implies that the behavior modifier—be he therapist, teacher, or parent—can alter antecedent and consequent events and hopefully in turn can alter the child's behavior. In contrast, a focus on intrapsychic conflicts, self-concept, and ego strength renders treatment more difficult and certainly less explicit. Since such treatment is less explicit, the procedures generally available to traditional therapists to change psychic conflicts are not easily taught, and, equally important, they are seldom—if ever—explicit enough to allow someone other than the therapist to promote any behavioral change. As will become obvious in later sections of this chapter, if the treatment procedures cannot be made explicit, therapeutic procedures will remain an art; they will remain extremely difficult to evaluate; and their implementation will be possible by only a very select group. Most importantly, if parents and teachers cannot be taught critical aspects of behavior change, it is very likely that any changes brought about by a therapist will be reduced or eliminated when contact with the therapist ends.

## Importance of Teachers and Parents as Behavior Modifiers

Techniques of behavior modification are usually most effective when they are employed by the very people who initially request that the behavior be changed and who are also the key people in the child's environment. If a problem existed in the home, the behavior modifier would work with the parent to help her change the child's behavior in the home. If problems existed both at home and at school, the behavior modifier would generally work on both fronts since, as will be emphasized later, one can change a child's behavior in one situation but have no effect in the other situation (Wahler, 1969). The parent or the teacher can exert a greater influence on the child than the psychologist himself as a psychologist might only see the child infrequently and often not in the critical situations where the problem behaviors exist. Consequently, the psychologist serves as a *consultant* to a parent or teacher concerning procedures for changing behavior, yet most frequently it is the parent or teacher himself who executes most of the behavior change procedures. Teachers and parents are the individuals who do in fact provide many of the antecedent and consequent events of the child's behavior and thus are in the most advantageous position to alter the child's behavior. The fact that the teacher implements the "treatment" or behavior change does not mean that the psychologist relinquishes responsibility with regard to the treatment. He is still responsible for seeing that appropriate procedures are executed and that the behavior is changed even though he himself does not deal directly with the child on a daily basis and may in fact see the child quite infrequently.

## The Normality of "Abnormal" Behavior

Assuming there is a focus on observable behavior, what behaviors are considerd "abnormal" and in turn worthy of modification? Every teacher is faced at some time with a child who seems different: a child who doesn't know how to mix well with others, a child who demands constant attention, a child who fidgets and chats incessantly with his neighbors, a child who misses school frequently, or a child who disrupts the class by jumping out of his seat and pinching other children. These children seem different and are often called abnormal. But what do we mean by abnormal? Abnormality can be conceptualized in a variety of ways, and in many respects one's view of abnormality determines one's approach to treatment. Consequently, it seems appropriate to describe the concept of abnormality in some detail and to emphasize the conceptual framework from which most of the articles in this book were derived.

Abnormal behavior can be conceived of as some deviation from a statistical norm. The very term "abnormal" suggests some deviation from a norm or an average. A deviant person, then, would be someone who is unlike everyone else—be he unusual in the sense that he has unusual problems or unusual intelligence. Unfortunately, the label, abnormality, then becomes almost synonymous with lack of conformity, and as a result, some professionals deem this definition inadequate. Abnormality may also be seen as a state of subjective unhappiness. However, there may be a plethora of people who would call a person abnormal, yet they would not see that person as unhappy. On the other hand, Ullmann and Krasner (1965) in presenting a psychological formulation of maladaptive behavior within a behavior modification paradigm noted the following:

> Maladaptive behaviors are learned behaviors, and the development and maintenance of a maladaptive behavior is no different from the development and maintenance of any other behavior. There is no discontinuity between desirable and undesirable modes of adjustment or between "healthy" and "sick" behavior. The first major implication of this view is the question of how a behavior is to be identified as desirable or undesirable, adaptive or maladaptive. The general answer proposed is that because there are no disease entities involved in the majority of subjects displaying maladaptive behavior, the designation of a behavior as pathological or not is dependent upon the individual's society. ... Behavior that one culture might consider maladaptive, be it that of the Shaman or the paranoid, is adaptive in another culture if the person so behaving is responding to all the cues present in the situation in a manner likely to lead to his obtaining reinforcement [rewards] appropriate to his status in that society. Maladaptive behavior is behavior that is considered inappropriate by those key people in a person's life who control reinforcers.* (p. 20)

In 1969, Ullmann and Krasner noted that:

*Reprinted with permission of Holt, Rinehart & Winston, Inc., from Leonard P. Ullmann and Leonard Krasner. *Case studies in behavior modification.* Copyright ©1965 by Holt, Rinehart & Winston, Inc., New York.

Behavior which is considered abnormal must be studied as the interaction of three variables: the behavior itself, its social context, and an observer who is in a position of power. No specific behavior is abnormal in itself. Rather an individual may do something (e.g., verbalize hallucinations . . . stare into space, dress sloppily) under a set of circumstances (e.g., during a school class . . .) which upsets, annoys, angers, or strongly disturbs somebody (e.g., . . . teacher, parent, or the individual himself) sufficiently that some action results (e.g., a policeman is called, seeing a psychiatrist is recommended, commitment proceedings are started) so that society's professional labelers (e.g., physicians, psychiatrists, psychologists, judges, social workers) come into contact with the individual and determine which of the current set of labels (e.g., schizophrenic reaction, sociopathic personality, anxiety reaction) is most appropriate. Finally, there follow attempts to change the emission of the offending behavior (e.g., institutionalization, psychotherapy, medication).* (p 21)

Before we go any further, let us question more extensively whether it really makes any difference what concept of abnormality we use or whether we use one at all. Does it help to be able to say to a teacher or a parent, "Yes, this child is abnormal" or "No, this child is not abnormal." Frequently, though not always, a teacher or parent comes to a professional not to ask if a child is abnormal but to ask what can be done about a certain behavior or set of behaviors. They *already* have the feeling that the child is unusual in one way or another. That is, they are not able to deal with him as they have deal with the difficulty the child presents—not to worry about the psychologist or psychiatrist is then to help the parent or teacher deal with the difficulty the child presents—not to owrry about whether the child is abnormal or not. However, a parent with one child or a new teacher may not know for sure if the child she is discussing really is very different from the small number of children with whom she has come in contact. Consequently, the question may not be "What can I do with this child?" but "Should I do anything with him to change his behavior?" In turn, they wish to know, "Does he deviate from the rest of the children of his own age? Is he ab-

---

*Reprinted with permission of Prentice-Hall, Inc., from Leonard P. Ullmann and Leonard Krasner. *A psychological approach to abnormal behavior.* Copyright © 1969 by Prentice-Hall, Inc., Englewood Cliffs, N.J.

normal or is he unusual? Do most children at this age display this behavior? Do most children talk at this age? What percentage of children walk at this age?" Any attempt to answer such questions depends upon the culture in which one lives, and as Ullmann and Krasner (1975) noted, the consideration of abnormality must also take into account the observer or the person in power who is to do the labeling (the physician, psychologist, or psychiatrist).

Equally important, the labeling of a person will depend upon the kind of cutoff point the labeler uses in his implicit or explicit definition of abnormality. That is, some psychologists might call a person abnormal if he behaved differently from 95% of the population, while another psychologist would call a person abnormal only if he behaved differently from 99% of the population. However, people differ on many behaviors and may be unusual in one sense and very normal in others. Consequently, if we are forced to deal with the issue of abnormality, we first must ask, "Abnormal in what *specific* respect?" Yet even if we ask ourselves about a *particular* behavior of a child, how do we tell whether it is abnormal? For example, how should we answer a teacher who asks us whether a child who is out of his seat 15% of the time is abnormal? We would first have to know the grade of the child, his sex, the type of lesson in which the out-of-seat behavior is displayed (teacher-directed or seat work where the children are supposed to work independently), and the kind of school system in which the child resides (e.g., southern, northern, a school on an Indian reservation, a city school in a ghetto, or a school in a wealthy suburb). Thus, our answer must be qualified by the particular subpopulation in which the child lives or goes to school. To develop an objective recording system which would account for such variables relevant to particular populations might seem impossible, and one might again say, "Who cares whether one tells the teacher or parent if the child is abnormal or not? The question is, does the behavior of the child bother the parent or the teacher?" One might simply abandon the label abnormal and tell the parent or the teacher that the issue of abnormality is irrelevant and a useless concern.

While the issue of abnormality is a thorny one which might be abandoned for the sake of simplicity and parsimony, the present authors feel it cannot be ignored. Like it or not, the public will continue to ask us if their children are abnormal. If we admit that many of the undesirable classroom behaviors exhibited by particularly disruptive children are learned, that they are not different in quality but only in quantity from behavior exhibited by any child,

and that such behavior can be unlearned, then how should we consider abnormality in a practical sense?

Let us examine more closely how a child might differ from his
peers. All children seek their teacher's praise, but some children want
more attention than usual. All children fidget and talk in class, but
some children are more talkative or fidgety than others. Thus, we can
say that children differ from their peers in terms of the amount or
*frequency* of the particular behaviors they display. Most children are
occasionally annoyed with their teachers or their classmates. Usually,
children express their annoyance with a brief comment, a sudden
look, or perhaps an occasional outburst. However, there are children
who fly into tantrums at the slightest provocation and children who
regularly lash out physically when other children call them names.
Thus, we can say that these children differ from other children in the
*intensity* with which they react to situations. Some children learn
very quickly while others learn so slowly that progress is barely
discernible. Thus, we can say that children differ according to the
*rate* at which they acquire new behaviors. In summary, the children
who are often labeled abnormal are not different from normal
children in the sense that they display behaviors which are strangely
unique to them. All children behave with varying frequencies and
intensities and learn at varying rates. We tend to label or designate a
child as abnormal when he exhibits some behavior or group of
behaviors at unusually high or low frequencies and intensities and
when he learns at an unusually high or low pace.

A child is often labeled abnormal primarily or solely on the basis
of a professional's clinical experience in the absence of objective
criteria. It seems that obtaining reliable objective indices of observable behavior will greatly aid the practitioner who is faced with
parents and teachers who ask "Is this child abnormal?" While ultimately the questions posed by the parent and teacher will involve
issues such as how do we *change* this behavior or that behavior,
normative data and knowledge of deviation from that norm should
prove useful. There is considerable research concerning behavioral
assessment in classrooms, and detailed methods of obtaining such
information will appear in the last chapter.

The articles which appear in this book approach the assessment
problem or what was formerly called diagnosis by focusing on
particular *target* behaviors. Most of the researchers have used frequency of certain observable behaviors as a focus for their studies
though some researchers working within the general behavior modification framework have used intensity as a measure, or at least a

supplementary measure, in their evaluation of treatment effects. The reader should note that generally there is no systematic attempt by behavior modifiers to place the children who are described in this book in particular diagnostic categories such as delinquency, hyperkinetic reaction[4] or unsocialized aggressive reaction.[5] However, as will be seen, particular behaviors of children who were labeled by other professionals as emotionally disturbed, retarded, delinquent, and schizophrenic have been changed by a number of behavior modification techniques. There is a very distinct advantage to focusing on target behaviors: namely, there is a specific focus for treatment. Instead of treating a disorder or a disease in a medical sense, a particular behavior or a series of behaviors is treated. The behavior modifier argues that even if a child displays a behavior pattern which is thought to have an organic origin like autism, retardation, or hyperactivity, the behaviors themselves can be treated as one would in any other behavior change program. As mentioned above, problem behaviors displayed by children described as autistic, retarded or hyperactive have been dramatically changed using a behavioral treatment approach. In contrast, when one views the child to be *mentally ill,* the child is often considered to suffer from a sickness that is due to an organic factor which acts like a germ. The germ must be removed before a healthy state can be regained. In addition, if one considers a child to be mentally ill, it is often assumed that the "illness" can be classified, like many other diseases, without taking into account social factors (Ullmann & Krasner, 1975).

## Treating Behaviors as Problems not Symptoms

It is true that certain childhood behavior problems do have definite chemical or physiological bases which now imply that medical treatment is in order. For example, one form of retardation called phenylketonuria is clearly due to an enzyme deficiency in the liver, and if this deficiency is detected early, retardation can be

---

[4]Hyperkinetic reactions consist of "restlessness in the classroom, impulsive action, and a difficulty in concentration and intellectual development" (Ulett & Goodrich, 1969).

[5]Children with purported personality growth disturbances who have "extremely poor control over their aggressive and sexual impulses and who have usually been poorly socialized by their parents and even subtly encouraged by the pleasure of their parents in the expressions of aggression" (Ulett & Goodrich, 1969).

avoided or arrested. Similarly, there is a form of mental retardation called Mongolism or Down's Syndrome which is caused by an extra chromosome. The childhood disorder, autism, which is characterized by severe social withdrawal, speech difficulties, eating problems, and a strange gait may be the result of genetic or biochemical problems. However, as mentioned earlier, the disruptive or unusual behaviors which children generally display in most classrooms are the result of a learning process and are not the symptoms of an underlying disease in a medical sense. Thus, the behavior is treated not as a *symptom* of a problem but as the problem itself. Some have said that direct treatment of a behavior is insufficient because the underlying causes of the problem are ignored. The disease or disorder will be expressed by a different symptom if one treats behaviors as the problem rather than treating "the underlying cause." Here again, one's conceptualization of abnormal is of critical importance for treatment. As Bandura (1968) aptly noted, all therapists—whether of a psychodynamic or behavior modification orientation—are seaching for causes in that they are looking for determinants of behavior! It is in the conception of the determinants, however, where real differences exist. Traditional therapists focus on libidinal or intrapsychic conflicts as the determinants of behavior, whereas behavior modifiers focus on eliciting stimuli and reinforcing events. Traditional therapists focus on early childhood factors, whereas behavior modifiers focus on current factors. The focus of the behavior modifier on current factors which control a child's behavior and on changing target behaviors, has not led to undesirable side-effects or what many have called "symptom substitution." In fact, Ward and Baker (1968) found that having teachers reinforce appropriate classroom behavior, i.e., treat the disruptive behaviors as problems not symptoms, has led to significant increases in appropriate classroom behavior; and no adverse effects were noticed after treatment when the children were tested with both overt behavioral indices as well as through assessment of fantasy.

## Behavioral Insight

In the same way that arguments have arisen over the types of causes of behavior that one should pursue, argument has arisen over the role of "insight" in behavior modification. As *all* therapists search for causes of behavior, *all* therapists are searching for insight into the problems of the people with whom they are dealing. However, the type or kind of insight may depend very heavily upon one's theoretical or conceptual framework. Insight in a traditional or psychodynamic sense refers to an understanding of the relationship between one's behavior and the conflicting forces in one's mind or psyche.

As will be seen from the forthcoming discussion, the behavior modifier uses a quite different conceptual framework from the traditional psychotherapist as he attempts to achieve insight or understanding of the case which will aid in his treatment plan. The behavior modifier tries to give his client insight into the factors which maintain his inappropriate or undesired behaviors in terms of specific reinforcing or rewarding stimuli, specific eliciting stimuli, and more global environmental factors called setting events. Since the articles in this book are generally based on the principles of learning as espoused by behavior modifiers, analysis of the steps taken in assessment and treatment is now in order.

## The Assessment of Target Behaviors and Their Environmental Determinants

A teacher who refers a child to a psychologist describes "the problem" as she sees it in rather general terms. Assuming the psychologist is a behavior modifier, he would then ask the teacher to pinpoint the behaviors upon which she bases her conclusion. For example, if the teacher complained that a child was odd or unusual because of his inability to get along with peers, the behavior modifier would then ask the teacher to specify exactly what the child does and how frequently the behaviors which she regards as unusual occur. The behavior modifier usually asks the teacher to deep a daily log of these specific behaviors for at least a week. The manner in which the behavior is recorded may vary from simple anecdotal records to rather precise recording of the frequencies (and occasionally intensity) of certain behaviors during a specified time unit, e.g., a half-hour period, an hour period, or even during a morning. In short, the initial step after the teacher refers the child to the behavior modifier is to specify as clearly as possible the particular types of behavior which are of concern to the teacher and to measure their frequency. These behaviors are then called "target behaviors" because they serve as the targets for remediation. (A more detailed examination of methods of classroom assessment appears in the last chapter of this book.)

The second major step in target assessment is to identify the variables which are responsible for the behaviors in question. More specifically, the psychologist asks the teacher to note what factors immediately precede and what factors immediately follow the target behaviors. The rationale for assessing factors which immediately precede or immediately follow the target behaviors is that a great deal of a child's behavior is the result of learning and that such learning takes place through respondent or classical conditioning and operant conditioning. Respondent or classical conditioning refers to the learning where a stimulus *preceding* a behavior or group of behaviors controls these behaviors. However, this sort of control is of a special nature in that there is an almost invariable relationship between the behavior and the stimuli which precede the behavior. Such behaviors are often called *involuntary* because when the stimuli are presented, the behaviors almost invariably occur (e.g., salivation, pupil dilation, fright, increase in heart rate), and it appears as if the organism had no choice in whether or not the behaviors occurred. A respondent behavior is generally not controlled by the stimuli which follow it. For example, pupil dilation (which occurs in response to a light) and salivation (which occurs in response to food), are usually not influenced by stimuli following the behaviors.[6] Examples of fearful behavior seen in schools which are often assumed to be classically conditioned are fears of dogs or hamsters and fear of speaking in front of others. While some behaviors are controlled by stimuli preceding the behavior, other behaviors—called operant behaviors—are influenced by the stimuli which *follow* them. The teacher should be alert to fearful behavior which is controlled by preceding stimuli because it may be very difficult to eliminate such fearful behavior by some of the major methods of behavior modification to be described in this book. These methods focus on the *consequences* rather than the antecedents of behavior. When certain stimuli follow a behavior, the behaviors increase in frequency. Stimuli which increase the frequency of the behaviors they follow are called positive reinforcers. Part of the job of the teacher and the psychologist is to find out what stimuli do serve as positive reinforcers for the undesired or unwanted behaviors. Once this is known, the positive reinforcers can be removed and the frequency of the disruptive behavior should be reduced. For example, if the teacher unwittingly attends to some

---

[6]However, under special conditions, behaviors generally characterized as involuntary, such as heart rate, blood pressure, and salivation, can be significantly influenced by the stimuli which follow them (Miller, 1969; Yates, 1975).

undesirable behavior by saying, "Johnny, why do you do that?" it is very likely that the teacher's comment serves to reinforce the undesirable behavior. Consequently, the teacher can be asked to cease questioning Johnny about why he engages in such behavior. In addition, the teacher and psychologist should try to discover what stimuli could serve as positive reinforcers for behaviors which should be increased in frequency. For example, the psychologist will want to know if teachers' praise or approval, stars, or grades will serve to increase the frequency of desirable behavior or if on occasion more potent reinforcers such as prizes are necessary to increase certain behaviors. While the use of the more potent reinforcers just described is rare, several articles in this book will discuss the utilization of systematic and extensive uses of powerful incentives such as money and comics. It is important to emphasize that these powerful incentive systems should be applied only after other possible reinforcers such as teacher attention are evaluated.

There are also certain stimuli which if made contingent upon behaviors will reduce the frequency of those behaviors. Such stimuli are called punishing stimuli, and the teacher should be aware of possible stimuli which could be used to punish or suppress behavior. As will be mentioned in the section on punishment, there are often very mild but interesting alternatives to criticism or to forms of physical punishment such as squeezing a child's arm or withholding recess which can be used to reduce disruptive behaviors in the classroom.

It has been stated that respondent behavior is controlled by stimuli which precede behavior and operant behavior is controlled by stimuli which follow behavior, and that the respondent behavior is often called involuntary while the operant behavior is called voluntary. However, operant behaviors and respondent behaviors often overlap, and the practical distinction between operants and respondents breaks down. For example, certain forms of anger and aggression may be elicited by a spanking or by a frustrating experience; but once the aggression is displayed, the reactions of the parent or teacher may further serve to maintain or reinforce the behavior. Thus, the distinction between operant and respondent behaviors should be seen as a convenient tool in conceptualizing behavior—not as a distinction which can be applied in every case. In fact, the present authors recommend that such a conceptualization be applied in general consideration of any case, but that particular types of behaviors may have peculiarities which must be considered; and as a result, the particular kinds of behaviors to be changed should be given as much, if not more, consideration than the general operant-respondent classification. The authors would hope that in the future those scientists who are working on behavior change procedures will be able to concentrate on finding the best ways to deal with particular kinds of behavior. For example, if research is directed at changing certain classes of behavior, such as aggression, withdrawal, swearing, and lying, then eventually we may be able to list a number of procedures which can best be used to decrease the frequency of each one of these groups of behaviors. At present, however, there has been a greater emphasis on the evaluation of various treatment procedures than on changing particular classes of behavior, and consequently, this book is organized around various treatment procedures rather than around target behaviors.

While the very name, behavior modifier, implies that there is going to be a focus on particular behaviors for amelioration, one should not disregard his "common sense" concerning problems which are referred to him. One can easily overlook physical or organic matters such as poor eyesight or hearing. Most importantly, the psychologist who is consulting with a teacher has to know something about academic or achievement assessment since a large percentage of the children referred to child guidance clinics and psychological centers have reading and other academic difficulties. Many psychologists focus on "emotional" or behavioral problems of such children and argue that such difficulties preceded the reading problems, but it is impossible to tell whether the reading problem preceded the social problems (usually called emotional or behavior problems) or vice versa. It is very unlikely that a child who is doing poorly academically will evidence great gains socially without intellectual or academic improvement. As is noted by Thomas, Nielsen, Kuypers, and Becker (1968), children with very poor academic skills who do not receive academic tutoring are not greatly aided by lavish amounts of praise for good classroom behavior. Consequently, the psychologist and teacher should ask themselves "To what extent are any of the problem social behaviors such as daydreaming, walking around the room, and talking to neighbors a result of not understanding what is going on in the classroom in academic matters?" If the child is not progressing well in reading, writing, arithmetic, or language development, a specific analysis of the problems in the particular subject matters where the child has problems is in order. If the psychologist or teacher does not feel that he or she has skills in the particular subject matter, he should ask for consultation from someone in that specialty area.

## BEHAVIOR MODIFICATION PROCEDURES

There are numerous behavior modification procedures existing today, but, in general, all such procedures can be viewed as concerted attempts either to increase or to decrease behavior. Such a dichotomy is somewhat arbitrary, as certain procedures may be used to increase some behaviors while on other occasions the same procedures may be used to decrease behaviors. For example, modeling can be used to teach cooperative behavior or to decrease fearful behavior. However, this method of classification whereby one looks at procedures to increase or decrease behaviors should be of use to those psychologists, teachers, or special educators who are faced with behavior change problems daily. Hopefully, they will be able to refer to such a classification and thus arrive at the particular procedure(s) best suited to their needs. Detailed analyses and discussions of many of these procedures are presented in later sections of this book.

### Procedures to Increase Behaviors

*Praise and Approval*
If a child already shows some evidence of a certain behavior that one wishes to increase such as paying attention, a teacher might simply walk over to the child and enthusiastically praise him while he is paying attention. The teacher will find that the child will pay attention for longer and longer periods of time (Becker, Madsen, Arnold, & Thomas, 1967; Drabman & Lahey, 1974; Kirby & Shields, 1972; Madsen, Becker, & Thomas, 1968). Approval may occur in many forms, e.g., a pat on the back, a smile, or saying, "That's good work!" While many teachers feel powerless in front of young children, research data clearly show that the positive words or gestures from a teacher which are made contingent upon a behavior can be extremely effective tools in changing a child's behavior. In addition, the child will probably like school more as he receives more positive attention from the teacher.

*Modeling*
One of the simplest and most straightforward ways to establish a behavior is to show the child how to do something and then ask him to repeat what you did. Certain athletic skills such as riding a bicycle or throwing a baseball are taught primarily in this fashion. However, modeling can also be a very effective method of obtaining desired

classroom behaviors. For example, a teacher may start teaching a child to print by showing him how to make certain movements with a pen and then asking the child to model her behavior. Similarly, a teacher may have one child perform a certain behavior and then ask another child to perform the behavior. The use of modeling to change a host of behaviors ranging from delay of gratification to aggression has been documented by Bandura (1969); Bandura, Grusec, and Menlove, (1967); Broden, Bruce, Mitchell, Carter, and Hall (1970); Brown, Reschly, and Wasserman (1974); Henderson, Swanson, and Zimmerman, (1975); and O'Connor (1969, 1972).

## Token Reinforcement Programs

A token reinforcement program generally involves three factors: (1) a set of instructions to the class about the behaviors that will be reinforced, (2) a means of making a potentially reinforcing stimulus— usually called a token—contingent upon behavior, and (3) a set of rules governing the exchange of tokens for back-up reinforcers such as prizes or opportunities to engage in special activities. Token reinforcement programs have been effectively utilized in mental hospitals with adult psychiatric patients (Ayllon & Azrin, 1968), with teenage children labeled childhood schizophrenic (Kaufman & O'Leary, 1972), with retarded children (Birnbrauer, Wolf, Kidder, & Tague, 1965), emotionally disturbed children (O'Leary & Becker, 1967), and with disruptive children in a "normal" class (O'Leary, Becker, Evans, & Saudargas, 1969). While token reinforcement programs have proven very successful in changing both the academic and social behavior of children in classrooms (O'Leary, 1977; O'Leary & Drabman, 1971), the use of tangible reinforcers such as prizes or toys is often called bribery. As normal practice, the use of prizes in token reinforcement programs in classrooms is definitely not bribery in the usual sense, i.e., trying to corrupt the conduct of a person. Nonetheless, the use of tangible reinforcers which are not natural to any classroom is not a procedure to be used in every class. They are extremely effective in changing behavior, but they should be utilized with care for their long-range use with children has only begun to receive attention, and the amateurish use of tangible extrinsic reinforcers may occasionally produce undesired behavioral effects.

While many token programs involve extrinsic reinforcers, i.e., reinforcers such as prizes, which are not usually found in a classroom or hospital ward, a number of token programs have utilized reinforcers which are natural to a classroom or hospital ward such as special privileges or special activities (Bushell, Wrobel, & Michaelis,

1968; McKenzie, Clark, Wolf, Kothera, & Benson, 1968; Osborne, 1969).

## Programmed Instruction

Programmed instruction is a way of arranging academic materials in logically sequenced small steps. Each step or frame of the program generally provides information, requires the student to respond to the information, and gives feedback to the student regarding the correctness of his response (Morrill, 1961; Skinner, 1963). With programmed instruction, a child can progress at his own rate, and the teacher can circulate among members of the class providing help where needed. The programmed instruction formats vary greatly from simple booklets with sequencing of materials (Holland & Skinner, 1961; Williams, Gilmore, & Malpass, 1968) to presentation of programmed mathematics material over television where a bedridden child can indicate his answer by dialing a phone which is connected to a central computer bank. In addition, some programmed instruction is presented via a machine which responds to a child's answers. If he gets an answer correct, the machine will type "correct" immediately following his answer. On the other hand, if he makes an error, the machine will go back into a sequence of materials and present the key concepts necessary for a child to advance (Atkinson, 1968).

## Self-Specification of Contingencies

Many of us occasionally say to ourselves that when and only when we finish a certain task, we will allow ourselves the privilege of purchasing a certain item or engaging in a certain behavior. This procedure of allowing oneself to engage in a certain behavior when one has finished a task has been discussed by Homme (1965). For example, if sitting in one's seat is a low probability behavior of a child and drawing at the blackboard is a high probability behavior of the child, then if the teacher allows the child to draw at the blackboard only after the child has been sitting at his seat for a certain period of time, the probability of the child's in-seat behavior should increase (Homme, DeBaca, DeVine, Steinhorst, & Rickert, 1963). There is some evidence to suggest that when *children* themselves specify that they should engage in certain academic tasks before allowing themselves to play in the free activity area of the room, the probability of their engaging in academic behavior increases (Lovitt & Curtiss, 1969). In token reinforcement programs it is probably wise to have children help in the selection of the behaviors to be reinforced in the class (Drabman, 1973); incentive programs in industry clearly show that involving the employees in the specification of and the pay for behaviors to be reinforced is better than simply having the management impose such a program on the employees (Lawler & Hackman, 1969). While self-specification of contingencies does not always lead to greater academic productivity than where the same contingencies are externally imposed in token programs (Felix-brod & O'Leary, 1973, 1974), children prefer to set their own contingencies, and having children set their own standards is undoubtedly a long-term goal of most parents and educators.

## Self-Reinforcement

The efficacy of self-reinforcement procedures in a classroom setting has received little attention, yet a number of studies with children in experimental settings bear on this issue. Bandura and Perloff (1967) demonstrated that self-administered consequences can, in fact, serve a reinforcing function. A child was given complete control over tokens which were exchangeable for prizes; when the child made the tokens contingent upon his behavior, the tokens served to maintain his behavior. Modeling plays a very important role in the transmission of self-reinforcing behavior (Bandura & Kupers, 1964). As summarized by Bandura (1969), the results of a series of modeling studies in the self-reinforcement area show that "people generally adopt the standards for self-reinforcement exhibited by exemplary models, they evaluate their own performances relative to that standard, and then they serve as their own reinforcing agents. For instance, those who have been exposed to models setting low standards tend to be highly self-rewarding and self-approving for comparatively mediocre performances. By contrast, persons who have observed models adhere to stringent performance demands display considerable self-denial and self-dissatisfaction for objectively identical accomplishments" (pp. 33-34). A teacher should bear such results in mind when she reinforces the behavior of children in her class, because presumably she can teach children to adopt high or low performance standards. That is, if the teacher reinforces only those behaviors which meet certain high standards, it is likely that the child will later be self-approving of behaviors which meet high standards.

## Establishment of Clear Rules and Directions

It is certainly true that simply making rules clear will not be effective in changing the behavior of many disruptive children (Madsen, Becker, & Thomas, 1968; O'Leary, Becker, Evans, &

Saudargas, 1969), but some children are helped by clear specification of the desired classroom behavior. The clear specification of classroom rules and occasional reviews of such rules can serve to prompt children to rehearse the rules themselves and, as observed in many classrooms, the children may remind others of the rules. Clear specification of rules is also an aid to classrooms where there is a great deal of change in the types of behaviors expected from one activity to another. For example, in the reading lesson, a teacher may expect much different behavior than during a science project. Not only do rules help a teacher to shift the kinds of classroom activities with ease, but allowing and expecting different behaviors during different lessons is probably good training for children. That is, they learn that certain behaviors are expected in one lesson but definitely prohibited in another. Such variation makes a classroom more interesting and pleasant for both the teacher and her students. Instead of learning to function in a completely unstructured classroom or a rigidly managed classroom, a child whose teacher expects and receives varying behaviors in different lessons is learning the type of self-control that will give him the greatest freedom and flexibility in the future.

When rules are made explicit, children must be reinforced for following them. Many children entering school have been reinforced by their parents for following a variety of instructions or rules made by their parents, and consequently, such children exhibit general "rule-following behavior" with only infrequent praise. However, most children who are "behavior problems" probably have not been consistently reinforced in the past for following rules or instructions, and it is incumbent upon the teacher to reinforce such children frequently when they do follow rules or instructions.

*Shaping*

Shaping is the procedure of reinforcing successive approximations to some desired terminal behavior. For example, if a child answers in class but only at a whisper, a teacher can praise the child when he answers with just a little more volume than usual. Later the teacher can reinforce answers that more closely approximate the desired terminal behavior, i.e., answering in a manner audible to both the teacher and to other students.

When a child or adolescent engages in behaviors which are particularly aversive or obnoxious, such as back-talk, thumbing one's nose at a teacher, or defying orders and requests, the teacher may find it very difficult to respond positively to any other appropriate behaviors the child makes during that class period or that particular day. While it is probably unwise to respond appropriately to good behavior which immediately follows a bad behavior, a teacher who "holds a grudge" against a child for a day and never responds to any of his positive behaviors may find it impossible to change his behavior. Simply, holding a grudge for a long period is incompatible with shaping.

*Passive Shaping*

If a child does not display a behavior when requested to do so or when another child has modeled the behavior for him, it may be necessary to help the child in performing the behavior by guiding him through the physical motions of the desired behavior. For example, if a child does not imitate any behavior—as is the case with some retarded children—the teacher can demonstrate raising her hand and then actually raise the child's hand and subsequently praise the child or give him a gold star. The term, passive shaping, is used because the child is essentially passive while the teacher actively aids the child in displaying the behavior. Passive shaping has been especially effective in establishing a variety of imitative behaviors in retarded children (Baer, Peterson, & Sherman, 1967). It also may be used to help a child learn to pour water from one container to another, to teach a child how to play a roll or a flam on a drum, or to teach a child certain ballet steps which are difficult to model simply.

## Procedures to Decrease Behavior

*Extinction*

When a teacher or parent stops making approval or some other form of attention contingent upon behavior, the behavior will frequently extinguish or decrease in frequency (Bijou, 1965). Many behaviors have been decreased when the teacher stops attending to them. Among those behaviors which have been successfully extinguished are tantrums (Zimmerman & Zimmerman, 1962), regressed crawling (Harris, Johnston, Kelley, & Wolf, 1964), vomiting (Wolf, Birnbrauer, Williams, & Lawler, 1965), and aggression in a classroom (Brown & Elliot, 1965). However, as will be emphasized repeatedly in this book, ignoring inappropriate behavior should be coupled with praise for appropriate behavior. Ignoring inappropriate behavior *without* praise for appropriate behavior is not only difficult for teachers to do, but it may be ineffective in a number of instances

(Madsen, Becker, & Thomas, 1968). Consequently, alternatives to ignoring such behaviors are presented later.

### Reinforcing Behavior Incompatible with Undesired Behavior

As just mentioned, when one extinguishes a behavior by not attending to that behavior, one should also reinforce or attend in a positive manner to the desired behavior. It is most helpful if one can reinforce a behavior which, if increased in frequency, would make the undesirable behavior less probable. For example, if a child is frequently talking and wandering around the classroom, it is helpful to reinforce academic behavior as the child cannot work on his academic material and at the same time talk and wander around the room. That is, the teacher will be reinforcing behaviors which are incompatible with the undesired behavior.

### Soft Reprimands

When simply ignoring a certain behavior does not serve to reduce such behavior, a reprimand which is audible only to the child being reprimanded may prove very effective in reducing the behavior of especially disruptive children (O'Leary & Becker, 1968; O'Leary, Kaufman, Kass, & Drabman, 1970). In contrast, when the reprimand is audible to a number of children in the class, the loud reprimand will generally serve either to maintain the disruptive behavior or to increase it. As will be noted in the section on punishment, it probably is best to reprimand a child just as he begins to display an undesired behavior rather than to reprimand him after he has been misbehaving for some time (Jones & Miller, 1974; Walters, Parke, & Cane, 1965). Interesting alternatives to a verbal reprimand such as taking away a slip of paper on which a child's name is written are presented by Hall, Axelrod, Foundopoulos, Shellman, Campbell, and Cranston, (1971).

### Timeout from Reinforcement

Teachers have long used the procedure of placing a child at the side of the room, in the back of a room, in a corner, or in a dunce's chair. Unfortunately, being placed in such a situation has a number of deleterious effects on the child, e.g., being the center of attention, being able to go through other children's pockets in the cloakroom, or getting out of doing an assignment. Timeout from reinforcement procedurally resembles the time-honored isolation procedures. However, timeout from positive reinforcement is a procedure in which some sources of positive reinforcement are eliminated for a specific period of time. For example, if a child enjoys being with others and displays disruptive behavior, he may be placed somewhere in the room where there are no objects of interest and where it is difficult for others to see him. In certain laboratory schools, hospitals, or classrooms for very disruptive children, he may even be placed in a small enclosed, lighted, ventilated cubicle at the side of the room—called a timeout room. Isolation in a room adjacent to a classroom is not a feasible or even a suggested procedure for most teachers and should be used only with extremely disruptive children and then only when qualified consultants can supervise the treatment program. However, in classes where children are extremely disruptive, timeout from reinforcement presents an alternative to some of the usual methods of punishment such as restriction on a ward or withdrawal of some privilege (Drabman & Spitalnik, 1973; Lahey, McNees, & McNees, 1973; Pendergrass, 1970).

*Relaxation*

Certain forms of behavior which are generally considered emotional may be treated by teaching a child how to relax when he becomes frustrated, agitated, or angered. In 1938, Jacobsen introduced a method for obtaining muscle relaxation which has now been incorporated into a number of current treatment procedures for adults. Relaxation has merit for it can be taught like any other skill. If the relaxation exercises have been well practiced, the person becomes relaxed when he says to himself, "Relax." Relaxation is thought to be incompatible with emotional behaviors such as fright, anger, or frustration. Since the verbal control of nonverbal behavior in children may be weak, and since controlled research on relaxation alone is almost nonexistent with children, at this point relaxation should simply be seen as a possible method by which a teacher or psychologist could aid a child in overcoming strong emotional reactions to fearful and frustrating situations. The use of relaxation is included here simply to alert teachers to a possible technique that might be used with a child who exhibits extreme reaction to a frustration or who displays fearful behavior. In the section on self-control later in this book, Robin, Schneider, and Dolnick (in press) illustrate the use of relaxation combined with discussions of problematic social situations that children may face.

*Gradual Presentation of Fearful Stimuli in Vivo*

If a child has a fear of school, he may be placed in real-life (in vivo) situations which are quite unlike and distant from the classroom and then be brought gradually closer and closer to the actual fearful stimulus, the classroom. Lazarus, Davison, and Polefka (1965) demonstrated the effectiveness of this procedure when it was combined with positive reinforcement for being in the classroom. Over a period of four and a half months, a nine-year-old school phobic boy was taken for a walk near the schoolhouse, went inside the schoolroom with the therapist, stayed in class with the therapist present, and finally stayed in class in the absence of the therapist. Similarly, Ayllon, Smith, and Rogers (1970) successfully treated an eight-year-old school phobic girl in 45 days. Since it is very difficult to determine whether a child is staying away from school as a ploy for avoiding work when in fact the child is not at all frightened, one must carefully assess the extent to which the problem is one of truancy or fear of school. Yates (1970) presents an excellent discussion of the various types of school phobia and an evaluation of treatment results of various procedures designed to have the child return to school. A lengthy discussion of the treatment of school phobias will not be presented since such treatment is usually carried out by a psychologist and since primarily case studies and not experimental analyses of the treatment of school phobias are available.

Brain-damaged children with fears of a public bus or the sight of a live dog have been successfully treated by gradual exposure to such fear arousing stimuli (Obler & Terwilliger, 1970). As the child made an approach to the feared object, he was immediately rewarded with candy, toys, or books. For example, if a child talked with the bus driver or put a token in the box on the bus, he was reinforced both socially and with some prize. According to parental ratings before and after treatment, the treatment was quite successful when compared with children who received no treatment.

One example of fearful behavior which a teacher could treat by using a gradual presentation of the fearful situation is the fear of speaking in class. The teacher might first have the child read to her in private, then to a friend, to a group of close friends, to a group in the class, and finally to the entire class. As the child is able to progress from one step to the next without fear, the teacher should make certain that the child receives some form of reinforcement for his successes.

*Desensitization*

A widely practiced technique which is used with adults who have fears and anxiety is desensitization. After completely relaxing a client, the client is asked to imagine or visualize a series of scenes which he finds anxiety provoking. After many trials where the client visualizes the anxiety producing scenes in a relaxed state, the client finds that the instances in his daily life which he visualized while relaxed no longer produce anxiety (Paul, 1966; Wolpe, 1958). Obviously, it would be difficult to have very young children visualize scenes which make them anxious, but desensitization has been used successfully with adolescents (Mann, 1972; Mann & Rosenthal, 1969).[7]

*Response Cost*

Response cost, point loss, or fines is a procedure often used in token programs. The usefulness of cost procedures in a classroom was suggested by McIntire, Jensen, and Davis (1968) in an after-school program for elementary and junior high school boys. Each child had a counter on which a teacher could either add or subtract points. The child gained points for correct answers and lost points for disruptive classroom behavior. "Whenever disruptive behavior occurred, the instructor could turn on the counter associated with that student's name and allow the counter to continue to subtract points until the instructor felt that the student had corrected himself" (pp. 3-4). The effectiveness of such cost procedures in a classroom setting was also documented by Kaufman and O'Leary (1972) in the children's unit of a psychiatric hospital. Children in the "cost" class received all their tokens (in the form of points) at the beginning of each rating period and then lost points when they were rated by a teacher. In contrast, children in the "reward" class did not have any points at the beginning of the class period. At the end of a lesson the teacher placed a rating (points) in the child's booklet which reflected the extent to which he followed classroom rules. Thus, the children in the reward group started with no points and earned them as the lesson progressed, whereas the children in the cost class started with all the possible points and lost them as the lesson progressed. Although both token programs were very effective in reducing disruptive behavior of children labeled "behavior disorder" and "childhood schizophrenic," the results of the reward and cost procedures were not different from one another, and no undesirable side-effects of the cost procedures were noted. The effectiveness of response cost is illustrated in this book by Iwata and Bailey (1974) in the punishment section; like Kaufman and O'Leary (1972), they found reward

[7]Desensitization, like relaxation, is not included here in the hope that teachers would attempt its use. It is included simply to alert teachers and psychologists to a procedure to be implemented by a psychologist which may be useful in decreasing fearful behavior.

and cost programs equally effective. Response cost in many situations could be combined with reinforcement for good behavior. For example, a teacher might reduce the amount of time a child could spend at recess whenever he behaved inappropriately. In addition, she could allow him extra minutes in the free activity corner whenever he completed an assignment on time.

## Medication

Medication for hyperactivity is probably the most common drug use seen by teachers in public schools. In fact, between 500,000 and 1,000,000 children are currently receiving stimulant medication for hyperactivity (Schrag & Divoky, 1975). Further, the use of medication is almost ubiquitous in schools for "emotionally disturbed" children or in psychiatric units of children's hospitals. It is true that drugs are not generally considered within a learning framework, but occasionally they may be a useful adjunct in behavior therapy to prompt behaviors that would not ordinarily occur. For example, a physician can prescribe medication which might make it more likely that a hyperactive child will sit in his seat and thereby allow the teacher to praise him more frequently for sitting still (Conners, Eisenberg, & Barcai, 1967; Conners, 1969). The use of stimulant drugs for hyperactivity has some disadvantages which are important. They sometimes have undesirable side-effects such as drowsiness, dryness of mouth, nausea, and suppression of height and weight. Furthermore, few, if any, studies have been done in a classroom which show that when a drug is removed, the behavior change produced by the medication is maintained. Unless special steps are taken to aid long-range behavior change, the undesirable behavior will probably return when the drug is withdrawn. Such a result should not be surprising, and the use of drugs should be seen simply as a method of prompting or artificially producing a behavior which can be further developed and maintained by methods available to the teacher. In contrast to drug treatment, a behaviorally oriented treatment approach actively teaches new behaviors and selectively increases or decreases the frequency of existing behaviors. Viewed as a prompting device, however, there is no reason why certain drugs could not be judiciously used in combination with behavior modification procedures to produce lasting behavior change (Pelham, in press).

## Self-Instruction

The effects of self-instruction were investigated by Luria (1963) who found that children with a particular brain dysfunction could not press a balloon when an external signal such as a light was flashed. When the children were taught to self-instruct (to say "Press" as they pressed the balloon), they could press the balloon without errors. Similarly, self-instruction has been shown to be of aid in both initiating and suppressing behavior (Bem, 1967; Meichenbaum, 1975; Meichenbaum & Goodman, 1969; Monohan & O'Leary, 1971; O'Leary, 1969; Robin, Armel, & O'Leary, 1975). Some teachers have taught children to control their own behaviors by saying sentences to themselves such as " 'i' before 'e' except after 'c,' " "Stop, look, and listen," or "Count to 10." The article by Bornstein and Quevillon (1976) illustrates the use of a self-instructional program in which Head Start children were taught to ask themselves questions, to provide answers to those questions, and to evaluate and praise themselves for appropriate behavior. Self-instruction, as well as the next procedure described, self-evaluation, can be used either to decrease or increase children's behavior. At present, however, most of the classroom research with these techniques has involved evaluations where they were used to decrease behavior.

## Self-Evaluation

Before a child can be taught to reinforce himself for a behavior or set of behaviors, he must learn to evaluate his behavior correctly. For example, in learning how to print, a child cannot effectively improve his printing by saying "good" or giving himself a star if he does not know whether his printing is good or bad or if it is better than previous samples of his printing. To teach a child to evaluate properly his own behavior, he must be taught to use some sort of standard by which he can measure his own behavior. For example, in teaching printing one can use a standard which a child traces and which he later copies. In teaching a child to match a tone when he plays a musical instrument, he can use a strobotuner which tells him if he is playing on pitch. As he plays the instrument on pitch, a certain signal would be seen on a screen, but if he plays off pitch, another signal would appear. Similarly, machines are available which teach children "good sense of rhythm." Children learn to press a button in unison with a series of clicks presented in different rhythmic patterns. If the child presses in unison with the clicks or if he can remember and later produce the rhythmic pattern, a light flashes indicating the correctness of his responses (Skinner, 1968). Where the standards for behavior are not as objective as in printing or in playing on pitch, the child must be taught to evaluate more subtle aspects of his behavior as in the case of judging whether a sentence or a paragraph he wrote is good.

It should be emphasized that there is a difference between one's self-evaluative and one's self-reinforcing behavior. A person may realize that his performance on a task has been very poor but still reinforce himself by allowing himself to have a certain reward or by engaging in a certain pleasurable activity. On the other hand, a child may continually see that his behavior is very good relative to some external standard yet deny himself pleasurable things except on rare occasions. Also, a person may deny himself reinforcers and make many self-derogatory statements (either overtly or covertly) because he fails to see that his behavior is quite acceptable. One advantage of teaching self-evaluative skills is that such behavior should make a child less dependent upon adults (Broden, Hall, & Mitts, 1971; Drabman, Spitalnik, & O'Leary, 1973; Turkewitz, O'Leary, & Ironsmith, 1975). If a child learns to make self-evaluative statements, he need not continually run to the teacher's desk and ask, "Is this good?" or "Is my paper nice?"

## General Principles of Behavior Change

### Schedules of Reinforcement

A schedule of reinforcement refers to the manner in which a reinforcer is made contingent upon a response. One can vary the number of responses between reinforcers or the time between reinforcers. A child may be rewarded for a fixed number of responses (e.g., five correct answers) or for a variable number of responses (e.g., on some occasions the child may be reinforced after three correct answers, while on other occasions he may be reinforced for five or eight correct answers). This difference between reinforcing a fixed number of behaviors and reinforcing a variable number of behaviors has led to the distinction, fixed ratio vs. variable ratio schedule of reinforcement, where the ratio refers to number of reinforcers divided by the number of responses required to receive a reinforcer. Both animal research and research with young children in an experimental setting have demonstrated that when a child is reinforced on a variable ratio basis, he will respond more rapidly than if he is reinforced on a fixed ratio basis. When the reinforcers are no longer made available to the child, the child who was trained on a variable ratio schedule of reinforcement will respond for longer periods of time (during extinction) than will a child who was trained on a fixed ratio schedule of reinforcement. One can also distinguish fixed vs. variable time or interval schedules of reinforcement. As the names imply, a fixed interval schedule of reinforcement refers to reinforcing a child for the first response just after a specified interval of time has passed. A variable interval schedule, on the other hand, refers to reinforcing a child for the first response after varying intervals of time, e.g., a teacher might reinforce the first correct answer of a child after 30 minutes, then after 15 minutes, and finally after 40 minutes. If a teacher wishes to reinforce a child systematically, she should probably do so on a variable ratio or variable interval schedule of reinforcement. In layman's terms, it appears better to "surprise" a child with reinforcers rather than to allow the child to predict that he will always get a reinforcer after a certain number of correct responses or after a certain number of minutes has passed if he were behaving appropriately.

*Satiation and Deprivation*

If one wishes to maximize the power of a reinforcer, he should assure himself that the child does not have ready access to such reinforcers. For example, if one wishes to use raisins as reinforcers in a tutoring session with a small child, one should be sure that the child has not consumed any quantity of raisins just before the tutoring sessions. If raisins were always available to the child, he would be satiated with them, and thus their reinforcing power would be minimized. Similarly, if a child is flooded with praise from a teacher or parent, the praise will lose its reinforcing value. While a teacher in a classroom of average size generally does not have to worry about too frequent delivery of praise, teachers who tutor children or who work with children in small groups should be attuned to the fact that their praise can lose its power if it is used too frequently. In order to make a tutor's praise most effective, it may even facilitate the tutoring session by having the child wait alone outside the tutor's office for a 5- or 10-minute period where he would have little to do. Gewirtz and Baer (1958) have demonstrated that deprivation can lead to strong adult reinforcing power whereas satiation will minimize such power.

## PREVENTION

Considering the small number of psychologists and other "mental health" personnel who are involved in treatment of children's problems in school settings, it seems both financially infeasible and practically impossible to ask professionals to deal with all the major problems that arise in a school. There are at least two possible approaches to the problem of providing adequate attention to problem children: (1) teachers, parents, paraprofessionals, and peers can be trained to handle problem situations which are currently dealt with by professionals, and (2) teachers, parents, paraprofessionals, and peers can be used more effectively to *prevent* problem situations from arising. Follow-Through programs which deal with children after they have been in Head Start are a step in the proper direction. Better teacher training with a focus on identification and remediation of problems in the classroom itself is certainly necessary. The use of peers to teach other children academic skills and the effective utilization of paraprofessionals are additional answers to the manpower problem. Let us discuss each of the methods of preventing academic and social problems in the classroom.

### Head Start and Follow-Through Programs

Head Start is an attempt by the federal government to give some children who are economically deprived an academic and social "head start"—to prevent academic failure and to prevent the development of inappropriate social behavior. Initial research evaluations of Head Start revealed that children who were in Head Start programs did score significantly better on measures of social and academic skills at the end of their Head Start experience than children who did not receive such experience. However, two years later the children who attended Head Start could not be distinguished from children who did not attend Head Start (Cicirelli, Cooper, & Granger, 1969). In an effort to capitalize on the gains made in Head Start, the federal government created Follow-Through, a first- and second-grade program for children who were in Head Start. Approximately 25 different approaches to Head Start and Follow-Through are now funded by the federal government, and these approaches are being evaluated to assess what effects the various programs have. Two programs, with a heavy behavior modification orientation, seem to be having very significant effects with diverse racial and ethnic groups in a number of geographical regions in the United States (*Behavior Today*, 1972). The Bushell program with headquarters at the University of Kansas and the Engelmann-Becker program at the University of Oregon both have a decided focus on academic programming and contingency management. Both programs involve workshops to teach the parents how to present some instruction to the children and how to reinforce the children for their efforts. That is, there is *follow-through* by the parents of what is taking place in the classroom. It is our impression that both the children and the parents are aided by such training, and it is likely that such training will reinforce or "follow-through" on those behaviors which were prompted by the Head Start program. If teachers and parents are not taught to follow-through by reinforcing desired academic and social behavior, the newly acquired academic and social behaviors will die. We can now optimistically say that most children can be "taught to be smart" (Becker, 1973), and with this knowledge many legislators are arguing for the institution of educational programs for all children between the ages of three and five. In fact, a bill was introduced into Congress by Congressman John Tunney (H.R., 15433) which proposed that the U.S. Department of Health, Education and Welfare give money to communities who wish to start their children in school earlier than the traditional kindergarten age. In short, Tunney wants all children to start school at age three (Tunney, 1970). Because of the national political pressure for day care centers, it is likely that such legislative efforts will be passed within the next 10 years. If so, many of the behavior problems currently seen in the classroom which are largely the result of poor academic skills may be prevented.

## Teacher Training

Even if Head Start and Follow-Through programs accomplished most of their objectives, there presumably would still be a number of social and academic problems which a teacher would have to face. Undoubtedly there are many highly skilled teachers who already can change behavior very effectively, even though they may never have heard of behavior modification. Unfortunately, the skills of such teachers will remain an art if the precise manner by which they change behavior is not made explicit. The behavior modification approach represents a concrete attempt to make explicit those procedures by which a teacher can change behavior. Possibly, the most important asset of the behavior modification approach is that it presents a conceptual framework for viewing the development of behavior and behavior change procedures. Since such a framework exists, the teacher can become a behavior analyst in his or her own right. Teachers should learn a set of principles for observing and changing behavior *on their own* in a systematic manner. If a general approach to behavioral change were learned, the teacher presumably could handle almost any problem as it arises in the classroom. Some of the principles presented in this book are so simple that one wonders why they are not already practiced throughout the country. It seems obvious that a teacher could (1) easily make the classroom rules clear, (2) give academic work that is commensurate with each child's skills, (3) frequently praise the children for their successes, (4) ignore children when they are involved in minor disruptions, (5) make explicit the consequences of severe disruptions, and (6) deal with each child consistently. Certainly, it is a waste of a psychologist's time and training to review such basic principles with individual teachers every time one has a problem. One method of eliminating this "Irrational state of affairs" (Baer, 1970) where consultation is provided to individual teachers as problems arise is to provide in-service training programs for groups of teachers already in the field. More importantly, the principles of behavior modification should be included in all undergraduate education curricula. In short, a behavior modification project larger than any yet tackled needs to be initiated—namely the changing of educational systems and curricula to include courses in behavioral principles and practical experience in the implementation of such principles.

Despite the occasional apparent simplicity of behavior modification procedures, one should be aware that the implementation of these procedures is not easy, and some of the effects of such procedures may seem counterintuitive. It is well known that some teachers upon hearing about behavior modification procedures say, "I've always been doing that. I reward my students when they are good." Obviously, such an answer reflects great naivete, because behavior modification procedures are much more complicated than that. Both the new teacher and the experienced teacher should recognize that research concerning the teacher's application of behavioral principles in the classroom has answered some questions quite definitively. However, in all of this research an emphasis has been placed not only on the implementation of behavioral principles but on very consistent implementation of such principles. It is hoped that the reader will sense the crucial importance of such consistency both conceptually and as it relates to the daily operations of a classroom.

## Paraprofessionals

Our society is becoming increasingly aware of the fact that many functions of personnel with professional titles could be performed by people without such titles. The term "paraprofessional" describes the people who work beside or along with ("para" meaning "beside") professional personnel but who are not trained in all aspects of the profession or who do not have a professional degree. Such an awareness has led to new schools for people working with professionals and new titles such as medical assistant, psychological assistant, and teacher assistant. For example, many functions of a physician can be performed by a physician's assistant who does not have a medical degree (M.D.) but who is trained to execute many technical tasks often done by physicians. Such functions might include performing preliminary medical examinations, maintaining patients' medical records, executing certain diagnostic tests, and performing resuscitation and other emergency procedures until a physician arrives.

Similarly, many functions of psychologists can be performed by someone without a doctorate (Ph.D.) in psychology, but who has been trained in specific technical tasks. For example, most testing functions and some teaching functions could be executed by a psychologist with a master's degree in psychology (M.A. or M.S.) or by a well trained person without college training (Ryback & Staats, 1970; Thomas, Nielsen, Kuypers, & Becker, 1968). Allerhand (1967) found that after three training sessions parents without high school degrees were as effective as psychology graduate students in administering two standard intelligence tests to Head Start children. Poser (1966) compared the effectiveness of psychiatrists (persons with medical degrees and additional psychiatric training), psychiatric social workers, and undergraduates in modifying the behavior of psychotic patients. Although the undergraduates had no special training in psychotherapy and although they were not told how to conduct their therapeutic sessions, patients seen by the undergraduates displayed greater gains than the untreated patients or the patients treated by the psychiatrists and psychiatric social workers. Rioch and her associates (1963) found that married women who received special training were able to change the behavior of their clients as well as professionals. The work of Allerhand, Poser, and Rioch should alert one to the possibility that paraprofessionals can definitely be used advantageously. If very specific procedures are found to deal with certain problems, trained housewives and undergraduates may perform a very useful function in psychological clinics, physical rehabilitation centers, and psychiatric hospitals. Kent and O'Leary (in press) found that teams consisting of clinical psychologists and former teachers were as effective in reducing classroom behavior problems of children as were clinical psychologists working alone. Their model involved having the clinical psychologists and teachers perform specific but somewhat different functions, and the model could readily be used to markedly increase the services available to children.

Paraprofessionals in school systems have made the public aware that properly trained paraprofessionals can perform certain skills as well as or better than permanently certified teachers. Paraprofessionals can grade papers, administer and score tests, record frequencies of behavior, dispense reinforcers, tutor children, and teach in circumscribed areas where the curriculum and its presentation are well defined. Such trained personnel obviously could be of benefit to almost any classroom situation. If paraprofessionals were used in all elementary schools as they are in Head Start and Follow-Through programs, the large numbers of children who lack academic and social skills when they arrive in third and fourth grade would be diminished greatly.

## Utilization of Peers as Therapeutic Agents

The fact that children can significantly influence the behavior of other children has long been known by professionals and laymen alike. Unfortunately, the therapeutic skills of children have not been used effectively by teachers. As will be evidenced in the section on peers as therapeutic agents, peers can successfully alter the behavior of other children in their classes (Graubard, Rosenberg, & Miller, 1971; Solomon & Wahler, 1973). Surratt, Ulrich, and Hawkins (1969) had a fifth grader record the amount of time four first graders were working appropriately. The first graders were reinforced with extra privileges for increasing amounts of time spent working and, as might be expected, the rate of studying or time spent working increased. Winett, Richards, Krasner, and Krasner (1971) had children rather than the teacher dispense tokens in a second-grade classroom and found that attending to the reading assignments increased in four of five children selected for observation in a normal public school classroom. The child-monitored token program took place while the teacher was conducting reading conferences with individual children, and the use of peers during this period—often referred to as "independent seat work"—offered a practical method of implementing behavior change programs when the teacher could not easily evaluate the children's behavior. Drabman (1973) even found that adolescents diagnosed schizophrenic were extremely effective in administering a classroom token program (awarding points) under the supervision of a teacher. Ulrich, Wallace, and Dulaney (1970) had elementary school children teach 18 30-month-old children to identify objects by name. The elementary school children were taught to present stimuli to the infants in a particular manner, to reinforce the infant with a piece of sugar-coated cereal, and to praise the infant when he made an appropriate vocalization or spoke correctly. All infants showed marked improvement following instruction by the elementary students. While the utilization of children as behavior modifiers as described in the last example does not bear directly on classroom management, the utilization of young children as behavior modifiers is certainly a method of preventing children from entering elementary school with poor language skills. Even if adult teacher aides are used increasingly in the school system, using children can be both beneficial to other children and highly desirable for the child behavior modifier in an educational sense. As adults, we know how much we ourselves learn when we are asked to explain or teach something to others. It should not be surprising that older students who teach younger students also learn something about the subject they are teaching. The use of junior high and high school students as tutors for elementary school children is also desirable since the student may find out long before he enters college whether he would enjoy a teaching career (Willis, Morris, & Crowder, 1972).

The aid of peers can also be enlisted in a more indirect fashion by reinforcing them for ignoring the disruptive behaviors of a particular child (Carlson, Arnold, Becker, & Madsen, 1968; Patterson, 1965). Carlson et al. reinforced the class for ignoring the tantrum behavior of a child, and points leading to a *class* party were made contingent upon the target child having no tantrums per half day of school. Evans and Oswalt (1968) reinforced the entire class when a single child answered questions correctly. They assumed that the class would reinforce the target child for his appropriate behavior, and that as a consequence the target child would show academic progress.

## SOCIAL ISSUES RELATED TO BEHAVIOR CHANGE PROGRAMS

Before considering the evidence concerning behavior modification procedures, several issues should be discussed which are often of paramount concern to all when initially exposed to behavior modification. The issues include the topics of labeling, teacher expectations, control and responsibility, and the sensitivity of the behavior modifier.

## Labeling

Special educators have worried about the influence on children of labels such as emotionally disturbed, retarded, schizophrenic, or delinquent (Hobbs, 1975). More specifically, they have been concerned that a child would be stigmatized by such a label, that people would react to him in accord with the label, and that the child in turn might continue to act the role depicted by the label he received. That is, the child would tend to act the part of an emotionally disturbed child if he were so labeled. Because of this concern, many schools have wisely used euphemistic names for classes of children often labeled retarded, emotionally disturbed, or schizophrenic. For example, classroom labels are now Transitional Classes, Project Help, Community Living and Learning, Project Achieve, Project Learn, etc. Though there is little research on this important problem, the new labels are probably a good idea.

## Teacher Expectations

The influence of teacher expectations on IQ scores was purportedly demonstrated by Rosenthal and Jacobsen (1966) who reported that simply telling a teacher that a child had potential for giftedness was related to a large IQ gain in one year—particularly in the first and second grades. This research has now been subjected to heavy criticism (Snow, 1969; Thorndike, 1969), and additional research has shown that giving a teacher differential expectancies about her children may influence her behavior in very diverse ways and that IQ scores of children do not always increase when the teacher is told that a child has a potential for being gifted. Given such an expectation, some teachers may spend more time with such a child while others appear to spend much less time with a child labeled gifted (Meichenbaum, Bowers, & Ross, 1969). Despite the absolute score a child receives on an intelligence test, it is probably always best to (1) present academic material to a child in a manner that enables him to succeed most of the time, (2) behave toward him in a manner that conveys the expectation that he can succeed, and (3) praise him heavily for his resulting good behavior.

## Control and Responsibility

Because of the inherent power of some of the behavior modification procedures, people sometimes feel that they are very dangerous tools. Scientific advances always carry the potential for evil doings and psychological advances make some people feel particularly uneasy. On the other hand, principles of behavior control have the potential for a great amount of good. Psychological research will proceed in this country as well as in other countries, and as the potential for behavioral change becomes greater and greater, the scientific community must ask itself if the changes it is helping to make are really beneficial. That is, with greater control comes greater responsibility. Many of the behavioral changes reported in the articles in this book are reflective of general wishes of teachers. Changing a child's behavior such as being in one's seat and paying attention is occasionally criticized by educational philosophers because the change seems irrelevant to some educational goals (O'Leary, 1972; Winett & Winkler, 1972). While being in one's seat and paying attention are not always inextricably related to learning, the child who is in his seat is more likely to receive effective help from the teacher. In short, having a child sit still and pay attention is but a first step in the progression toward many educational goals. As evidenced by the articles in this book, children are taught more with greater precision in shorter periods of time than has formerly been possible. Yet one must question whether such goals are the critical aims of education. More importantly, just what behaviors should be taught? While many of the studies in behavior modification have focused on deviant children or adults, it is likely that future work will be addressed to enhancing diverse behaviors of normal children. For example, creativity, sensitivity to others, logical thinking, musical skills, and knowledge of economics are but a few of the behaviors which may well receive attention in the next decade by behavior modifiers. Sharing and cooperative behavior have already begun to be investigated by psychologists including those with an avowed behavior modification emphasis. Behavior modification can be a tool to maintain a poor educational system; it can be a tool for enhancing the positive aspects of our current system; or it can be helpful in creating new systems. Obviously, it can only be a tool in creating new educational systems if teachers and researchers take a critical look at both the short-term and long-range results of existing systems. Whenever a powerful tool for rapidly changing behavior exists, such as behavior modification, it is imperative that the long-term goals of our educational system be evaluated carefully.

## Sensitivity

Shaping behavior requires a great deal of sensitivity to small nuances in behavior change and in environmental change. The teacher or therapist must notice and reinforce any small approximations to the desired terminal behavior. If one is to teach behaviors which will be maintained by the natural environment in which a child lives, a teacher or parent must be sensitive to the *actual* practices of the child's parents and peers instead of the *purported* practices of such persons. That is, one must be sensitive to the kinds of behaviors which really will receive rewards in the home and community—not just what parents say would be good for their children. Before one attempts to change a behavior of a client or a child in a classroom, a great deal of sensitivity is necessary to decide what the parent or teacher really desires. For example, a parent may come to a psychologist purportedly to seek aid for her child, but in reality, she has come to discuss her own problems. Similarly, a teacher may come to a school psychologist ostensibly to talk about a child who is not progressing satisfactorily, when, in fact, she may be most interested in finding out where she can get help for herself about a personal problem. A parent may come to a teacher to discuss her child but may be even more interested in finding out how she can obtain state aid, welfare, or food stamps. Since some people are reticent to bring up such problems, a behavior modifier—be he psychologist, teacher, social worker, or psychiatrist—should be very careful to ascertain why his help is being sought lest he find himself overzealously changing a behavior which was only of peripheral concern to the person seeking aid. In summary, while the behavior modifier must be aware of the experimental principles which he can apply to human problems, he must also be sensitive to the feelings and attitudes of his client or student, and to be effective, he must be warm and spontaneous. While teachers and therapists have always tried to be warm and loving, their love has often been rather haphazardly focused.

Another facet of sensitivity concerns a therapist's or teacher's warmth and emotional responses to a child. To be a good modifier of behavior one cannot simply dispense attention in a mechanical or machine-like fashion. One must give such attention in a spontaneous, warm manner. Equally important, one must be aware of a child's feelings and desires so that when the child is excited over success—be it ever so small—the teacher will respond immediately in a sincere fashion. That is, the teacher must have some empathy for the child.

The teacher or therapist who is maximally effective probably frequently exhibits a variety of affective behaviors—she is soft and gentle on one occasion while on another she is ebullient and ecstatic with excitement about a child's progress. She probably reprimands occasionally but in a firm manner indicating or intimating that there will be some consequence if the child does not cease his activity. More importantly, when she is approving, she also acts as if she really means it. When such warmth and love are systematically channeled, their potential for changing behavior is enhanced immeasurably.

# 2
# *Teacher Attention*

The way teachers attend to their pupils determines in large measure what the children will do. A teacher's smiles, words of encouragement, praise, evaluations, and silence are powerful allies in affecting how the students behave and change socially and academically. Because of this, teacher attention is perhaps the most basic of all influences on students' behavior, and the systematic use of attention should characterize every teacher's classroom repertoire. When a child is not learning or behaving productively, there are many ways of changing the child's behavior, but systematic teacher attention should be either the first procedure tried or a central component of other procedures. Positive forms of teacher attention, such as praise, are valued by most children. Therefore, when a teacher responds to a desirable behavior with praise, the frequency of that behavior usually tends to increase over time. Similarly, when a teacher ignores a nonproductive behavior by looking away and remaining silent, that behavior is likely to occur less frequently in the future.

The preceding comments may seem patently obvious and the procedure embarrassingly simple. Certainly all teachers variously attend to and ignore their students. However, using this attention systematically and effectively requires skill and awareness on the teacher's part. Prior to implementing a praise and ignore procedure, or any other behavior change procedure for that matter, the behaviors to be changed must be clearly defined so that the teacher will know not only what to respond to but also whether the procedure s/he employs is effective. As will be seen in most of the articles in this book, the behaviors of concern are described carefully enough so that two or more people can agree with precision that the behaviors have or have not occurred. Although the precision of research reports is usually unnecessary for general application of behavioral procedures, specific rather than global characterizations of the child's behavior will help a teacher implement these procedures most effectively. For example, it is much easier for a teacher to notice how often a child smiles or says that he would like to take a paper home than it is to assess the child's self-confidence (see chapters 1 and 9 for further discussion of assessment issues).

The behaviors which the teacher has defined as important for the child's progress will probably include behaviors to be increased in frequency as well as behaviors to be decreased in frequency. For example, the teacher may want Sara to complete more of her work, to volunteer more answers to questions, to make fewer requests to go to the bathroom, and to spend less time at the teacher's desk. If Sara is praised for completing her work and for volunteering answers, she will probably do so more often. By ignorning Sara when she is at the teacher's desk and when she asks to go to the bathroom, the teacher will find that these behaviors will occur less frequently.

Sara's behavior will not change overnight but must be gradually shaped. To shape a behavior, the teacher should determine the level at which Sara is presently able to perform and then praise her for successive improvements. Suppose Sara is now completing only one of her five daily assignments. By giving her shorter assignments, the teacher can make it very likely that Sara will be successful at completing all her work and can encourage and praise Sara's accomplishments. The length of the assignments and the teacher's criterion for praise may be gradually increased until Sara is regularly completing full length assignments. Shaping a behavior requires careful planning. The teacher who sets initial goals which are too high will have nothing to praise; the teacher who expects instant results will be discouraged and may give up. The end result will be the same: the child's behavior will not improve.

With behaviors which the teacher decides to systematically ignore, such as Sara's frequent visits to the teacher's desk, improvement will also be gradual. In fact, the problem may become worse before it improves. When Sara's source of satisfaction for coming to the desk is removed, she may at first solicit the teacher's attention more often, and only when it is clear that completing assignments is the only reliable way to attract the teacher's attention will she stop coming to the desk. Thus, ignoring must be consistent, or Sara will merely learn that being persistent or noisier when she comes to the desk will eventually attract the teacher's eye. By simultaneously praising behaviors which are incompatible with the ignored behavior (e.g., praising Sara for sitting at her own desk), the effects of ignoring will be improved.

Several suggestions for maximizing the effectiveness of teacher attention are discussed in the articles in this chapter. For example, praise should be as spontaneous and sincere as possible. When a teacher significantly increases the frequency of her praise, especially if the children involved have been constant sources of aggravation, s/he may feel somewhat awkward and artificial. Care must be taken not to communicate these feelings to the children. To foster sincerity, comments to the children should vary in content and specify the behaviors being praised (see Madsen, Becker, & Thomas, 1968, for examples). The effectiveness of praise will be enhanced if the child's improved behavior is praised very shortly after it occurs. For example, a child's progress in completing assignments will be faster if the teacher corrects and praises each completion as it occurs rather than waits until the end of the day. Certainly, teachers cannot respond immediately to every good behavior; and praising a child on Friday for cooperating well with other children on Thursday is clearly preferable to not praising the child at all. The teacher should also take into account what type of praise is effective for the particular child. Some children respond well to physical contact and affection, while others (often older children) might find a hug aversive but would be delighted with a complimentary note on the completed paper.

Consistently ignoring a behavior which is annoying can be very difficult. Herein lies one of the pitfalls of misusing teacher attention (particularly ignoring). Many teachers who believe they are "ignoring" misbehavior may, in fact, be inadvertently reinforcing the behavior they wish to decrease, either by occasionally forgetting to ignore the response or by unwittingly attending to the behavior, often nonverbally. Attention from a teacher need not be praise or a pat on the back to be reinforcing. Being able to engage a teacher in a brief, perhaps even unpleasant, conversation or catching the teacher's eye can increase the frequency of a child's behavior. An instance that occurred recently in a special class for first-grade behavior problem children illustrates this point. The teacher in this class used her attention systematically in a highly skilled manner. However, in one case she unknowingly developed a behavior pattern resulting in high rates of low intensity disruption in the classroom. A child would misbehave in some minor way, such as tapping his pencil. The teacher would glance briefly at the source of the disruption and then ignore the incident. The child would immediately engage in a highly positive behavior, such as working diligently; and since the teacher's private, if not public, attention was still focused on the child, she would praise him for his hard work. Minor disruptions were increasing in the classroom as a consequence of this sequence of behavior which terminated with praise. The teacher altered her behavior by completely ignoring minor disturbances and by praising the children only when good work was not immediately preceded by misbehavior, and the minor disturbances lessened in frequency. This example again emphasizes that using teacher attention successfully requires skill, careful observation, and recognition of the subtle interplay between praise and ignoring.

Finally, teachers can foster productive behavior in a child by praising the appropriate behavior of another child sitting nearby. For example, imagine a situation in which two children are sitting next to each other. One child is busily working; the other is playing with a toy in his desk. The teacher would probably elect to ignore the playing; however she wants to see that child working also. If she praises the child who is doing his work, she will often find that the other child will stop his playing and return to his assignment. It is not clear whether this procedure is effective because the teacher's comment serves as a cue for good behavior, whether the problem child models the behavior of the child being praised, or whether the child who is attending to his work is less likely to respond to the fact that his neighbor is playing. In any event, this form of teacher attention has proved successful (Broden, Bruce, Mitchell, Carter, & Hall, 1970) and can serve as an additional tool for improving behavior.

Some other important facts should be considered when attempting to decrease the frequency of a behavior by ignoring it. Clearly, dangerous and destructive behaviors cannot be ignored. Behaviors which appear to be maintained by powerful influences outside the teacher's control, such as attention from peers, probably will not decrease and may occur more and more frequently if ignored by the teacher. If, for example, a girl's trips to the teacher's desk are reinforced by winks from her boyfriend in the front row, she will probably continue this behavior even though the teacher ignores her. On the other hand, if the student is primarily interested in some personal attention from the teacher, ignoring may be very effective. When a behavior appears to be reinforced by someone other than the teacher, the teacher might consider trying some form of mild punishment rather than ignoring the response. Punishment will be discussed in detail in the next chapter.

While teachers are concerned about how effective various procedures are, they are also rightfully concerned about how much time and effort are involved in implementing a procedure. Learning the skills associated with the systematic use of teacher attention may require that a teacher concentrate on and alter habitual patterns of behavior and, in that sense, will demand extra effort from a teacher until those skills are acquired. However, the judicious implementation of praise and ignoring does not mean that the teacher must spend more time attending to the children. Most teachers find that they spend a great deal of time interacting with problem children primarily in reaction to the disruptions the child is causing. It can be said with reasonable certainty that a teacher need spend no more, and will probably spend less, time with the difficult children if the *pattern* of those interactions is altered. Instead of reminding Bill to return to his eating, telling him to stop bothering his neighbors, reprimanding him for shooting paper clips with a rubberband, and only occasionally praising his completed assignments, the teacher should attempt to reverse this ratio of attending to negative rather than positive behaviors. Productive behaviors should be the ones to catch the teacher's eye; disruptions should be ignored. In most cases, this altered pattern of interaction will yield desirable results without requiring substantially more interaction with the problem child. With improvements in the behavior of classroom troublemakers, the teacher will be able to divide his or her time more equitably among all the students.

The articles which follow illustrate in a controlled manner and in normal classrooms many of the points mentioned above. The work of Madsen, Becker, and Thomas (1968) is a classic demonstration of the effects of using teacher attention systematically. The report contains many excellent practical examples of how to establish classroom rules, to praise, and to ignore. One of the most important points made by Madsen et al. (1968) is that ignoring disruptive behavior is not an effective procedure unless accompanied by praise for appropriate behavior. In addition, teacher A was able to alter the pattern of her attention so that by the end of the study she was spending 25% less time responding to social behaviors than she had initially, and the two problem children in her class were displaying 70% less disruptive behavior.

The dramatic effects of altered attention patterns are replicated with an older child in the Kirby and Shields (1972) article. The reader should not be confused by the term "adjusting fixed-ratio schedule." By this, the authors simply meant that at any one point the student had to complete a certain ("fixed") number of problems to receive praise, and this number was gradually increased ("adjusted") over time as the student demonstrated his ability to complete more work. This procedure is comparable to those discussed earlier for shaping behavior from its existing level to a more productive level or form. Note the comment made by the authors in describing the interaction between Tom, the seventh-grade students, and his teacher prior to the study. Tom typically did not work unless his teacher reminded him or stood next to him. After a few minutes or when the teacher left, he stopped working until she again reprimanded him. In effect, the teacher was directing her attention to Tom only when he was not studying, and non-study behaviors were indeed occurring at a high rate. This pattern represents a common form of the misuse of teacher attention while at the same time shows the powerful effect attention has on behavior. Unlike the other two studies in this section, the Kirby and Shields (1972) study focused on changing an academic rather than a social behavior. Interestingly, both Tom's rate of correct math solutions and the extent to which he paid attention during class were monitored even though Tom was praised only for correct answers. The fact that his attending behavior improved when he was praised for correct answers suggests that teachers may be able to focus directly on the academic behaviors which are of ultimate concern and find correlated improvement in more social behaviors such as attending.

The Drabman and Lahey (1974) article is included for several reasons. This study demonstrated that systematically attending to a problem child's behavior did *not* adversely affect other children in the class but, on the contrary, fostered better behavior in the rest of the class and also resulted in better relations between the problem child and her peers. In addition, the procedure used was a simple evaluative feedback given in the form of a rating every 10-15 minutes, a clearly effective procedure requiring very little effort on the teacher's part. The present authors have found that a good rule of thumb with any problem behavior is to begin with the simplest procedures involving the least amount of extra reward and to intervene with more complex programs only if the simpler procedures prove to be ineffective.

In summary, the systematic use of teacher attention is a very effective way to change children's behavior. In spite of its relatively simple and natural appearance, the procedure requires skill to implement with maximum success. Teachers should consider altering their patterns of interaction with children rather than dramatically increasing the frequency of those contacts. Complex, time-consuming efforts may not be needed to curtail classroom disruptions; even a simple feedback procedure can lead to significant improvement in classroom behavior. Finally, of all the procedures discussed in this book, the systematic use of teacher attention is the one that we feel all teachers should be using routinely with all their students.

# Article 1
## Rules, Praise, and Ignoring:
## Elements of Elementary Classroom Control*

CHARLES H. MADSEN, JR., WESLEY C. BECKER,
and DON R. THOMAS †

**Abstract**: An attempt was made to vary systematically the behavior of two elementary school teachers to determine the effects on classroom behavior of Rules, Ignoring Inappropriate Behaviors, and showing Approval for Appropriate Behavior. Behaviors of two children in one class and one child in the other class were recorded by observers, as were samples of the teachers' behavior. Following baseline recordings, Rules, Ignoring, and Approval conditions were introduced one at a time. In one class a reversal of conditions was carried out. The main conclusions were that: (a) Rules alone exerted little effect on classroom behavior, (b) Ignoring Inappropriate Behavior and showing Approval for Appropriate Behavior (in combination) were very effective in achieving better classroom behavior, and (c) showing Approval for Appropriate Behaviors is probably the key to effective classroom management.

Modern learning theory is slowly but surely increasing its potential for impact upon social problems. As problems in social development and interaction are more closely examined through the methods of experimental analysis, the importance of learning princi-

*Reprinted by permission from the *Journal of Applied Behavior Analysis,* Vol. 1, No. 2, 1968, 139-150. Copyright 1968 by the Society for the Experimental Analysis of Behavior, Inc.

†We wish to express our appreciation to the teachers involved, Mrs. Barbara L. Weed and Mrs. Margaret Larson, for their cooperation in a study which involved using and applying procedures which at times made their teaching duties very difficult. Gratitude is expressed to the Director of Elementary Education, Unit District #116, Urbana, Illinois, Dr. Lowell M. Johnson, and to the principals of Thomas Paine and Prairie Schools, Richard Sturgeon and Donald Holste. This study was supported by Grant HD-00881-05 from the National Institutes of Health.

ples in everyday life becomes clearer. The potential contribution of these developments to childrearing and education appears to be especially significant. This report is a part of a series of studies aimed at demonstrating what the teacher can do to achieve a "happier," more effective classroom through the systematic use of learning principles. The study grows out of a body of laboratory and field research demonstrating the importance of social reinforcers (smiles, praise, contact, nearness, attention) in establishing and maintaining effective behaviors in children. Extensive field studies in experimental nursery schools by Wolf, Bijou, Bear, and their students (e.g., Hart, Reynolds, Baer, Brawley, & Harris, 1968; Allen, Hart, Buell, Harris, & Wolf, 1965; Bijou & Baer, 1963) provided a background for the extension of their work by the present authors to special and typical elementary classrooms. In general, we have found to date that teachers with various "personalities" and backgrounds can be trained systematically to control their own behavior in ways which will improve the behavior of the children they are teaching. (Becker, Madsen, Arnold, & Thomas, 1967). We have also found that teachers can "create" problem behaviors in the classroom by controlling the ways in which they respond to their pupils (Thomas, Becker, & Armstrong, 1968; Madsen, Becker, Thomas, Koser, & Plager, 1968). It is hoped that field studies of this sort will contribute to more effective teacher training.

The present study is a refinement of an earlier study of Becker et al. (1967), in which the behavior of two children in each of five classrooms was recorded and related to experimentally controlled changes in teacher behaviors. The teachers were instructed and guided to follow a program which involved making classroom rules explicit, ignoring disruptive behaviors unless someone was getting hurt, and praising appropriate classroom behaviors. Under this program, most of the severe problem children under study showed remarkable improvements in classroom behavior. However, that study lacked certain controls which the present study sought to correct. First, the teachers in the earlier study were in a seminar on behavior theory and practice during baseline conditions. Some target children improved during baseline, apparently because some teachers were beginning to apply what they were learning even though they had been requested not to do so. Second, public relations and time considerations did not make it possible to introduce the components of the experimental program one at a time (rules, ignoring, and praise) to better study their individual contributions. Third, a reversal of teacher behavior was not attempted. Such a reversal would more conclusively show the importance of teacher's behavior in producing the obtained changes. Fourth, extensive recordings of teacher behavior under all experimental conditions were not undertaken in the earlier study. The present study attempted to deal with each of these problems.

# METHOD

## Procedures

Teachers in a public elementary school volunteered to participate in the study. After consultation with teachers and observation of the children in the classroom, two children with a high frequency of problem behavior were selected for study in each class. Previously developed behavioral categories (Becker et al., 1967) were modified for use with these particular children and baseline recordings were made to determine the frequency of problem behaviors. At the end of the baseline period the teachers entered a workshop on applications of behavioral principles in the classroom which provided them with the rationale and principles behind the procedures being introduced in their classes. Various experimental procedures were then introduced, one at a time, and the effects on the target children's behaviors observed. The experiments were begun in late November and continued to the end of the school year.

## Subjects

### Classroom A
There were 29 children in Mrs. A's middle-primary (second grade) room who ranged in school progress from mid-first-grade level to early-third-grade level. Cliff and Frank were chosen as the target children.

Cliff was chosen because he displayed no interest in school. In Mrs. A's words, "he would sit throughout entire work periods fiddling with objects in his desk, talking, doing nothing, or misbehaving by bothering others and walking around the room. Lately he has started hitting others for no apparent reason. When Cliff was required to stay in at recess to do his work, he would complete the work in a short time and it was usually completely accurate. I was unable to motivate him into working on any task during the regular work periods." Cliff is the son of a university professor who was born in Europe and immigrated when Cliff was 5-yrs. old. Cliff scored 91 on an early (CA 5-3) intelligence test. This score was discounted by the examiner because of language problems. His group IQ scores rose steadily (CA 5-9, IQ 103; CA 6-2, IQ 119; CA 7-1, IQ 123). His achievement scores indicated a low second-grade level at the beginning of the present study. Cliff was seen by the school social worker throughout the entire first grade and throughout this entire study.

Cliff was observed early in the year and it was noted that he did not respond once to teacher's questions. He played with his fingers, scratched himself repeatedly, played in his desk, paid no attention to the assignment and had to stay in at recess to finish his work. Almost continually he made blowing sounds and talked to himself. On occasions he was out of his seat making noises and talking. He would leave the room without permission. Before the study began the observers made the following notes: "What a silly kid, writing on the bottom of his shoes, writing on his arms, blowing kisses at the girls. He was vying for the attention of the girl behind him, but she ignored him. . . . Poor Cliff! he acts so silly for his age. He tried to talk to the other kids, but none of them would pay attention to him. . . . Cliff seems concerned with the little girl beside him (girl behind him last week). He has a sign on his desk which reads, 'Do you love me?'. . . ."

Frank was described by his teacher as a likeable child. He had a record of misbehavior in the classroom and intense fighting on the playground. He was often out of his seat talking to other children and did not respond to "discipline." If someone was reprimanded for doing something, Frank would often do the same thing. Test scores indicated an IQ of 106 (Stanford-Binet) and achievement level just under beginning second grade at the start of school (average California Achievement Test scores 1.6 grades). The school psychologist noted that Frank's mother was a person "who willingly permitted others to make decisions for her and did not seem able to discipline Frank." Father was absent from the home during the entire year in the Air Force.

*Classroom B*

Twenty children were assigned to Mrs. B's kindergarten room. Two children were observed initially; one moved from the community shortly after baseline was taken, leaving only Stan for the study.

Stan was described as coming from a truly pathetic home environment. The mother was not married and the family of four children subsisted on state aid. One older brother was enrolled in a special class for the educable retarded. At the beginning of the year, Stan's behavior was characterized by the teacher as "wild." She reported that, "Stan would push and hit and grab at objects and at children. He had no respect for authority and apparently didn't even hear directions. He knew how to swear profusely, and I would have to check his pockets so I would know he wasn't taking home school equipment. He would wander around the room and it was difficult to get him to engage in constructive work. He would frequently destroy any work he did rather than take it home."

The difficult home situation was made manifest during the month of March. Stan had been absent for two weeks and it was reported that his mother was taking her children out of public school and placing them in a local parochial school. Investigation by school personnel indicated that Stan's mother had moved the children into a relative's home and had gone to the hospital to have another illegitimate baby. A truancy notice was filed for all four children including Stan. Following legal notice the children were returned to school.

### Rating of Child Behavior

The same rating schedule was used in both classrooms except that Isolate Play was added to the list of Inappropriate Behaviors for the kindergarten. Since the children were expected to be involved in structured group activities during observation periods, going off by oneself to play with the many toys or materials in the room was considered inappropriate by the kindergarten teacher. Inappropriate Behavior was defined as the occurrence of one or more of the behaviors listed under Inappropriate Behavior in Table 1 during any observation interval.

Observers were trained in the reliable use of the rating schedule before baseline recordings began. Training consisted of practice in use of the rating schedule in the classroom. Two observers would each rate the same child for 20 min and then return to the research office to compare their ratings and discuss their differences with their supervisor. Training was continued until reliability was above 80% on each behavior code. Training lasted approximately two weeks. Reliability was determined periodically throughout the study by dividing the number of agreements by the number of agreements plus disagreements. An agreement was defined as a rating of the same

## Table 1. Behavioral Coding Categories for Children.

I.   Inappropriate Behaviors

   A.   *Gross Motor.* Getting out of seat, standing up, running, hopping, skipping, jumping, walking around, moving chair, etc.

   B.   *Object Noise.* Tapping pencil or other objects, clapping, tapping feet, rattling or tearing paper, throwing book on desk, slamming desk. Be conservative, only rate if you can hear the noise when eyes are closed. Do *not* include accidental dropping of objects.

   C.   *Disturbance of Other's Property.* Grabbing objects or work, knocking neighbor's books off desk, destroying another's property, pushing with desk (only rate if someone is there). Throwing objects at another person without hitting them.

   D.   *Contact (high and low intensity).* Hitting, kicking, shoving, pinching, slapping, striking with object, throwing object which hits another person, poking with object, biting, pulling hair, touching, patting, etc. Any physical contact is rated.

   E.   *Verbalization.* Carrying on conversations with other children when it is not permitted. Answers teacher without raising hand or without being called on; making comments or calling out remarks when no questions have been asked; calling teacher's name to get her attention; crying, screaming, singing, whistling, laughing, coughing, or blowing loudly. These responses may be directed to teacher or children.

   F.   *Turning Around.* Turning head or head and body to look at another person, showing objects to another child, attending to another child. Must be of 4 second duration, or more than 90 degrees using desk as a reference. Not rated unless seated. If this response overlaps two time intervals and cannot be rated in the first because it is less than 4 second duration, then rate in the interval in which the end of the response occurs.

   G.   *Other Inappropriate Behavior.* Ignores teacher's question or command. Does something different from that directed to do, including minor motor behavior such as playing with pencil or eraser when supposed to be writing, coloring while the record is on, doing spelling during the arithmetic lesson, playing with objects. *The child involves himself in a task that is not appropriate.* Not rated when other Inappropriate Behaviors are rated. Must be time off task.

H. *Mouthing Objects.* Bringing thumb, fingers, pencils, or any object in contact with the mouth.

I. *Isolate Play. Limited to kindergarten* free-play period. Child must be farther than 3 feet from any person, neither initiates or responds to verbalizations with other people, engages in no interaction of a non-verbal nature with other children for the entire 10 second period.

II. Appropriate Behavior
   Time on task; e.g., answers question, listens, raises hand, works on assignment. Must include whole 10 second interval except for Turning Around responses of less than 4 second duration.

behavior class in the same observation interval. Average reliability over children, behavior classes, and days for the 69 occasions (out of 238) on which it was checked was 81%. Single day reliabilities ranged from 68% to 96%. Reliabilities were checked in each phase of the study.

Instructions to observers followed those used by Becker et al. (1967). In essence, the observers were not to respond to the children, but to fade into the background as much as possible. Teachers, as well as children, quickly learned not to respond to the observers, although early in the study one observer was attacked by a kindergarten child. The observer did not respond to the behavior and it quickly disappeared. Experimental changes were initiated without informing observers in an attempt to control any observer bias. However, the changes were often dramatic enough that observer comments clearly reflected programmed changes in teacher's behavior.

The target children were observed for 20 minutes per day, three days a week. In the middle-primary class, observations were taken when the children were engaged in seat work or group instruction. In the kindergarten class, observations were made when structured activities, rather than free play, were expected. Each observer had a clipboard, stopwatch, and rating sheet. The observer would watch for 10 seconds and use symbols to record the occurrence of behaviors. In each minute, ratings would be made in five consecutive 10-second intervals and the final 10 seconds would be used for recording comments. Each behavior category could be rated only once in a 10-second interval. The primary dependent variable was percentage

**Table 2. Coding Definitions for Teacher Behaviors.**

Appropriate child behavior is defined by the child rating categories. The teacher's rules for classroom behavior must be considered when judging whether the child's behavior is Appropriate or Inappropriate.

I.   Teacher Approval following Appropriate Child Behavior
  A.  *Contact.* Positive physical contact such as embracing, kissing, patting, holding arm or hand, sitting on lap.
  B.  *Praise.* Verbal comments indicating approval, commendation or achievement. Examples: that's good, you are doing right, you are studying well, I like you, thank you, you make me happy.
  C.  *Facial attention.* Smiling at child.

II.  Teacher Approval following Inappropriate Child Behavior
  Same codes as under I

III. Teacher Disapproval following Appropriate Child Behavior
  A.  *Holding the child.* Forcibly holding the child, putting child out in the hall, grabbing, hitting, spanking, slapping, shaking the child.
  B.  *Criticism.* Critical comments of high or low intensity, yelling, scolding, raising voice. Examples: that's wrong, don't do that, stop talking, did I call on you, you are wasting your time, don't laugh, you know what you are supposed to do.
  C.  *Threats.* Consequences mentioned by the teacher to be used at a later time. If _____ then _____ comments.
  D.  *Facial attention.* Frowning or grimacing at a child.

IV.  Teacher Disapproval following Inappropriate Child Behavior
  Same codes as under III

V.   "Timeout" Procedures[a]
  A.  The teacher turns out the lights and says nothing.
  B.  The teacher turns her back and waits for silence.
  C.  The teacher stops talking and waits for quiet.
  D.  Keeping in for recess.
  E.  Sending child to office.
  F.  Depriving child in the classroom of some privilege.

VI.  Academic Recognition
  Calling on a child for an answer. Giving "feedback" for academic correctness.

[a]These are procedural definitions of teacher behaviors possibly involving the withdrawal of reinforcers as a consequence of disruptive behaviors which teacher could not ignore.

of intervals in which an Inappropriate Behavior occurred. Since the varieties of Inappropriate Behavior permitted a more detailed analysis with the schedule used, the presentation of results is focused on them, even though functionally their converse (Appropriate Behavior) was the main behavior being manipulated.

## Ratings of Teacher Behavior

Ratings of teacher behavior were obtained to clarify relationships between changes in teacher behavior and changes in child behavior. Recordings of teacher behavior were also used by the experimenters to help the teachers learn the contingent use of Approval and Disapproval Behaviors. The teacher rating schedule is presented in Table 2. Teacher behaviors were recorded by subclasses in relation to child behaviors. That is, the record would show whether a teacher response followed Appropriate child classroom behavior or whether it followed one of the categories of Inappropriate Behavior. Responses to all children were rated. Teacher behavior was scored as the frequency of occurrence of a specified class of behavior during a 20 minute interval. Teacher ratings were either recorded during one of the periods when a target child was being rated by another observer, or immediately thereafter when only one observer made both ratings. Teacher behavior was rated on the average of once a week. except during experimental transitions, when more frequent ratings were made. The number of days teacher behavior was rated under each condition is given in Table 3. Most recorded teacher behavior (about 85%) fell in the *Verbal* Approval or Disapproval categories. For this reason we have used the term *Praise* interchangeably with Approval Behaviors and *Criticism* interchangeably with Disapproval Behaviors.

Reliability of measures of teacher behavior were checked approximately every other rating day (21 of 42 occasions for the two teachers) by dividing the agreements as to time interval and behavior codes by the agreements plus disagreements. Average reliability over behavior classes, teachers, and days was 84% with a range from 70% to 96% for individual day measures.

## Experimental Conditions

In the middle-primary class (Class A) the experimental conditions may be summarized as consisting of *Baseline*; introduction of *Rules;*

*Rules* plus *Ignoring* deviant behavior; *Rules* plus *Ignoring* plus *Praise* for appropriate behavior; return to *Baseline*; and finally reinstatement of *Rules, Ignoring,* and *Praise.* In the kindergarten class (Class B) the experimental conditions consisted of *Baseline;* introduction of *Rules; Ignoring* Inappropriate Behavior (without continuing to emphasize rules); and the combination of *Rules, Ignoring,* and *Praise.*

The various experimental procedures were to be used by the teachers for the classroom as a whole throughout the day, not just for the children whose behavior was being recorded, and not just when observers were present.

*Baseline.*

During the Baseline period the teachers conducted their classes in their typical way. No attempt was made to influence their behavior.

*Rules*

Many people would argue that just telling children what is expected should have considerable effect on their behavior. We wished to explore this question empirically. Teachers were instructed individually and given written instructions as follows:

> The first phase of your participation in the use of behavioral principles to modify classroom behaviors is to specify explicit rules of classroom conduct. When this is done, there is no doubt as to what is expected of the children in your classroom. However, do not expect a dramatic shift in classroom control, as we all know that knowing the prohibitions does not always keep people from "sin." This is the first phase in the program and inappropriate behavior should be reduced, but perhaps not eliminated. The rules should be formulated with the class and posted in a conspicuous location (a chart in front of the room or a special place on the chalkboard where they will not be erased). Go over the rules three or four times asking the class to repeat them back to you when they are initially formulated and use the following guidelines:
>
> (a) Make the rules short and to the point so they can be easily memorized.
>
> (b) Five or six rules are adequate. Special instructions for specific occasions are best given when the occasion arises. Children will not remember long lists of rules.
>
> (c) Where possible phrase the rules in a positive not a negative manner (for example, "Sit quietly while working,"

rather than, "Don't talk to your neighbors"). We want to emphasize positive actions.

(d) Keep a sheet on your desk and record the number of times you review the rules with the class (strive for at least four to six repetitions per day). Remember that young children do not have the retention span of an adult and frequent reminders are necessary. Let the children recite the rules as you ask them, rather than always enumerating them yourself.

(e) Remind the class of the rules at times other than when someone has misbehaved.

(f) Try to change no other aspects of your classroom conduct except for the presentation of the rules at appropriate times.

Teacher tally sheets indicated that these instructions were followed quite explicitly. The average number of presentations of rules was 5.2 per day.

*Ignoring Inappropriate Behavior*

The second experimental phase involved Ignoring Inappropriate Behavior. In Class A, repetition of rules was also continued. Individual conferences to explain written instructions were given both teachers. Both teachers were given the following instructions:

The first aspect of the study was to make expectations explicit. This you have been doing over the past few weeks. During the next phase of the study you should learn to *ignore* (do not attend to) behaviors which interfere with learning or teaching, unless of course, a child is being hurt by another, in which case use a punishment which seems appropriate, preferably withdrawal of some positive reinforcement. Learning to ignore is rather difficult. Most of us pay attention to the violations. For example, instead of ignoring we often say such things as the following: "Johnny, you know you are supposed to be working"; "Sue, will you stop bothering your neighbors"; "Henrieta, you have been at that window for a long time"; "Jack, can you keep you hands off Bill"; "Susie, will you please sit down"; "Alex, stop running around and do your work"; "Jane, will you please stop rocking on your chair."

Behaviors which are to be ignored include motor behaviors such as getting out of seat, standing up, running, walking around the room, moving chairs, or sitting in a contorted manner. Any verbal comment or noise not connected with the assignments should also be ignored, such as: carrying on conversations with other children when it is not permitted, answering questions without raising hands or being called on, making remarks when no questions have been asked, calling your name to get attention, and extraneous noises such as crying, whistling, laughing loudly, blowing noise, or coughing. An additional important group of behaviors to be ignored are those which the student engages in when he is supposed to be doing other things, e.g., when the child ignores your instructions you are to ignore him. Any noises made with objects, playing with pencils or other materials should be ignored, as well as, taking things from or disturbing another student by turning around and touching or grabbing him.

The reason for this phase of the experiment is to test the possibility that attention to Inappropriate Behavior may serve to strengthen the very behavior that the attention is intended to diminish. Inappropriate Behavior may be strengthened by paying attention to it even though you may think that you are punishing the behavior.

*Praise for Appropriate Behavior*

The third phase of the experiment included individual contacts with teachers to encourage and train Praising of Appropriate Behavior. The Praise instructions to the teachers were as follows:

The first phase included specifying explicit rules, writing them on the board and reviewing them 4-6 times per day. The second phase was designed to reduce the amount of attention paid to behaviors which were unwanted by ignoring them. This third phase is primarily directed toward *increasing* Appropriate Behaviors through praise and other forms of approval. Teachers are inclined to take good behavior for granted and pay attention only when a child acts up or misbehaves. We are now asking you to try something different. This procedure is characterized as "catching the child being good" and making a comment designed to reward the child for good behavior. Give praise, attention, or smile when the child is doing what is expected during the particular class period in question. Inappropriate Behavior would not be a problem if all children were engaging in a great deal of study and school behavior, therefore, it is necessary to apply what you have learned in the workshop.

Shape by successive approximations the behavior desired by using praise and attention. Start "small" by giving praise and attention at the first signs of Appropriate Behavior and work toward greater goals. Pay close attention to those children who normally engage in a great deal of misbehavior. Watch carefully and when the child begins to behave appropriately, make a comment such as, "You're doing a fine job, (name)." It is very important during the first few days to catch as many good behaviors as possible. Even though a child has just thrown an eraser at the teacher (one minute ago) and is now studying, you should praise the study behavior. (It might also decrease the rate of eraser throwing.) We are assuming that your commendation and praise are important to the child. This is generally the case, but sometimes it takes a while for praise to become effective. Persistence in catching children being good and delivering praise and attention should eventually pay off in a better behaved classroom.

Some examples of praise comments are as follows:

I like the way you're doing your work quietly (name).

That's the way I like to see you work _____ .

That's a very good job _____ .

You're doing fine _____ .

You got two right _____ , that's very good (if he generally gets no answers right).

In general, give praise for achievement, prosocial behavior, and following the group rules. Specifically, you can praise for concentrating on individual work, raising hand when appropriate, responding to questions, paying attention to directions and following through, sitting in desk and studying, sitting quietly if noise has been a problem. Try to use variety and expression in your comments. Stay away from sarcasm. Attempt to become spontaneous in your praise and smile when delivering praise. At first you will probably get the feeling that you are praising a great deal and it sounds a little phony to your ears. This is a typical reaction and it becomes more natural with the passage of time. Spread your praise and attention around. If comments sometimes might interfere with the ongoing class activities then use facial attention and smiles. Walk around the room during study time and pat or place your hand on the back of a child who is doing a good job. Praise quietly spoken to the children has been found effective in combination with some physical sign of approval.

General Rule: Give *praise* and *attention* to behaviors which facilitate learning. Tell the child what he is being praised for. Try to reinforce behaviors incompatible with those you wish to decrease.

The teachers were also instructed to continue to ignore deviant behavior and to repeat the rules several times a day.

Additional training given teachers consisted of: (a) discussion of problems with suggested solutions during weekly seminars on behavior analysis, and (b) specific suggestions from the experimenter on possible alternative responses in specific situations based on the experimenter's observations of the teachers during experimental transitions, or based on observer data and notes at other times when the data showed that the teachers were not on program.

Additional cues were provided to implement the program. Cards were placed on the teachers' desks containing the instructions for the experimental phase in which they were engaged.

*Reversal*

In Class A the final experimental conditions involved an attempt to return to Baseline, followed by a reinstatement of the *Rules, Praise,* and *Ignore* condition. On the basis of the earlier observations of Teacher A, we were able to specify to her how frequently she made disapproving and approving comments. The success of this procedure can be judged from the data.

## RESULTS

Percentage of observation intervals in which Inappropriate Behaviors occurred as a function of conditions is graphed in Figs. 1 and 2. Major changes in Inappropriate Behaviors occurred only when Praise or Approval for Appropriate Behaviors was emphasized in the experimental procedures. A $t$ test, comparing average Inappropriate Behavior in conditions where Praise was emphasized with those where Praise was not emphasized, was significant at the 0.05 level ($df = 2$).

Before examining the results more closely, it is necessary to inspect the data on teacher behavior. Table 3 gives the frequency of classes of teacher behaviors averaged within experimental conditions. Since day-to-day variability of teacher behavior was low for the measures used, these averages fairly reflect what went on.

Introduction of Rules into the classroom had no appreciable effect on Inappropriate Behavior.

Ignoring Inappropriate Behaviors produced inconsistent results. In Class A the children clearly became worse under this condition: in Class B little change was apparent. Both teachers had a difficult time adhering to this condition, and Teacher A found this phase of the

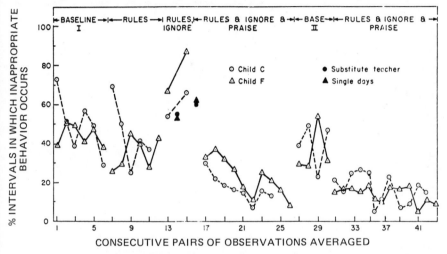

**Fig. 1. Inappropriate behavior of two problem children in Classroom A as a function of experimental conditions.**

experiment very unpleasant. Table 3 shows that Teacher A was only able to reduce critical comments from an average of one per 1 minute to an average of three in 4 minutes. Teacher B cut her critical comments in half. In view of these difficulties, the present results cannot be taken as a clear test of the effects of responding with Disapproval to Inappropriate Behaviors.

The failure to eliminate Disapproval Reactions to Inappropriate Behaviors in Phase Three of the experiment, adds some ambiguities to the interpretation of the Phase Four data for Teacher A. The Rules, Ignore, and Praise condition for Teacher A involved both a reduction in critical comments (Ignoring) as well as a marked increase in Praise. As demonstrated previously (Becker et al., 1967), this combination of procedures is very effective in reducing inappropriate classroom behaviors, but we still lack a clear isolation of effects. The data for Teacher B are not confounded with a simultaneous shift in frequency of Disapproval and Approval Reactions, but they are made less interpretable by a marked shift in Academic Recognition (defined in Table 2) which occurred when the shift in

Praise was made. Since Academic Recognition does not show any systematic relations to level of Appropriate Behaviors elsewhere in the study, we are not inclined to interpret this change as showing a causal effect. A best guess is that the effective use of Praise gave the teacher more time to focus on academic skills.

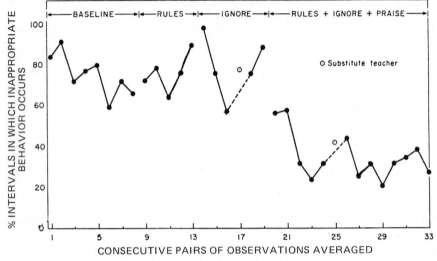

Fig. 2. Inappropriate behavior of one problem child in Classroom B as a function of experimental conditions.

The reversal operation for Teacher A quite clearly shows that the combination of Praising and Ignoring exerts a strong control over Appropriate Behaviors.

As with Academic Recognition, no attempt was made to control how frequently the teacher used procedures labeled "Timeout" (defined in Table 2). The frequency data reported in Table 4 indicates that during Baseline, Teacher A, especially, used "Timeout" procedures to try to establish control (usually turning off the lights until the children were quiet). The changes in the frequency of use of "Timeout" procedures are not systematically related to the behavior changes graphed in Figs. 1 and 2.

In summary, the main results indicate: (a) that Rules alone had little effect in improving classroom behavior, (b) the functional status of Ignoring Inappropriate Behavior needs further clarification, (c) the combination of Ignoring and Praising was very effective in achieving better classroom behavior, and (d) Praise for Appropriate Behaviors was probably the key teacher behavior in achieving effective classroom management.

The effects of the experimental procedures on individual classes of behavior for the two children in Class A are presented in Table 4. The data in Table 4 illustrate that with a few exceptions the effects on individual classes of behavior are similar to those for Inappropriate Behavior as a whole.

**Table 3. Teacher Behavior—Averages for Experimental Conditions (Frequency per 20-min Observation).**

| Teacher A Behavior Classes | Baseline I | Rules | Rules + Ignore | Rules + Ignore + Praise I | Baseline II | Rules + Ignore + Praise II |
|---|---|---|---|---|---|---|
| Approval to Appropriate | 1.2 | 2.0 | 0.0 | 18.2 | 2.5 | 12.5 |
| Approval to Inappropriate | 8.7 | 0.8 | 2.0 | 1.2 | 4.0 | 5.1 |
| Disapproval to Inappropriate | 18.5 | 20.5 | 15.7 | 4.1 | 9.8 | 3.5 |
| Disapproval to Appropriate | 0.9 | 0.7 | 1.0 | 0.3 | 0.9 | 0.0 |
| Timeout | 3.3 | 1.4 | 1.7 | 0.4 | 0.0 | 0.1 |
| Academic Recognition | 26.5 | 23.6 | 46.3 | 52.4 | 45.4 | 45.6 |
| Days observed | 15 | 8 | 3 | 11 | 4 | 9 |

| Teacher B Behavior Classes | Baseline | Rules | Ignore | Rules + Ignore + Praise |
|---|---|---|---|---|
| Approval to Appropriate | 19.2 | 14.1 | 19.3 | 35.2 |
| Approval to Inappropriate | 1.9 | 0.9 | 0.3 | 0.0 |
| Disapproval to Inappropriate | 16.9 | 22.1 | 10.6 | 10.8 |
| Disapproval to Appropriate | 0.0 | 0.0 | 0.0 | 0.0 |
| Timeout | 1.5 | 1.5 | 0.3 | 0.4 |
| Academic Recognition | 14.5 | 5.1 | 6.5 | 35.6 |
| Days observed | 8 | 6 | 6 | 10 |

# DISCUSSION

## Technical Considerations

The problems of gaining good data and maintaining adequate experimental control in an ongoing classroom in a public school have not all been recognized as yet, much less solved. The greatest difficulty encountered was that of maintaining stable control over some important variables while others were being changed. When these variables involve aspects of teacher behavior, the problem becomes one of helping the teacher maintain discriminative control over her own behavior. Daily feedback from the experimenter, based on the observer ratings, can help in this task (i.e., show the teacher the up-to-date graph of her behavior). Also, providing the teacher with a small counter to help monitor her own behavior can be helpful (Thomas, et al., 1968). Most difficult to control in the present study was teacher's Disapproving Reactions to Inappropriate Behaviors during the Ignore Phase of the experiment. Teacher A

Table 4.  **Percentage of Intervals in which Behaviors Occur: Averages for Two Children in Classroom A by Experimental Conditions.**

| Behavior Classes (1) | Experimental Conditions | | | | | |
|---|---|---|---|---|---|---|
|  | Baseline I | Rules | Rules + Ignore | Rules + Ignore + Praise I | Baseline II | Rules Ignore Praise |
| Inappropriate |  |  |  |  |  |  |
| Behavior (2) | 46.8 | 39.8 | 68.5 | 20.5 | 37.6 | 15.1 |
| Gross Motor | 13.9 | 11.3 | 32.7 | 5.9 | 15.5 | 4.1 |
| Object Noise | 3.5 | 1.4 | 1.3 | 0.5 | 1.9 | 0.8 |
| Disturbing Other's Property | 3.3 | 1.8 | 1.9 | 0.7 | 0.7 | 0.3 |
| Turning Around | 21.6 | 9.9 | 11.4 | 9.1 | 12.8 | 7.6 |
| Verbalizations | 12.0 | 16.8 | 21.8 | 6.5 | 8.0 | 3.5 |
| Other Inappropriate Behavior | 10.9 | 7.8 | 16.5 | 3.9 | 7.8 | 2.6 |
| Mouthing Objects | 5.5 | 2.9 | 3.5 | 0.7 | 0.2 | 0.1 |

(1)    Contact occurred less than 1% of the time and is not tabulated here.

(2)    The sum of the separate problem behaviors will exceed that for Inappropriate Behavior, since the latter measure does not reflect the possibility that more than one class of problem behaviors may occur in an interval.

became very "upset" as her classroom became worse. One solution to this problem might be a pre-study in which the teacher is trained in effective management techniques, and then taken through a series of short periods where both Approval and Disapproval are eliminated and one or the other reinstated. The teacher would then have confidence that she can effectively handle her class and be better able to tolerate short periods of chaos (if such periods did occur). She would also have had sufficient training in monitoring her own behavior to permit more effective control.

No attempt was made to program the frequency of various classes of Academic Recognition behaviors. Since such behavior may be important in interpreting results, and was found to vary with some experimental conditions, future work should strive to hold this behavior constant also.

The present study emphasized the importance of contingencies between student and teacher behaviors, but did not measure them directly. While producing similar effects on two children in the same classroom and one child in another classroom, and showing correlated changes in teacher behaviors (including a reversal operation), more powerful data are potentially obtainable with a different technology. Video-tape recordings could enable the use of present coding techniques to obtain contingency data on all classroom members over longer observation periods. Just as the children adapted to the presence of observers, a class could be adapted to the presence of a TV camera man. Costs could be trimmed by saving only some sample tapes and reusing others after reliability ratings are obtained. The current observation procedures (short of having an observer for each child) cannot readily be extended to include simultaneous coding of teacher and child behavior without over-taxing the observers. The present findings, and related studies in this series, are sufficiently promising to warrant an investment in more powerful recording equipment.

## Teacher Reactions

*Teacher A.*

Initially, Mrs. A generally maintained control through scolding and loud critical comments. There were frequent periods of chaos, which she handled by various threats.

When praise was finally added to the program, Mrs. A had these reactions: "I was amazed at the difference the procedure made in the atmosphere of the classroom and even my own personal feelings. I realized that in praising the well-behaved children and ignoring the bad, I was finding myself looking for the good in the children. It was indeed rewarding to see the good rather than always criticizing. . . . I became convinced that a positive approach to discipline was the answer."

*Teacher B.*

During Baseline Mrs. B was dispensing a great deal of praise and approval to her classroom, but it was not always contingent on Appropriate Behavior. Her timing was wrong and inconsistencies were apparent. For example, on one occasion two children were fighting with scissors. The instigator was placed under a table away from the rest of the class and left there for 3 minutes. After 3 minutes Mrs. B took the child in her arms and brought her back to the group even though she was still emitting occasional loud screams. Mrs. B would also ignore behavior for a period of time and then would revert to responding to Inappropriate Behavior with a negative comment; she occasionally gave Approval for Inappropriate Behavior. The training given in seminar and discussions with the experimenter led to an effective use of contingencies. Teacher B was also able to use this training to provide instructions and training for her aide to eliminate problems which arose in the final phase of study when the aide was continuing to respond to Disruptive Behaviors.

## Changes in the Children

Cliff showed little change until Mrs. A started praising Appropriate Behavior, except to get worse during the Ignore phase. He was often doing no academic work, talking to peers, and just fiddling away his time. It took considerable effort by Mrs. A to catch Cliff showing praiseworthy behavior. As the use of praise continued, Cliff worked harder on his assigned tasks, learned to ignore other children who were misbehaving, and would raise his hand to get teacher's attention. He participated more in class discussions. He was moved up to the fastest arithmetic group.

Frank showed little change in his "hyperactive" and "inattentive" behaviors until praise was introduced. Frank responded rapidly to praise. After just two days in the "praise" phase, Frank was observed to clean his desk quietly and quickly after completing a handwriting assignment. He was able to finish a task and study on his own until the teacher initiated a new activity. He began to ask for extra assignments and volunteered to do things to help his teacher. He had learned to sit quietly (when appropriate), to listen, and to raise his hand to participate in class discussion, the latter occurring quite frequently.

Stan slowly improved after contingent praise was instituted, but some of the gains made by Mrs. B were in part undone by the teacher aide. The aide was described as playing policeman and it took special efforts by the teacher to get her to follow the program. Mrs. B summarized the changes in Stan as follows: "Stan has changed from a sullen, morose, muttering, angry individual into a boy whose smile seems to cover his whole face." He became very responsive to teacher praise and learned to follow classroom rules, to pay attention to teacher-directed activities for long periods of time, and to interact with his peers in a more friendly way.

## Implications

This replication and refinement of an earlier study by Becker, et al., (1967) adds further confidence to the assertion that teachers can be taught systematic procedures and can use them to gain more effective behaviors from their students. Unless teachers are effective in getting children "ready to learn," their technical teaching skills are likely to be wasted. Knowledge of differential social reinforcement procedures, as well as other behavioral principles, can greatly enhance teachers' enjoyment of the profession and their contribution to effective development of the students.

The reader should note that while we formally recorded the behavior of a few target children, teacher and observer comments indicated dramatic changes in the whole "atmosphere" of the classroom and in the teachers' enjoyment of their classes.

# REFERENCES

Allen, K.E., Hart, B.M., Buell, J.S., Harris, F.R., & Wolf, M.M. Effects of social reinforcement on isolate behavior of a nursery school child. In L.P. Ullmann and L. Krasner (Eds.), *Case studies in behavior modification.* New York: Holt, Rinehart & Winston, 1965. Pp. 307-312.

Becker, W.C., Madsen, C.H., Jr., Arnold, Carole R., & Thomas, D.R. The contingent use of teacher attention and praise in reducing classroom behavior problems. *Journal of Special Education,* 1967, 1, 287-307.

Bijou, S.W., & Baer, D.M. Some methodological contributions from a functional analysis of child development. In L.P. Lipsitt and C.S. Spiker (Eds.), *Advances in child development and behavior.* New York: Academic Press, 1963. Pp. 197-231.

Hart, Betty M., Reynolds, Nancy J., Baer, Donald M., Brawley, Eleanor R., & Harris, Florence R. Effect of contingent and non-contingent social reinforcement on the cooperative play of a preschool child. *Journal of Applied Behavior Analysis,* 1968, 1, 73-76.

Thomas, D.R., Becker, W.C., & Armstrong, Marianne. Production and elimination of disruptive classroom behavior by systematically varying teacher's behavior. *Journal of Applied Behavior Analysis,* 1968, 1, 35-45.

Madsen, C.H., Jr., Becker, W.C., Thomas, D.R., Koser, Linda, & Plager, Elaine. An analysis of the reinforcing function of "Sit Down" Commands. In Parker, R.K. (Ed.), *Readings in educational psychology.* Boston: Allyn and Bacon (in press).

# Article 2
# Modification of Arithmetic Response Rate and Attending Behavior in a Seventh-grade Student* †

FRANK D. KIRBY and FRANK SHIELDS

Abstract: An adjusting fixed-ratio schedule of praise and immediate correctness feedback produced increases in a seventh-grade student's arithmetic response rate. Percentage of time spent in attending behavior also increased collaterally. Removal of the treatment led to decreases in both arithmetic response rate and collateral attending behavior. Reinstatements of the procedure again produced increases in both types of behavior. It was suggested that the present procedure of directly modifying arithmetic response rate requires less time and effort than working indirectly through modifying attending behavior.

Recent studies have shown that operant conditioning techniques can be useful in improving children's classroom behaviors. Several of these studies have focused on either increasing study behavior or increasing academic response rate. Hall, Lund, and Jackson (1968) demonstrated that study behavior is subject to teacher attention contingencies. Bushell, Wrobel, and Michaelis (1968) modified study behavior utilizing a token system and group contingencies. Walker and Buckley (1968) conditioned attending behavior by providing points for increasing intervals of attending behavior. The points

*Reprinted by permission from the *Journal of Applied Behavior Analysis,* Vol. 5, No. 1, 1972, 79-84. Copyright 1972 by the Society for the Experimental Analysis of Behavior, Inc.

†This study is based on a thesis submitted to the Department of Psychology, Humboldt State College, in partial fulfillment of the requirements of the Master of Arts degree. The authors wish to express appreciation to Dr. Paul Ness of the College Elementary School, without whose cooperation this study would not have been possible.

could be exchanged for a model of choice at the end of the treatment period. Surrat, Ulrich, and Hawkins (1969) utilized an elementary student to monitor the study behavior of a group of students. A light on the student's desk was on during study behavior and off during non-study behavior. Using back up reinforcers for light-on time, they increased time spent in study.

The main purpose of increasing study behavior is to achieve collateral increases in academic performance. The forementioned studies modified attending or study behavior but did not systematically measure changes in academic response rate or accuracy. One of the problems in attempting to increase academic response rate indirectly by modifying study behavior is the time and effort involved in monitoring study behavior. Someone must monitor the behavior of the child almost constantly. A more direct approach to academic performance may be more efficient.

Academic response rate has been directly modified by Lovitt and Curtiss (1968, 1969). These studies demonstrated increases in academic response rate as a result of verbalizing in addition to writing correct answers and of self-imposed as opposed to teacher-imposed reinforcement contingencies. Changes in percentage of study behavior were not systematically measured.

The present study was designed to measure the combined effects of an adjusting fixed-ratio schedule of immediate praise and immediate correctness feedback on the arithmetic response rate of a seventh-grade student and to measure possible collateral changes in study behavior. The subject was rewarded for increasing units of arithmetic work in a manner similar to the procedure used by Walker and Buckley (1968) wherein the subject was rewarded for increasing intervals of time spent in study.

## METHOD

### Subject

Tom, a 13-year-old boy enrolled in the seventh grade at Humboldt State College Elementary School, was of average intelligence as measured by the Wechsler Intelligence Scale for Children, receiving a Full Scale Score of 96. Before the study, Tom was observed for a period of two weeks. During this time, he exhibited a great deal of non-attending behavior and his arithmetic work was poor. Tom frequently exhibited non-attending behavior until his teacher reminded him to work or went over to his desk and watched him. Tom would then work for a few minutes, but if his teacher left, he would become easily distracted. Tom seldom completed class assignments and tended to make many errors, especially with arithmetic problems

## Procedure

After consultation with Tom's teacher, it was decided to use a 20 minute time block each day in an experiment designed to help Tom increase his arithmetic achievement and attending behavior. The study was conducted in Tom's normal classroom every day from 11:30 to 11:50 a.m. During this time the experimenter presented Tom with a worksheet consisting of 20 multiplication problems to compute. Examples of the types of problems used are shown in Table 1. Complexity order # 1 represents a one digit number times another one digit number (1 X 1), etc.

Random selection was used to determine the content for each worksheet. The problems were placed on individual cards and placed in one of nine boxes, each box contained problems of the same complexity. Two problems were drawn from each box for each of the 24 worksheets used during the study, giving each worksheet 18 problems. The remaining problems were then placed in one box and two more problems were selected for each of the 24 worksheets, so

Table 1.  Examples of the Multiplication Problems Used in the Present Study.

| Complexity Order | No. of Digits | Examples | Number |
|---|---|---|---|
| 1. | 1 X 1 .............. | 2 X 6, 4 X 8 .............. | 56 |
| 2. | 1 X 2 .............. | 3 X 12, 5 X 43 ............ | 56 |
| 3. | 1 X 3 .............. | 8 X 754, 9 X 362 .......... | 56 |
| 4. | 2 X 1 .............. | 54 X 7, 32 X 5 ............ | 56 |
| 5. | 2 X 2 .............. | 34 X 65, 75 X 12 .......... | 56 |
| 6. | 2 X 3 .............. | 23 X 143, 59 X 641 ........ | 56 |
| 7. | 3 X 1 .............. | 645 X 4, 781 X 3 .......... | 56 |
| 8. | 3 X 2 .............. | 893 X 34, 619 X 15 ........ | 56 |
| 9. | 3 X 3 .............. | 156 X 723, 916 X 416 ...... | 56 |

that each worksheet contained 20 problems. The problems were arranged in order of increasing complexity for each worksheet, i.e., 1 X 1, 1 X 2, 1 X 3, 2 X 1, 2 X 2, *etc.*

Two measures of behavior were recorded: the number of correct problems solved per minute and the percentage of total time spent in attending behavior. The number of correct problems solved was recorded by the experimenter each time Tom turned in a unit of work. The amount of time spent in problem solving included only the time he spent at his desk while completing the 20 problems and did not include the time he took to bring his work to the experimenter for correction, be assigned a new set of problems to solve, and return to his desk. Tom completed the entire worksheets of 20 problems each day of the experiment.

An independent observer was used to record Tom's attending behavior. The observer was seated in the classroom, approximately 18 feet from Tom's right-hand side, out of the way, but with an unobstructed view of the subject. From this position the observer recorded Tom's behavior every 10 seconds, recording only behavior exhibited at the tenth second. The observer used a stopwatch, held in her left hand, clearly marked, to determine the intervals. Attending behavior included: looking at or writing on the assigned page, looking at the teacher or experimenter when appropriate, talking to the teacher or experimenter, walking from his desk to the experimenter's desk and back to his own, and standing at the experimenter's desk while his paper was being corrected and a new assignment given. All other behavior was recorded as non-attending. If Tom completed the worksheet before the end of the assigned 20 minutes, the observer noted the time and stopped recording. This procedure was used throughout the study. The reliability of the observer was checked 10 times with another observer, three times before the start of the study and seven times during the study. The two observers sat in opposite corners at the rear of the room during reliability checks. The results showed a 98% agreement between observers, with a range from 95% to 100%. Percentage of agreement was determined by dividing the number of Agreements by the total number of observations.

## Design

The study was conducted over a period of 24 school days and was divided into four phases.

| Phase | Days |
|---|---|
| Baseline ................................. | 1-5 |
| Treatment 1 ............................. | 6-13 |
| Reversal ................................ | 14-19 |
| Treatment 2 ............................ | 20-24 |

*Baseline.*

During the baseline phase, Tom was presented each day with a different arithmetic worksheet of 20 problems. His instructions were as follows:

> "Here is your arithmetic worksheet for today, you have 20 minutes to complete it, then I will collect it."

The problems were corrected and returned the following day with the number correct at the top. No praise was given Tom, by either the teacher or the experimenter during the 20 minute period.

*Treatment 1*

During this phase, Tom was presented each day with a different arithmetic worksheet of 20 problems. The instructions given Tom during this phase were as follows:

> "Here is your arithmetic worksheet for today, when you have completed _____ problems, bring your paper over to my desk and I will check your answers. You have 20 minutes to complete the worksheet."

Tom was given praise and the correct answers marked subsequent to the correction of each unit of work using an adjusting fixed-ratio schedule. Initially this involved reinforcement for every two problems completed. Then, the experimenter gradually increased the units of work or number of problems completed by Tom before delivering reinforcement. Correct answers were designated but Tom was not shown how to work any problems or where he had made errors.

Examples of praise used by the experimenter included:

1. "Good work"
2. "Excellent job"
3. "Great, you got 14 right today"
4. "All right, you didn't do too well today, but tomorrow you will do better"

5. "Since you did so well today it won't be necessary to have your work checked as often tomorrow"
6. "And keep up the good work; you can work more problems at a time now"

For the first two days of Treatment 1, Days 6 and 7, Tom was given praise and the correct answers each time he completed two problems. During Days 8 and 9, the number of problems completed at one time was increased to four. Then, for Days 10 and 11, the number was increased to eight. Finally, for Days 12 and 13, no reinforcement was given until Tom had completed 16 problems.

*Reversal*
During this phase, Tom was given a different arithmetic worksheet of 20 problems each day with the same instructions used during baseline. His paper was corrected and returned the following day with the number correct at the top. No praise was given Tom by either the experimenter or the teacher.

*Treatment 2*
Each day, Tom was given a different arithmetic worksheet of 20 problems with the same instructions used during Treatment 1. Praise and correct answers were given Tom in the same manner as in Treatment 1, using an adjusting fixed-ratio schedule. The number of problems completed by Tom before presenting himself to the experimenter to have his work checked was increased from five for Day 20, to 10 for Day 21, 15 for Day 22, and all 20 problems for the last two days.

## RESULTS

As can be seen in Fig. 1, during baseline Tom's mean correct answer rate was 0.47 per minute. During Treatment 1, the rate increased to a mean of 1.36 correct answers per minute. During reversal, the rate decreased to 0.98 and during Treatment 2, climbed to a mean of 1.44.

Collateral changes also occurred in attending behavior. Figure 2 shows that during baseline Tom spent a mean of 51% of his time in attending behavior. During Treatment 1, mean percentage of attending behavior rose sharply to 97%. There was a slight decrease during reversal to 82%, followed during Treatment 2 by an increase to 97%.

It should be noted that Tom's behavior could not be recorded for Day 18 (reversal) because he left the room and completed the problems in the hallway.

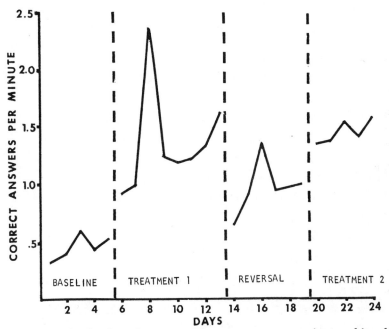

Fig. 1. The number of correct arithmetic answers per minute achieved by the subject throughout the study.

## DISCUSSION

The results demonstrate the combined effectiveness of the present adjusting fixed-ratio schedule of praise and immediate correctness feedback in increasing the subject's arithmetic response rate and associated attending behavior. When Tom's rate of correct problem solving was increased through systematic reinforcement, incompatible behaviors of non-attending decreased. It remains to be shown whether or not working directly on increasing attending behavior would have produced comparable improvement in arithmetic response rate.

One advantage of working directly on academic response rate instead of indirectly through increasing attending behavior is the time and effort involved in monitoring the two forms of behavior. Working directly on arithmetic response rate, as in the present study, does not require the teacher constantly to monitor the student's study behavior. The only requirement of the teacher is immediately to correct the paper when presented and supply a short expression of praise upon returning the paper. While the adjusting ratio schedule of

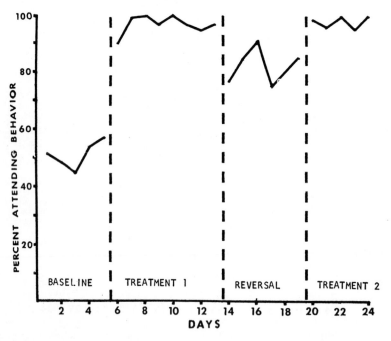

Fig. 2. Percentage of total time the subject spent in attending behavior throughout the study.

reinforcement requires frequent contact with the student during early phases requiring small units of work, it requires no extra effort during later phases when large units of work are assigned. The present study indicates that large units of work can be required rather quickly without deterioration in either academic response rate or related attending behavior. It is interesting to note that during reversal, when all praise and immediate correctness feedback was withheld, the subject maintained a much higher level of arithmetic achievement and attending behavior than before Treatment 1.

Though the praise and immediate correctness feedback were provided by the experimenter in this study, the classroom teacher, a selected pupil from the class (or even from another class), or a parent volunteer could easily perform the same function.

# REFERENCES

Bushell, Don, Jr., Wrobel, Patricia Ann, & Michaelis, Mary Louise. Applying "group" contingencies to the classroom study behavior of preschool children. *Journal of Applied Behavior Analysis,* 1968, 1, 55-61.

Hall, R. Vance; Lund, Diane, & Jackson, Deloris. Effects of teacher attention on study behavior. *Journal of Applied Behavior Analysis,* 1968, 1, 1-12.

Lovitt, Thomas C., & Curtiss, Karen A. Effects of manipulating an antecedent event on mathematics response rate. *Journal of Applied Behavior Analysis,* 1968, 1, 329-333.

Lovitt, Thomas C., & Curtiss, Karen A. Academic response rate as a function of teacher-and self-imposed contingencies. *Journal of Applied Behavior Analysis,* 1968, 1, 49-53.

Surratt, Paul R., Ulrich, Roger E., & Hawkins, Robert P. An elementary student as a behavior engineer. *Journal of Applied Behavior Analysis,* 1969, 2, 85-92.

Walker, Hill M., & Buckley, Nancy K. The use of positive reinforcement in conditioning attending behavior. *Journal of Applied Behavior Analysis,* 1968, 1, 245-252.

# Article 3
# Feedback in Classroom Behavior Modification: Effects on the Target and her Classmates* †

RONALD S. DRABMAN and BENJAMIN B. LAHEY

Abstract: A behavior modification program that employed feedback with no additional contingencies was initiated and withdrawn in an ABAB design on a target child within a classroom. The disruptive behavior of the target child as well as that of her peers was monitored. Additionally, the sociometric status of the target child was recorded. Finally, the positive and negative comments made to the target by her teacher and her peers were related to initiation and withdrawal of the feedback contingency. Results indicate that (1) feedback alone may be an effective behavior modification procedure, (2) the disruptive behavior of the target's classmates changed, even though they were not directly treated, (3) sociometric status of the target was altered by behavioral contingencies, (4) positive comments by classmates to the target increased, and (5) negative comments from the teacher to the target child decreased.

Behavior modification with children in the classroom has had remarkable success (O'Leary & Drabman, 1971). However, several

*Reprinted by permission from the *Journal of Applied Behavior Analysis,* Vol. 7, No. 4, 1974. Copyright 1974 by the Society for the Experimental Analysis of Behavior, Inc.

†This study was partially supported by Grant #1- R03-MH24502-01 from the National Institute of Mental Health to the first author and Grant #1-R03-MH21948-01 from the National Institute of Mental Health to the second author. Our thanks to William Hunt, team leader, and Gregory J. Jarvie who served as observers in this study. The cooperation of Mrs. Cohen, principal, and Miss Below, teacher, at the Park Maitland school is gratefully acknowledged. The authors would also like to thank Richard Tucker and Margaret Hanratty Thomas for reading earlier versions of this manuscript and Ed Shirkey for his help in the statistical analysis.

theoretical and practical questions remain to be answered. An important theoretical question involves the part that feedback plays in a successful behavioral program. Feedback can be defined as information provided to the subject about the appropriateness of his response. Usually, classroom programs involve feedback to the subjects plus some other behavioral intervention such as backup rewards contingent on certain types of feedback. Drabman (1973) showed that with an entire classroom of very disruptive children, feedback alone may not be an effective control. But many behavior modification studies involve only a single disruptive child. Is it possible that in some of these studies, feedback alone without the additional contingency would have been sufficient to ensure the behavioral change? For example, in Patterson's studies (e.g., Patterson, 1965; Patterson & Brodsky, 1966; Patterson, Jones, Whittier, & Wright, 1965), where a hyperactive child earned points exchangeable for candy for him and his classmates, what would have happened if the child had earned only points and not candy? Another example was provided by Ramp, Ulrich, and Dulaney (1971), who put a light on a student's desk. Ignition of this light (feedback) indicated to the student that his time in delayed punishment was increased. Might the student have behaved just as well simply to avoid the negative feedback? Was the additional punishment necessary?

Related to this is another theroretical issue. Can classmates of a target child be used as untreated controls or are they also indirectly affected by the treatment? Patterson et al. (1965) suggested that controls in the same classroom might not be appropriate. Bolstad and Johnson (1972) tried to use classmates as an untreated control and found that the classmates seemed to change, even though they were not involved in the experimental manipulation. Kazdin (1973) found with retarded children in special two-person groups, each group with a tutor, that behavioral consequences to one could affect the other. Because Bolstad and Johnson (1972) did not attempt to verify their conclusions experimentally, and Kazdin (1973) used retarded children in special circumstances, the question of the untreated classmates' change needs to be investigated further.

These theoretical questions intertwine with some very important practical considerations. Often, teachers and school psychologists do not initiate needed behavioral programs because they are afraid of possible negative effects to the untreated children. Although negative effects have not been reported in the behavioral literature, very little is known about the effects of behavioral procedure on the target's classmates. Besides the question of the classmates' behavior, there are also important unanswered questions regarding the relationships between the target child and his peers. For example, does the target child's sociometric status change as a result of the contingency system? Or, does the verbal behavior of the target's classmates towards the target change when the contingencies are introduced?

The present study sought to provide rudimentary answers to these theoretical and practical questions. A behavior modification program that employed feedback with no additional contingencies was initiated and withdrawn in an ABAB design on a target child within a classroom. The disruptive behavior of the target child, and that of her peers, was monitored. Additionally, the sociometric status of the target child was recorded. Finally, the positive and negative comments made to the target by her teacher and her peers were related to initiation and withdrawal of the feedback contingency.

## METHOD

### Subject

A 10-year-old female, Charlotte, was brought to the attention of the authors by school authorities because of inappropriate behavior in her classroom. Her teacher and principal reported that she was the most disruptive child in her class and that she had no friends. In general, she was teased or ignored by her classmates. Independent observation confirmed the initial reports provided by the teacher and principal.

### Teacher

The teacher was regularly employed by the private school that Charlotte attended. She taught Social Studies to Charlotte and 12 other similarly aged students from 8:45 to 9:30 A.M. every day. The students went individually on to their next class after 9:30.

### Observation Procedures

Two undergraduates, enrolled in a practicum in research techniques, served as observers. They entered the classroom before the class began and stayed for the entire class period Mondays through Thursdays. Because of the undergraduates' schedules, observation did not take place on Fridays. Observations were made on a 20-second observe, 10-second record basis. Except for reliability checks, the observers were randomly assigned each day to monitor either Charlotte or her classmates for 5 minutes each in random order. The observation system used was similar to that developed by O'Leary and his associates for assessment of classroom behavior (Drabman, 1973; Drabman, Spitalnik, & O'Leary, 1973; O'Leary, Kaufman, Kass, & Drabman, 1970). It included the following categories of disruptive behavior:

1.    Out of Chair:   movement of the child from her chair when not permitted or requested by the teacher. No part of the child's body is to be touching the chair.
2.    Touching:   using material object as an extension of the hand to touch others' property.
3.    Playing:   child uses her hands to play with her own or community property when such behavior is incompatible with learning.
4.    Noise:   child creating any audible noise other than vocalization.
5.    Non-Compliance:   failure to initiate the appropriate response requested by the teacher.
6.    Time off Task:   child does not do assigned work for entire 20-second interval. For example, child does not write or read when so assigned.
7.    Vocalization:   any unpermitted audible sound emanating from the mouth.
8.    Orienting:   turning or orienting response is not rated unless the child is seated and the turn must be more than 90° using the desk or teacher's position as a reference point.
9.    Aggression:   child makes movement towards another person so as to come into contact with him, whether directly or by using a material object as an extension of the hand.

One of the major dependent measures was the mean number of these disruptive behaviors observed per 20-second interval.

## Positive and Negative Comments

Every word spoken specifically to Charlotte by either her peers or teacher was recorded by the observers. This was not a difficult task because the frequency was low. These comments were shown to two groups of naive college student judges who were told:

Charlotte is a little girl in the fourth grade, her teachers tell us that she is quite shy and has few friends; in fact, most of the children don't like her. I am going to show you a group of cards and on each card will be printed a comment made to Charlotte by one of the children in her class [by her teacher]. I want you to put these cards in three stacks; one stack should contain those comments which reveal positive feelings towards Charlotte; the second should contain those comments which reveal negative feelings towards Charlotte and the third stack should contain those comments upon which you are unable to decide if they are positive or negative feelings. In making your decision please remember that Charlotte is considered a very unpopular little girl.

This description of Charlotte given to the judges helped put the teacher and student comments into context. This was an attempt to decrease the amount of comments on which the judges could not decide. The observers, who were present in the classrooms as the comments were made, also rated the comments. They agreed on 100% of the comments judged to be in either the positive or negative categories, although they placed far fewer of the comments into the "unable to decide" category. However, their proportions of positive and negative comments were about the same as that of the judges.

## Sociometric Data

Twice each week (on Tuesdays and Fridays) the teacher was asked to read to the class, in random order, three sociometric questions:

1. If you were on Apollo 17 as an astronaut and you were going on a long, long trip to the moon, who would you want to take along? Remember to choose only one person that you would want to be with for a long time; a person you could get along with very well.

2.  You are doing a hard job and you need someone who is very responsible and grown-up, whom would you pick? Remember to pick only one person and to pick a very grown-up person.
3.  If I asked you to help me pick a person to receive today's happy face award, whom would you pick? Remember to pick only one person and pick a very deserving person.

The children responded by coloring in the desk of the person they selected on a map of the class (Drabman, Spitalnik, & Spitalnik, 1974). Each child was allowed to vote only once per question and children could not vote for themselves.

## Procedure

The four phases of this study were as follows: (a) Baseline I, (b) Feedback I, (a) Baseline II, (b) Feedback II.

*Baseline I.* (10 school, eight observation days).
During Baseline I, no experimental manipulations were introduced. Before observers were introduced, the teacher had been asked to practice limiting her praise or disciplinary interactions to individual children. She was asked to continue this throughout the study. The teacher also began asking the sociometric questions twice weekly during Baseline I.

*Feedback I.* (18 school, 13 observation days).
During this phase, a timer was placed in the classroom. The teacher set it to ring after the initial 15 minutes of class and then after each succeeding 10 minutes. Therefore, it rang four times during a class session. The teacher explained to Charlotte that she would give Charlotte a rating each time the timer rang. These ratings would be from zero, for very poor behavior, to 10, for very good behavior. At the end of the class, the teacher would quietly tell Charlotte her total score for the day. The rest of the class was not informed of this procedure. Since teacher behavior was being monitored, the teacher was not instructed how to determine the ratings or whether to praise or reprimand Charlotte when delivering feedback. The teacher was asked to rate Charlotte on how well she thought Charlotte had behaved during the rating period. When the timer rang, the teacher would reset the timer, walk over to Charlotte,

and quietly inform the child of that period's rating. Sociometric questions were continued in this phase.

*Baseline II.* (Eight school, 7 observation days).

This phase replicated Baseline I. The timer was removed from the class and feedback discontinued. Charlotte was simply told "we are not going to use the timer any more, but I expect you to continue being good." Sociometric questions continued to be asked.

*Feedback II.* (11 school, 9 observation days).

This phase replicated Feedback I. The timer was brought back into the classroom and feedback began again. Charlotte did not ask why the timer was returned and the teacher did not mention it. The sociometric questions were also continued in this phase.

## Reliability of Observation

Before entering the classroom, the observers were trained with a group of observers for other projects for 10 weeks in simulated classroom conditions. Observers were not allowed to enter the classroom until their average reliability with randomly assigned partners was above 65%. When both observers recorded the same disruptive behavior within a 20-second interval, a perfect agreement was recorded. The ratio of the number of perfect agreements over the number of agreements plus disagreements served as a percentage measure of reliability. Baseline I was not initiated until the observers had been in the classroom for several days. Reliability was normally calculated for 5 minutes daily on each of two randomly chosen children. Reliability for the 47 school and 37 observation days study averaged 86%.

## RESULTS

### Disruptive Behavior

Figure I shows the average number of disruptive behaviors for Charlotte and her classmates. Charlotte, who was the most disruptive child in the class, averaged 1.39 disruptive behaviors per 20-second interval during Baseline I. The rest of the class averaged 0.714 disruptive behaviors per interval. After the Feedback I contingency was initiated, Charlotte's inappropriate behavior decreased markedly to 0.498; her classmates also decreased their average, to 0.550. Return to Baseline II brought Charlotte's disruptive behavior up to 1.77 and also raised the average of the other pupils to 0.780. The Feedback II contingency lowered Charlotte's behavior to 0.370 disruptive behaviors per 20-second interval and lowered her classmates' average to 0.503. In general, as Fig. 1 shows, Charlotte was

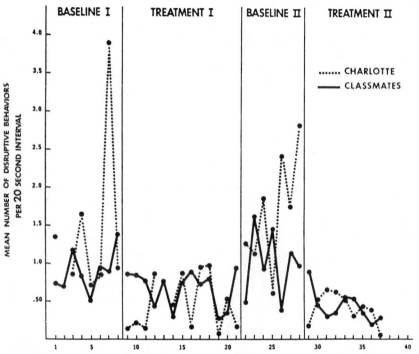

Fig. 1. Mean number of disruptive behaviors per 20-sec interval for Charlotte and her classmates across days observed. Missing data points indicate that Charlotte was absent that day.

more disruptive than her peers during baseline conditions and less disruptive than her peers during treatment phases. This was true even though her classmates' behavior also was changing when treatment was initiated and withdrawn. Although only Charlotte was exposed to the contingencies, repeated measures analysis of variance indicated that the changes in her classmates' disruptive behavior were significant ($F$ [3,33] = 4.04; $p < 0.05$).

## Sociometric Ratings

During the two-week Baseline I phase, the sociometric questions were administered five times. Charlotte received a total of two votes. During the four-week Feedback I phase, the sociometric questions were administered eight times. Charlotte received 11 votes. For these two phases, a normal approximation to the binomial indicated that the proportion of votes attained in the treatment phase surpassed the level of significance required by a one-tailed test, but failed to reach the level required by the more appropriate two-tailed test ($z = 1.67$; $p < 0.10$). Importantly, however, all 11 of these votes occurred during the last 2.5 weeks (five presentations) of the Feedback I phase. For these last 2.5 weeks, during which Charlotte established a continued pattern of appropriate behavior, the proportion of votes obtained during Feedback I was significantly greater than the proportion obtained during Baseline I ($z = 2.15$; $p < 0.05$). The sociometric questions were administered twice during the one-week return to Baseline II. Charlotte did not receive any votes during this phase. Around this time, the children reported being very bored by the questions and began to color in their maps before the teacher read the questions. Their responses also became much less variable. Sociometric questions were administered four times during Feedback II. Charlotte failed to receive any votes during this phase. The votes Charlotte did receive in Phases I and II were approximately equally distributed among the three sociometric questions.

## Positive and Negative Comments

*Classmates*
The comments spoken individually to Charlotte were recorded by the observers. Ten college students were asked to sort the randomly ordered classmate comments into positive comments, negative comments, and comments on which they could not decide. The greatest number of positive selections for any classmate comment spoken in a baseline phase was six of the possible 10. Six votes, therefore, were used as a conservative criterion of a positive or negative comment. Thus, only comments on which at least six judges agreed were used in the analysis. The classmates' positive and negative comments were divided into those spoken during baseline or feedback phases. The frequency of positive comments averaged 0.14 per class period during baseline and 0.76 per period during feedback

phases. Statistically controlling for the differential opportunity to emit comments during the baseline and feedback phases, a normal approximation to the binomial revealed that the proportion of positive comments spoken to Charlotte by her peers was significantly ($z = 2.50; p < 0.05$) greater during the feedback phases.

Negative comments directed toward Charlotte from her classmates did not significantly change with the contingencies ($z < 1$). The frequency of negative comments averaged 1.36 per class period during baseline and 1.00 per period during the feedback phases.

*Teacher*

Teacher comments were categorized in a similar manner to classmates' comments. A different set of 10 college-student judges was used for the teacher comments. Teacher positive comments directed towards Charlotte were extremely rare in either baseline or treatment conditions. The frequency of teacher-initiated positive comments was zero per class during the baseline phases and 0.10 per class during the feedback phases. They did not occur at a rate that would be consistent with statistical analysis. The frequency of teacher-initiated negative comments was 0.71 per class session during the baseline phases and 0.24 per class during the feedback phases. A normal approximation to the binomial indicated that the proportion of negative comments delivered to Charlotte by her teacher was significantly less during the feedback conditions ($z = 2.11; p < 0.05$).

## DISCUSSION

The present results indicate that feedback may play an important role in behavioral procedures involving a target child within a classroom. Frequency of teacher praise remained very low throughout the study. Additionally, the college-student observers reported that the teacher delivered feedback "accurately, but with little emotion." Therefore, feedback alone was probably responsible for Charlotte's behavior change. We do not feel that feedback is something qualitatively different from other forms of verbal reinforcement or punishment. Certainly, operationally it is not. The point is that both clinical and experimental uses of behavior modification often assume that feedback is necessary but not sufficient for behavioral change. This study has demonstrated that such an assumption may not be tenable. Feedback may be both necessary and sufficient for behavior change. In the future, single-target behavioral studies that include feedback plus some other variable may be unsatisfactory unless they contain a control that can adequately isolate the effects of feedback alone. Without this control, the relative contribution of feedback to the treatment remains unclear.

As a cautionary note, Ayllon and Azrin (1964) demonstrated that instructions alone were able to modify the behavior of hospitalized patients. But, the effects were short-lived. Without backup reinforcement, the patients began to revert to their inappropriate behavior. It is possible that the effects of feedback might also be transient. If the treatment phases had been longer than 18 and 11 school days, the effects of feedback might have disappeared. Although the data cannot answer this question, the teacher reported that using the feedback system led to Charlotte's continued good behavior throughout the remainder of the school year. Perhaps the changes in teacher and student verbal behavior are partially responsible.

The second theoretical question raised was whether classmates could be effectively used as untreated controls in behavior modification research. The answer seems to be: "No." The disruptive behavior of Charlotte's classmates was significantly altered, even though none of them was directly involved in the treatment procedure. Using classmates as untreated controls may lead to inaccurate assessment of the treatment's effectiveness.

On the more practical side, Charlotte's sociometric status did change with the original initiation and withdrawal of the feedback contingency, but did not recover when treatment was again instituted. However, the lack of recovery seemed to be more a function of the inadequacy of the assessment instrument, rather than actual change in the pupil's attitudes towards Charlotte. The children reported boredom with the task and began to fill out the maps in a stereotypic manner before the questions were even asked. Future studies combining behavior modification and sociometric methods should probably use a wider variety of questions. However, it is important that all questions that are asked during treatment should also be asked during baseline. Even slight variations may not be comparable.

Probably the most interesting findings had to do with the comments made to Charlotte by her teacher and peers. Similar to earlier research (Drabman, 1973), Charlotte's improved behavior did not automatically lead to more positive comments from her teacher. Teachers must be instructed (and probably monitored) if they are to provide appropriate verbal reinforcement. The teacher did use fewer negative comments when Charlotte was better behaved during the feedback phases. In contrast, the pupils did emit more positive comments to Charlotte during the treatment phases, although they did not significantly decrease their negative comments. Perhaps this is a hopeful sign. Ideally, one may want a child to receive both positive and negative comments from classmates. A child who receives only positive or only negative comments from classmates might not be considered an appropriate playmate. The optimal combination of positive and negative comments remains a question for future research. However, even when Charlotte was one of the best-behaved children in the classroom, she still received more negative than positive comments. Pupils may model their overall ratio of comments on that of the teacher. If this is true, training teachers to show approval becomes even more critical.

Finally, it is not known how often behaviorally oriented clinical or school psychologists are guilty of using a more powerful technique when a less powerful one would be effective. What is the probability that if Charlotte were brought to a behaviorally oriented therapist, he would have initiated a more costly and time-consuming treatment procedure such as a token economy? The present results indicate that a precautionary measure should be taken before initiating the more-powerful treatment procedure. Therapists should first attempt to change behavior without major environmental manipulations. Only when the data indicate that a more radical technique is called for should one be used.

# REFERENCES

Ayllon, T., & Azrin, N.H. Reinforcement and instructions with mental patients. *Journal of the Experimental Analysis of Behavior,* 1964, 7, 327-331.

Bolstad, O.D., & Johnson, S.M. Self-regulation in the modification of disruptive behavior. *Journal of Applied Behavior Analysis,* 1972, 5, 443-454.

Drabman, R.S. Child versus teacher administered token programs in a psychiatric hospital school. *Journal of Abnormal Child Psychology,* 1973, 1, 68-87.

Drabman, R., Spitalnik, R., & O'Leary, K.D. Teaching self-control to disruptive children. *Journal of Abnormal Psychology,* 1973, 82, 10-16.

Drabman, R., Spitalnik, R., & Spitalnik, K. Sociometric and disruptive behavior as a function of four types of token economies. *Journal of Applied Behavior Analysis,* 1974, 7, 93-101.

Kazdin, A.E. The effect of vicarious reinforcement on attentive behavior in the classroom. *Journal of Applied Behavior Analysis,* 1973, 6, 71-78.

O'Leary, K.D., Kaufman, K.F., Kass, R.E., & Drabman, R.S. The effects of loud and soft reprimands on the behavior of disruptive students. *Exceptional Children,* 1970, 37, 145-155.

O'Leary, K.D., & Drabman, R.S. Token reinforcement programs in the class-room: A review. *Psychological Bulletin,* 1971, 75, 379-398.

Patterson, G.R. An application of conditioning techniques to the control of a hyperactive child. In L. Ullmann and L. Krasner (Eds.), *Case studies in behavior modification.* New York: Holt, Rinehart & Winston, 1965, Pp. 370-375.

Patterson, G.R., & Brodsky, G.D. A behavior modification program for a boy with multiple problems. *Journal of Child Psychology and Psychiatry,* 1966, 7, 277-295.

Patterson, G.R., Jones, R., Whittier, J., & Wright, M.A. A behavior modification technique for the hyperactive child. *Behaviour Research and Therapy,* 1965, 2, 217-226.

Ramp, E., Ulrich, R., & Dulaney, S. Delayed timeout as a procedure for reducing disruptive classroom behavior: A case study. *Journal of Applied Behavior Analysis,* 1971, 4, 235-239.

# 3
## Classroom Punishment

Investigations of the effects of punishment in the classroom have been meager. The dearth of experimentation has been due to the ethical concern of researchers and the practical limitations in the application of punishment to children. In addition, until very recently, psychologists have espoused the *legend* that punishment is an extremely ineffective means of controlling behavior (Solomon, 1964). In this respect, Walters, Parke, and Cane (1965) noted that parents have probably been wiser than the experts. We now know that punishment does suppress or weaken behavior and that the effectiveness of punishment is determined by factors including the timing of punishment, the presence of an alternative to the punished response, the scheduling of punishment, and the relationship of the punishing agent to the one being punished.

Before considering the evidence regarding punishment, a definition of terms is in order. Punishment has been defined as following a behavior with a consequence which reduces the future probability of that behavior or, alternatively, as making an aversive stimulus contingent upon a response. The aversive stimulus is defined as something the child will work to avoid or terminate. For example, children often do their chores to avoid being spanked or to terminate nagging from parents. In laboratory studies, children will press buttons to avoid or terminate loud tones. In these cases, spanking and the loud tones are the aversive stimuli. In practice, however, few investigators actually determine in advance whether their subjects will work to escape or avoid the presumably aversive stimulus which is used in their studies. Instead, a stimulus is picked which the investigators *presume* a child would attempt to escape or avoid (and thus by definition would be aversive), and the stimulus (e.g., a tone) is made contingent upon some behavior which the investigators wish to weaken. Consequently, most research on punishment deals with testing various stimuli which are assumed to be aversive to see if they will weaken a response. In addition, the withdrawal of a positive reinforcer is considered a form of punishment. If a teacher removes a child from a pleasant classroom or an activity which the child obviously likes whenever he displays inappropriate behavior, the operation is called "time-out from positive reinforcement." If a child loses points toward recess time when he misbehaves, the point loss is termed "response cost" because the misbehavior costs him a certain number of minutes in recess. In summary, punishment here refers to two types of procedures: (1) presentation of a stimulus presumed to be aversive, or (2) the removal of a presumed positive reinforcer when the subject performs some response one wishes to weaken.

Although there now is considerable evidence indicating the effectiveness of punishment in weakening or suppressing a response, many investigators still fear that adverse side-effects will result from punishment. While it is true that certain applications of punishment may produce fearful and neurotic-like behavior (Masserman, 1943; Wolpe, 1958), procedures which produce undesirable side-effects can be avoided. In order to minimize negative side-effects, certain guidelines should be followed: (1) use punishment sparingly, (2) make it clear to the child why he is being punished, (3) provide the child with an alternative means of obtaining some positive reinforcement, (4) reinforce the child for behaviors incompatible with those you wish to weaken, (5) avoid physical punishment if at all possible, (6) avoid punishing while you are in a very angry or emotional state, and (7) punish at the initiation of a behavior rather than at its completion.

Some of the reasons why punishment should be used sparingly include the following: A teacher or parent who frequently uses punishment becomes less effective at changing behavior because (1) he or she loses positive reinforcing value, and (2) control through punishment weakens as the child adapts or becomes immune to the punishment being used. In addition, an adult who shakes or slaps a child provides inadvertently an aggressive model for the child. For example, a parent who always uses physical punishment when he or she is angry provides the child with an example which the child might follow at some later point when angry—namely physically assaulting the target of his or her own anger. Furthermore, the excessive use of punishment in a particular situation can cause the situation itself to become aversive, and the child will begin to stay away from the scene of repeated negative experiences. For example, a parent or teacher who continually criticizes a child on the basketball court for his poor playing may find that the child quickly begins to avoid the court. Similarly, if a child receives repeated criticism in school, he may cut classes and/or become truant. Even if he does not avoid school altogether, he may avoid school participation in a variety of other ways, e.g., not paying attention, day dreaming, and being restless. Even worse, as Skinner (1968) noted, a child who receives a great deal of punishment may counterattack:

> If the teacher is weak, the student may attack openly. He may be impertinent, impudent, rude, or defiant. His verbal behavior may be obscene or profane. He may annoy the teacher and escape punishment by doing so surreptitiously—by groaning, shuffling his feet, or snapping his fingers. . . . Physical attacks on teachers are now common. . . . Vandalism is another form of counterattack which is growing steadily more serious. . . . A much less obvious but equally serious effect of aversive control is plain inaction. The student is sullen, stubborn, and unresponsive. He "blocks." He refuses to obey. (p. 98)

Nonetheless, there are occasions in which punishment may be a necessary procedure in a classroom. Many of the aforementioned dangers can be eliminated by the judicious use of mild forms of punishment, especially in conjunction with positive means of behavior change. The following four articles document the effectiveness of four different types of punishment: (1) soft reprimands, (2) reprimands coupled with praise and prompts to behave appropriately, (3) social isolation, and (4) response cost or point loss.

The most common form of classroom punishment is a verbal reprimand. Reprimands are used daily by almost all teachers. Despite their frequent use, the effects of reprimands have rarely been systematically investigated because many researchers fear being labeled punishment advocates if reprimands are found to be effective. This fear has had the fortunate effect of prompting investigators to search for positive means of behavior change, and these searches will hopefully continue. However, practically speaking, teachers will undoubtedly use reprimands as long as they face classroom bickering, cursing, and disruptions.

Generally, when teachers reprimand children, they do so in a manner that enables many of the children in the class to hear the reprimand. The study by O'Leary, Kaufman, Kass, and Drabman (1970) documents the effectiveness of an alternative mode of reprimanding for reducing disruptive behavior, viz., soft reprimanding or reprimanding in a manner so that only the child concerned can hear the reprimand. The latter form works best in a class or during an activity where the teacher can move rather freely around the class, e.g., when correcting work, when using programmed instruction, or when the teacher is talking or lecturing as she walks around the classroom. Soft reprimands are probably most effective when combined with frequent praise for appropriate behavior and when the intensity and tone of the teacher's reprimand are not severe. A soft reprimand is preferable to a loud reprimand, although the reprimand audible to many children may on occasion be effective—especially when combined with frequent forms of positive teacher attention. When disruptive behavior cannot be ignored, a soft reprimand should be one of the first types of punishment a teacher uses to deal with the problem and should ordinarily be utilized before trying loud reprimands and social isolation (time-out from reinforcement).

The study by Jones and Miller (1974) illustrates how a combination of (1) quick, mild negative attention followed by (2) reinforcement of others who are behaving appropriately, as well as (3) reinforcement of the offending child shortly after he or she begins behaving appropriately is related to a reduction in disruptive behavior. As Jones and Miller noted, other studies using very *infrequent* praise with reprimands, such as frequently telling children to sit down (Madsen, Becker, Thomas, Koser & Plager, 1968), or high frequency disapproval (Thomas, Becker & Armstrong, 1968) can lead to *increases* in disruptive behavior. In sum, the message for a teacher seems clear: frequent praise seems to enhance the effects of verbal reprimands in reducing disruptive classroom behavior and may in fact be necessary if negative attention is to have the desired effect on disruptions.

It is surprising that no increases in the negative attention of the teachers were reflected in the Jones and Miller data. The absence of an increase may have been due to weekly rather than daily data collection. Alternatively, increased reinforcement of children other than the target students and prompting of appropriate behavior may have partly resulted in the decrease in disruptive behavior. Consequently, while the evidence suggests that a combination of verbal reprimands and praise is effective in reducing disruptive behavior, more data is necessary before the combination of teacher behavior advocated by Jones and Miller should be definitely adopted. McAllister, Stachowiak, Baer, and Conderman (1969), however, did find such a combination of praise and reprimands effective in reducing inappropriate talking and turning around in a secondary school classroom.

The Lahey, McNees, and McNees (1973) study illustrates the use of timeout from reinforcement with a 10-year-old student. When this student made obscene remarks, he was placed in a timeout room for a minimum of five minutes. In this case, the timeout room was a well-lighted, 4 by 10 ft. room connected to the classroom. As mentioned earlier, timeout refers to the removal of some source of positive reinforcement for a specified period of time. Timeout in the form of isolation in a room adjacent to a classroom is not feasible or suggested for any but the most serious classroom problems since the procedure can often lead to public alarm regarding misuse of behavioral procedures. In this study, however, the obscenities uttered by the 10-year-old student were so frequent that had they not been dramatically reduced, the boy might have been forced to withdraw from the special class. In cases like this, alarm concerning timeout may be obviated in part by effective communication with the child, parent, and principal before implementing the procedure.

Social isolation, of course, is difficult to use with adolescents since many teachers could not physically place a teenager in a timeout room if the teenager refused to go on his own. Fortunately, the child in this study was only 10, and he resisted going to the timeout room only occasionally. Another practical obstacle to the use of timeout is the likelihood that a child will scream and bang on the timeout room door. This problem is usually handled by requiring a minimum period of quiet before the child can leave the timeout room (e.g., one minute in the Lahey et al. study) and ignoring any noises that occur. To deal with problems of refusing to go to timeout and banging on the timeout room door, a variation of the basic timeout procedure has been used very successfully by the present authors.* The child is told that he must go to timeout for 15 minutes of quiet because he hit another child. If he goes to timeout by himself immediately, he earns five minutes off his quiet time. If he quiets down as soon as he enters timeout, he earns another five

*Personal communication, W. Pelham, 1975.

minutes off his quiet time. Note that the child is rewarded for controlling his behavior and is therefore not in an entirely punitive situation. Such a procedures is similar to one used by parents when they reduce the punishment if the child is honest about admitting his transgression.

Several comments are in order regarding the child and procedures described in the Lahey et al. article. The combination of tics, facial twitches, and uttering of obscene statements is often described as "Gilles de la Tourette's syndrome." While this child had not been aided by medical treatment, it should be noted that a drug, Haloperidol, has been effective in treating some children with this problem (Shapiro & Shapiro, 1968). However, even if medication were effective in partially reducing the tics and obscenities, additional intervention might be necessary to reduce the obscenities to a near zero rate.

Finally, the teacher who uses timeout should recognize that timeout should be gradually eliminated rather than abruptly terminated. As was the case in this study, when timeout is abruptly withdrawn, the child may revert to his former behavior. While timeout is being gradually eliminated, strong emphasis should be placed on reinforcing positive alternatives to punished behaviors, such as cooperating with others and completing class work. In addition, some alternatives to timeout, such as soft reprimands and loss of privileges, should be used when timeout is being eliminated.

Many individuals using token programs ask whether tokens can be taken away consequent on inappropriate behavior without adverse side-effects. More specifically, the concern has been that a response cost procedures might lead to increases in aggression, avoidance of the class, and dislike of the teacher. These questions were addressed by Iwata and Bailey (1974) who compared a reward token program with a cost token program in a math class. In the cost program, each student began the class with 10 tokens in his or her cup, and tokens were removed for violating classroom rules. In the reward program, students began with empty cups and earned tokens for complying with the rules. Iwata and Bailey found that the programs were equally effective in reducing classroom rule violations and off-task (inattentive) behavior, as well as producing increases in the number of problems completed. Furthermore, there were no differences in students' preference for reward or cost programs after the students had experienced both.

There was a slight tendency for the teacher to be more approving when she used a reward program than when she used a cost program.

This difference, although small, should not be taken lightly, for a teacher using a cost program without observers or experimenters to monitor his/her behavior may feel even freer to give criticism without hesitation. Special efforts should be taken to prevent this possible increase in teacher criticism or disapproval when a cost program is employed. It is also possible that reward programs sensitize teachers to praiseworthy positive behavior rather than classroom disruptions. This sensitization could in turn lead to increases in teacher praise.

Most importantly, as Iwata and Bailey noted, only when students in cost programs have been given "free" tokens at the beginning of class have investigators found no differences between reward and cost programs. On the other hand, when students earn the tokens which are later removed, cost programs produce less reduction in inappropriate behavior than reward programs. Finally, though not here investigated, a combination of reward and cost procedures in which students earn tokens for many prosocial and academic behaviors and lose tokens for only a small number of inappropriate behaviors is probably the most desirable method of operating a token program where it is absolutely necessary to deal with high rates of inappropriate behavior. In classes where this is not the case, however, it is probably wise to use a reward only system since the effect on positive teacher behavior is most salient in this type of program.

# Article 4
# The Effects of Loud and Soft Reprimands
# on the Behavior of Disruptive Students* †

K. DANIEL O'LEARY, KENNETH F. KAUFMAN,
RUTH E. KASS, and RONALD S. DRABMAN

Abstract: Two children in each of five classes were selected for a 4 month study because of their high rates of disruptive behavior. During a baseline condition the frequency of disruptive behaviors and teacher reprimands was assessed. Almost all teacher reprimands were found to be of a loud nature and could be heard by many other children in the class. During the second phase of the study, teachers were asked to use primarily soft reprimands which were audible only to the child being reprimanded. With the institution of the soft reprimands, the frequency of disruptive behavior declined in most of the children. Then the teachers were asked to return to the loud reprimand and a consequent increase in disruptive behavior was observed. Finally, the teachers were asked to again use soft reprimands, and again disruptive behavior declined.

A number of studies demonstrate that teacher attention in the form of praise can reduce disruptive classroom behavior (Becker, Madsen, Arnold, & Thomas, 1967; Hall, Lund, & Jackson, 1968; Madsen, Becker & Thomas, 1968; Walker & Buckley, 1968). In these studies, praising appropriate behavior was usually concomitant with ignoring disruptive behavior. In addition, shaping appropriate behavior or reinforcing successive approximations to some desired teminal behavior was stressed. Despite the generally positive results

*Reprinted by permission from *Exceptional Children,* October 1970, 37, 145-155.

†The research reported herein was performed in part pursuant to Biomedical Sciences Support Grant No. 31-8200-C, US Public Health Service, 1967-69.

obtained when a teacher used these procedures, a closer examination of the studies reveals that (a) they were not always effective (Hall et al., 1968), (b) the teacher did not actually ignore all disruptive behavior (Madsen et al., 1968), and (c) in one class of disruptive children, praising appropriate behavior and ignoring disruptive behavior resulted in classroom pandemonium (O'Leary, Becker, Evans, & Saudargas, 1969).

One might argue that where praising appropriate behavior and ignoring disruptive behavior prove ineffectual, the teacher is not appropriately shaping the children's behavior. Although such an argument is theoretically rational, it is of little solace to a teacher who unsuccessfully attempts to reinforce approximations to desired terminal behaviors. Furthermore the supposition that the teacher is not appropriately shaping ignores the power of peers to reinforce disruptive behavior. Disregard of disruptive behavior is based on two premises—that it will extinguish if it is not reinforced and that praising appropriate behavior which is incompatible with disruptive behavior will reduce the frequency of the latter. However, even when a teacher ignores disruptive behavior, other children may reinforce it by giggling and smiling. These peer reactions may occur only occasionally, but they may make the disruptive behavior highly resistant to extinction. Thus, the teacher may ask what she can do when praise and ignoring are not effective. The present studies were designed to assess one alternative to ignoring disruptive behavior: reprimanding the child in a soft manner so that other children in the classroom could not hear the reprimand.

The effectiveness of punishment in suppressing behavior of animals has been amply documented (Solomon, 1964). Similarly, the effectiveness of punishment with children in experimental settings has been repeatedly demonstrated (Parke & Walters, 1967). However, experimental manipulations of punishment or reprimands with disruptive children have not often been investigated in applied settings. One attempt to manipulate teacher reprimands was made by O'Leary and Becker (1968) who varied aspects of teacher attention and found that soft reprimands were effective in reducing disruptive behavior of a class of first-grade children during a rest period. Since soft reprimands seemed to have no adverse side effects in the study and since ignoring disruptive behavior is not always effective, further analyses of the effects of soft reprimands seem promising.

Soft reprimands offer several interesting advantages over loud ones. First of all, a soft reprimand does not single out the child so that his disruptive behavior is made noticeable to others. Second, a soft reprimand is presumably different from the reprimands that disruptive children ordinarily receive at home or in school, and, consequently, it should minimize the possibility of triggering conditioned emotional reactions to reprimands. Third, teachers consider soft reprimands a viable alternative to the usual methods of dealing with disruptive behavior. Two experiments are presented here which assessed the effects of soft reprimands.

## EXPERIMENT I

Two children in a second-grade class were selected for observation because of their high rates of disruptive behavior. During a baseline condition, the frequency of disruptive behaviors and teacher reprimands was assessed. Almost all reprimands were loud, i.e., many children in the class could hear them. During the second phase of the study, the teacher was asked to voice her reprimands so that they would be audible only to the child to whom they were directed. The third phase of the study constituted a return to the teacher's former loud reprimand. Finally, during the fourth condition, the teacher was requested to again use soft reprimands.

### Subjects
Child D was described as nervous and restless. He bit his nails, drummed his fingers on his desk, and stuttered. He was often out of his seat talking and bothering other children. D avoided any challenging work. He was quick to argue and was known to get into trouble in the neighborhood.

Child S was described as uncooperative and silly. He paid little attention to his work, and he would often giggle and say things out loud. His teacher said that he enjoyed having other children laugh at him and that he acted in this manner to gain attention.

### Observation
Before base period data were collected, college undergraduates were trained over a 3-week period to observe in the classroom. During this time, the observers obtained reliabilities of child observations exceeding 70 percent agreement. There were two undergraduate observers. One observed daily, and the other observed less frequently, serving as a reliability checker. The observers were instructed to neither talk nor make any differential responses in order to minimize their effect on the children's behavior.

Each child was observed for 20 minutes a day during the arithmetic lesson. Observations were made on a 20-second observe, 10-second record basis: The observer would watch the child for 20 seconds and then record in 10 seconds the disruptive behaviors which had occurred during that 20-second period. The disruptive behaviors were categorized according to nine classes modified from the O'Leary and Becker study (1967). The nine classes of disruptive behavior and their associated general definitions are:

1. *Out-of-chair:* Movement of the child from his chair when not permitted or requested by teacher. No part of the child's body is to be touching the chair.
2. *Modified out-of-chair:* Movement of the child from his chair with some part of the body still touching the chair (exclude sitting on feet).
3. *Touching others' property:* Child comes into contact with another's property without permission to do so. Includes grabbing, rearranging, destroying the property of another, and touching the desk of another.
4. *Vocalization:* Any unpermitted audible behavior emanating from the mouth.
5. *Playing:* Child uses his hands to play with his own or community property so that such behavior is incompatible with learning.
6. *Orienting:* The turning or orienting response is not rated unless the child is seated and the turn must be more than 90 degrees, using the desk as a reference point.
7. *Noise:* Child creating any audible noise other than vocalization without permission.
8. *Aggression:* Child makes movement toward another person to come into contact with him (exclude brushing against another).
9. *Time off task:* Child does not do assigned work for entire 20-second interval. For example, child does not write or read when so assigned.

The dependent measure, mean frequency of disruptive behavior, was calculated by dividing the total number of disruptive behaviors by the number of intervals observed. A mean frequency measure was obtained rather than frequency of disruptive behavior per day since the length of observations varied due to unavoidable circumstances such as assemblies. Nonetheless, only three of the 27 observations for child D lasted less than 20 minutes and only four of the 28 observations for child S were less than 20 minutes. Observations of less than 10 minutes were not included.

*Reliability*

The reliabilities of child observations were calculated according to the following procedure. A perfect agreement was scored if both observers recorded the same disruptive behavior within a 20-second interval. The reliabilities were then calculated by dividing the number of perfect agreements by the number of different disruptive behaviors observed providing a measure of percent agreement. There were three reliability checks during the base period (Loud I) and one during the first soft period for child D. There were two reliability checks during the base period and one reliability check during the first soft period for child S. The four reliability checks for child D yielded the following results: 81, 72, 64, and 92 percent agreement; the three for child S resulted in: 88, 93, and 84 percent agreement.

The reliability of the observations of the teacher's loud and soft reprimands to the target children was also checked. On two different days these observations were taken simultaneously with the observation of the target children. One reliability check was made during the base period and one check was made during the first soft period. A perfect agreement was scored if both observers agreed that the reprimand was loud or soft and if both observers scored the reprimand in the same 20-second interval. The consequent reliabilities were 100 percent and 75 percent during the base period and first soft period respectively.

## Procedures

*Base Period (Loud I)*

During the base period the teacher was asked to handle the children as she normally would. Since few, if any, soft reprimands occurred during the base period, this period was considered a loud reprimand phase.

*Soft Reprimands I*

During this phase the following instructions were given to the teacher:

1.  Make reprimands soft all day, i.e., speak so that only the

child being reprimanded can hear you.

2.  Approximately one-half hour before the observers come into your room, concentrate on using soft reprimands so that the observers' entrance does not signal a change in teacher behavior.

3.  While the observers are in the room, use only soft reprimands with the target children.

4.  Do not increase the frequency of reprimands. Reprimand as frequently as you have always done and vary only the intensity.

5.  Use soft reprimands with all the children, not just the target children.

## Loud Reprimands II

During this phase the teacher was asked to return to loud reprimands, and the five instructions above for the soft period were repeated with a substitution of loud reprimands for soft ones.

## Soft Reprimands II

During this final period, the teacher was asked to return to the soft reprimand procedures.

## Results

### Child D

Child D displayed a marked reaction to soft reprimands. The mean frequency of disruptive behavior during the four conditions was: Loud I, 1.1; Soft I, 0.8; Loud II, 1.3; Soft II, 0.9. A reversal of effects was evident. When the loud reprimands were reinstated disruptive behavior increased while disruptive behavior declined during the second soft period (Fig. 1). In addition, in order to more closely examine the effects of the two types of reprimands, there was an assessment of the frequency of disruptive behaviors in the two 20-second intervals after a reprimand, when another reprimand had not occurred in one of the two intervals. The results revealed that the average number of disruptive behaviors in these two intervals during the four conditions was: Loud I, 2.8; Soft I, 1.2; Loud II, 2.6; and Soft II, 1.6.

*Child S*

Child S also displayed a marked reaction to soft reprimands. The mean frequency of his disruptive behavior during the four conditions was: Loud I, 1.4; Soft I, 0.6; Loud II, 1.1; Soft II, 0.5. Again a reversal of effects was evident when the loud reprimands were reinstated. The average number of disruptive behaviors in the two 20-second intervals just after a reprimand was made was as follows during the four conditions: Loud I, 2.9; Soft I, 1.5; Loud II, 2.1; Soft II, 0.9.

*Teacher*

Although teacher A was asked to hold constant the incidence of her reprimands across conditions, the mean frequency of her reprimands to child D during the four conditions was: Loud I, 7; Soft I, 5; Loud II, 12; Soft II, 6. Similarly, she also had difficulty in holding constant her reprimands to child S across conditions as the following data show: Loud I, 6; Soft I, 4; Loud II, 8; Soft II, 3. Thus, there is some possibility that the increase in disruptive behavior during the second loud phase was a consequence of increased attention to the behavior per se, rather than a consequence of the kind of attention given, whether loud or soft. As the disruptive behavior increased, teacher A felt it impossible to use the same number of reprimands that she had used during the soft period.

Because the frequency of loud reprimands was greater than the frequency of soft reprimands, one could not conclude from Experiment I that the loudness or softness of the reprimands was the key factor in reducing disruptive behavior. It was clear, however, that if a teacher used soft reprimands, she could use fewer reprimands and obtain better behavior than if she used loud reprimands.

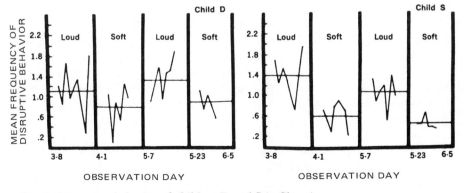

Fig. 1. Disruptive behavior of children D and S in Class A.

## EXPERIMENT II

Experiment II was conducted to assess the effects of loud and soft reprimands with the frequency held constant and to test whether all the children's disruptive behavior decreased when the teacher used soft reprimands. Experiment II is divided into three parts. Part I followed the same ABAB paradigm described in Experiment I (Loud, Soft, Loud, Soft), but Parts II and III involved variations which will be described later.

### Part I

*Subjects*
Class B, Grade 2: Child Z was a large boy who said that he wanted to be a bully when he grew up. He was the only child in the class who deliberately hurt other children. He constantly called out answers without raising his hand and his work habits were poor. Child V was extremely talkative. He loved to be with other children and he was always bursting with something to say. He was also mischievious, but never intentionally hurt anyone. His work habits were poor and his papers were never completed.
Class C, Grade 3: Child E was an extremely nervous child. When she directed all her energy to her studies she could perform well. However, she was very undependable and rarely did her work. She was in and out of her seat and talked endlessly. Child W was a disruptive child whose reaction to most situations was to punch, kick, throw things, and to shove others out of his way. He did little work and devoted his time to such activities as chewing his pencils and punching holes in his papers.

*Observation*
The observational procedures described earlier in Experiment I were identical to those used in Experiment II. Each target child was observed during a structured academic lesson for 20 minutes each day on a 20-second observe, 10-second record basis. The nine classes of disruptive behavior were the same as those in Experiment I with some definitial extensions and a slight change in the definition of aggression. The dependent measure was calculated in the same manner as described in Experiment I.
To minimize the possibility of distance as the key factor in reprimanding the children, the target children in both classes were

moved near the front of the room so that the teacher could administer soft reprimands without walking a great distance. This seating arrangement made it easier for the teacher to reprimand the target children either loudly or softly and decreased the possibility of the teacher's serving as a cue for appropriate behavior by her walking to the child.

The occurrence of loud and soft reprimands was recorded throughout the study by a teacher-observer. As mentioned previously, the teachers were asked to hold the frequency of reprimands constant both to the target children and to the class throughout the study. The teacher was also asked to hold other behaviors as constant as possible so that behaviors such as praise, "eyeing down" a child, and reprimands to the class as a whole would not confound the results. A graduate student observed almost daily and gave the teachers feedback to ensure adherence to these requirements.

In addition to observations on target children, daily observations of disruptive behavior were taken on all the other children by a sampling procedure for one hour each day. Each nontarget child was observed consecutively for 2 minutes. The observer watched the children in a predetermined order each day, looking for the disruptive behaviors that had been observed in the target children.

## Reliability

The reliabilities of child observations for both the target children and the class samples were calculated according to the procedures discussed in Experiment I. There were three reliability checks during the base period for both target children and the class sample. The average reliability for the target children was 84 percent and for the class sample was 79 percent. Nine additional reliability checks of the observations averaged 79 percent for the target children and 82 percent for the class sample.

The reliability of the observations during the base period of loud and soft reprimands used by Teacher B was 79 percent and 80 percent respectively. The reliability of the observation of loud and soft reprimands used by Teacher C was 82 percent and 72 percent respectively.

## Results

Because there were definite decreasing trends of disruptive behavior during both soft conditions for three of the four target children, the average of the mean levels of disruptive behavior during the last five days of each condition for the target children are reported in Table 1. There were changes in children's behavior associated with changes in teacher behavior (see Fig. 2). There was a decrease in the children's disruptive behavior in the soft reprimand phase and then an increase in the disruptive behavior of three of the four children during the reinstatement of loud reprimands. Finally, the second soft period was marked by a decrease in disruptive behavior. Although the disruptive behavior of child V did not

**Table 1. The Average of the Mean Levels of Disruptive Behavior During the Last Five Days of Each Condition for the Target Children.**

| Subjects | Condition | | | |
|---|---|---|---|---|
|  | *Loud I* ($\bar{X}=1.3$) | *Soft I* ($\bar{X}=0.9$) | *Loud II* ($\bar{X}=1.2$) | *Soft II* ($\bar{X}=0.3$) |
| Child Z | 1.0 | 0.9 | 1.3 | 0.8 |
| Child V | 1.7 | 1.4 | 1.3 | 0.6 |
| Child E | 0.9 | 0.6 | 1.1 | 0.4 |
| Child W | 1.6 | 0.8 | 0.9 | 0.3 |

increase during the reinstitution of loud reprimands, a reduction of disruptive behavior was associated with each introduction of soft reprimands—particularly during the second soft phase. Consequently, soft reprimands seemed to influence the reduction of disruptive behavior of each of the four children. A mean reduction of 0.4 and 0.7 disruptive behaviors was associated with each introduction of soft reprimands for these children.

In order to demonstrate that the reduction of disruptive behavior was not a function of changes in frequency of reprimands, the frequencies of loud and soft reprimands are provided in Table 2. Although there was some slight reduction of reprimands for individual children during the soft reprimand phases, the teachers were able to hold the frequency of reprimands relatively constant across days and conditions, despite an obvious change in the children's behavior. The mean total reprimands, loud and soft, during the four conditions were as follows: Loud I, 5.7; Soft I, 4.6; Loud II, 5.3; Soft II, 3.7. Also of particular significance was the constancy of praise comments across conditions. There was an average of less than one praise comment per day given to each child in each of the four conditions. It can be inferred from these data that soft reprimands can be influential in modifying classroom behavior of particularly disruptive children.

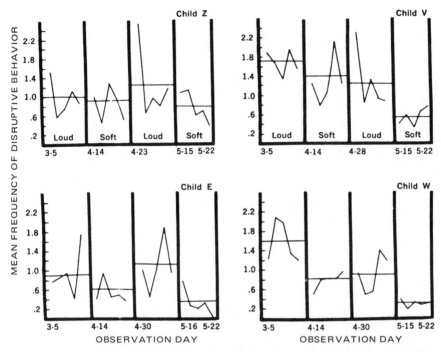

**Fig. 2. Disruptive behavior of children Z and V in Class B and children E and W in Class C.**

The data from the class samples taken during the last five days of each condition did not show that soft reprimands reduced disruptive behavior for the whole class. Because of the variability within conditions and the lack of any clear relationship between type of reprimands and level of disruptive behavior, those data are not presented here. However, the changes in the behavior of the target children are evident when one considers that the mean frequency of disruptive behavior for the class sample B was .9 throughout the experiment and .8 during the second soft condition. The mean frequency of disruptive behavior for the class sample C was .6 throughout the experiment and .5 during the second soft condition. Thus one should note that the disruptive behavior of the four target children during the second soft period was less than the level of disruptive behavior for the class.

**Table 2. Average Frequency of Loud and Soft Reprimands Per Day.**

| Condition | Type of Reprimand to Child Z | | Condition | Type of Reprimand to Child V | |
|---|---|---|---|---|---|
| | *Loud* | *Soft* | | *Loud* | *Soft* |
| Loud I | 3.8 | 2.0 | Loud | 6.8 | 2.2 |
| Soft I | 0.6 | 2.6 | Soft | 0.5 | 6.7 |
| Loud II | 3.0 | 1.7 | Loud | 3.5 | 1.0 |
| Soft II | 0.1 | 2.6 | Soft | 0.1 | 3.6 |
| Condition | Reprimand to Child E | | Condition | Reprimand to Child W | |
| | *Loud* | *Soft* | | *Loud* | *Soft* |
| Loud I | 3.5 | 0.6 | Loud | 3.3 | 0.7 |
| Soft I | 0.4 | 5.0 | Soft | 0.4 | 2.3 |
| Loud II | 5.7 | 0.9 | Loud | 5.3 | 0.3 |
| Soft II | 0.2 | 3.4 | Soft | .04 | 4.6 |

## Part II

Two target children and a class sample were observed in the class of a third-grade teacher. A baseline (Loud I) of disruptive behavior was obtained in this class during a structured academic lesson using the procedures described in Experiment I. In the second phase of the study (Soft I) the teacher was asked to use soft reprimands, just as the other teachers had done. Because of the infrequency of her reprimands in the second phase, the teacher was asked to double her use of soft reprimands in phase three (Soft II-Double). During phase four (Loud II), she was asked to maintain her more frequent use of reprimands but to make them loud. Both child and teacher observations were made in accord with the procedures described in Part I of Experiment II.

### Subjects
Child B was reported to be a happy extrovert who was a compulsive talker. Child R was described by his teacher as a clown with a very short attention span.

### Reliability
The reliability of child observations was obtained for the target children on seven occasions, and the reliability of the class sample on

five occasions. The resultant average reliabilities were 87 percent and 87 percent, respectively.

The reliability of the observations of teacher behavior was checked on two occasions during the base period and once during the first soft period. The average reliability of the observations of loud and soft reprimands was 82 percent and 72 percent, respectively.

*Results*

Child B's disruptive behavior declined from 1.6 during the last five days of baseline (loud reprimands) to 1.3 during the last five days of soft reprimands. In contrast, child R's disruptive behavior increased from 1.5 in the last five days of baseline to 1.9 during the last five days of soft reprimands (see Fig. 3). With the instructions to increase the use of soft reprimands during phase three (Soft II-Double), child B's disruptive behavior showed a slight drop to 1.1 while child R's increased slightly to 2.0. The return to loud reprimands was associated with an increase to 1.8 for child B and almost no change for child R.

The increase in child R's disruptive behavior from the loud to the first soft condition cannot be attributed to the soft reprimands. In fact, the change appeared to be due to a decrease in both loud and soft reprimands. Even with the instructions to double the use of soft reprimands, the teacher observations reported in Table 3 indicate that the frequency of total reprimands during the double soft phase was less than during baseline. However, since child R's disruptive behavior did not increase with the return to loud reprimands, the

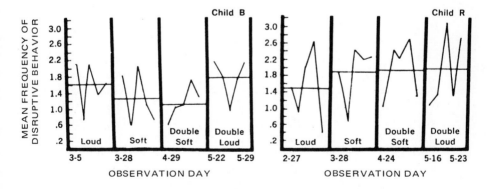

Fig. 3. Disruptive behavior of children B and R in Class D.

experimental control over R's behavior was minimal or nonexistent. On the other hand, child B's disruptive behavior appeared to lessen with the use of soft reprimands.

Again, the data from the class sample did not show that soft reprimands reduced disruptive behavior for the whole class. Those data will not be presented here in detail. The mean frequency of disruptive behavior for the class sample throughout the experiment was .62.

**Table 3. Average Frequency of Loud and Soft Reprimands Per Day.**

| Condition | Type of Reprimand to Child B | | Condition | Type of Reprimand to Child R | |
|---|---|---|---|---|---|
| | Loud | Soft | | Loud | Soft |
| Loud I | 2.0 | 0.4 | Loud | 1.5 | 0.2 |
| Soft I | 0.5 | 1.0 | Soft | 0.2 | 0.0 |
| Soft II | | | Double | | |
| (Double) | 1.8 | 1.1 | soft | 0.0 | 0.8 |
| Loud II | 3.1 | 2.3 | Loud | 2.5 | 0.0 |

| Condition | Reprimand to Child D | | Condition | Reprimand to Child J | |
|---|---|---|---|---|---|
| | Loud | Soft | | Loud | Soft |
| Loud | 4.5 | 1.3 | Loud | 1.3 | 0.2 |
| Soft | 0.2 | 3.2 | Soft | 0.0 | 2.2 |

*Discussion*

The failure to decrease child R's disruptive behavior by soft reprimands may have been due to his very deficient academic repertoire. He was so far behind his classmates that group instruction was almost meaningless for him. It is also possible that the teacher felt frustrated because of increases in child R's disruptive behavior when she used soft reprimands; teacher D found them particularly difficult to use. She stated, "It was difficult for me to give soft reprimands as I feared they were a sign of weakness. The walking and whispering necessary to administer soft reprimands to the disruptive child were especially strenuous for me. As the day wore on, I found that my patience became exhausted and my natural tendency to shout like a general took over." Also of particular note was an observer's comment that when verbal reprimands were administered, whether in a loud or soft phase, they were rarely if ever soft in intensity. In summary, teacher D's data showed that soft reprimands did reduce disruptive behavior in one child. Because of lack of evidence for any consistent use of soft reprimands to the second child, nothing can be said conclusively about its use with him.

## Part III

In a third-grade class of a fourth teacher, two target children and a class sample were observed during a structured academic activity. A baseline of disruptive behavior was obtained in the class with procedures identical to those of Experiment I. In the second phase of the study, the teacher was asked to use soft reprimands, just as the other teachers had done. Because of some unexpected results following this second phase, the general nature of the study was then changed and those results will not be presented here. Both child and teacher observations were made according to the procedures described in Part I of Experiment II.

### Subjects
Child D was a very intelligent boy (135 IQ) who scored in the seventh-grade range on the reading part of the Metropolitan Achievement Test but he was only slightly above grade level in mathematics. His relations with his peers were very antagonistic.

Child J was occasionally considered disruptive by his teacher. However, he did not perform assigned tasks and would often pretend to be working while he actually was not.

### Reliability
The reliability of child observations was obtained for the target children on 15 occasions, and the reliability of the class sample was obtained on three occasions. The resultant average reliabilities were 88 percent for the observations of the target children and 91 percent for the observations of the class sample.

The reliability of the observations of teacher behavior was checked on two occasions during the base period and once during the soft period. The average reliability of the observations of loud and soft reprimands on these three occasions was 78 percent and 79 percent respectively.

*Results*

Child D's disruptive behavior increased from .9 during the last five days of baseline (loud reprimands) to 1.0 during the last five days of soft reprimands. Child J's disruptive behavior increased from .4 to .8 from baseline to the soft reprimand period (see Fig. 4). There was no change in the class sample from baseline to the soft reprimand period. The mean frequency of disruptive behavior for the class sample during the loud and soft phase was .6 and .5 respectively.

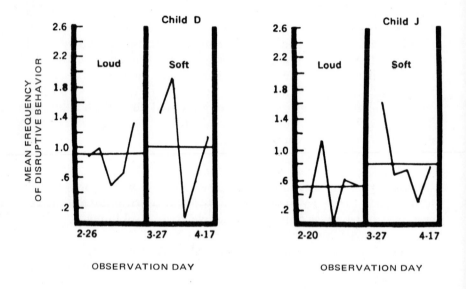

Fig. 4. Disruptive behavior of children D and J in Class E.

As can be seen in Table 3, teacher E's behavior with child D and child J did appear to have been influenced by the experimental instructions.

*Discussion*

The reasons that soft reprimands failed to decrease disruptive behavior in this class are not clear. Several factors may have been important. First of all, teacher E was always very skeptical about the possibility that soft reprimands could influence disruptive behavior whereas the other teachers were willing to acknowledge the probability of their influence. Second, it is possible that the children learned to control the teacher's behavior since a soft reprimand had to be made while the teacher was close to the child. That is, a child might realize that he could draw the teacher to his side each time he misbehaved during the soft reprimand period. In addition, this teacher tolerated more disruptive behavior than the other teachers, and her class was much less structured. Probably most important, she wished to investigate the effectiveness of various types of instructional programs rather than soft reprimands.

## CONCLUSIONS

These two experiments demonstrated that when teachers used soft reprimands, they were effective in modifying behavior in seven of nine disruptive children. Because of a failure to document the proper use of soft reprimands by one teacher (D) to one child, it is impossible to assess the effectiveness on that child. Of particular significance was the finding that soft reprimands seemed to be associated with an increase in disruptive behavior of one—and possibly two—target children in one teacher's class although the soft reprimands did not influence the level of disruptive behavior for the class as a whole. The results of Experiments I and II lead to the conclusion that with particularly disruptive children a teacher can generally use fewer soft reprimands than loud ones and obtain less disruptive behavior than when loud reprimands are used.

The authors wish to make clear that they do not recommend soft reprimands as an alternative to praise. An ideal combination would probably be frequent praise, some soft reprimands, and very occasional loud reprimands. Furthermore, it is always necessary to realize that classroom management procedures such as praise and types of reprimanding are no substitute for a good academic program. In the class where soft reprimands were ineffective for both target children, a type of individualized instruction was later introduced, and the disruptive behavior of both the target children and the class sample declined.

Because soft reprimands are delivered by a teacher when she is close to a child it is possible that a soft reprimand differs from a loud one in other dimensions than audibility to many children. Although observations of teachers in this study did not reveal that teachers made their soft reprimands in a less harsh, firm, or intense manner than their loud reprimands, it might be possible for a teacher to utilize soft reprimands in such a manner. If the latter were true, soft reprimands might require less teacher effort than loud reprimands. Ultimately soft reprimands might prove more reinforcing for the teacher both because of the relatively small expenditure of effort and the generally positive and sometimes dramatic changes in the children's behavior. The inherent nature of the soft reprimand makes its use impossible at all times, particularly when a teacher has to remain at the blackboard or with a small group in one part of the room. As one teacher mentioned, "I had to do more moving around, but there appeared to be less restlessness in the class."

In sum, it is the authors' opinion that soft reprimands can be a useful method of dealing with disruptive children in a classroom. Combined with praise, soft reprimands might be very helpful in reducing disruptive behavior. In contrast, it appears that loud reprimands lead one into a vicious cycle of more and more reprimands resulting in even more disruptive behavior.

## REFERENCES

Becker, W.C., Madsen, C.H., Jr., Arnold, C., & Thomas, D.R. The contingent use of teacher attention and praise in reducing classroom behavior problems. *Journal of Special Education,* 1967, 1, 287-307.

Hall, R.V., Lund, D., & Jackson, D. Effects of teacher attention on study behavior. *Journal of Applied Behavior Analysis,* 1968, 1, 1-12.

Madsen, C.H., Becker, W.C., & Thomas, D.R. Rules, praise, and ignoring: Elements of elementary classroom control. *Journal of Applied Behavior Analysis,* 1968, 1, 139-150.

O'Leary, K.D., & Becker, W.C. Behavior modification of an adjustment class: A token reinforcement program. *Exceptional Children,* 1967, 33, 637-642.

O'Leary, K.D., & Becker, W.C. The effects of a teacher's reprimands on children's behavior. *Journal of School Psychology,* 1968, 7, 8-11.

O'Leary, K.D., Becker, W.C., Evans, M.B., & Saudargas, R.A. A token reinforcement program in a public school: A replication and systematic analysis. *Journal of Applied Behavior Analysis,* 1969, 2, 3-13.

Parke, R.D., & Walters, R.H. Some factors influencing the efficacy of punishment training for inducing response inhibition. *Monographs of the Society for Research in Child Development,* 1967, 32, (1, Serial No. 109).

Solomon, R.L. Punishment. *American Psychologist,* 1964, 19, 239-253.

Walker, H.M., & Buckley, N.K. The use of positive reinforcement in conditioning attending behavior. *Journal of Applied Behavior Analysis,* 1968, 1, 245-250.

# Article 5
# The Effective Use of Negative Attention
# for Reducing Group Disruption in
# Special Elementary School Classrooms* †

FREDERICK H. JONES and WILLIAM H. MILLER

Abstract: In a private school for behaviorally deviant children, 2 teachers who led orderly discussions were designated as "comparison teachers" and two whose discussions were characterized by excessive disruptiveness were designated "target teachers." Appropriate and disruptive student behaviors as well as positive, neutral, and negative teacher attention contingent upon each class of student behavior were recorded. In an ABA design with follow-up, intervention consisted of training the target teachers to dispense negative attention contingent upon student disruptiveness in a manner similar to that of the most effective comparison teachers. Intervention reduced disruptiveness in the target classrooms, and follow-up indicated that skills learned by target teachers were being used effectively 3 months later. Comparison teachers decreased use of negative attention throughout the year without loss of classroom control.

A common behavioral problem in special elementary and junior high school classrooms is high-rate, low-intensity student disruptive-

*Reprinted by permission from *The Psychological Record,* 1974, 24, 435-448.

†The procedure and preliminary results of this study were presented at the workshop entitled "The socialization of children with behavior and learning disorders" at the annual meeting of the American Orthopsychiatric Association, Washington, D.C., March, 1971. The research was carried out while the senior author was serving a clinical internship at the Neuropsychiatric Institute, U.C.L.A. Center for the Health Sciences, supported by NIMH Training Grant #2 TO 1 MH 7593-10. Research was carried out at the Laurence School, Van Nuys, California, under the supervision and support of the Director of the Laurence School, Mr. Marvin Jacobson, his associates, Mrs. Sonya Braverman and Mrs. Grace Lee, and psychological consultant Mrs. Lillian B. Vogel. The full cooperation of the teaching staff and the efforts of the two volunteer raters, Mrs. Bertha Kas and Mrs. Dena Davis, are gratefully acknowledged.

ness during a group instruction period. Such disruptions typically include interrupting, talking to one's neighbor, laughing, making inappropriate remarks, or making noise with objects. In some cases such behavior becomes so frequent and intrusive as to undermine the teacher's efforts to conduct a coherent lesson.

Traditionally, operant control of such behavior has been conceptualized in terms of three classes of teacher consequences: positive reinforcement, ignoring or nonreinforcement, and punishment. The vast majority of the classroom control studies have focused upon the use of differential reinforcement of other behavior (DRO), i.e., ignoring targeted inappropriate behaviors in conjunction with the systematic or free-operant reinforcement of appropriate behaviors incompatible with the problem behaviors. While generally successful, this paradigm has on occasion produced an undesirable increase in classroom disruptiveness (Hammerlynck, Donley, & Heller, 1967; Becker, Madson, Arnold, & Thomas, 1967). This occasional failure of DRO highlights the need to explore effective and appropriate uses of punishment to supplement DRO in special circumstances.

While the literature on the systematic use of punishment in the classroom is particularly sparse (Neale, 1969; Baer, 1970), studies have reported the successful use of time-out (Patterson, Ray, & Shaw, 1968; Walker, Mattson, & Buckley, 1969; Mattos, Mattson, Walker, & Buckley, 1969), soft nonpublic reprimands (O'Leary, Kaufman, Kass, & Drabman, 1970), loss of tokens (Barrish, Saunders, & Wolf, 1969), loss of name slips (Hall, Axelrod, Foundopoulos, Shellman, Campbell, & Cranston, 1971), marks signifying 5 minutes of after-school time (Hall et al., 1971), and verbal disapproval (McAllister, Stachowiak, Baer, & Conderman, 1969; Hall et al., 1971). Several of these procedures have liabilities, however, for use with the kinds of high-rate, low-intensity disruptions that typically undermine a classroom discussion. Time-out, for example, constitutes a major disciplinary intervention which would represent "overkill" in relation to the behaviors being considered here and which would greatly disrupt classroom continuity if utilized frequently. Such interventions as nonpublic reprimands, removal of tokens or name slips, and the giving of marks signifying after-school time tend to be too slow and cumbersome to deal effectively with the brief disruptions typical of a vigorous discussion. In such situations the use of some form of contingent disapproval or *mild social punishment* would appear to be a promising means of behavioral control.

The literature suggests, however, that there may well be some pitfalls to the use of mild social punishment which need to be acknowledged and examined. For example, Madsen, Becker, Thomas, Koser, and Plager (1968) found that "sit-down" commands given by the teacher to children who were out of their seats, a kind of disapproval resembling that used successfully by others (McAllister et al., 1969; Hall et al., 1971) produced an *increase* in the frequency of out-of-seat behavior, thereby functioning as reinforcement rather than punishment. And in another study Thomas, Becker, and Armstrong (1968) found that high-intensity disapproval in the form of yelling, belittling, grabbing, spanking, or shaking increased the frequency of classroom disorder as much as threefold when delivered in a setting in which positive reinforcement for competing responses was lacking.

The objectives of the present study were to analyze patterns of consequences for student disruptions dispensed by two teachers in a special elementary school who complained of having highly disorderly class discussions and to compare these patterns of consequences with those dispensed by two teachers who led orderly discussion. Discrepancies between the two groups of teachers were used as the basis for developing a training procedure for the less effective teachers. Preliminary observations indicated that the way in which mild social punishment was used by the two groups of teachers was an important differentiating variable.

## METHOD

### Subjects

The teachers and students of four classrooms in a private school for educationally handicapped children in Los Angeles served as *S*s. The students were Caucasian males from a middle- to upper-middle-class suburban area of the city, and all of these students exhibited learning or adjustment disorders, the majority exhibiting both. Most had been disruptive in public schools prior to transferring to the private school. Ages ranged from 9 to 14 years, and I.Q. was within the normal range. There were approximately 10 students per class.

## Scoring and Reliability

Group behavior was scored in each of the four classrooms using a 15-second interval recording system during the first, middle, and last 5-minute segments of a weekly 30-minute discussion period. The dependent variables were the frequency of disruptive student behavior and the frequency of appropriate student responses in the 15 minutes of each discussion during which data were taken. Disruptive student behavior was scored when a student emitted any of the following three classes of behavior: (a) interrupting another student, (b) talking to his neighbor without first being recognized by the teacher, or (c) disrupting non-verbally by getting out of his chair, throwing an object, knocking over furniture, or rolling a pencil for 3 seconds or more. Appropriate student responding was scored whenever a student participated in the discussion after first being recognized by the teacher. Scorers scanned the entire class while taking data and recorded only the first instance of each of the four classes of targeted student behavior that occurred during any 15-second time segment. Thus there were 16 scoreable student behaviors per minute (appropriate student response and three classes of disruptive student behavior x four 15-second intervals) and 240 such events per discussion (60 appropriate responses and 180 disruptive responses).

In addition to scoring the four classes of student behavior, Os also scored teacher consequences for each of these student behaviors. Three classes of teacher consequences were scored; (a) positive attention, (b) ignore or no attention, and (c) negative attention. *Positive attention* was scored when the teacher oriented toward the student whose behavior was being tracked and delivered a verbal or physical response indicating acceptance or appreciation of the student's response. This could be simply attending to the child as he spoke, smiling and nodding, or verbally acknowledging or affirming the child's contribution. *Negative attention* was scored whenever the teacher oriented toward the student whose behavior was being tracked and delivered a verbal or physical response indicating disapproval. This could be a gesture such as the raising of a finger to the lips or raising the hand to remind an interrupting student to raise his hand if someone else was talking, or it could be a verbal signal that the child was out of order, ranging from saying the student's name to the repetition of a class rule or a stern lecture. Facial expressions alone were not scored. *Ignore* was scored when the teacher failed to orient to the behavior of the child being tracked by the scorer.

Two volunteer housewives were trained in the scoring system and reached criterion reliability of 90% for student behaviors and 80% for teacher consequences prior to the beginning of baseline. The $O$s were given no information as to the nature or timing of the interventions. Approximately nine reliability checks of each $O$'s data were made during the course of the experiment by a criterion scorer, and they were spaced so that at least one check was run on each of the two $O$s each month. Booster training sessions were also held monthly and preceded reliability checks by at least 1 week in all cases. Independence of scoring was achieved by the criterion scorer sitting behind and to the left of $O$ at the back of the class.

Reliability was calculated for appropriate student responding and disruptive student behavior (collapsing the three types of disruptive behavior) as well as for each of the three classes of teacher consequences for disruptive behavior. Reliability was not calculated for consequences of appropriate student responding, since the teachers' response was positive attention over 99% of the time (almost by definition) and since this would have unduly inflated reliability figures for teacher consequences. The reliability index used was the percentage of agreement between the volunteer and criterion scorers' totals for each of the five variables across all 15 minutes of data for a given classroom on a given day (dividing the smaller total by the larger total.). The median and range of these percentages are presented below. In addition, since the ranges of percentages were sometimes excessive as a result of the large effect on percentage figures of a single instance of disagreement during discussions in which only two or three instances of a given type of teacher consequence occurred, a product/moment correlation of the volunteer and criterion scorer's totals for each variable across all reliability checks is also presented. The reliability for each variable was as follows: (a) Appropriate Student Responding: median 94.1%, range 75-100%, r = 98.1; (b) Disruptive Student Behavior: median 94.1%, range 81.9-100%, r = 99.0; (c) Positive Attention: median 83.3%, range 67-100% r = 91.7; (d) Ignoring: median 87.5%, range 74.6-100%, r = 97.2; (e) Negative Attention: median 83.3%, range 50-100%, r = 86.6.

## Procedures

An experimental procedure, which will be referred to as a "contrasted comparison group" design, was employed in which two teachers who complained of excessive disruptiveness during group discussions were designated as *target* teachers, and two teachers who led orderly discussions were designated as *comparison* teachers. An ABA design with follow-up (ABAC) was employed with the target teachers, and the comparison teachers served as controls. Two unique functions of the comparison group in this design were as models of effective functioning to aid in the pinpointing of discriminating variables between the two groups of teachers and as sources of continuous feedback on the extent to which the target teachers approximated effective functioning as a result of training.

Behavior was observed once weekly in each of the four classrooms in a group discussion period. Preliminary observations indicated that the topic of discussion made no difference in the rate and type of disruptive behavior with one exception: Disruptiveness increased markedly during discussions of classroom disruptiveness. Consequently, teachers were instructed to hold discussions on any topic of interest except discipline problems. Typical discussions centered around social studies lessons, science lessons, current events, the planning of field trips, and a school carnival. Seating arrangements varied from week to week in the various classes with desks usually arranged in a "horseshoe" configuration and less often in rows.

## Experimental Conditions

*Baseline (A)*

Baseline data were taken once weekly for six weeks in both the comparison and target classrooms beginning in December. The teachers were requested to conduct their classroom discussions oblivious to the presence of the raters. Four adaptation sessions were held prior to baseline in which $O$s recorded data just as they would during the experimental treatments.

*Intervention (B)*

Training sessions were held after school on days in which weekly data were taken for six weeks until the effects of the intervention had stabilized and the teachers reported that they were no longer learning anything new from the training sessions. Baseline in this contrasted comparison group design had served to pinpoint aspects of behavioral management which differentiated the target from the comparison teachers, and this information subsequently served as the basis for the design of the intervention procedure. Analysis of the baseline data showed that: (a) both the target and comparison teachers had approximately the same frequency of appropriate behavior during classroom discussions, and the teacher consequence for this appropriate behavior was positive attention over 99% of the time; (b) the target teachers had a frequency of disruptive student behavior over twice that of the comparison teachers on the basis of interval sampling. In fact, tallies of disruptive behavior showed the target teachers to have as much as 10 times that of the comparison teachers; (c) the target teachers and the comparison teachers dispensed approximately the same amount of positive attention and negative attention for inappropriate behaviors; and (d) the target teachers ignored inappropriate student behavior at a frequency almost four times that of the comparison teachers. Thus while the frequency of negative attention was the same for both groups, disruptive student behavior was followed by negative attention 33% of the time in the comparison teachers' discussions and only 11% of the time in the target teachers' discussions. Anecdotal observations also indicated that the topography of negative attention was very different in the target and comparison classrooms. While the same amount of appropriate student behavior occurred in both the target and comparison classrooms, in the target classroom appropriate behavior was "buried" in intrusive and distracting verbalizations which the teacher tolerated or attempted to overlook for the most part. Only when the target classrooms reached a high level of disruptiveness did the teachers intervene with negative attention, and at such times the negative attention was delivered at a high intensity and in such a manner as to bring the discussion to a complete halt. In comparison classrooms, limits were set in a fundamentally different fashion. The comparison teachers tended to deliver negative attention quickly and mildly following student disruptions so that one instance of disruptiveness was rarely followed by another one. Consequently, disruptiveness rarely reached a high intensity, and the teachers' negative attention also rarely reached a high intensity.

Intervention consisted of training the target teachers to deliver contingent negative attention during the discussion periods in a manner analogous to that of the comparison teachers. This was done in conjunction with differential reinforcement of appropriate behavior at which the target teachers demonstrated skill prior to intervention. Training emphasized: (a) correct identification of potentially disruptive behavior, (b) development of a repertoire of brief verbalizations and gestures signifying that the child was out of order,

(c) physical proximity to and orientation toward the disruptive student, (d) quick teacher responding following disruptive student behavior so that negative attention often interrupted disruptiveness before it could elicit peer attention or approval, (e) facial expression and tone of voice consistent with disapproval, (f) immediate attention to and reinforcement of a student who was behaving appropriately following the giving of negative attention, and finally (g) reinforcement (and prompting, if necessary) of appropriate participation of the offending child as soon as possible following attention to the appropriate student. The primary focus of the training, therefore, was upon a sequence or chain of behavior that ended in reinforcement of appropriate student behavior even when the sequence was initiated by disruption and involved the systematic use of mild social punishment.

A role-playing procedure was developed in which $E$s and target teachers participated in mock discussions during which the "students" were highly disruptive. All participants took turns being "teacher" and "student," and whenever the "teacher" was unable to control the disruptiveness of the "students," the discussion was stopped. At that point, the group jointly devised an effective teaching strategy for that situation based upon principles of reinforcement and $E$s' observations of the use of negative attention by the comparison teachers. This strategy was then practiced by the "teacher" and the "students" repeated the original series of events until the "teacher" reported mastery. Training sessions were held at the end of the school day following the taking of weekly data so that the data would reflect only those effects of teacher training that had carried over for a period of one week. During the experiment the children in the various classrooms were not informed of any changes in classroom policy.

As a result of training, the target teachers typically dealt with disruptiveness in the classroom during intervention by placing themselves in the proximity of the disruptive student and by quickly and assertively delivering short, low-intensity verbalizations such as "just a second," "wait your turn," "that's enough," and "not now," or by hand gestures toward the offending student, accompanied by his name or by touching the student or taking the distracting object. Lengthy reprimands or raising of the voice were relatively infrequent, since during role-playing such teacher behavior tended to stimulate disruptiveness. Highly provocative student behavior received "time-out," and teacher training included such situations in order to prepare the teachers for any eventuality.

*Reinstatement of Baseline (A)*

The target teachers were instructed to ignore disruptive student behavior until it became intense in a manner approximating the pattern of classroom interaction during baseline. To assist the target teachers in carrying out this assignment, one role-playing session was held in which they practiced ignoring disruptive student behavior. As an additional means of controlling the manner in which negative attention was dispensed during reversal, a cueing procedure was developed for use in the target classrooms during discussions. Each of the target teachers' mean baseline rate of negative attention was randomly scheduled throughout the half-hour discussion period, and whenever negative attention was scheduled to occur, *E* held up a colored card in the back of the classroom. The teacher was instructed as follows: "When the card is up, provide negative attention the next time a child earns it. Provide no negative attention unless the card is up." However, due to the teachers' unwillingness to relinquish their newly acquired means of behavioral control during the remainder of the week, both teachers were permitted to practice the systematic use of negative attention during other class periods.

*Follow-up (C)*

At the end of the reversal procedure, the target teachers were assembled and told simply that they were to conduct their classrooms for the remainder of the school year as they saw fit. Follow-up lasted six weeks until the end of the school year. A more extended follow-up during the summer and the following year had to be abandoned, since two of the four teachers left the staff for personal reasons.

## RESULTS

### Teachers' Behavior

Figure 1 shows the frequency of positive attention, ignoring, and negative attention contingent upon disruptive student behavior for each of the four teachers collapsed by pairs of sessions. The effect of the intervention procedure can be seen primarily in the change in the frequency of ignoring across treatments for the target teachers. The intervention procedure radically reduced the frequency of ignoring for the target teachers, and the reversal procedure produced an increase in the frequency of ignoring of rule-breaking for the target teachers to approximately 60 percent of baseline. By the time of follow-up, the rate of ignoring for the target teachers was less than during baseline or reversal but greater than during intervention.

The frequency of positive attention and negative attention for rule-breaking failed to differentiate the target and comparison teachers across treatments. Interestingly, the frequency of negative attention of the target teachers did not increase during intervention even though their training focused upon its systematic use.

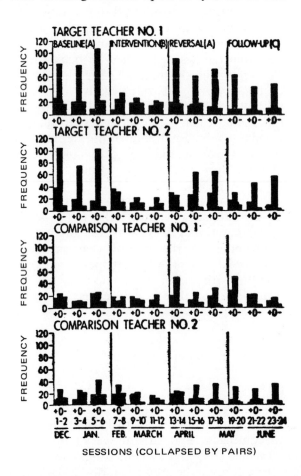

Fig. 1. Frequency of Positive Attention (+), Ignoring (0), and Negative Attention (−) contingent upon disruptive student behavior for each classroom across Baseline (A), Intervention (B), Reinstatement of Baseline (A) and Follow-up (C) collapsed by pairs of sessions.

*Children's behavior*

Figure 2 shows the frequency of disruptive student behavior for each of the four teachers collapsed by pairs of sessions. The frequency of disruptive student behavior for the target teachers decreased during intervention, increased during reversal to 60 percent of baseline, and decreased again during follow-up. The extent of the covariation between the frequency of disruptive student behavior and the frequency of ignoring of disruptive student behavior was striking for both the target and comparison teachers. A product/moment correlation of the session totals of disruptive student behavior and teacher ignoring of disruptive student behavior was calculated for each teacher across treatments. The correlations for Target Teachers #1 and #2 were .92 and .94, respectively, and the correlations for Comparison Teacher #1 and #2 were .88 and .69.

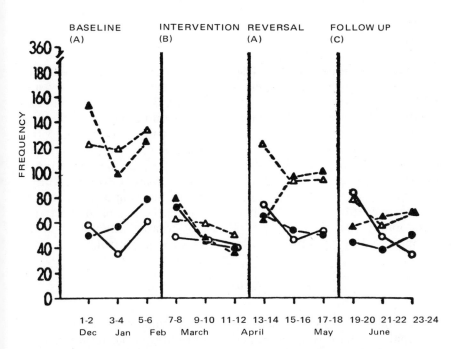

Fig. 2. Frequency of disruptive student behavior for each classroom across Baseline (A), Intervention (B), Reinstatement of Baseline (A), and Follow-up (C) collapsed by pairs of sessions.

The frequency of appropriate student responding failed to differentiate the comparison and target teachers across treatments. The mean frequencies for the four teachers during the study ranged from 19 to 25 per session.

Reversal provided a test of the effect of teacher training upon the frequency of disruptive student behavior. It also highlighted one of the mechanisms by which the training had its effect. The forced distribution of the baseline rate of negative attention in the target classrooms during reversal so that individual instances of student disruptiveness were infrequently and inconsistently followed by negative attention produced an increase in student disruptiveness and an increase in the ignoring of student disruptiveness analogous to the situation which existed during baseline. Apparently this abrupt thinning of the schedule of negative attention following only six weeks of intervention was enough to undermine the capacity of negative attention to prevent disruption, other factors remaining constant.

## Longitudinal Trends

One longitudinal trend is discernible in the contingency data for the comparison teachers. Whereas both Comparison Teachers #1 and #2 gave negative attention for approximately 33 percent of instances of disruptive student behavior during baseline and intervention (December to March), by the time of follow-up (May to June) this figure had decreased to 8 percent and 17 percent, respectively. No loss of classroom control accompanied this decline. The elevation in the frequency of ignoring during follow-up relative to intervention for the target teachers (Fig. 1) parallels this thinning of the schedule of negative attention by the comparison teachers, and in the target classrooms as well this fading of the use of negative attention was not accompanied by an appreciable loss of classroom control.

## DISCUSSION

Training of the target teachers in the systematic and effective use of negative attention in conjunction with differential reinforcement of appropriate student behavior produced data indicating both a decrease in the ignoring of disruptive student behavior and a decrease in the frequency of disruptive student behavior. Reversal and follow-up data confirmed that the contingency variable effecting the changes in the frequency of disruptive student behavior across treatments was the manner in which negative attention was dispensed by the target teachers. Follow-up data also indicated that the skills learned during intervention were still being used effectively three months later in the absence of retraining prior to follow-up. Longitudinal data from the comparison teachers' classrooms indicated a decline in negative attention relative to the frequency of inappropriate student behavior as the year progressed, without any accompanying loss of classroom control. This latter finding suggests that the consistent and effective application of negative attention over the course of the school year in conjunction with differential reinforcement of appropriate behavior may train students in habits of group participation which progressively frees the teacher from a reliance upon aversive contingencies.

However, the question is open as to why the use of negative attention as operationalized in the training procedure proved to be effective. As mentioned earlier, teacher training emphasized a sequence of behaviors on the part of the target teachers, which included early recognition of disruptive behavior, physical proximity to the disruptive student, brief but forceful negative attention as soon as possible after onset of disruptive student behavior, an immediate redirection of attention to a student responding appropriately, and eventual reinforcement of the offending student as soon as he exhibited appropriate behavior. Within this framework a variety of mechanisms of behavioral control may have been operating.

One explanation for the effectiveness of the training procedure is that it increased the consistency of the target teachers' use of negative attention by training them to discriminate disruptive behavior and to dispense negative attention each time it occurred. Assuming that negative attention was functioning as punishment, this would produce a richer schedule of punishment which would be expected to suppress disruptiveness. A second explanation for the effectiveness of the training procedure is that it altered the topography of negative attention for the target teachers so that their use of negative attention subsequently functioned as punishment, whereas previously it had not. A third explanation of the effectiveness of the training procedure is that it taught effective timing of negative attention so that the teachers interrupted student disruptiveness and thereby eliminated peer reinforcement. Other things being equal, this might be expected to put disruptiveness on extinction.

While the data do not permit a separation of these various

mechanisms of behavioral control, some clarification is possible on the basis of *Es'* informal observations of the classrooms during baseline and intervention, which served as the basis of the successful teacher training procedure, and on the basis of their experience with the teacher training procedure itself. Briefly, it would appear that all three mechanisms were operating. In terms of the teachers' consistency, it was noted during baseline, as mentioned earlier, that the target teachers did not typically intervene with negative attention until disruptiveness had reached a high level. Only at the point at which all order was lost would these teachers intervene with negative attention. At such times negative attention was delivered at a high intensity and often to several individuals in the relatively punitive form of yelling, criticism, threats, and lectures. At this point all activity came to a halt, and following the teachers' reassertion of "control," the discussion began again, slowly at first and then building into another crescendo. The high frequency of ignoring of disruptiveness by the target teachers during baseline occurred while the discussion was in the process of deteriorating, and negative attention occurred only at the end of a long series of disruptions. In contrast, the comparison teachers handled disruptiveness in a fundamentally different fashion by consistently giving mild negative attention as soon as disruptions occurred so that class disruptiveness never had a chance to build. The fact that the frequency of negative attention by the target and control teachers was the same during baseline is probably only a coincidence.

While the consistency modeled by the comparison teachers served as a basic element of the training procedure, so also did the topography of negative attention as employed by them. In contrast to the high-intensity negative attention which characterized the efforts of the target teachers to regain control when they had their "backs against the wall," the comparison teachers tended to use mild negative attention, such as a hand gesture or a few words, to stay calm but to be firm and to react *quickly*. Furthermore, the effectiveness of the comparison teachers' use of negative attention seemed to be greater when they were standing very close to the offending student. Consequently, training stressed the building of a repertoire of brief, effective verbalizations and gestures signifying negative attention, calmness in the face of provocation, quickness of responding following the onset of disruptiveness, and proximity to the disruptive student. During training, lengthy verbalizations and displays of strong emotion tended to produce increased disruptiveness and feelings reported by the "students" that they had "won" or "gotten the teacher's goat." Such lengthy verbalizations often included the repetition of classroom rules which were all well known to begin with.

As training progressed, the skills and reflexes of the teachers improved to the point where rather than consequating disruptiveness with negative attention, they often interrupted it. Thus rather than competing with peer reinforcement following disruptiveness, the target teachers were often able to eliminate the stimulus for peer responding. This increase in skill did not have a major impact on the frequency of disruptive student responses, perhaps since effective contingency management had already greatly suppressed the frequency of student disruptiveness. However, those gains made during the second half of intervention may in part be attributable to extinction caused by the general decrease in opportunities for peer reinforcement informally noted by $E$s. Perhaps the most noticeable effect of the increase in the quickness of teacher responding, however, was in the increased smoothness of the discussion, since the student-teacher interactions involving disruption and negative attention were of shorter duration and were therefore less intrusive.

The present data raise one additional question concerning the abruptness with which the frequency of student disruptiveness changed from baseline to intervention and from intervention to reversal—especially since the teachers reported that they were dispensing negative attention systematically throughout the week except during the weekly discussion while the reversal was being carried out. It is highly probable that much of the effect of the use of negative attention was caused by stimulus control rather than considerations of contingency management or response interference alone. Indeed, the rapidity with which the target teachers could lose control of the class and then regain it as a function of the effectiveness of her use of negative attention was often noted by $E$s, especially as the teachers were first gaining mastery of their newly learned skills in the classroom. This might indicate that the students were able to judge quite quickly and precisely the relative cost and payoff of disruptive behavior on the basis of the experience of one or two of their classmates. If so, the effective use of negative attention served not only as a contingency to the offending student but also as a discriminative stimulus to his classmates.

The findings of the present study stand in apparent contrast to those of Madsen et al. (1968), who found that disapproval in the form of "sit down" commands by teachers to students who were out of their seats tended to increase the frequency of out-of-seat behavior. A possible answer to this contradiction is given in the description of the nonverbal elements of negative attention which were built into the teacher training procedure, such as assertiveness, proximity to and orientation toward the offending student, quickness of responding, and quickly diverting attention to a student who was responding appropriately. Experience with the training procedure indicated that these nonverbal elements had to be present along with the verbal component for the negative attention to have its desired effect. The role-playing procedure gave the teachers practice in integrating the elements of this complex verbal-motor skill of effectively dispensing negative attention. Before this skill was mastered, a great many of the teachers' attempts at negative attention during training failed and often led to greater disruptiveness.

The findings of the present study also stand in contrast to much of the classroom control literature which focuses exclusively upon DRO behavior and supports the findings of Hammerlynck et al. (1967) and Becker et al. (1967) that DRO alone may in certain situations produce an increased level of disruptiveness. During baseline in the present study the target teacher reinforced as much appropriate, on-task behavior as did the comparison teachers while ignoring vast amounts of disruptiveness. This pattern of responding proved highly ineffectual in the face of large amounts of student disruption and peer reinforcement for that disruption. This finding highlights the need for teachers to integrate a wide range of social skills covering various aspects of positive reinforcement, extinction and punishment in order to be able to deal with the various patterns of student disruptiveness typical of most classrooms.

While not presuming to present a guide to effective group behavioral management, the present study does describe a means of remediating a common classroom problem, and it outlines a quick and simple method of imparting the teaching skills required for its use. This analysis of disruptive classroom behavior and the proposed teacher training program may provide a useful tool for training teachers in effective classroom management both at the university level and in "in-service" settings, and it may add a particularly useful skill to the behavior repertoires of substitute teachers. Perhaps more importantly, the intervention focuses exclusively on the social skills of the teacher so that once learned, its implementation represents no cost to the teacher in terms of individualized programs and reinforcers, records, and consultation time.

# REFERENCES

Baer, D.M., A case for the selective reinforcement of punishment. In C. Neuringer & J.L. Michael (Eds.), *Behavior modification in clinical psychology*. New York: Appleton-Century-Crofts, 1970.

Barrish, H., Saunders, M., & Wolf, M. Good behavior game: Effects of individual contingencies for group consequences on disruptive behavior in a classroom. *Journal of Applied Behavior Analysis*, 1969, 2, 119-124.

Becker, W.C., Madsen, C.H., Arnold, C.R., & Thomas, D.R. The contingent use of teacher attention and praise in reducing classroom behavior problems. *Journal of Special Education*, 1967, 1, 287-307.

Hall, R.V., Axelrod, S., Foundopoulos, M., Shellman, J., Campbell, R.A., & Cranston, S. The effective use of punishment to modify behavior in the classroom. *Educational Technology*, 1971, 11, 24-26.

Hammerlynck, L.A., Donley, M., & Heller, D. Modification of high base rate verbal behavior by behavioral contacts. Unpublished manuscript, University of Oregon, 1967.

Madsen, C.H., Becker, W.C., Thomas, D.R., Koser, L., & Plager, E. An analysis of the reinforcing function of "sit down" commands. In R.K. Parker (Ed.), *Readings in educational psychology*. Boston: Allyn & Bacon, 1968.

Mattos, R.L., Mattson, R.H., Walker, H.M., & Buckley, N.K. Reinforcement and aversive control in the modification of deviant classroom behavior. *Academic Therapy*, 1969, 5, (1).

McAllister, L.W., Stachowiak, J., Baer, D., & Conderman, L. The application of operant conditioning techniques in a secondary school classroom. *Journal of Applied Behavior Analysis*, 1969, 2, 277-285.

Neale, D.C. Aversive control of behavior. *Phi Delta Kappan*, February 1969, 335-338.

O'Leary, K.D., Kaufman, K., Kass, R.E., & Drabman, R. The effects of loud and soft reprimands on the behavior of disruptive students. *Exceptional Children*, 1970, 37, 145-155.

Patterson, G.R., Ray, R.S., & Shaw, D.A. Direct intervention in families of deviant children. *Oregon Research Institute Research Bulletin*, 1968, 8 (9).

Thomas, D.R., Becker, W.C., & Armstrong, M. Production and elimination of disruptive classroom behavior by systematically varying teacher's behavior. *Journal of Applied Behavior Analysis*, 1968, 1, 35-45.

Walker, H.M., Mattson, R.H., & Buckley, N.K. Special class placement as a treatment alternative for deviant behavior in children. In F.A.M. Benson (Ed.) *Modifying deviant social behaviors in classroom settings*. Eugene: University of Oregon Press, 1969.

# Article 6
## Control of an Obscene "Verbal Tic" through Timeout in an Elementary School Classroom*

BENJAMIN B. LAHEY, M. PATRICK McNEES, and MARGARET C. McNEES†

Abstract: A classroom teacher modified the behavior of a 10-year-old student who had a high rate of obscene vocalizations accompanied by facial twitches. In the first phase, the subject was instructed to repeat rapidly the most frequent obscene word in four daily 15-minute sessions. This procedure reduced the frequency of obscene vocalizations, but not to an acceptable level. Subsequently, the teacher was able effectively to control the target behavior using a timeout procedure.

Since the development of simple effective techniques of behavior modification there has been a trend toward the remediation of a variety of behavior problems in the classroom. Teachers have been trained to deal successfully with problems that would have previously required referral to outside agencies (e.g., Hall, Fox, Willard, Goldsmith, Emerson, Owen, Davis, & Porcia, 1971; Becker, Madsen, Arnold, & Thomas, 1967; Reynolds, & Risley, 1968). This paper deals with a classroom teacher's use of a timeout procedure to control successfully an unusual and extremely disruptive behavior.

The child was a problem because he recurrently uttered obscene words and phrases (usually a four-letter euphemism for sexual intercourse) accompanied by facial twitches. This behavior had been

*Reprinted by permission from the *Journal of Applied Behavior Analysis,* 1973, Vol. 6, No. 1, 101-104. Copyright 1973 by the Society for the Experimental Analysis of Behavior, Inc.

†Thanks are given to Susan Lahey for her help with reliability checks.

a problem for two years before the start of the study, in spite of treatment by a physician and a psychologist. It closely matched descriptions of previously studied behaviors referred to as "verbal tics" or "Gilles de la Tourette's Syndrome" (Clark, 1966; Feldman, & Werry, 1966; Rafi, 1962; Yates, 1958). Although these terms have been the subject of a great deal of unsubstantiated speculation and theory, several experimental reports that used these terms were reviewed for suggestions as to a possibly effective technique for controlling the behavior. This is not at all to say that the child "had" a "verbal tic," but that his behavior resembled other behaviors that had been so labeled.

Clark (1966) worked with three adults who repeatedly said obscenities accompanied by bizarre motor behaviors. He reported the complete elimination of these behaviors in two of the three subjects by instructing them continually to repeat the obscenities until they could no longer do so. This procedure, variously referred to as "massed practice," "negative practice," and "reactive extinction" (which is referred to simply as "instructed repetition" in this study), has also been successfully applied to high-frequency motor behaviors. Yates (1958) was able sharply to reduce the frequency of facial and stomach tics through instructed repetition, and Rafi (1962) had similar results with a head-jerking tic. Feldman and Werry (1966), however, found that instructed repetition increased the frequency of a head-jerking tic, as well as increasing the frequency of another untreated tic, while a third tic that had not bothered the subject for some time before therapy returned.

Instructed repetition was the first procedure used in the present study but, because it was not completely effective in this case, a timeout procedure was then used. Timeout was chosen because it is a simple technique, easy to carry out, and has been shown to be an effective method for reducing the frequency of problem behaviors in a large number of previous studies. For example, Bostow and Bailey (1969) reduced the frequency of the loud vocal behavior of a retarded adult and the aggressive behavior of a retarded child using timeout; Tyler and Brown (1967) controlled the misbehaviors of institutionalized delinquents; and Barton, Guess, Garcia, and Baer (1970) improved the eating behaviors of retarded children with this technique. Leitenberg (1965) reviewed most of the literature on this procedure.

## METHOD

### Subject and Target Behavior

The subject was a 10-year-old male with a Stanford-Binet IQ of 76. At his parent's request, he was enrolled in an elementary level class of "educable mentally retarded" children due to his disruptive behavior. Usually, the subject said a single obscene word accompanied by a stutter, an eye-blink, and a vertical head-jerk. But, because there was considerable variation in the amplitude and intelligibility of the utterances, the target behavior was defined as any vocalization other than an intelligible non-obscene word. These vocalizations were almost always intelligible obscene words during baseline, but were rarely intelligible by the end of the study. Four interobserver reliability checks were taken, as indicated by arrows on Fig. 1. A reliability coefficient was calculated by dividing the smaller frequency count for the hour-long data collection period by the larger. Reliability ranged between 0.86 and 1.00, with a mean of 0.91.

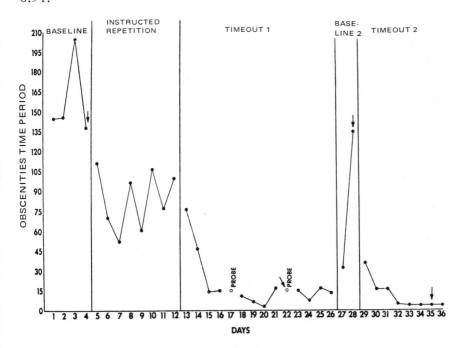

Fig. 1. Frequency of target behavior in each experimental condition.

## Procedure

All phases of the procedure were carried out in a classroom for "educable mentally retarded" children by the teacher. A second observer was present on four occasions for the purpose of establishing reliability.

## Baseline

The frequency of the target behavior was recorded for four consecutive days. Data were recorded during baseline and throughout the study between the hours of 9 and 10 a.m., but all contingencies used in later phases were in effect throughout the school day.

## Instructed Repetition

For eight consecutive school days, the subject was taken to a separate room by the teacher for four daily 15-minute sessions and instructed to repeat rapidly the most frequent obscene word. Whenever he stopped, the instructions were repeated until the 15-minute period was over with no rest periods. Often, these instructions had to be "emphatically" repeated several times before the subject would begin or continue; accordingly, the frequency of responses varied widely from session to session. Both pupil and teacher stated that they strongly disliked these sessions and the behavior of the other children changed during this phase as well. Although data were not recorded, the teacher reported an increase in the frequency of complaints about the subject's behavior and that on a number of occasions some students sympathized with the subject when he emerged from instructed repetition sessions, while others criticized him.

## Timeout

On the thirteenth day, a timeout contingency was instituted. This was carried out during the entire school day for 14 school days. During this phase, the subject was immediately placed in a timeout room for a minimum of 5 minutes and until he was quiet for 1 minutes after every target behavior. The timeout room was a well lighted 4- by 10-foot room connected to the classroom, which had originally been used for typing instruction. The subject was told of the contingency at the beginning of the phase. In the beginning, the subject was escorted to the timeout room without any statement or eye-contact from the teacher, but later he went to the room when told to do so. On a very few occasions he had to be pulled into the room. The room was stripped of all objects and locked to prevent further disruption while he was in timeout.

## Probe Trials

During the timeout contingency, the subject spent a great amount of time in the timeout room. Although data were recorded while the subject was in the timeout room as well as when he was out, there was a possibility that the frequency of the target behavior was influenced in some way by the time spent in the timeout room. For this reason, probe trials were conducted on Days 17 and 22. The probe trials consisted of hour-long periods of data collection, during which the timeout contingency was not in effect. No comment was made to the subject as to this (or any succeeding) change in contingency. As stated before, this did not constitute a separate phase of the procedure, but the probe trials were interspersed during the timeout phase.

## Baseline Two

Following the timeout phase, the conditions of baseline were reintroduced. No contingency of any sort was in effect throughout the entire school day. The results of the second baseline made it unnecessary to continue this phase for more than two consecutive school days.

## Timeout Two

Following the second baseline, the conditions of the first timeout phase were reintroduced for eight days.

## RESULTS AND DISCUSSION

As can be seen in Fig. 1, the subject's baseline rate of target behaviors was approximately twice per minute. During the instructed repetition phase of the procedure, there was an immediate drop in the frequency of target behaviors. On the average, the frequency during instructed repetition was approximately half that of the frequency during the baseline period. But, because the frequency was not reduced to an acceptable level and because the procedure was aversive to the teacher, the timeout procedure was introduced.

The timeout contingency reduced the frequency of target behavior to a level below that of the instructed repetition phase. Although they were not systematically recorded, the teacher reported that the amplitude and articulation of the target behaviors also decreased during timeout to the point that they were rarely intelligible. During this phase, the subject's parents reported that, for the first time in two years, he had gone an entire weekend without saying an intelligible obscene word, and that they had taken him out into public for the first time in as many years.

Because the target behavior was not considered a problem at this level by the subject's parents and teacher, a second baseline was introduced that produced an immediate increase in the frequency of the target behavior. Following the second baseline, the lower frequency was quickly recovered in the second timeout phase.

The timeout contingency remained in effect for two weeks after the collection of data was discontinued and the teacher reported that the frequency of target behaviors remained at the same level. During the third and fourth weeks, the timeout room was used for another purpose for an hour each day. The teacher reported that the frequency of the target behavior returned to Baseline 1 levels, but only during that hour. School then ended for the summer.

These data should not be taken to mean that instructed repetition is a less effective technique than timeout for the modification of such behaviors. Before reaching such a conclusion, several aspects of instructed repetitions would have to be systematically varied (e.g., frequency of sessions, length of sessions, method of instructing, etc.), and more subjects would have to be studied. It was concluded, however, that for several reasons timeout was the more desirable procedure in this case. These reasons included the fact that instructed repetition was aversive to both the teacher and the subject, that timeout required less of the teacher's classroom time, and that a substitute teacher was required while the teacher was out of the classroom during instructed repetition. Most importantly, the technique was quickly effective in this case.


# REFERENCES

Barton, E.S., Guess, D., Garcia, E., & Baer, D.M. Improvement of retardates' mealtime behaviors by timeout procedures using multiple baseline techniques. *Journal of Applied Behavior Analysis*, 1970, 3, 77-84.
Becker, W.C., Madsen, C.H., Jr., Arnold, R., & Thomas, D.R. The contingent use of teacher attention and praise in reducing classroom behavior problems. *Journal of Special Education*, 1967, 1, 287-307.
Bostow, D.E., & Bailey, J.B. Modification of severe disruptive and aggressive behavior using brief timeout and reinforcement procedures, *Journal of Applied Behavior Analysis*, 1969, 2, 31-37.
Clark, D.F. Behavior therapy of Gilles de la Tourette's syndrome. *British Journal of Psychiatry*, 1966, 112, 771-778.
Feldman, R.B., & Werry, J.S. An unsuccessful attempt to treat a ticquer by massed practice. *Behaviour Research and Therapy*, 1966, 4, 111-117.
Hall, R.V., Fox, R., Willard, D., Goldsmith, L., Emerson, M., Owen, M., Davis, F., & Porcia, E. The teacher as observer and experimenter in the modification of disputing and talking-out behaviors. *Journal of Applied Behavior Analysis*, 1971, 4, 141-149.
Leitenberg, H. Is time out from positive reinforcement an aversive event? *Psychological Bulletin*, 1965, 64, 428-441.
Rafi, A.A. Learning theory and the treatment of tics. *Journal of Psychosomatic Research*, 1962, 6, 71-76.
Reynolds, N., & Risley, T. The role of social and material reinforcers in increasing talking of a disadvantaged school child. *Journal of Applied Behavior Analysis*, 1968, 1, 253-262.
Tyler, V.O., & Brown, G.D. The use of swift brief isolation as a group control device for institutionalized delinquents. *Behaviour Research and Therapy*, 1967, 5, 1-9.
Yates, A.J. The application of learning theory to the treatment of tics. *Journal of Abnormal and Social Psychology*, 1958, 56, 175-182.

# Article 7
# Reward versus Cost Token Systems:
# An Analysis of the Effects on
# Students and Teacher*

BRIAN A. IWATA and JON S. BAILEY [†]

Abstract: The effects of reward and cost token procedures on the social and academic behavior of two groups of elementary special-education students were assessed using a reversal design. Behavioral observations of three target subjects in each group revealed that both procedures were about equally effective in reducing rule violations and off-task behavior. Records kept on the daily arithmetic performance of all subjects showed that output doubled in both groups during the token phases, although accuracy remained unchanged. When students were allowed to choose either contingency, no pattern of preference was established. Small differences were found in teacher behavior: the reward procedure led to an increase in approval comments but cost procedures produced no changes in teacher behavior.

In recent years, the token economy has emerged as a powerful tool in behavior management (Kazdin & Bootzin, 1972; O'Leary & Drabman, 1971; Paul, 1969). Although the range of subjects, settings, target behaviors, dispensing and recording procedures, and type of

*Reprinted by permission from the *Journal of Applied Behavior Analysis,* 1974, Vol. 7, No. 4, 567-576. Copyright 1974 by the Society for the Experimental Analysis of Behavior, Inc.

[†]We would like to thank Jim Apgar for his assistance in conducting this study and the following persons who served as observers: Gary Barr, Trine Billingsby, Donna Braziel, Linda Leonard, Joetta Long, and Mimi Sapp. We also wish to acknowledge Mrs. Jane Forster, special education teacher, and Mr. John MacElwee, principal, of Leonard Wesson Elementary School, Tallahassee, Florida, for their cooperation and help throughout the study.

back-up reinforcers has varied widely, the procedures appear to produce reliable and replicable changes in behavior. The majority of these studies has emphasized what might be called a "reward" system of reinforcement, i.e., the subjects are rewarded with tokens when they have met some present criterion behavior; nontarget behavior receives no tokens.

Although several experimenters have reported the successful use of token systems based on response cost in reducing undesirable behavior (Broden, Hall, Dunlap, & Clark, 1970; Burchard, 1967; Phillips, 1968; Phillips, Phillips, Fixsen, & Wolf, 1971; Weisberg, Lieberman, & Winter, 1970; Winkler, 1970), others, viewing fines or cost as similar to punishment, have felt that the use of these techniques may lead to deleterious "side effects," such as increased aggression and escape behavior, which have typically been associated with punishment (Azrin, & Holz, 1966).

Two direct comparisons between reward and cost procedures have yielded mixed results. McLaughlin and Malaby (1972) found that contingent point gain for quiet behavior produced lower rates of inappropriate verbalizations than did contingent point loss of inappropriate verbalizations on the part of fifth and sixth graders. Kaufman and O'Leary (1972), on the other hand, found no differences between reward and cost procedures in a psychiatric hospital school setting. Their results showed similar decreases in disruptive behavior and increases in academic performance for both the reward and the cost groups.

One purpose of the present study was to compare the effects of reward and cost token procedures on student social and academic behavior. A second purpose was to look at preference by the students for either a reward or cost token system. During one phase of the study, students were given a choice as to which contingency (reward or cost) they preferred. Finally, records were kept of the teacher's verbal approval and disapproval in order to detect possible differential effects on teacher behavior that may result from the use of the two procedures.

## METHOD

### Subjects and Setting

Fifteen elementary school students in a special-education class (mean age 10 years, mean IQ 70), who, according to teacher reports, exhibited a moderate to high degree of off-task and disruptive behavior, served. Based on prebaseline observations and teacher recommendations, the students were divided into two groups of seven (Group R-C) and eight (Group C-R) students respectively, of about equal arithmetic ability. Three students from each group were selected as targets for concentrated data collection on the basis of prebaseline observations because they exhibited the greatest amounts of off-task behavior. Experimental sessions were conducted each morning over a three-month period during a 40-minute math class while students were engaged in individual seat work.

## Observation

Daily observations were conducted during the first 30 minutes of the math period. Each of two observers was responsible for recording the behavior of three target students plus the teacher's verbal interaction with those three students. Observations were made on a continuous 10-second interval basis, with the exception of the last 10-second interval of each minute, which was reserved for making written comments.

The two categories of student behavior employed in the present study were:

1. *Off-task:* Visual nonattention to one's materials for more than 2 seconds, unless the student was either talking to the teacher (with permission) or had his hand raised above his head.

2. *Rule violation:* the violation of one or more of the following teacher-prepared rules. (a) We remain seated during math class. (b) We raise our hands to get help from the teacher. (c) We do not talk or disturb our neighbor. (d) We may go to the bathroom when no one else is using it.

Since the categories were not mutually exclusive, it was possible for both categories to be scored during any 10-second interval. However, only one instance of each category was recorded for a student during an interval.

The two categories of teacher behavior observed were:

1. *Teacher approval:* any verbal form of individual or group approval that was audible to the observer.

2. *Teacher disapproval:* any verbal form of individual or group disapproval that was audible to the observer.

## Reliability

To assess the accuracy of the observers' records, frequent reliability checks were made by an independent observer. Reliabilities were calculated for each of the four separate categories of behavior by dividing the total number of agreements by the total number of agreements plus disagreements. An agreement was scored if both observers recorded the same behavior within the same 10-second interval. A disagreement was scored if one observer recorded a behavior and the other did not. Instances in which both observers agreed that no behavior occurred were not counted as agreements when computing reliabilities. The inclusion of such instances would result in spuriously high reliability, especially with regard to low-frequency behaviors.

## Academic Measures

Arithmetic materials consisted of the Singer Math Series (Random House), which is composed of several kits, each containing a number of problem cards, 20 problems per card. Daily records were kept of all 15 subjects' performance during math period. After each session, the students papers were graded either by the teacher or by an observer, and daily performance was recorded in terms of both the number of problems completed and the percentage correct.

## Experimental Procedures

### Prebaseline
Observations were begun during math period four weeks before formal data were collected. During this time, the teacher was not given any instruction regarding the enforcement of rules and was merely told to operate in her usual manner.

### Baseline I
During this phase, an apparatus consisting of a cassette-taped series of short-duration auditory tone signals was introduced to familiarize the class with it. The apparatus divided the 40-minute math class into 10 intervals ranging from 3 to 5 minutes in duration. One signal was delivered at the beginning of the first interval and at the end of each of the first nine intervals. The end of the tenth

interval was marked by four signals in rapid succession.

On the first day of baseline, the teacher reviewed the class rules and handed out writing materials and arithmetic folders that contained the math card on which each child was currently working. The students were then instructed to begin work at the sound of the first signal and to stop when they heard four signals in rapid succession. At the end of the math period, students engaged in a 15-minute mid-morning break, for snacks and juice. Children who could afford to do so paid a dime; those who were on a free breakfast and lunch program were given a free snack.

*Token I*

On the first day of the token program (Session 27), the teacher followed the usual procedures of handing out folders and reviewing the class rules. In addition, a cup was placed on the table in front of each student. Students in Group R-C (reward-cost) received empty cups; students in Group C-R (cost-reward) received cups containing 10 tokens (obtained from Peabody Language Development Kit). The teacher then explained to the children that she wanted to see how well they could obey the class rules. Students in Group R-C were told that they could earn 10 tokens for following the rules during math class. Students in Group C-R were told they could keep the 10 tokens already given to them if they followed the rules, but that they had to have at least six tokens in their cups by the end of math class in order to earn a snack. The teacher also informed the students about "surprise days," on which the three or four students who had earned the most tokens since the last "surprise day" would be eligible for a special bonus. Since students did not know when "surprise days" were to be held, it was important that they try to accumulate as many tokens as possible from day to day.

Throughout the math period, the signal apparatus served as a cueing device for the teacher. At the sound of each signal, the teacher placed one token in the cup of each student in Group R-C who had not violated any rules during the previous interval, and withdrew one token from the cup of each student in Group C-R who had violated one or more rules during the previous interval. The final occasion for delivering or withdrawing tokens was indicated by the four signal series at the end of the math class.

At the end of the math period, observers counted the number of tokens in each student's cup and the experimenter recorded the daily totals on the bulletin board chart. All tokens and materials were then collected and snacks were served to those students who met the criteria. Students who were not eligible to receive a snack were permitted to engage in free-time activities of a neutral type (e.g., stacking blocks, playing with an abacus) in a different section of the classroom.

On the sixth day of the first token phase (Session 32), the criterion for a snack was raised from six to eight tokens and remained at this level for the duration of Token I. "Surprise days" were held following Sessions 32 and 37 during the Token I phase. On the first surprise day, three students had achieved perfect scores (60 tokens). It was therefore decided that on all subsequent surprise days, students with perfect scores would be eligible for a reward. The surprises consisted of a large variety of inexpensive toys and candy, ranging in price from 29 to 63 cents.

*Baseline II*

On the morning of the thirty-eighth session, the teacher announced that the token program would be discontinued for an indefinite amount of time due to a temporary inability to furnish free snacks and prizes. Procedures during this phase were the same as those followed during Baseline I.

*Token II*

The token program was re-instituted at Session 45. The procedures were similar to those used in the Token I phase, with the following exception. The group that previously earned tokens (Group R-C) was now the cost group and Group C-R became the reward group. The criterion for a snack was raised from six to eight tokens on the third day of this phase (Session 47), and one surprise day was held following Session 49.

*Choice*

Beginning at Session 55 and continuing for two additional sessions, each subject was given a daily choice between the reward and cost contingencies. On the basis of the students' choices, new reward and cost groups were formed daily.

## RESULTS

### Reliability

Reliability data were obtained for 40 of the 54 experimental sessions, yielding an overall mean of 87 percent and the following means for separate categories: rule violations—88 percent; off-task—86 percent; teacher approval—85 percent; teacher disapproval—90 percent. In addition to the 40 regular checks, four additional observations were made by a trained observer participating in another project who had no knowledge of the present study. These checks produced an overall mean of 92 percent, and the following category means: rule violations—84 percent; off-task—87 percent; teacher approval—98 percent; teacher disapproval—100 percent. Agreements on nonoccurrence of the behaviors were not included in these calculations.

## Social Behavior

The mean percentages of intervals in which off-task behavior and rule violations were exhibited by the target subjects are presented in Fig. 1, along with the group means for each experimental condition. Individual graphs were quite consistent with the group data. During Baseline I, the means for off-task behavior for Groups R-C and C-R were 30 percent and 32 percent, respectively; the mean for rule violations was 9 percent for both groups. With the institution of Token I, rule violations dropped to below 1 percent for both groups. Off-task behavior also decreased for both groups, especially after the increase in criterion from six to eight tokens. When the token system (Baseline II was withdrawn), off-task behavior increased for both groups to levels comparable to those of the previous baseline; only small increases in rule violations were observed. During the Token II phase, when the contingencies for Group R-C and C-R were reversed, rule violations again decreased to 1 percent or below for both groups and off-task behavior dropped to below 5 percent for both groups after the increase in criterion from six to eight tokens. During the final condition (Choice), each student was allowed to choose either the reward or the cost contingency. Although the main purpose of this phase was to assess preference, rather than the effectiveness of the reward and cost procedures, rule violations and off-task behavior continued at a low level (2% or less) for both the reward and cost groups.

Data on the net number of tokens earned by all subjects revealed Group R-C averages of 92 and 83 during the Token I and Token II phases, respectively, and Group C-R averages of 97 and 88 tokens. It appeared that Group C-R averaged more tokens than did Group R-C, and that reward and cost procedures had little or no effect on token earnings.

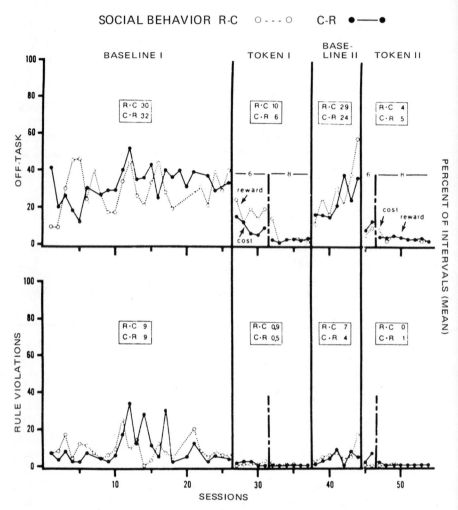

Fig. 1. Mean percent of intervals of off-task behavior and rule violations for Group R-C (Reward-Cost, N=3) and Group C-R (Cost-Reward, N=3). Group means for each condition are provided in boxes. The reward and cost groups during the token phases are indicated by arrows, and the change in criterion from six to eight tokens is indicated by a broken vertical line during Token I and Token II.

## Arithmetic Performance

The mean numbers of problems completed per session and the percentage of problems correct for all subjects in Groups R-C and C-R are presented in Fig. 2. There was little difference between the groups during Baseline I in the number of problems completed. The

means for Groups R-C and C-R during the first baseline were 19 and
21 problems, respectively. When Token I contingencies were put into
effect, the output for Group C-R soon more than doubled, while the
output for Group R-C increased only slightly at first. However, after
the increase in token criterion, the performance of Group R-C rose
to about the same level as Group C-R. When the contingencies were

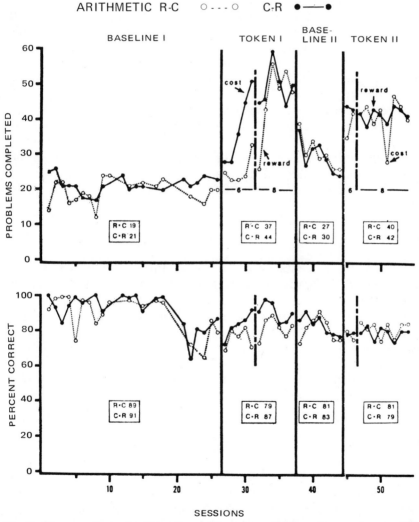

Fig. 2. Mean number of arithmetic problems completed and percent correct for
Group R-C (Reward-Cost, N=7) and Group C-R (Cost-Reward, N=8). Group means
for each condition are provided in boxes. The reward and cost groups during the
token phases are indicated by arrows, and the change in criterion from six to eight
tokens is indicated by a broken vertical line during Token I and Token II. The
nonrepetition and cheating control procedures were instituted in Session 20.

removed, arithmetic output decreased, and by the end of Baseline II, both groups had returned to Baseline I levels of performance. Output increased once again during the Token II phase and remained at a high level for both groups throughout the final Choice condition.

The data on the accuracy of problem solving revealed a drop for both groups beginning with Session 20 during the Baseline I phase. Before this session, the teacher did not allow a student to proceed to a new math card until he completed all problems on his present card correctly. Thus some students were working on new cards, while others were repeating the same material. In addition, the observers began to notice an increase in cheating by the students (the answers to the problems could be found on the backs of the math cards). Beginning with Session 20, students who completed a math card proceeded to a new card, regardless of their score. The teacher also clipped pieces of cardboard to the backs of the cards, so that the answers could not be seen.

As shown in Fig. 2, reward and cost contingencies had little or no effect on the accuracy of arithmetic performance, which remain between about 80 and 90 percent for the entire study.

## Teacher Behavior

The mean percentages of intervals during which the teacher delivered verbal approval and disapproval to the target subjects are presented in Fig. 3. It can be seen that she delivered few comments of either a positive or negative type. Her Baseline I means for approvals and disapprovals were less than 2 percent of all observation intervals for both groups. Although she continued to maintain low levels of reinforcement throughout the study, there were small (less than 2%) but noticeable increases in approval for Group R-C during Token I (reward) and toward Group C-R during Token II (reward).

## Student Choices

The final experimental condition was limited to three sessions due to the end of the school year. However, results of the 15 subjects' choices during this phase showed no consistent pattern of preference toward either reward or cost. Over the three-day period, four subjects consistently chose reward, five subjects consistently chose cost, and six subjects switched their choice at least once.

## DISCUSSION

Present results indicated that both reward and response-cost token systems can be highly effective procedures in maintaining classroom social and academic behavior; in terms of student behavior, there appeared to be no differential effects resulting from the use of either contingency. Both procedures led to similar decreases in the percentage of classroom rule violations and off-task behavior of all students observed, even though the contingencies were not directly applied to the latter category.

A further indication of the success of the reward and response-

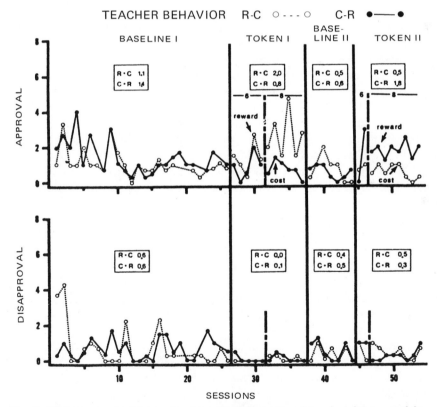

Fig. 3. Mean percent of intervals of teacher approval and teacher disapproval for Group R-C (Reward-Cost, N=3) and Group C-R (Cost-Reward, N=3). Group means for each condition are provided in boxes. The reward and cost groups during the token phases are indicated by arrows, and the change in criteria from six to eight tokens is indicated by a broken vertical line during Token I and Token II.

cost procedures was the twofold increase in academic output during the Token phases. Such a large change in behavior is perhaps also an indicator that academic output may be a more relevant measure of student behavior than the amount of time spent on-task, especially for students who behave appropriately most of the time. Three students who were not chosen for observation because of their good behavior, for example, went from Baseline I averages of 19, 22, and 32 problems completed per session to Token I averages of 64, 64, and 82 problems, respectively. The changes in arithmetic output are also representative of the beneficial "ripple effects" that may accrue from the application of contingency systems in general. Increases in the number of arithmetic problems completed were observed as a result of contingencies applied to classroom rule violations. Conversely, Ayllon and Roberts (1974) demonstrated that classroom disruptive behavior can be reduced by direct reinforcement of reading performance.

Perhaps the most meaningful measure of student behavior is actual academic achievement. Although the present procedures produced no change in arithmetic accuracy, the students were progressing at higher rates due to the fact that they were covering twice as much material in the same amount of time. A number of factors may have been responsible for the lack of gain in arithmetic accuracy. First, the present contingencies applied only to rule violations. Thus, students received no payoff for doing correct work. Second, when the teacher changed her former procedure of requiring students to answer all problems correctly before proceeding to a new card, the students may have taken this as a cue that it was more important to work rapidly than to work accurately. The institution of the Token I phase shortly after the teacher's change in procedures may have further led the students to believe that some type of contingency was being placed upon academic output. Finally, as the material became more difficult with each succeeding card, the students may not have had sufficient academic skills to progress satisfactorily without repeated instruction.

One of the major objections to the use of response cost has been that it may lead to detrimental side effects, such as increased aggression or behavior that enables one to avoid or escape the cost condition. The present results failed to support either of these contentions. Since aggressive behavior on the part of students was included in the rule violations category, increased aggression during the cost conditions would have appeared as an increase in rule violations for Group C-R during Token I, and an increase for Group

R-C during Token II. Such increases did not occur. In fact, during both token phases, the cost groups engaged in fewer rule violations than the reward groups (see Fig. 1). Absences from class also failed to establish cost as an aversive event. The combined absences for both groups under reward conditions averaged 0.48 per session, and absences under cost conditions were only slightly higher at 0.57 per session. Finally, data obtained from the Choice condition indicated that subjects found the cost contingency to be at least as "desirable" as the reward contingency, if not more so. Although more subjects chose reward on the first day, cost was chosen more frequently on both of the following days.

In light of the conflicting results regarding the negative side effects of response cost, several factors or procedural differences may be associated with the presence or absence of these side effects. Kaufman and O'Leary (1972) mentioned a few, namely: the latency between the occurrence of the inappropriate behavior and the time at which the fine is levied, the value of the back-up reinforcers, the reinforcing value of the behavior that is being shaped, and the subjects' dislike toward the reinforcing agent. A further difference may be whether or not the tokens that are subtracted were initially given freely or earned contingently. The token dispensing procedures employed in both the present study and the Kaufman and O'Leary (1972) experiment were noncontingent, i.e., students were given "free" tokens that were removed contingent on the occurrence of inappropriate behavior. On the other hand, Boren and Colman (1970) and McLaughlin and Malaby (1972), both of whom reported negative results in conjunction with response cost, employed a system in which the tokens removed had previously been earned contingent on the occurrence of appropriate behavior. Thus, a more punishing or aversive situation may be created when earned reinforcers are removed than when noncontingent reinforcers are removed.

A final point that deserves consideration regarding the relative merits of reward and cost is the effect that these procedures may have on the reinforcing agent. In the present study, the teacher delivered higher percentages of verbal approval toward the reward groups during the Token I and Token II phases. This effect was also replicated during the Choice condition. Thus, it appears that reward procedures may lead to slightly greater amounts of teacher approval than do cost procedures. There appeared to be no consistent indication that reward led to fewer disapprovals than response cost, or that response cost led to an increase in disapprovals over baseline rates. Although these results should be considered highly tentative, due to both the teacher's low baseline of reinforcement and the exceedingly small changes in her behavior, it is conceivable that a teacher's behavior may be greatly affected as a result of implementing reward or cost procedures in the classroom. In turn, large changes in teacher behavior, especially in a negative direction, may have adverse effects on student behavior, the net effect being either that the teacher's verbal behavior undermines the positive effect of the tokens or that the teacher must continuously rely on the token system for control in the absence of a system of social reinforcers toward which she can fade.

## REFERENCES

Ayllon, T., & Roberts, M.D. Eliminating discipline problems by strengthening academic performance. *Journal of Applied Behavior Analysis,* 1974, 7, 71-76.

Azrin, N.H., & Holz, W.C. Punishment. In W.K. Honig (Ed.), *Operant behavior: areas of research and application.* New York: Appleton-Century-Crofts, 1966. Pp. 380-447.

Boren, J.J., & Colman, A.D. Some experiments on reinforcement principles within a psychiatric ward for delinquent soldiers. *Journal of Applied Behavior Analysis,* 1970, 3, 223-233.

Broden, M., Hall, R.V., Dunlap, A., & Clark, R. Effects of teacher attention and a token reinforcement system in a junior high school special education class. *Exceptional Children,* 1970, 36, 341-349.

Burchard, J.D. Systematic socialization: a programmed environment for the habilitation of antisocial retardates. *Psychological Record,* 1967, 17, 461-476.

Kaufman, K.F., & O'Leary, K.D. Reward, cost, and self-evaluation procedures for disruptive adolescents in a psychiatric hospital school. *Journal of Applied Behavior Analysis,* 1972, 5, 293-309.

Kazdin, A.E., & Bootzin, R.R. The token economy: an evaluative review. *Journal of Applied Behavior Analysis.* 1972, 5, 343-372.

McLaughlin, F.T., & Malaby, J. Reducing and measuring inappropriate verbalizations in a token classroom. *Journal of Applied Behavior Analysis,* 1972, 5, 329-333.

O'Leary, K.D., & Drabman, R. Token reinforcement programs in the classroom: A review. *Psychological Bulletin,* 1971, 75, 379-398.

Paul, G.L. Chronic mental patient: current status—future directions. *Psychological Bulletin,* 1969, 71, 81-94.

Phillips, E.L. Achievement Place: Token reinforcement procedures in a home-style rehabilitation setting for "predelinquent" boys. *Journal of Applied Behavior Analysis,* 1968, 3, 213-223.

Weisberg, P., Lieberman, C., & Winter, K. Reduction of facial gestures through loss of token reinforcers. *Psychological Reports,* 1970, 26, 227-230.

Winkler, R.C. Management of chronic psychiatric patients by a token reinforcement system. *Journal of Applied Behavior Analysis,* 1970, 3, 47-54.

# 4
# *Modeling*

Children learn by observing others. The process of imitating a behavior which has been modeled by someone else is an ongoing part of development. Little girls imitate their mothers when they "dress up" in high heels and wear lipstick. Parents sometimes model profane responses to frustrating situations and are not always pleased to find how quickly their children's vocabularies increase. Modeling is important in teaching skills such as tying shoes or saving money. The impact of television as a model for children has received extensive documentation and attention (Liebert, Neale, & Davidson, 1973). For example, Friedrich and Stein (1973) showed that nursery school children became less obedient and less tolerant of frustration after viewing aggressive cartoons. Exposure to prosocial films (*Mister Roger's Neighborhood*), however, resulted in higher levels of persistence.

Little doubt remains that modeling significantly influences learning. A vast body of experimental literature exists which clearly identifies ways of enhancing the effects of modeling (Bandura, 1969). Variables which seem particularly important include the sex, status, humanness, likeability, and age of the model; the observed consequences of the model's behavior; the degree to which the child is attending to the model; and the feedback the child receives when he imitates the model. Unfortunately, extensions of laboratory findings into the classroom setting are still few in number. The articles selected for this section illustrate three quite different ways in which modeling can be used systematically: to foster interaction with other children, to increase question asking, and to change the mode of interaction between a teacher and her students. Note that in each instance the focus of the intervention is on increasing desirable behavior.

Social withdrawal, especially in the early years, can severely limit the development of interpersonal skills which are becoming increasingly important if a child is to cope successfully in an ever more populated world. Concerned with this issue, O'Connor (1972) evaluated the efficacy of using a filmed sequence of peer interactions which gradually became more active and complex to alter the behavior of socially isolated nursery school children. Not only was the film model a significant influence on the children, but it was perhaps even more successful than having an adult come into the classroom to systematically attend to and shape the interactions of isolate children. Whether such a filmed modeling procedure can be effective with older children is uncertain, but it would seem important to use models who are similar to the observers, who demonstrate a gradual increase in skill, and who provide their own narrative sound track.

Along with social skills, linguistic skills are among the most complex in the human repertoire. As such, they are more easily demonstrated or modeled than they are systematically shaped. Henderson, Swanson, and Zimmerman (1975) provide us with another example of how televised modeling can influence children's behavior, in this case causal question asking (i.e., queries of the "why?" "how come?" or "what would happen if?" variety). Preschool children who were exposed to a modeling film in which adults were praised for causal question asking in turn asked more causal questions than children who viewed a film which did not show question asking. Zimmerman and Pike (1972) also found that modeling significantly influenced question asking in a study where the model was a teacher conducting a story period with a small group of second-grade children. The teacher-model also praised the children for asking questions. The use of modeling *and* praise was more effective than the use of praise alone. That modeling significantly added to the effect of praise replicated O'Connor's (1972) finding with socially isolated children.

Children are not the only people whose behavior can be changed by exposure to a model. Brown, Reschly, and Wasserman (1974) were consulting with a teacher and her class of emotionally disturbed children. After establishing a successful self-reinforcement procedure for two children, the authors elected to model the systematic use of attention in the classroom. This intervention was undertaken without the express permission of the teacher although she had agreed to the authors' presence in the class and their intervention with the children. Brown et al.'s recognition of the ethical issue involved in such a procedure should be particularly noted. Nonetheless, the effects of modeling were clear as the teacher significantly increased her positive interactions with her students.

In all three studies presented in this chapter, the effects of praise and/or instructions were enhanced by the presence of a model. The implication that what people do may be more influential than what people say is supported by the work of Bryan and Walbek (1970). They exposed children to one of several kinds of models. The model either kept all of his winnings from a game or donated some to charity. In addition, the models verbalized either charitable feelings, greedy feelings, or neutral feelings. The children's post-experimental verbalizations corresponded to the verbalizations of the model; but the children's own charitable behavior, or the lack of it, conformed to the model's behavior regardless of the moral position preached by the model. That is, the actions of the model spoke louder than his words. Thus, the teacher should attend to her own behavior because it serves as a model for her students, and she should attempt to maintain consistency between what she says and what she does. For example, a teacher who encourages politeness will be most successful if she is careful to say "Please" and "Thank you." If an adult or peer practices one thing but preaches another, the child is more apt to model the act itself rather than the verbally advocated desired behavior.

It is unfortunate that a procedure which so successfully modifies behavior has not been applied more systematically or frequently to influence classroom behavior. A number of possibilities exist for the creative implementation of modeling. For example, teachers are often confronted with children who have unproductive responses to academic failure, e.g., ripping paper, refusing to work, or disrupting the class. The present authors have found that when teachers model failure and appropriate ways of coping with failure, children not only respond in kind but thoroughly enjoy the realization that teachers are not always perfect.

# Article 8
# Relative Efficacy of Modeling, Shaping, and the Combined Procedures for Modification of Social Withdrawal* †

ROBERT D. O'CONNOR

Abstract: Thirty-three social isolates were selected from four nursery school populations according to teacher ratings and behavioral samples obtained by trained $O$s. In a 2 X 2 factorial design, half of the children viewed a 23-minute modeling film depicting appropriate social behavior, while the other half viewed a control film. Half of the subjects in each film condition then received social reinforcement contingent upon the performance of peer interaction behaviors. Modeling was shown to be a more rapid modification procedure than was shaping, and the interaction levels produced through modeling, with or without the addition of shaping, were more stable over time. In the follow-up assessments, modeling $S$s remained at the level of nonisolates, while shaping and control $S$s returned to isolate level.

The apparent utility of behavioral approaches to psychotherapy has brought about a general and increasingly enthusiastic acceptance

*From *Journal of Abnormal Psychology,* 1972, Vol. 79, No. 3, 327-334. Copyright 1972 by the American Psychological Association. Reprinted by permission.

†Much of this research was conducted while the author held Predoctoral Research Fellowship 1FOIMH 43, 284-01, MILH from the National Institute of Mental Health, and was further supported by the Department of Psychology and the Children's Research Center at the University of Illinois, Champaign, Illinois.

The author wishes to express his gratitude to the teachers at the Child Development Laboratory Nursery School, University of Illinois; the Children's Research Center Nursery School, University of Illinois; the Cooperative Nursery School, Urbana, Illinois; and the Playtime Nursery School, Urbana, Illinois, as well as to his colleagues and friends at the University of Illinois who provided essential assistance in conducting the investigation.

of treatment procedures based upon principles of learning. A number of crucial contributions to the behavior modification literature have recently emphasized experimental demonstrations of therapeutic change and thereby have lent scientific support to the rapidly advancing behavior therapy movement (e.g., Bandura, 1969, Eysenck, 1964; Franks, 1969; Kanfer & Phillips, 1970; Krasner & Ullman, 1965; Wolpe & Lazarus, 1966). While these and other convincing elaborations have accelerated the trend toward clinical behaviorism in general, only quite recently have $E$s begun to assess the relative efficacy of the various behavioral approaches. The present study compares the outcomes of two of the major procedures in behavior modification, applied both singly and in combination. Moreover, it evaluates the long-term effects of the observational acquisition of social skills as influenced by naturally occurring and/or programmed reinforcement.

The efficiency of symbolic modeling as a means of modifying social withdrawal was demonstrated in an earlier study by the author (O'Connor, 1969). Social isolates were shown a modeling film designed to transmit social competencies and simultaneously reduce fear of interaction with peers. The film had been staged in the $S$s' nursery school rooms, employing six actors of nursery school age. It was found that a single viewing of the film increased isolate childrens' social interaction to the level of nonisolates. The efficiency of behavior change produced by the 23-minute modeling film was quite impressive, compared to the lengthy procedures usually involved in shaping. Given that behavior is largely *maintained* by its consequences, it was speculated that social reinforcement might serve to maintain behavioral changes induced through modeling.

While the efficiency and durational outcome of differential treatment procedures are important considerations to which the present study was directed, the nature of the disorder selected for modification is of no small consequence in psychopathology and personality development. A nursery school child who exhibits gross deficits in social interaction might be labeled a "preschizophrenic personality" in some diagnostic systems (Cameron, 1963). Whatever one's orientation to diagnostics and etiology, it may nonetheless be noted that very little "normal" development can occur in the absence of social interaction. The preschool isolate foregoes immeasurably significant learning experiences and is quite conceivably acquiring a set for social avoidance which may be maintained over long periods of time, perhaps indefinitely, by the anxiety-reducing properties of solitary play. Children with very limited social competence are typically mistreated by their peers, the result being that severely withdrawn children are likely to undergo aversive conditioning when they occasionally hazard interactions with peers. It appears that social withdrawal in preschool children is a phenomenon of interest to students of child development as well as those generally concerned with the amelioration of critical behavior disorders.

The notion of "early prevention" can be equally well applied to the present situation, within a behavioral framework, in that elimination of behavioral deficits in early childhood safeguards against the development of more pervasive dysfunctions. This last consideration points to a final note of interest in the present study, that is, by taking much of our current behavior change skills into clearly "preventive" social situations, we might gain our greatest opportunity for meaningful social impact (Cowan, Gardner, & Zax, 1967; O'Connor, 1972; O'Connor & Rappaport, 1970; Rappaport & O'Connor, 1970; Sarason & Ganzer, 1969). This investigation was intended to examine questions of treatment efficacy within such a socially relevant natural setting.

## METHOD

### Selection of Isolates

Teachers in each of four local nursery schools were asked to identify the most socially withdrawn children in their classes in rank order. Those in the most "isolated" 25% were then observed over 64 randomly scheduled time intervals, and those who were observed to interact with peers no more than 15% of the time (10 out of the 64 intervals) were selected for inclusion in the study. The use of these criteria therefore combined the historically based summary judgments of teachers and objective observations of the withdrawal behavior itself. A total of 12 teachers provided data for the preliminary identification of 80 isolates from a total school population of 320 children. Of these 80, 41% (33) were observed in peer interaction with frequencies below the predetermined 15% isolate level. Consistent with the earlier study, 60% of the isolates were female.

The behavioral assessment of interaction was conducted by six trained $O$s. The $O$s were randomly assigned to classrooms to observe the ongoing nursery school behavior of the teacher-rated isolates as well as an equal number of randomly chosen nonisolates. The $O$s were assigned in pairs for 25% of the observations to permit estimation of reliability. The $O$s were not informed of the status of any given child throughout the study, that is, they were not informed of the isolate-nonisolate status of children during the pretest and were not informed of $S$s' condition assignment throughout the remaining assessment periods. The nonisolates observed during the pretest later served as an additional baseline ("normal" interaction level) against which to compare the behavior of treated and non-treated isolates. Reliabilities (percentage of agreement across time intervals) ranged from 70% to 100% for any given pair of $O$s and averaged 91% across all $O$ pairings.

Five categories were included in the observational assessment. Proximity to, visual contact with, verbal behavior toward, and interaction with another child were recorded. Interaction in this context was defined as any behavior directed toward another child which leads to reciprocal behavior on the part of the other child. The fifth category of these observations focused on the number of children involved in any peer interactions of the $S$. The interaction category was considered of primary importance, since interactions were the behavior class of dominant interest and the other categories are either dependent on or indicants of the occurrence of social interaction. This category was therefore the one chosen for all analyses.

### Pretest and Follow-up

Observation sessions were randomly scheduled throughout free-play periods during the nursery school day and consisted of 15-second intervals, 3 seconds per category, 4 minutes per observational session. Postfilm assessments took place at similarly random freeplay times. The time sampling apparatuses were comprised of transistor-ized circuits set into clipboards with special lights set to blink every 3 seconds.

### Treatment Conditions

Three treatment conditions and one control condition were included in the study. Isolate children were assigned to one of the four conditions shown in the following figure after having been matched in sets of four according to pretest interaction scores and randomized across groups by sets such that each child was randomly assigned to a matched "partner" within each of the three other groups. The residual $S$s were randomly assigned to conditions.

Figure 1 indicates that $S$s viewed either the modeling film or the control film and were either externally reinforced for social inter-action thereafter or not. The assignment procedure insured equal means, range, and variance in all groups' "base rates." The same sorts of high anxiety responding to $E$ (some children were socially avoidant to the point of refusing to leave the schoolroom with anyone) and frequent absences that occurred in the earlier study occurred to some extent in the present one, such that the final group $N$s became 9, 7, 8, 7, respectively, as shown in Fig. 1.

|  | EXTERNAL REINFORCEMENT | NO EXTERNAL REINFORCEMENT |
|---|---|---|
| MODELING FILM | MODELING AND SHAPING N = 7 | MODELING ONLY N = 9 |
| CONTROL FILM | SHAPING N = 8 | CONTROL N = 7 |

Fig. 1. Condition assignments of all isolate-rated Ss.

## Shaper Training

The "shapers" had all received classroom instruction in and had experience with operant procedures. It was assumed that these trained graduate students would more uniformly apply the syste-matic reinforcement required in shaping than would nursery school teachers. It is often the case that teachers actually reinforce children for consistent attention to adults, thereby reducing the possibility for peer interaction. Strangers, furthermore, have been shown to be more effective reinforcers in general than are parents (Stevenson, Keen, & Knights, 1963), and teachers may well be less effective change agents for similar reasons. All four of the shapers were females, in light of additional findings which have indicated greater social control over this age group for female $E$ s (e.g., Stevenson, 1961).

Each of the shapers was randomly assigned a group of $S$s from each of the two shaping conditions (postmodeling film and post-control film). The shapers were unaware of these condition assignments. The number of shaping sessions varied across $S$s because of competing activities in the different nursery schools, but the research plan called for each child to receive a total of 5 hours of praise and attention, during a 2 week period, upon the occurrence of successive approximations to social interaction. A few children actually received somewhat less than 5 hours of social reinforcement because of interruptions imposed either by the teacher or the child. All but five children, however, received the full 5 hours of shapings, and no child received less than 3 hours of shaping.

The *modeling* film, identical with that used in the present author's 1969 study, consisted of 11 scenes depicting the social interactions of nursery school children, presented in a sequence which systematically graduated the activity level and the number of children engaged in the interaction. In each scene, a "model" child is shown joining an ongoing social activity, ranging from one other child reading a book and making comments, to several children vigorously tossing large paper blocks around the room. There are six different models, two male and four female, who make such self-initiated entrances into an interaction, and in each case the descriptive soundtrack points out the particular behaviors performed by the model as well as the positive responses of the other children. The observing children had no contact with an $E$, beyond the instruction, "You can sit here and watch a movie on TV while I go finish my work." Children viewed the film on a TV set through which the film was back projected. As in the earlier study, this method of presentation appeared to heighten $S$s' attention to the film, presumably due to children's general habituation to TV viewing.

The *control* film was again the Marineland dolphin film from the O'Connor 1969 study, with its lack of human behavior and focus on acrobatic fish. Its accompanying soundtrack was taken from Debussy's "L'après midi d'un Faune." The control film is of approximately the same length and interest value as the modeling film.

It may be noted in Fig. 1 that two of the conditions constitute a replication of the 1969 study during the pre- and posttest phases here. More than simply a replication, however, these two groups' results provided a test of the generalizability of the modeling film across four different nursery school settings and populations. The fact of *exact* setting familiarity was thus absent in the present modeling conditions, although the general class of behaviors modeled in the 1969 film is similar to that found in most nursery schools, as are the physical stimuli.

## Posttreatment Assessment

Following the postfilm assessment, there were two additional treatment conditions, shaping and modeling plus shaping. Both of these manipulations began immediately after the postfilm assessment. Aside from behavior change comparisons across treatments, durational outcome was assessed for all groups, a consideration included in the earlier study.

The assessment periods can be most readily clarified from Fig. 2 in the Results section below. Each group was assessed for level of social interaction on four occasions, labeled pretest, Assessment 1, Assessment 2, and Assessment 3. These assessment periods provided a pre- to posttreatment change measure and a follow-up assessment

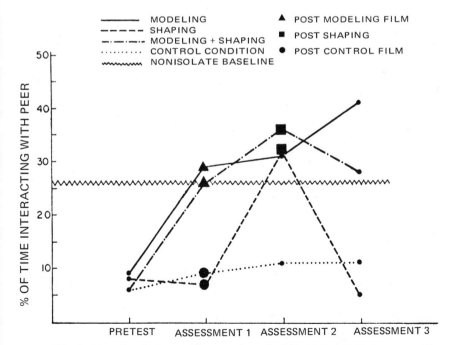

Fig. 2. Mean level of social interaction of all Ss × Conditions, across all assessment phases.

over time for each group and treatment. The time periods between all assessment phases averaged 3 weeks with a range from 1 week to 4. For two groups (modeling and control), the Assessment 3 measure is redundant in some sense, that is, it follows a follow-up of given treatment effect, whereas for the remaining two groups (shaping and modeling plus shaping) the third assessment is the sole measure of durational outcome following the shaping treatment effect. Each group was nonetheless, observed at all four time periods in order to provide for same-time comparisons. In the modeling and control conditions, Assessment 2 and Assessment 3 are both follow-up measures of durational outcome. In all planned analyses, the appropriate, that is, posttreatment-of-interest scores were compared. The 3 week periods between assessments were considered optimal, in terms of approximating the "standard" time for noticeable behavior change in earlier shaping studies (e.g., Allen, Hart, Buell, Harris, & Wolf, 1964).

## RESULTS

Behavioral effects of treatments employed in the present study as well as tests of their efficiency and durational outcome are presented below. Figure 2 represents the mean percentages of time spent in peer interaction for all $S$s, in all conditions, at each phase of the study.

The overall analysis of variance with repeated measures indicated that main effects for treatment conditions ($F = 4.74$, $p < .01$) and for assessment periods ($F = 7.52$, $p < .003$) were significant, as was the Treatment Group $\times$ Assessment Phase interaction ($F = 2.34$, $p < .03$). The reader can readily see in Fig. 2 that these significance figures are accounted for by controlled similarity among pretest scores and within-group changes which differ across groups at various assessment periods.

### Replication of Modeling Effect

The effects of the modeling film are demonstrated by comparing the combined interaction levels of the two groups of children who saw the modeling film with those of the two groups who saw the control film. The planned statistical comparison (pre- to post-modeling film groups vs. pre- to postfilm groups [control]) reveals a highly significant modeling film effect ($t - 2.81$, $p < .005$). This is a

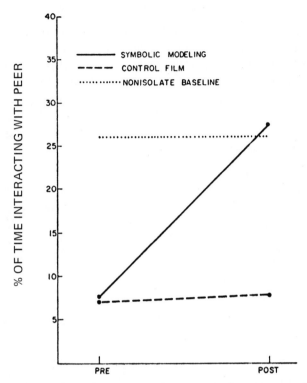

Fig. 3. Mean level of social interaction displayed by Ss in the modeling film and control film conditions before and after the viewing session.

clear replication of results obtained in the earlier research (O'Connor, 1969) and can more readily be seen in a separate graph comparable to the figure in the report of the 1969 study.

As Fig. 3 shows, children in the modeling condition increased their social responsivity markedly. Their postfilm level of interaction was similar to that of the 80 nonisolates observed earlier.[1] The behavior of children who viewed the control film was unchanged.

---

[1] The 80 randomly chosen nonisolates interacted 26% of the time, on the average, which is comparable to the 29% average of nonisolates in the 1969 study. This average is across all four nursery schools, whose "norms" were 21%, 22%, 27%, and 32%, respectively. These data indicate that there is some consistency across nursery schools in the level of social interaction displayed by nonisolate children. Although there was a range of 11% in the "normal" interaction level among the four schools in the study, there was no statistical interaction effect on the scores of isolates in any phase of the study.

Again there was a remarkable consistency across $S$s in the modeling film groups, with all 16 $S$s showing increases in peer interaction after viewing the modeling film. Children who viewed the control film showed only randomly directed changes in the posttest.

**Table 1. Planned Comparisons.**

| Comparison: Groups/assessment phases | ± | $p$ |
|---|---|---|
| 1. All modeling $S$s (post-pre) vs. all control-film $S$s | 2.81 | <.005 |
| 2. Shaping (FU$_1$ post) vs. control (FU$_1$ post) | 2.56 | <.01 |
| 3. Modeling + shaping (FU$_1$ post) vs. modeling (FU$_1$ post) | − .25 | >.4 |
| 4. Shaping (FU$_1$ pre) vs. modeling + shaping (FU$_1$ pre) | .30 | >.25 |
| 5. Shaping (FU$_1$ post) vs. all modeling film $S$s (post-pre) | − .69 | >.4 |
| 6. Shaping (FU$_2$ FU$_1$) vs. modeling + shaping (FU$_1$ post) | 2.49 | <.01 |
| 7. Shaping (FU$_2$ FU$_1$) vs. modeling (FU$_1$post) | 2.94 | <.005 |
| 8. Modeling + shaping (FU$_2$ FU$_1$) vs. modeling (FU$_1$ post) | .69 | >.1 |

Note.—FU equals follow-up

Eight increased, six decreased, and one remained at the same level of interaction. The changes, furthermore, were of small magnitude, from +10% to - 10% time spent interacting with peers. Viewers' familiarity with the exact setting depicted in the modeling film was apparently not a necessary factor in the observational learning process, and the film's efficacy appears to be generalizable across settings.

## Comparison and Outcome

From the overall analysis, it was possible to extract a number of interesting planned comparisons between groups at the various treatment and durational outcome phases of the study. These are shown in Table 1. Aside from the modeling versus control effect already mentioned, the following results appear to be of major interest. First, the group effect of shaping as compared to changes over that period among control $S$s (Comparison 2) was highly significant. Not only did the rate of social interaction among $S$s in the shaping condition increase at the time of postshaping observations in terms of the group mean, but seven of the eight $S$s in the group showed increments which ranged up to +75% time spent in peer interaction. This is an impressively consistent indication of social reinforcement effects on the behavior of isolates, since some past research has suggested that "development of social play behaviors may require much longer periods of reinforcement (Harris, Wolf, & Baer, 1964)," for some children. It may be that the success of shaping, across $S$s, in the present study was partly due to the training and skills of the shapers. Other factors, such as the novelty of the shaper's presence, the intermittent scheduling of sessions, or the repertoire of the $S$s may have differentially affected the outcome here.

The overall effect of the shaping procedure was equally consistent in the modeling plus shaping condition, with six of those seven $S$s showing increased peer interaction in the postshaping assessment. By averaging across $S$s the number of interactions per shaping session, it was possible to view the two shaping conditions by group. Fig. 4 represents these combined results within the two groups' shaping sessions. These two groups do not differ significantly, that is, interaction increments during

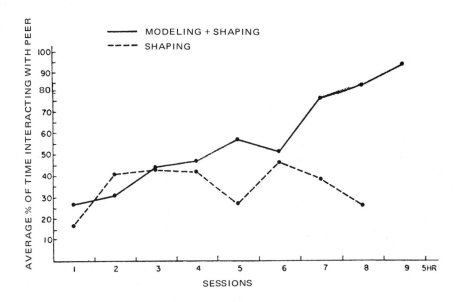

Fig. 4. Mean level of social interaction reached in each shaping session for Ss in the shaping and modeling plus shaping conditions.

shaping sessions were not significantly greater for Ss who had viewed the modeling film than for those who had viewed the control film. Furthermore, there were no significant differences between the treatment effects of modeling plus shaping versus modeling alone, nor between the treatment effects of shaping versus modeling plus shaping.

There were, however, highly significant differences among these treatments at the follow-up phases. Comparisons 6 and 7 in Table 1 indicate highly significant differences in durational outcome across treatments. These analyses, along with the functions shown in Fig. 2, reveal that the high levels of social interaction achieved in the modeling and modeling plus shaping conditions remained stable over time, but that the effects of shaping alone were no longer evident at the time of the follow-up assessment. Shaping did not seem to add anything to modeling alone where durations of effect were considered. The modeling and modeling plus shaping groups did not differ significantly in the follow-up assessment. In fact, the modeling group showed a slight increment from the postfilm assessment to the follow-up, while the modeling plus shaping group showed a slight decrease over the follow-up period. This difference is not significant, but its direction is interesting.

## DISCUSSION

That behavior is largely a function of its consequences and can be modified through manipulation of the reinforcement value of its outcome has become a truism. It is not at all surprising, therefore, that peer interaction can be increased by carefully manipulating the reinforcement contingencies related to those behaviors. The more compelling questions arising from the present data have to do with the relatively more efficient and longer lasting effects of symbolic modeling.

One possible explanation may lie in limitations of the shaping procedures employed in this study. It is surely possible that a more extended shaping period might have produced more durable patterns of social behavior. The Allen et al. (1964) study showed maintenance over time of the shaping effect with one S. It might also be speculated that "fading" and other systematic attempts to prolong reinforcement control might have produced more lasting changes. Since Ss in the shaping conditions reached their peak levels of social interaction during the third or fourth shaping session, and the shapers attempted to employ fading and intermittent reinforcement techniques as much as possible in a nonlaboratory setting, it would appear that neither of these hypotheses are supported in the present data, however.

An alternative explanation of the differential effects found here pivots around the learning versus performance distinction proposed in social learning theory (Bandura, 1968a, 1969; O'Connor, 1969b, 1971). It may be that behavior modifiers are often concerned only with manipulating the performance of behaviors readily available within the repertoire of $S$s, rather than with the transmission of new responses. Learning can be viewed not simply as an alteration in the probability of and discriminative stimuli for the performance of responses an $S$ *can* already emit, but also as the acquisition of novel responses or cognitive rearrangements of simple components of a complex behavior. Within such a theoretical framework, the systematic presentation of modeled stimuli which may represent social behaviors absent from the repertoire of the $S$ would be expected to increase $O$'s social *capability,* given an attention-controlling situation and an absence of competing or confusing stimuli. By exposing the viewer to increasingly more active interaction, presumably graduating the anxiety-evoking content of the presentation in a relaxed non-performance situation, the treatment would be expected to produce a reduction in anxiety or avoidance behavior. This effect has been termed "vicarious desensitization" elsewhere (O'Connor, 1971) and the predicted "disinhibition" has been demonstrated in several studies (Bandura, 1968b). By following each modeled sequence of appropriate interaction behavior with an obviously positive consequence in the film, a vicarious reinforcement effect would be expected to facilitate $O$'s performance of the behaviors modeled. These elements were all included in the modeling treatment conditions of the present study and appear to have produced the predicted results in the posttreatment data. Perhaps the simple manipulation of overt behavior through contingency management overlooks, in the case of severe deficits, the cognitively mediated elements that provide self-controlled cues which help maintain social behavior across a variety of classroom situations. If this were the case, the behavior would not likely be maintained by way of $S$s' initiation and responsivity beyond the externally controlled period. The present data support this assumption as well.

Still another consideration, the locus of reinforcement during shaping, might have been at least partially responsible for the outcome here. Enhancing the social interaction of peers through the responses of reinforcing adults may be somewhat contradictory, since each delivery of praise and attention requires the child to withdraw from peer interaction to some extent. Future research might well focus on reinforcement delivered more naturally from within the context of the desired performance of behavior. In the present study it may have been the case that this "distraction effect" was responsible for both the variation in experimental control during shaping sessions and the absence of performance maintainance beyond the treatment period. Serious consideration of the choice of change agent in terms of controlling for distraction and other reinforcement counteracting properties might well be included in future research.

That adding shaping to modeling did not produce significantly greater effects than did modeling alone was a somewhat surprising outcome. It might have been assumed that these powerful procedures would have an additive effect and that reinforcement would have stabilized peer interaction resulting from the modeling presentation. Neither of these assumptions appear to be validated in the present results. It may be that there was something of a ceiling effect, such that once a child had acquired interaction behaviors through modeling he was likely to perform enough peer interaction to "use up" most of the available situations in which he *could* interact. This possibility seems in line with the similarly small variance in levels of interaction evidenced by nonisolates in all five of the nursery school populations observed in the present line of research. Since most $S$s who viewed the modeling film reached this consistent "norm" level immediately, further increments may be statistically unlikely regardless of additional treatment procedures.

While some elements of observational learning have been defined (Bandura, 1968c, 1969; O'Connor, 1971) and specific interactions between reinforcement and "external" social control identified (Bandura & Barab, 1971; Peterson & Whitehurst, 1971; Steinman, 1970), there remains a set of interesting and unanswered questions in both areas. Perhaps the most pressing indication of the need for further experimentation is that which accrues directly from the success of behavior modification procedures in general. Whether to use modeling or shaping techniques or combinations of the two in nursery school rooms comprises only one example of the concerns facing the consumers of behavioral research. The very fact that such procedures can obtain powerful effects is sufficient to encourage teachers, parents, and other professionals to employ them across numerous behaviors and situations. The present study indicates that there is yet a great need for further basic and comparative study before readers can begin to utilize the findings of behavioral research efficiently and with confidence.

# REFERENCES

Allen, K.E., Hart, B.M., Buell, J.S., Harris, F.R., & Wolf, M.M. Effects of social reinforcement on isolate behavior of a nursery school child. *Child Development,* 1964, 35, 511-518.

Bandura, A.   A social learning interpretation of psychological dysfunctions. In P. London & D. Rosenhan (Eds.), *Foundations of abnormal psychology.* New York: Holt, Rinehart and Winston, 1968.(a)

Bandura, A. Modeling approaches to the modification of phobic disorders. In R. Porter (Ed.), *The role of learning in psychotherapy.* London: Church, 1968.(b)

Bandura, A. Social learning theory of identificatory processes. In D.A. Goslin (Ed.), *Handbook of socialization theory and research.* Chicago: Rand McNally, 1968.(c)

Bandura, A. *Principles of behavior modification.* New York: Holt, Rinehart and Winston, 1969.

Bandura, A., & Barab, P.G. Conditions governing nonreinforced imitation. *Developmental Psychology,* 1971, 5, 244-255.

Cameron, N. *Personality development and psychopathology.* Boston: Houghton-Mifflin, 1963.

Cowan, E., Gardner, E., & Zax, M. *Emergent approaches to mental health problems.* New York: Appleton-Century-Crofts, 1967.

Eysenck, H.J. *Experiments in behavior therapy.* New York: Macmillan, 1964.

Franks, C.M. *Assessment and status of the behavior therapies and associated developments.* New York: McGraw-Hill, 1969.

Harris, F.R., Wolf, M.N., & Baer, D.M. Effects of adult social reinforcement on child behavior. *Young Children,* 1964, 20, 8-17.

Kanfer, F.H., & Phillips, J.S. *Learning foundations of behavior therapy.* New York: Wiley, 1970.

Krasner, L., & Ullmann, L.P. *Research in behavior modification.* New York: Macmillan, 1965.

O'Connor, R.D. Modification of social withdrawal through symbolic modeling. *Journal of Applied Behavior Analysis,* 1969, 2, 15-22.(a)

O'Connor, R.D. Modeling treatment of non-behavior disorders. Paper presented at 41st Annual Meeting of the Midwestern Psychological Association, Chicago, May 1969.(b)

O'Connor, R.D. Stimulus contiguity/mediational modeling theory: Application and outcome. Paper presented at the Annual Meeting of the Society for Research in Child Development, Minneapolis 1971.

O'Connor, R.D., & Rappaport, J. Application of social learning principles to the training of ghetto blacks. *American Psychologist,* 1970, 7, 659-661.

O'Connor, R.D. *Social learning and community: A psychological approach to mental health.* New York: Holt, Rinehart and Winston, 1972, in press.

Peterson, R.F., & Whitehurst, G.J. A variable influencing the performance of generalized imitative behaviors. *Journal of Applied Behavior Analysis,* 1971, 4, 1-9.

Rappaport, J., & O'Connor, R.D. The psychological center in a psychology department. Paper presented at the Symposium on the Psychological Center, 78th Annual Meeting of the American Psychological Association, Miami, September 1970.

Sarason, J.G., & Ganzer, V.J. Social influence techniques in clinical and community psychology. In C.D. Spielberger (Ed.), *Current topics in clinical and community psychology.* Vol 1. New York: Academic Press, 1969.

Steinman, W.M. Generalized imitation and the discrimination hypothesis. *Journal of Experimental Child Psychology,* 1970, 10, 79-99.

Stevenson, H.W. Social reinforcement with children as a function of CA, sex of E and sex of S. *Journal of Abnormal and Social Psychology,* 1961, 1, 147-154.

Stevenson, H., Keen, R., & Knights, S. Parents and strangers as reinforcing agents for children's performance. *Journal of Abnormal and Social Psychology,* 1963, 2, 183-186.

Wolpe, J., & Lazarus, A. *Behavior therapy techniques.* Oxford: Pergamon Press, 1966.

# Article 9
# Inquiry Response Induction in Preschool Children through Televised Modeling*†

RONALD W. HENDERSON, ROSEMARY SWANSON, and BARRY J. ZIMMERMAN

Abstract: Social variables such as modeling and reinforcement of modeled behaviors have been demonstrated to influence conceptual and linguistic responses of children under laboratory conditions. Television is a pervasive force in the lives of children, and modeling is inherent in the medium. This study was, therefore, conducted to determine if language forms involving the use of causal questions can be induced through televised modeling. Subjects were three, four, and five year old Papago Indian children. Experimental children viewed video tapes in which causal questions were modeled and reinforced in interaction sequences involving Papago adults and costumed animal characters adapted from Papago folklore and legends. Controls viewed placebo tapes of activities unrelated to the target behaviors. Highly significant differences in causal question-asking favored experimental children on both posttest and retention measures. Questions asked by child who viewed the series of video tapes were highly original, and clearly did not reflect simple mimicry.

The ability to ask questions is recognized as an important aspect of a child's linguistic and intellectual development. Investigators have stressed the role of question-asking in intellectual development

*An extended version of a brief report published in *Developmental Psychology*, 1975, 11 (4), 523-24. Copyright 1975 by the American Psychological Association. Reprinted by permission.

†This project was supported in part by Grant No. OCD-CB-479 from the Children's Bureau in the Office of Child Development. The opinions expressed herein do not necessarily reflect the position or policy of the Office of Child Development, and no official endorsement by these agencies should be inferred.

(Cazden, 1970), problem-solving (Blank & Covington, 1965), and inquiry processes (Suchman, 1964). Descriptive studies of the development of question forms reveal that some types of questions are developed later than others in children's repertoires of linguistic capabilities (Piaget, 1955; Ausubel & Sullivan, 1970). Question forms which develop later are considered "more mature" than those which develop earlier (Torrence, 1972). The earlier question forms, sometimes characterized as nominal physical questions, are largely those which call for the names of objects or persons, or which refer to the physical attributes of objects (Rosenthal, Zimmerman & Durning, 1970; Torrence, 1972). Why and how questions, or those which call for causal relations, develop somewhat later (Piaget, 1955; Ausubel & Sullivan, 1970).

Descriptive research has also been fairly consistent in showing that the progression of question-asking capabilities is somewhat slower in lower socioeconomic and minority group populations than in more "advantaged" white populations (McCarthy, 1930; Davis, 1932; Ausubel & Sullivan, 1970; Martin, 1970).

Considering the acknowledged importance of question-asking as an inquiry skill which may enable the child to obtain information from the environment, to the benefit of his intellectual development, surprisingly little research has been conducted to identify conditions which may contribute to the development of rule-governed syntactic regularities involved in the generation of interrogative utterances. Theoretical speculation about the development of children's use of increasingly mature syntactic forms ranges from maturational views which minimize the influence of environmental contributions to children's development of syntax, to positions which hold that environment plays a major role in this development (Leach, 1972).

The social learning position posits that children abstract linguistic rules from regularities in the speech of models in the environment (Bandura, 1969). This proposition has found support in research in which a diverse range of rule-governed linguistic behaviors have been influenced directly through the exemplification of specified language structures by live models (Zimmerman & Rosenthal, 1974). In these studies child observers were required to induce a particular property or rule from a highly diverse or complex modeling sequence, and to generalize this property to new and different conceptual tasks. Generalization beyond the specific training task was achieved by randomly varying nonrelevant aspects of the task on which the model performed. Among the language responses which have been influenced through these procedures are children's use of passive and prepositional sentence constructions (Bandura & Harris, 1966; Odom, Liebert, & Hill, 1968), verb tense (Carroll, Rosenthal, & Brysh, 1972; Rosenthal & Whitebook, 1970), and sentence length and complexity with both monolingual and bilingual children (Harris & Hassmer, 1972). Modeling procedures have also been employed successfully to induce a range of interrogative responses when employed by experimenters in laboratory situations (Zimmerman & Pike, 1972), and by parents of children in the primary grades (Henderson & Garcia, 1973; Henderson & Swanson, 1974). This body of literature convincingly demonstrates that children can and do abstract rules for specified linguistic forms from the speech regularities of live models.

In addition to live models, there are multiple sources of vicarious influence in the environments of children. One of the principal potential sources of influence is television, which has taken its place alongside parents, teachers, and peers as a potent agent of socialization (Lyle, 1972; Leifer, Gordon, & Graves, 1974). Most of the recent research on the effects of television on children's development has focused on social behavior and attitudes (Surgeon General's Scientific Advisory Committee on Television and Social Behavior, 1972; Leifer, Gordon, & Graves, 1974), but the *Sesame Street* venture has also prompted interest in the effects of television on cognitive skills. Programming such as that employed in *Sesame Street* has been shown effective in teaching simple associative skills, such as rote counting or discriminating and labeling stimuli such as letters and numerals, but it has not been notably successful in imparting complex concepts and rule-governed responses (Bogatz & Ball, 1971).

Since modeling is implicit in the medium of television, it is important to determine whether or not this potential source of environmental influence is capable of facilitating the acquisition of linguistic rules governing the generation of linguistic forms involved in inquiry processes. Modeling procedures employed in research on the observational learning of conceptual behavior differ considerably from the fragmented programming format of *Sesame Street,* which affords the viewer little opportunity to observe repeated instances, while non-relevant aspects of the task are systematically varied.

The task of the present research was to determine if modeling procedures based on practices employed in previous studies with live models could induce question-asking responses in preschool Papago Native American children. The question category selected for study and the children who participated in the experiment were chosen to provide an especially stringent test of the effects of televised modeling on the production of rule-governed inquiry responses. Questions dealing with causal relations are relatively mature for children of this age (Torrence, 1972), and question-asking in general is not a highly developed skill in most young Papagos, because asking questions is not promoted as a means of obtaining information in traditional Papago culture (Joseph, Spicer, & Chesky, 1949; Henderson & Swanson, 1974).

## METHOD

### Subjects

Thirty-nine Papago Indian children who constituted the entire population of preschool children in Head Start centers of two reservation communities in southern Arizona were randomly assigned to experimental and control conditions. Some of the children were monolingual speakers of English, some were bilingual in Papago and English, and a few were essentially monolingual in Papago. All subjects were from low-income families. Children in the experimental group ranged in age from 3 years 9 months, to 5 years 3 months, with a mean age of 4 years 3 months. Control subjects ranged in age from 3 years 11 months to 5 years 5 months, with a mean of 4 years 6 months.

### Materials

Programming of video taped stimulus presentations was based on social learning principles. Papago adult females interacting with costumed animal characters adapted from Papago folklore and legends modeled the use of causal questions and positively reinforced the production of causal questions. Causal questions were defined as interrogative utterances beginning with the phrases "why," "how come," or "what would happen if," and seeking information about relationships or causal processes. Total instruction for causal question production consisted of three video tapes of approximately ten minutes duration each. Video taped interaction sequences in which causal question-asking was modeled and reinforced centered around large achromatic cartoon-like posters depicting activities from traditional and contemporary Papago life, and unusual behavioral performances on the part of one of the characters. Situations, characters, and visual stimuli were varied across modeled exemplars of causal questions, while the provision of some variation of the verbally stated rule "questions start with question words and get answers," and the delivery of positive reinforcement for question production were held constant. Three placebo tapes of approximately ten minutes duration each were prepared for presentation to the control group. Placebo tapes depicted interesting activities unrelated to the target behavior.

A criterion instrument especially constructed for this study consisted of a set of 20 chromatic drawings depicting a variety of culturally relevant situations and characters. The drawings were presented in a game format, with the child's object being to see if he or she could ask a question about each picture. Each response was scored as a causal question, non-causal question, statement, or non-response. Non-causal questions received one point, and causal questions were scored two points. Spearman-Brown split-half reliabilities for the instrument were .99 for the pretest and .99 for the posttest, and .99 for the retention test.


## Procedure

Following assignment to experimental and control conditions, all subjects were pretested on the criterion instrument. Testing was conducted individually by bilingual Papago examiners who administered the test in the preferred language of each child. When all subjects had been pretested, experimental children viewed a series of three instructional video tapes which depicted a range of models asking causal questions and being differentially reinforced for asking such questions. No reinforcement was provided for other types of utterances. During this same period the control subjects were exposed to the placebo tapes which demonstrated performances unrelated to the target behavior of causal question-asking. Both experimental and control children viewed the tapes individually in a trailer adjacent to the Head Start centers. For each child, approximately three to four days intervened between the viewing of successive tapes in the series. The entire experimental and control treatment extended over a period of approximately one month.

At the conclusion of the experimental and placebo treatments, all children were posttested on the criterion instrument. The test was administered once again as a retention measure during the period between 5 and 10 days following the posttest. By this time, however, a shortage in operating funds had necessitated the early termination of the school year for one center. Therefore, retention data could be obtained only on children at one site.

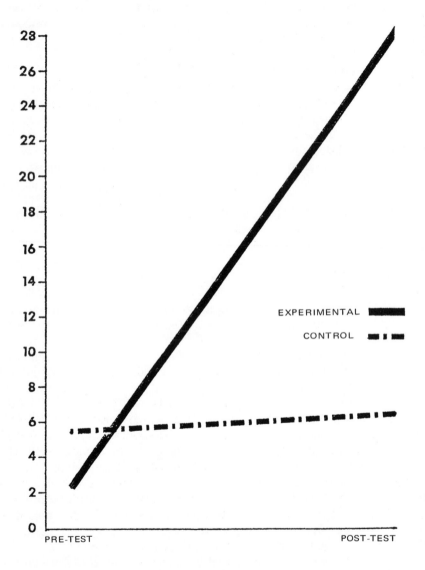

Fig. 1. Question-asking means for Pre- and Post-trials

## Experimental Design

Pre- and post-performance data on all children who participated in both testing phases were analyzed using a 2 (treatment) × 2 (age) × 2 (sex) × 3 (trials) repeated measures analysis of variance design for unequal $N$. A separate analysis of performance measures on only those children for whom retention scores were also obtained employed a 2 (treatment) × 2 (age) × 2 (sex) × 3 (trials) repeated measures ANOVA for unequal $N$.

## RESULTS

Figure 1 shows the mean performance scores of experimental and control children on pre- and post-administrations of the criterion instrument.

The analysis of variance revealed a significant main effect for groups ($F = 8.58$, $df\ 1/39$, $p < .006$), and for trials ($F = 34.76$, $df\ 1/38$, $p < .001$). The interaction term for groups X trials was also significant ($F = 31.83$, $df\ 1/38$, $p < .001$). These results confirm the prediction that question-asking responses could be induced through televised modeling.

The mean performance scores of those experimental and control children on whom retention scores were obtained are displayed in Fig. 2. The analysis of variance of these data recorded a significant effect for groups ($F = 11.20$, $df\ 1/31$, $p < .002$), trials ($F = 15.82$, $df\ 2/61$, $p < .001$), and the group X trial interaction ($F = 16.81$, $df\ 2/61$, $p < .001$). These results indicate that children who were exposed to televised modeling of inquiry statements maintained their advantage over controls on the retention measure.

The number of causal and non-causal questions asked by experimental and control children on the pre-, post-, and retention-trials of the experiment were also tabulated. Table 1 presents the tabulated totals for both groups on all trials. The question-asking performance, especially for causal questions, was very low for both groups on the pretest, and continued at a low level for controls on subsequent trials. It should be further noted that all but one of the pretest questions asked by the experimental group were attributable to one child. Experimental effects, however, were clearly not attributable to the performance of a few children, since 83% of the children in the experimental group made gains, and 67% of them gained 20 or more points.

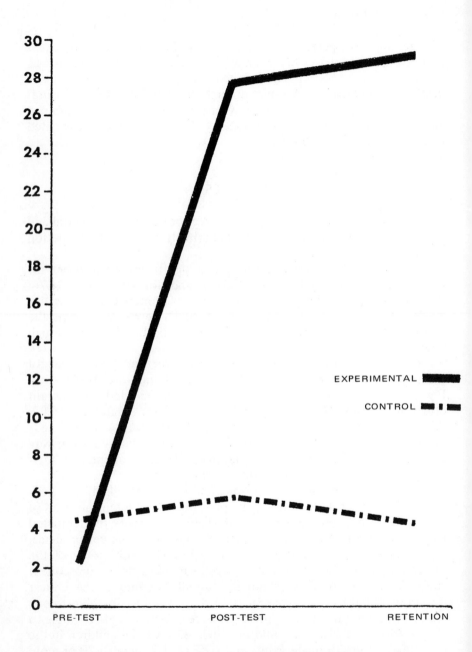

Fig. 2. Question-asking means for Pre-, Post-, and Retention Trials

## DISCUSSION

The results of this investigation show clearly that interrogative linguistic constructions were induced through televised modeling procedures. These findings lend support to the social learning position that children abstract regularities from the speech of models to which they are exposed and are able to incorporate these forms appropriately in their own linguistic responses. The fact that findings previously reported for the influence of live models on children's syntactic construction also appear to hold true for televised models has practical as well as theoretical implications. The potential power of televised models to influence the linguistic performance of children is demonstrated by the fact that children in this investigation were considerably younger than those who served as subjects in any of the previously reported studies of modeling influences on linguistic responses. The English language skills of children in this population are not well developed. They live in circumstances of extreme isolation and socialized within a cultural tradition that has not traditionally emphasized question-asking as a means of inquiry. Parents of these children, nevertheless, now recognize the value of such skills in dealing with the Anglo-dominated governmental and educational bureaucracies, and want their children to acquire such skills. With the availability of video cassettes, it would be feasible to provide stimulation for the development of a wide range of linguistic and conceptual behaviors which may be valued, but for which the requisite conditions for development may be too infrequent or haphazard in the natural environment to be effective.

Table 1. Question Totals for Pre-, Post-, and Retention Trials.

|  | Pre | | Post | | Retention | |
|  | C | N-C | C | N-C | C | N-C |
|---|---|---|---|---|---|---|
| Experimental Group | 21 | 11 | 333 | 10 | 322 | 14 |
| Control Group | 39 | 53 | 46 | 40 | 6 | 21 |

Many psycholinguists seem to equate imitative or observational learning with simple mimicry (Chomsky, 1965; Slobin, 1968). Zimmerman and Rosenthal (1974) have reviewed a number of modeling studies which demonstrate that exact mimicry constitutes a very small proportion of the outcome performances in such investigations. The present study lends support to that conclusion. First, direct mimicry was virtually impossible, because the stimulus materials differed considerably in content and organization from the stimulus materials used in training. As a result it was necessary for the children to generalize from the situations they had seen depicted on television, to a quite different set of circumstances. Moreover, at least two days intervened between viewing of the final tape and testing. The variety of questions asked by different children in response to identical stimulus materials on the performance test is vividly displayed by the following examples of responses:

Sample responses to card #12:
    What would happen if the ladder would fall down and break their legs?
    How come that boy is climbing up the tree?
    How come that little girl is trying to get up and get the orange?
    What if he fell?
    What would happen if the ladder fell on the boy?
    Why is the girl climbing the tree?
    How come the monster took them (cherries) all off?
    Why did the boy take his shoes and socks off?

Sample responses to card #14:
    How come the cat is playing with the yarn?
    Why is the boy watching the kitties?
    What would happen if the mouse bit him?
    How come the kitty is crying?
    Why is the boy scaring the mouse?
    How come the mouse ran out of the house?
    Why would the mouse get mad at the little boy?

Sample responses to card #15:
    What if the father would kick the mother?
    How come the chicken is afraid of these people?
    Why are they chasing the chickens?
    How come the girl is not wearing shoes?

Sample responses to card #16:
    How come the horse won't get up and go?
    Why is the boy trying to get the horse up?

How come that man is pulling the donkey's teeth?
Why is the boy pulling the horse when he don't want to get up?
How come the horse is sitting back?
Why did the boy make the horse sit down?
Why won't the man pick the horsey up?
How come the horse wouldn't go to the man?

Obviously these responses do not represent direct mimicry of the language displayed by characters in the television episodes viewed by the children in the experimental group. Neither could it be argued convincingly that the questions are stereotyped versions of the modeled performances. From these results it seems clear that children's development of skill in asking questions is amenable to the influence of television models.

## REFERENCES

Ausubel, D.P. *Theory and problems of child development* (2nd Ed.). New York: Grune and Stratton, 1970.

Bandura, A. *Principles of behavior modification.* New York: Holt, Rinehart and Winston, Inc., 1969.

Bandura, A., & Harris, M.B. Modification of syntactic style. *Journal of Experimental Child Psychology,* 1966, 4, 341-352.

Blank, S.S., & Covington, M. Inducing children to ask questions in problem solving. *Journal of Educational Research,* 1965, 59, (1), 21-27.

Bogatz, G.A., & Ball, S. *The second year of Sesame Street: A continuing evaluation.* Vol. 1 & 2, Princeton, New Jersey: Educational Testing Service, November 1971.

Carroll, W.R., Rosenthal, T.L., & Brysch, C.G. The social transmission of grammatical parameters. *Journal of Educational Psychology,* 1972, 63 (6), 589-596.

Cazden, C.B. Children's questions: Their forms, functions and roles in education. *Young Children,* 1970, 25 (4), 202-220.

Chomsky, N. *Aspects of the theory of syntax.* Cambridge, Mass.: M.I.T. Press, 1965.

Davis, E.A. The form and function of children's questions. *Child Development,* 1932, 3, 57-74.

Harris, M.B., & Hassemer, W.G. Some factors affecting the complexity of children's sentences: The effects of modeling, age, sex, and bilingualism. *Journal of Experimental Child Psychology,* 1972, 13, 447-455.

Henderson, R.W., & Garcia, A.B. The effects of a parent training program on the question-asking behavior of Mexican-American children. *American Educational Research Association,* 1973, 10, (3), 193-201.

Henderson, R.W., & Swanson, R.A. The application of social learning principles in a field setting: An applied experiment. *Exceptional Children,* 1974, 41, 53-55.

Joseph, A., Spicer, R.B., & Chesky, J. *The desert people: A study of the Papago Indians.* Chicago: University of Chicago Press, 1949.

Leach, E.A. Adult-child dialogue: Some diagnostic implications. *Acta Symbolica,* 1972, 3 (1), 46-49.

Leifer, A.D., Gordon, N.J., & Graves, S.B. Children's television more than mere entertainment. *Harvard Educational Review,* 1974, 44 (2), 213-245.

Lyle, J. Television and daily lives: Patterns of use (overview). In *Television and Social Behavior, Vol. 4,* Washington, D.C.: U.S. Government Printing Office, 1972.

Martin, F. Questioning skills among advantaged and disadvantaged children in first grade. *Psychological Reports,* 1970, 27, 617-618.

McCarthy, D. Language development of the pre-school child. Minneapolis: University of Minnesota, Institute of Child Welfare, 1930, No. 4.

Odom, R.D., Liebert, R.M., & Hill, J.H. The effects of modeling cues, reward, and attentional set on the production of grammatical and ungrammatical syntactic construction. *Journal of Experimental Child Psychology,* 1968, 6, 131-140.

Piaget, J. *The language and thought of the child.* New York: World Publishing Company, 1955.

Rosenthal, T.L., & Whitebook, J.S. Incentives versus instruction in transmitting grammatical parameters with experimenter as a model. *Behavior Research and Therapy,* 1970, 8, 189-196.

Rosenthal, T.L., Zimmerman, B.J., & Durning, K. Observationally induced changes in children's interrogative classes. *Journal of Personality and Social Psychology,* 1970, 16 (4), 681-688.

Sloban, D. Imitation and grammatical development in children. In N.S. Endler, L.R. Boulter, and H. Osser (Eds.) *Contemporary issues in developmental psychology.* New York: Holt, Rinehart and Winston, 1968, 437-443.

Suchman, J.R. The child and the inquiring process. In A.H. Passow and R.R. Leper (Eds.), *Intellectual development: Another look.* Washington, D.C.: Association for Supervision and Curriculum Development, 1964.

Surgeon General's Scientific Advisory Committee on Television and Social Behavior. *Television and growing up: The impact of televised violence.* Washington, D.C.: Government Printing Office, 1972.

Torrence, E.P. Influence of alternate approaches to pre-primary educational stimulation and question-asking skills. *Journal of Educational Research,* 1972, 65 (5), 204-206.

Zimmerman, B.J., & Pike, E.O. Effects of modeling and reinforcement on the acquisition and generalization of question-asking behavior. *Child Development,* 1972, 43, 892-907.

Zimmerman, B.J., & Rosenthal, T.L. Observational learning of rule-governed behavior by children. *Psychological Bulletin,* 1974, 81 (1), 29-42.

# Article 10
# Effects of Surreptitious Modeling
# upon Teacher Classroom Behaviors*

DAVID BROWN, DANIEL RESCHLY, and HOWARD WASSERMAN†

The effects of observational learning upon subsequent social and intellectual behaviors have been demonstrated amply (Bandura, 1971; Rosenthal & Zimmerman, 1970). This research has revealed the profound influence of models upon a wide variety of behaviors that include aggressiveness, phobic reactions, grammatical structure, rule learning, etc. However, to date little research has been completed that concerns the problem of the possible use of modeling procedures as a means to change teachers' behaviors. The present study is a report of an effort to change a teacher's behavior in a natural classroom setting.

The authors were requested to consult with the teacher of a classroom for emotionally disturbed children as part of a practicum in a graduate class on behavior modification consultation. Briefly, the teacher previously had requested assistance to deal with the "hyperactive" and disruptive behavior of two students. Even though the teacher had requested such assistance, she refused to accept advice offered by the school counselor on one occasion and by the special education consultant on another. Two of the authors were placed in this classroom for the purpose of observing "emotionally

*Reprinted by permission from *Psychology in the Schools,* 1974, 11 (3), 366-369.

†The authors wish to express appreciation to Dr. Ralph Wetzel who provided assistance and encouragement during the project.

disturbed" students and applying behavior modification techniques.

An initial interview with the teacher established her extreme resistance to various behavior modification plans, although she was receptive to the plan of allowing the authors to observe in the classroom and interact with the children. Instead of the behavioral techniques favored by the authors the teacher insisted upon the necessity of psychotherapy in combination with chemotherapy (Ritalin) in dealing with the disruptive students. Implicit in her recommendations was the desire to minimize direct teacher involvement in any intervention plan.

Classroom observation established the fact that the two students were definitely not hyperactive, and moreover, led to an intuitive judgment that the teacher maintained a very low rate of positive contacts with individual or groups of students.

Based upon the above observations, two intervention plans were instituted. The first involved the establishment of self-reinforcement contingencies for the two disruptive students. Briefly, this involved stating criteria for reward and allowing the students to decide whether the rewards had been earned. The self-reinforcement plan was successful (see Brown, Reschly, & Wasserman, 1974) even though it was carried out with no teacher assistance.

The second intervention plan, which was the major purpose of the study reported herein, involved an attempt to use modeling procedures as a means to increase the frequency of positive pupil-teacher contacts. Specifically, the frequency of positive contingent social reinforcement was determined before and after such behaviors were modeled by the authors.


## METHOD

The authors were in the classroom described above for the purpose of observing the behavior of two disruptive children. This arrangement provided the opportunity to observe carefully the frequency of teacher-initiated positive contingent social reinforcement. The frequency of occurrence of teacher praise and number of times the teacher moved away from the seat at her desk were gathered on five occasions (see Fig. 1): probes 1, 2, and 3 prior to modeling, probe 4 immediately after modeling, and probe 5, 4 weeks after modeling. All data were collected during the first 90 minutes of the school day.

Reliability of observations was obtained, during the second and fifth probes, by comparing the ratings of two observers who operated independently within the classroom. Observations of teacher behavior were made during the first 90 minutes of the school day. Agreements of 100% on probe two and 95% on probe five were obtained.

Modeling out-of-seat behavior and the contingent application of praise was implemented on two occasions, day 31 and day 32. The teacher was not informed previously of this intervention procedure, hence she was given no cue to direct her attention toward the model. The teacher remained in the chair behind her desk at all times during the 90 minutes of modeling on both days and seemingly was occupied with class-related work. The model (one of the authors) continuously moved about the classroom and quietly interacted with students. When students attended to their assigned tasks the model moved closer to the student, occasionally placed a hand on their shoulder, and praised good working behaviors (the model enumerated the positive work behaviors manifested).

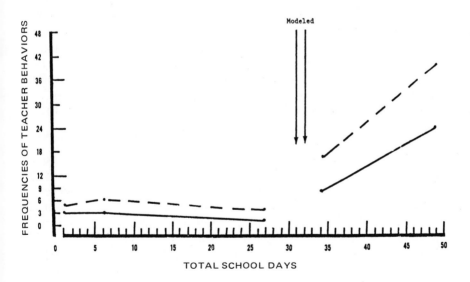

Fig. 1. Frequency of times teacher came out from behind her desk (•——•) and times teacher positively interacted with students (•— —•).

## RESULTS

As can be seen from Fig. 1 the mean number of times the teacher left her desk and frequency of praise for children prior to modeling were 2.3 and 4.3 respectively. Immediately after modeling intervention the teacher came out from behind her desk 8 times and the incidence of praise increased to 17 during the 90-minute interval. The frequency of these behaviors was 25 and 40 respectively 4 weeks after the initial modeling.

The above results were analyzed statistically through application of the Fisher Exact Method (Walker & Lev, 1953). Frequencies of both teacher praise and number of times she spent away from her desk were found to be significant ($p < .02$).

## DISCUSSION

The modeling of interaction with students and praise for student work had a dramatic effect upon the frequency of these behaviors with this particular teacher. While it was impossible to control carefully a number of potentially confounding variables (see Campbell & Stanley, 1963), it seems highly likely that the substantial change in teacher behavior was more than mere coincidence. It is clear from the data reported herein that a set of inappropriate teacher behaviors apparently had existed for a long time (as was substantiated by the principal), and that after modeling conditions considerably more appropriate behaviors were adopted.

Bandura (1971) has demonstrated amply the importance of a number of variables associated with the stimulus value of the model. Factors such as perceived competence, prestige, age, and sex are potential influences upon the effectiveness of a model. However, it should be emphasized that the model in this situation in all likelihood did not possess these important characteristics in any greater degree than the typical consultant to a classroom teacher. The model was rather young (under 30), a graduate student in school psychology, and relatively inexperienced in educational settings. All of these facts were known to the teacher. It seems unlikely that these results were simply due to a model-status factor that exceeds or is beyond that of the typical consultant.

These results seem to have a number of implications for the use of a consultation model by school psychologists, curriculum supervisors, counselors, and others. When overt suggestions for changing teacher behaviors may be excessively threatening, or likely to be rejected for other reasons, some form of covert influence might be attempted. The increasing acceptance of observation and interaction with problem children in the classroom by psychologists and counselors, rather than interacting only on a one-to-one basis outside of the class, provides the opportunity for the kind of covert influence exercised in this study. Even though no directional cues or attention cues were provided, the modeling appeared to have an effect. This procedure avoided a possible confrontation over methods to deal with children and further reduced the "expert-client" relationship that often interferes with effective consultation. On the basis of the above data covert influence, or what we like to call "surreptitious modeling," appears to be a promising procedure for counselors and psychologists in working with classroom teachers.

A caution should be expressed concerning the use of an influence technique such as covert modeling without a prior agreement between the consultant and consultee. In some cases a consultant is requested to help a teacher with problems related to overall professional performance, e.g., discipline in the classroom. In such cases the covert modeling that has been described herein appears to be well within an explicit agreement establishing a helping relationship between the consultant and consultee. However, in cases in which the initial reason for consultation is a third party such as an individual child, consultant modeling for the purpose of influencing the teacher's behavior should be undertaken only when an agreement that specifies possible effects, procedures, etc., is made.

## REFERENCES

Bandura, A. *Social learning theory.* New York: General Learning Press, 1971.

Brown, D., Reschly, D., & Wasserman, H. The modification of "hyperactivity" via self-management procedures. Unpublished manuscript, University of Arizona, 1973.

Campbell, D., & Stanley, J. *Experimental and Quasi-Experimental Designs For Research.* Chicago: Rand McNally, 1963.

Rosenthal, T., & Zimmerman, B. Modeling by exemplification and instruction in training conservation. Unpublished manuscript, University of Arizona, 1970.

Walker, H.M., & Lev, J. *Statistical inference.* New York: Holt, Rinehart and Winston, 1953.

# 5
## *Children as Change Agents*

We have discussed many procedures which teachers may use to modify children's behavior. This chapter focuses on the ways children themselves can influence their environment. The effects children have on their parents, teachers, and especially on their peers are powerful and varied. Children imitate the dress styles, language, and social behavior of their peers. Such imitation is viewed as advantageous when, for example, a withdrawn child becomes more outgoing by observing his socially confident friends. Unfortunately, children also model less desirable behavior, e.g., drug abuse, cheating, and aggression. Just as "fitting in" or imitating peer group behavior has rewarding outcomes for children, "doing better than" or competing with fellow students is also an avenue of peer influence. The successful use of competition for modifying behavior is dramatically demonstrated in the Soviet educational process (Bronfenbrenner, 1970, pp. 51-69). Beginning in first grade, Soviet children are systematically taught to compete with each other. Competition occurs between rows or other groupings rather than between individuals, and the entire group benefits from fostering appropriate academic and social behavior in its members. This approach resembles that illustrated by Long and Williams (1973) and by the structure of competition in many American academic and athletic contests. In addition to exerting influence via modeling and competition, children modify each other's behavior by providing explicit consequences. For example, children offer and withdraw their friendship based on whether a child shares toys or "acts the bully." Membership in a street gang may be made contingent upon a youth's demonstration of courage and skill in fighting. The class clown is often rewarded with giggles and the best students are the first ones picked for spelling teams.

It is clear that in the natural environment, peers are one of the greatest sources of reinforcement and punishment for other children. It is equally clear that children do not always influence others in beneficial ways. The following article by Solomon and Wahler (1973) provides strong support for the assumption that children respond primarily to their peers' inappropriate behavior and offer little attention for desirable behaviors. As importantly, Solomon and Wahler demonstrated that responsible students can be taught in a short time to alter their interactions with disruptive children and thereby effect substantial reductions in problem behavior. Five sixth graders were trained to attend to appropriate behavior and ignore the disruptions of five problem children in the same class. Although other children and the teacher did not significantly change their behavior with respect to the problem children, the child change agents were successful, particularly in ignoring disruptions.

Graubard, Rosenberg, and Miller (1971) also taught children to respond to others in ways which increased positive interactions and decreased negative interactions. This report differs from Solomon and Wahler (1973) in that the child change agents were not "responsible and popular" children but rather were children from special education classes who were often teased, ridiculed, and ignored by their "normal" peers and who were the first to be accused of wrong-doing by many teachers. Two examples of how deviant junior high school children changed the behavior of important people in their environment by using a variety of positive attention and ignoring procedures are described. Since these children spent three of the seven periods per day in regular classes, one experiment focused on improving the children's interactions with their regular class teachers. The students were able to increase the amount of praise and decrease the number of negative comments from these teachers by, for example, asking for extra assignments and ignoring any provocations from the teachers. The second experiment shows how the same special class children were able to modify their relations with "normal" children. The effects of using these children as change agents was clearly beneficial for all concerned.

The last article (Willis, Morris, & Crowder, 1972) in this section documents the effectiveness of a procedure which is being used with ever increasing frequency, namely peer tutoring. Eighth grade volunteers tutored fourth graders who were experiencing serious reading problems. Tutoring was conducted on a daily basis for a 15-week period. When tangible back-up reinforcers were added to praise and tokens for successful reading, reading rate increased. Thus, with supervision, the tutors effectively administered a simple token program and produced significantly greater gains in the reading levels of their tutees than would have been predicted from previous low rates of learning.

The use of children as change agents has distinct advantages. Peer attention is a powerful reinforcer, and all would agree that directing this attention toward desirable forms of behavior, such as sharing and reading, is more beneficial than allowing the predominant mode of responding to disruptions to continue. Students may also be in a better position to observe peer behavior than the teacher and can thereby provide support for the efforts of their classmates more immediately and more frequently than the teacher could. As Graubard et al. (1971) pointed out, teaching deviant children to change the behavior of others has salutory consequences for both parties involved. By using positive forms of control, problem children may develop more positive feelings about themselves. In the process of changing others, the child changes his/her own behavior and receives positive feedback for these changes.

Some important issues must be addressed, however, if peer influence is to be used systematically. The seriousness of these issues increases as the influence and training to use that influence becomes more direct and individualized. Peer influence is presumed to be a powerful factor in the success of group reinforcement procedures (e.g., Long & Williams, 1973), but no one child is singled out as a "therapist" who is trained to alter the behavior of a specific child (e.g., Solomon & Wahler, 1973). When children are asked to assume the responsibility for another child's behavior, whether academic or social behaviors are concerned, parental consent and especially close supervision are warranted. The child change agents should be carefully selected. When children evaluate and reward their peers (Willis et al., 1972), the possibility exists that the evaluations will be harsh or that the child "client" will exert undue pressure for the "therapist" to give high evaluations. Precautions, such as a system of fines for the evaluator or the use of an elected evaluator (Phillips, Wolf, & Fixsen, 1973), should be considered.

An additional ethical issue is raised by the Graubard et al. (1971) article. In the first experiment, teachers' behavior was observed and altered without their express knowledge or consent. When children are being trained to interact differently with teachers and that training is a part of the children's school or therapy program, consent may not be necessary although cooperation from the teacher certainly could enhance the effectiveness of the program. When observations are being made as part of a research project, informed consent from the teachers is required.

In sum, using children as change agents has both advantages and disadvantages. Children learn to pay closer attention not only to the behavior of others but also to their own behavior. Although supervision is necessary, peer influence is a powerful source of reinforcement for other children, and if it can be directed toward appropriate ends, fewer children would need professional attention.

# Article 11
# Peer Reinforcement Control of
# Classroom Problem Behavior*†

ROBERT W. SOLOMON and ROBERT G. WAHLER

**Abstract**: Peer and teacher interactions with five "disruptive" children were studied in an elementary school classroom. The intent of the study was to analyze experimentally peer reinforcement control of the disruptive children's problem behaviors. Social attention provided by all peers was found to be directed exclusively to the problem behaviors during baseline. Following baseline, several manipulations of selected peer social attention demonstrated the reinforcement function of this stimulus class.

Naturalistic approaches to child behavior modification have typically emphasized adult control of the problem child's actions. Thus, the majority of investigators have examined interactions between parents and their children (e.g., Patterson, Cobb, & Ray, in press) or between teachers and their pupils (e.g., Madsen, Becker, & Thomas, 1968). Based partly on information derived from these assessments, training programs have been devised to shift adult social attention from the children's problem behavior to their more

*Reprinted by permission from the *Journal of Applied Behavior Analysis,* Vol. 6, No. 1, 1973, 49-56. Copyright 1973 by the Society for the Experimental Analyses of Behavior, Inc.

†This study was supported in part by a grant from the Knox Children's Foundation. The authors wish to express their appreciation to this Foundation and to Aileen Lowery, Ursula Bothyl, and Diane Childress, who served as observers in this study.

desirable actions. As the majority of studies showed, such shifts can produce sizable therapeutic changes in the children's behavior.

Unfortunately, a third source of social contingencies, present in both home and school settings, has received little systematic inquiry. This source, provided by the behavior of the problem child's peer group, has been described as an important determinant of deviant and normal child behavior (O'Leary & O'Leary, 1972). Both Patterson, Littman, and Bricker (1968) and Wahler (1967) demonstrated that peer reinforcement controls normal child behaviors in preschool settings. Other investigators have shown that peers might also support the deviant behaviors of children. Two investigations (Buehler, Patterson, & Furness, 1966; Duncan, unpublished) presented data indicating quite systematic peer approval following the antisocial behaviors of delinquent children, but very little following the children's prosocial responses. While neither of these studies attempted to evaluate the function of these peer consequences, it is probable that the peers did contribute support to the antisocial behaviors.

It is unfortunate that the above investigations of peer influence in the maintenance of problem child behavior have not been replicated in ways that would allow experimental analyses of peer influence. Additional investigations have either assumed that peers contribute to the control of child behavior, or have merely used peers as dispensers of non-social reinforcers. For example, Patterson and Brodsky (1966) attempted to modify the aggressive behavior of a 5-year-old boy through a point system applied to the boy and his peer group following non-aggressive interactions by either party. Although the boy's aggressive interactions declined, the causal roles of peer behavior and the adult controlled point system were confounded. In further work, Patterson, Shaw, and Ebner (1969) attempted to study the peer therapist problem by enlisting the aid of a single peer. This child was trained to dispense points and social approval following the classroom "work" behavior of an inattentive problem child. The procedures was followed by improvement in the problem child's attention, but the differential roles of peer social behavior and the non-social point system were confused. Finally, Surratt, Ulrich, and Hawkins (1969) showed that an elementary student could effectively alter the study behavior of younger children through monitoring and distributing non-social reinforcers for the children's classroom work.

The above investigations certainly demonstrate that peers can be incorporated as instrumental agents in behavior modification programs. However, it has not yet been shown how peers contribute to the initial maintenance of deviant child behavior and how this natural social influence might be altered to produce behavior modification. Thus, two questions generated by the previously reviewed findings require empirical investigation: (1) Do peers deliver reinforcement to members of their group for behaviors considered deviant by adults? and (2) Can the social reinforcement of peers be controlled by adults to produce changes in the problem behaviors of particular children? The present study was designed to analyze experimentally both of these assumptions.

## METHOD

### Subjects

Ten children, selected from a sixth-grade classroom in a rural county school, were chosen on the basis of teacher and principal reports of disruptive pupil behavior.

Discussion with the principal and teacher revealed that much of the disruptive classroom behavior was produced by five boys (out of a total of 30 children of both sexes). Informal observations supported this assumption; these children frequently violated classroom rules involving talking, out-of-seat behavior, and play. Thus, it appeared reasonable to designate the five boys as sample problem children. These subjects are now referred to as target subjects.

Since one goal of the present study was to evaluate peer control of problem child behavior, the second phase of subject selection involved choosing potential "therapists." Given that the therapists would operate as trained dispensers of social attention, two factors seemed important criteria for subject selection: (1) that the peers be of high social reinforcement value for the target subjects, and (2) that the peers be likely to cooperate with the adult-directed training program. Assuming that peer popularity is a good index of social reinforcement value, initial selection of peer therapists was conducted through a class-wide administration of a sociometric survey of student popularity (similar to one used by Lesser [1959]). Finally, the teacher was asked to rank order the most popular children in terms of "willingness to cooperate with adults." The top five in this rank ordering were chosen as potential peer therapists (three boys and two girls). These subjects are referred to as control subjects.

## Setting

All observations were conducted during the social studies period of each classroom day. This setting was selected for two reasons: (1) teacher reports indicated that problem behavior was reliably evident during the period and; (2) teacher rules as to what constituted problem and desirable behavior were clearest during this period. As the next section indicates, a precise understanding of teacher rules was critical to the scoring of dependent measures of target subject behavior.

When asked to provide a complete list of "musts" and "must nots" for this period, the teacher confidently presented the following items that referred to all pupils: must raise hand before talking; must stay in seat unless given permission to do otherwise; must not manipulate objects irrelevant to reading and writing.

## Dependent and Independent Variables

*Dependent measures*

After a number of informal observations of the target subjects, discussions between the teacher and observers led to the formulation of six behavior categories that appeared to describe adequately the behavior of target subjects. These categories could refer to both problem behavior and desirable behavior, depending on the teacher's explicit set of classroom rules during the social studies period. Considering these rules, each behavior category could be scored as problem (p) or desirable (d) as follows:

*Action (A  p or d)*

This category referred to non-verbal interaction with objects occurring at the target subjects' desks. On virtually all occasions, behavior such as reading, writing, gesturing, and manipulation of combs, nail files, and rubber bands defined the categories. Only reading and writing were considered as desirable behaviors (d). All other object manipulations were considered rule violations (p).

*Talking (T  p or d)*

Speech composed this category. These behaviors, occurring as rule violations (p), were most often mentioned by the teacher as instances of classroom disruptive behavior. Talking that did not violate the teacher's rule was considered desirable (d).

*Out of Seat (OS  p or d)*

These categories were scored whenever target subjects left their desks. As a (p) score, this category was also mentioned frequently by the teacher as a major contributor to classroom disruption. When this category occurred following teacher permission it was considered desirable (d).

*Independent measures*

Control peer behaviors constituted the broadly defined independent variable. Control subject behavior was defined as a single broad stimulus category, referred to as social attention. This category was composed of any verbal behavior or physical contact if, in the observer's judgment, these behaviors involved a target subject.

Two other sources of social attention were also recorded, primarily to evaluate their contribution to the therapeutic program. These sources, provided by teacher and "other peer" behavior were defined in the same manner as the control peer social attention category.

## Sampling Techniques and Response Units

Each target subject's behavior was sampled in 6-minute periods. That is, every 30-minute observation was broken into five periods and one target subject was randomly assigned per period. Observers thus shifted their attention every 6 minutes, sequentially monitoring each target subject and social reactions to his behavior.

Scoring of target subject behavior categories and their social contingencies was accomplished by segmenting the categories into 10-second units. Observers discriminated the units through a large wall clock containing a sweep second hand. The observers were instructed to record the first category occurring in a time interval, including social attention provided by any or all of the three stimulus sources. Thus, for each 10-second unit, only one of the six possible behavior categories could be scored; social consequences for this category could, however, be scored for control peers, other peers, and the teacher. Pilot work revealed that this procedure produced the largest amount of information at acceptable levels of observer reliability.

## Procedure

### Baseline

Before beginning the observational scoring, classroom seating arrangements were modified so that one control subject was seated adjacent to one target subject. This arrangement (conducted randomly) ensured that control subjects were now in a position to influence target subjects.

Observers were stationed in the back of the classroom and on opposite sides of the room. When their records indicated agreement levels of 80% on all response and stimulus classes, the formal baseline observations began. At this point, one observer was randomly selected as the "data collection" observer and her partner served as a reliability check.

### Peer training

Control peer training in behavior modification techniques was initiated at the conclusion of baseline. This involved a group meeting among the five control peers, their teacher, and the authors. The children were asked to "help" target subjects to improve their school performance, which was in fact, poor. All control peers immediately agreed to do so. The authors then pointed to the target subjects' disruptive behavior as a cause of their poor performance. Following a brief explanation of differential reinforcement and extinction concepts, the children were told how they could reduce disruptive behavior and increase the occurrence of more appropriate classroom behavior. At this point, a video-taped baseline session was presented and the children were encouraged to "spot" instances of $p$ and $d$ behavior as produced by target subjects. In addition, they were asked to discuss the social contingencies for these behaviors in terms of strengthening and weakening functions of these events.

Finally, the children were given specific instructions concerning their role as behavior modifiers. They were told that they must ignore any $p$ behavior by target subjects and respond positively to the $d$ behavior. To facilitate this discrimination, the children were instructed to score their reinforcement of $d$ behavior by marking a plus (+) on a sheet of paper; if they inadvertently responded to $p$ behavior, a minus (–) must be recorded. The teacher was then designated as the children's "trainer." At the end of each school day the teacher would meet with the control subjects and discuss their records.

*Experimental strategies*

An ABAB single subject design was used to assess the reinforcement role of peer attention in the expected outcomes of this study. Following baseline (a) and peer training (b), the control peers were instructed to resume their baseline reactions to target subject behavior (a); when the effects of this intervention were apparent, the control subjects were again instructed to produce their "therapeutic" contingencies (b). These steps ensured three systematic manipulations of the primary independent variable (control peer attention).

## RESULTS

### Observer Reliability

Observer agreement was calculated for each of the six behavior categories and each of the three stimulus categories. To do so, agreements or disagreements were tabulated for each 10-second interval containing a category. Reliability was then determined by the formula: agreements/disagreements + agreements. Agreement percentages varied from 80 to 100% (mean agreement over all sessions was 87%).

### Target Subject Behavior

Figure 1 describes the mean number of problem ($p$) behavior units produced by the target subjects over all periods of the study. Reference to the first baseline period clearly confirms the "disruptive" reputations of the target subjects; for most sessions, $p$ behavior accounted for more than 80% of the 10-second intervals.

Following the training of control subjects as behavior modifiers, a gradual and clear reduction in $p$ behavior was evident over the 12 sessions of Treatment I. A further examination of Fig. 1 also demonstrates the causal role of the treatment operations in determining the reductions. One replication of the baseline phase (Baseline II) and one replication of the treatment phase (Treatment II) were associated with predictable increments and decrements in $p$ behavior.

Table 1 presents the data of Fig. 1 in percentage form, compressed for each target subject over the various baseline and treatment sessions. These data indicate that the treatment effect was observed

**Table 1. Percent Problem ($p$) Behaviors Produced by Target Subjects Over All Baseline and Treatment Periods.**

| Target Subjects | Baseline I | Treatment I | Baseline II | Treatment II |
| --- | --- | --- | --- | --- |
| 1 | 81 | 43 | 70 | 30 |
| 2 | 87 | 52 | 75 | 41 |
| 3 | 79 | 55 | 71 | 40 |
| 4 | 81 | 43 | 69 | 25 |
| 5 | 68 | 17 | 46 | 10 |

for each target subject. Thus, it is apparent that the mean data plotted in Fig. 1 reflect the behaviors of all target subjects.

## Control Peers, Other Peers, and Teacher

The principal question of interest in this study was an evaluation of peer influence in the maintenance and modification of the previously described $p$ behavior of target subjects. Figure 2 provides some interesting data in this respect. In examining Baseline 1, it is strikingly apparent that all peers were differentially responsive to the $p$ behavior of target subjects; 100% of their social attention was made contingent upon $p$ behavior. The teacher, while less likely than peers to respond to $p$ behavior, also provided a good proportion of attention for these behaviors.

The reinforcement function of control peer attention is also demonstrated in Fig. 2, bearing in mind the data of Fig. 1. Figure 1 shows that target subject $p$ behavior dropped sharply during Treatment I. As the Treatment I section of Fig. 2 indicates, only the control peers changed their social attention contingencies in a direction expected to produce reductions in $p$ behavior. Other peers maintained their social attention at 100% for $p$ behavior, and teacher social attention actually increased for $p$ behavior. In all further periods of the study, control peer social attention shifted in perfect accordance with directions for them to respond and not respond to $p$ behavior, while the other peers continued to attend almost solely to $p$ behavior. Thus, it seems reasonable to conclude that the fluctuations in $p$ behavior shown in Fig. 1 were primarily a function of contingency changes in control peer attention. The control peers not only contributed to the maintenance of $p$ behavior, they were also the central agents in the modification of that behavior.

MEAN 10-SECOND UNITS OF PROBLEM BEHAVIOR/OBSERVATION

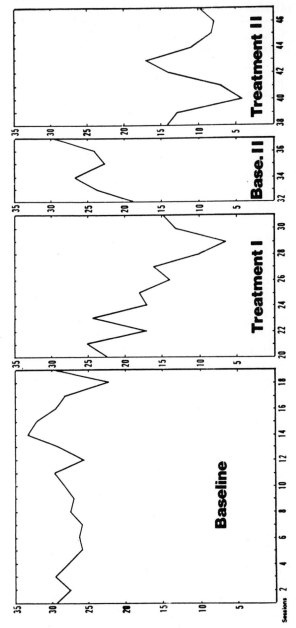

**Fig. 1.** Mean number of problem behavior units produced by target subjects over all baseline and treatment periods.

Table 2. Mean Number of social attention units continguous with problem (p) and desirable (d) behaviors of target subjects.

| | Behavior Category | Baseline I | Treatment I | Baseline II | Treatment II |
|---|---|---|---|---|---|
| Control peers | p | 2.54 | 0.82 | 4.60 | 0.08 |
| | d | 0.00 | 0.23 | 0.00 | 0.59 |
| Other peers | p | 3.20 | 3.63 | 4.47 | 2.17 |
| | d | 0.00 | 0.00 | 0.10 | 0.00 |
| Teacher | p | 0.65 | 1.13 | 0.33 | 0.28 |
| | d | 0.26 | 0.08 | 0.33 | 0.55 |

However, these data do not reflect the extent of this shift in terms of the actual number of peer reinforcements provided for these behaviors. Table 2 describes the mean number of social attention units provided by control peers, other peers, and teacher for $p$ and $d$ behavior over all periods of the study. While these data for other peers and teacher follow more or less from the percentage data of Fig. 2, the control peer means add further information. The comparison of mean changes between Baseline and Treatment I shows a substantial reduction in control peer attention to $p$ behavior; however, simultaneously these peers provided only a small increase in their attention to $d$ behavior. Further examination of other baseline and treatment periods in the study continue to confirm these contrasts in control peer attention. Thus, while these peers were remarkably successful in reducing their attention to $p$ behavior, they were not so efficient in dispensing approval for $d$ behavior.

## DISCUSSION

This investigation confirmed its two major hypotheses: (1) our data showed how peers operate in a setting where children are known to produce behavior considered deviant by adults. In line with the findings of other investigations (e.g., Buchler et al., 1966), the peers in the present study were almost exclusively attentive to deviant actions produced by problem children: prosocial behaviors produced by these children were completely ignored. (2) the present findings also indicated that it is possible to shift the above social contingen-

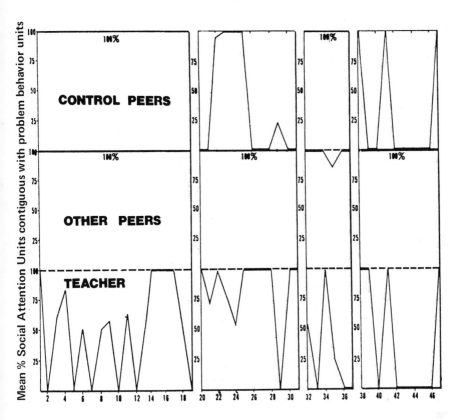

Fig. 2. Mean percent of control peer, other peer, and teacher social attention units contiguous with target subject problem behavior units.

cies such that some peers no longer pay attention to the deviant behaviors. When this operation was performed, the problem children produced less deviant behavior and emitted more prosocial behaviors. In other words, peers who typically supported the deviant behavior of their group members, could also modify that behavior in a direction desirable to adults (i.e., teachers).

No doubt the most valuable feature of this study is pragmatic. It comes as no great surprise that children do reinforce deviant behaviors of their group members, although, the extent to which they did so in this study is somewhat alarming. However, to demonstrate that peers can also modify these behaviors under adult direction has far-reaching implications. Some children tend to produce deviant behaviors in settings where adult intervention is impossible or unlikely. For example, school truancies and stealing may have low likelihoods of immediate detection by adults and thus their modification is difficult. However, while adult intervention is often unlikely for these behaviors, such may not be true for peer interventions. As the present findings suggest, it is probably not unreasonable to suggest that peers do support these "difficult to modify" behaviors. If that indeed proves to be the case, then ways of changing social interactions among these children should certainly be pursued. Granted that some influential members of a peer group can be directly influenced by adults, one might imagine the development of "peer therapist" programs designed specifically to deal with deviant child behaviors typically supported by the peer group.

## REFERENCES

Barker, R.G., & Wright, H.F. *Midwest and its children.* New York: Harper and Row, 1955.

Buehler, R.E., Patterson, G.R., & Furness, R.M. The reinforcement of behavior in institutional settings. *Behaviour Research and Therapy,* 1966, 4, 157-167.

Duncan, D.F. *Verbal behavior in a detention home.* Unpublished manuscript, Juvenile Hall, Olatha, Kansas, 1969.

Lesser, G.S. The relationship between various forms of aggression and popularity among lower class children. *Journal of Educational Psychology,* 1959, 50, 20-25.

Madsen, C., Becker, W., & Thomas, D. Rules, praise and ignoring: elements of elementary classroom control. *Journal of Applied Behavior Analysis,* 1968, 1, 139-150.

O'Leary, K.D., & O'Leary, S.G. *Classroom management: the successful use of behavior modification.* New York: Pergamon Press, Inc., 1972.

Patterson, G.R., & Brodsky, G. A behavior modification program for a boy with multiple problems. *Journal of Child Psychology and Psychiatry,* 1966, 7, 277-295.

Patterson, G.R., Cobb, J.A., & Ray, R.S. A social engineering technology for retraining aggressive boys. In H. Adams and L. Unikel (Eds.) *Georgia symposium in experimental clinical psychology,* Volume II. Pergamon Press, (in press).

Patterson, G.R., Littman, R., & Bricker, W. Assertive behavior in children: A preliminary outline of a theory of aggressive behavior. *Monograph of Society for Research in Child Development,* 1967, 32, 1-43. (VI)

Patterson, G.R., Shaw, D., & Ebner, M.J. Parents, teachers, and peers as behavior modifiers. *Oregon Research Bulletin,* 1969.

Surratt, P.R., Ulrich, R.E., & Hawkins, R.P. An elementary student as a behavioral engineer. *Journal of Applied Behavior Analysis,* 1969, 2, 85-92.

Wahler, R.G. Child-child interactions in free field settings; some experimental analyses. *Journal of Experimental Child Psychology,* 1967, 5, 278-293.

# Article 12
# Student Applications of Behavior Modification to Teachers and Environments or Ecological Approaches to Social Deviancy*† ‡

PAUL S. GRAUBARD, HARRY ROSENBERG, and MARTIN B. MILLER

This paper describes how social deviance and maladaptive behavior can be alleviated through the use of behavior modification techniques. In the two experiments reported here a novel approach was taken: the "normals" were treated to increase their tolerance for deviant behavior.

This approach was developed as a result of our concern at seeing individuality and creativity suppressed in "exceptional" children, who were expected to conform to rules of the dominant culture. These children are often the tragic victims of our society. Under the mantle of "helping," society has stigmatized these children with labels such as "mentally retarded," "psychotic," and "schizophrenic."

*From Graubard, P.S., Rosenberg, H., & Miller, M.B. Student applications of behavior modification to teachers and environments or ecological approaches to social deviancy. In E.A. Ramp & B.L. Hopkins (Eds.), *A New Direction for Education: Behavior Analysis 1971, Vol. 1.* The University of Kansas: Support and Development Center for Follow Through, Department of Human Development, Lawrence, Kansas, 1971. Reprinted by permission with the following abridgements: Experiments II and IV and associated references omitted.

†Grateful acknowledgement is made to the following teachers and administrators who made this work possible: James Moore, Richard Rasner, Clifford Denham and Charles Richmond. Also appreciated are Breena Overton and Ann Dell Duncan, for their insightful and critical readings of the manuscript. Our special appreciation to the children who were good students and even better teachers.

‡ Not for distribution or reproduction without the explicit, written permission of the authors.

They have been subjected to loss of privacy, to public ridicule, to involuntary detention in training schools and hospitals and to loss of prestige and privileges. In many cases, this "help" also leads to physical abuse (James, 1969). This phenomenon is also compounded by racism and class bias. In our opinion, it is no accident that special education classes, child guidance clinics, mental hospitals, and training schools are filled with youth of minority group status far out of proportion to their actual numbers in the population.

For an understanding of our approach, first imagine that a child has absented himself for thirty-seven days of an eighty day school term. If he is referred to a guidance counselor or clinical psychologist, the medical label, (which usually tends to preempt all others), can be applied to him. He will be viewed and designated as "school phobic," "emotionally disturbed" or "sick" to some degree. A dean of discipline or probation officer would label and treat the same child as a "juvenile delinquent," "incorrigible youth" or "youth in need of supervision." Other citizens might view this absentee behavior as "wrong" and would recommend moral lessons dealing with the rewards of virtue and respect for diligence.

In contrast, some members of a counterculture might define this same truancy as heroic behavior to be encouraged, as it seems to violate an oppressive law.

Thus, the problem of maladaptive behavior (or what is popularly called emotional disturbance) can be reasonably interpreted in the language of psychopathology, of learning theory, or of social deviancy. The social deviancy model, long popular in anthropology, has seen little use in the field of applied behavior analysis. This is unfortunate, as it is a model which carries many implications for both understanding and ameliorating behavior problems.

In 1934, Benedict noted in her study of comparative cultures the ease with which people that would be considered abnormal in America were functional in other cultures. It did not matter what kind of "abnormality" she looked at—those which indicated extreme instability or those which were more in the nature of character traits like sadism, or delusions of grandeur—there were still well described cultures in which these abnormals could function at ease and with honor. These people apparently functioned without danger, or difficulty to their society.

If one agrees that given behaviors are not good, bad, healthy or pathological in themselves, and that any component of behavior is either adaptive or maladaptive for a specific culture, then "non-normative," "pathological," and "social deviant" become equivalent terms. Use of this conceptualization demands examination of: (1) the specific behavior; (2) the perceiver of the behavior; and (3) the effect of the behavior upon the perceiver.

Theories and methods generated by the field of ecology are of great value here, as they view man within the ecosystem or context of his environment. Ecologists do not conceptualize or treat "emotional disturbance." They attempt to describe behavior which is a mismatch between surroundings and individuals or groups. The implication is that behavior, behavior analysis, and planning strategies to reduce conflict can be conducted only in the originating habitat. It is the "goodness of fit" of behaviors to specific environments that must be scrutinized. Rabkin and Rabkin (1969) say that it is the interface (described as the meeting of two social systems, including the context or background of their encounter) and the clash between cultures, that is in need of change when clinical intervention is requested. The behavior of neither the behaver nor the perceiver in isolation from this interface is the target. The behaver, whether a member of either minority or majority groups should be considered with reference to culture—specific factors. This is particularly true if we take the pluralistic ideals of our society and the rights of minority groups seriously. In our opinion, aberrant behavers constitute a minority group as meaningful as groups composed of ethnically different members of the population.

In the field of mental health, we usually find one group—usually that within the dominant, established culture—which labels the behavior of individuals from another group as disturbed. Those so labeled usually come from a political or social minority. Both Szasz (1970) and Rhodes (1969) discuss the political underpinnings of mental health labeling in current society.

The treatment of "social deviants" by "normals" cannot be extensively documented here. The theme of cruelty to underdogs runs through the social history of Western society and is extensively detailed in our literature (e.g., Chekhov's *Ward Six*, 1965) and the harrassment of "deviants" can be seen on any playground as "normal" children torment a "different" child. Thus, if we work with the "goodness of fit" model, to change the behavior of "normals" may be of equal importance to changing the behavior of "deviants." Change in the interface between conflicting groups is the most significant factor.

The behavioral literature is replete with examples of how behavior modification has been used to change the behavior of the social deviant (e.g., any issue of *Journal of Applied Behavior Analysis*).

There are few examples in the literature where deviants, as part of a planned process of change, were taught to modify the behavior of normals.

We feel that it is necessary to teach deviants to change other people, not only for self-protection, but also because the positive use of power leads to self-enhancement and positive feelings about the self. If children are to be more than recipients of someone's benevolence, they must learn how to operate on society, as well as to accept being operated upon. Moreover, our clinical data indicated that in the process of learning to change others, the "deviant" changes his own behavior and receives feedback and reinforcement for this change.*

The two experiments described in this paper took place in an agricultural community in the San Joaquin Valley in California. "Anglos" comprise the predominant group within the town, although there is a large Chicano population and a small Black community. Each experiment describes a special application of our approach. These experiments are reported as representative of our method and we assume a much wider spectrum of possible applications than is illustrated here.

## EXPERIMENT I:
## CHILDREN-MODIFIED TEACHER BEHAVIOR

This experiment took place in a school which had a reputation for being hostile to the special education program in general and towards adolescent minority group children in particular. Experience had shown that it was extremely difficult to reintegrate special education children into the mainstream of that particular school. It was felt that many regular class teachers scapegoated special education children. Supervisors' directives that all children, including special education children, were to be treated equally, had little effect.

The goal of the special education program was to reintegrate its members into regular classes of the school. The children spent more time with each of the regular class teachers than any professional consultant or administrator could, and had the greatest personal interest in changing their teachers. They were, therefore, expected to

*Video tape records are available for inspection, upon appropriate inquiry from Harry Rosenberg, Visalia Schools, 200 South Dollner, Visalia, California 93277.

exert the most influence over their teachers, if given an effective technology.


## Method

*Subjects*

Seven children with an age range of 12 to 15 were selected as behavior engineers. Two children were Caucasian, two were Black and three were Chicanos. Each engineer was assigned two clients (teachers), and each had the responsibility of accelerating praise rates and decelerating negative comments and punishment by the teachers.

*Procedure*

The class day in the school was organized into seven 43-minute periods. Special education children met with a special class teacher three periods a day and were integrated into the regular classes for four periods daily.

Instruction and practice in behavior modification theory and techniques were given during one period a day by the special class teachers. Initially, instruction was on a one-to-one basis, but later the whole class worked together on practicing their newly learned skills. The children were told that they were going to participate in an experiment. Scientific accuracy was stressed as being extremely important. Students were directed to record all the client-teacher's remarks during the pilot period of two weeks. Through consensual validation of the class and special education staff, these comments were sorted into positive or negative groups.

Techniques taught to the children included making eye contact with teachers and asking for extra help and, further, children were taught to make reinforcing comments such as: "Gee, it makes me feel good and work so much better when you praise me," and "I like the way you teach that lesson." They also were taught to use reinforcing behavior such as sitting up straight and nodding in agreement as teachers spoke. These techniques and phrases were used contingent upon teacher performance. The pupils were also taught to perform the "Ah Hah" reaction (so notably described by Fritz Redl) as follows: When a pupil understood an assignment, he was to ask the teachers to explain it once again. In the middle of the second explanation the student exclaims "Ah Hah! Now I understand; I could never get that point before."

Pupils were also taught to break eye contact with the teacher during a scolding, to ignore a teacher's provocation, to show up early for class, and to ask for extra assignments. These techniques were explicitly taught and practiced repeatedly. Simulation techniques and role playing were employed. Video tapes were used extensively so that other children could monitor their performance and, under both class and teacher promptings, adjust those factors that were targets for change.

*Reliability*

Each of the seven students was observed in action. At various times, an observer-aide unobtrusively recorded his own version of positive and negative contacts within the teacher-student interface. These records were later compared with those of the student-participants for the same observation periods.

On positive contacts from teacher-clients, the range of correlations between student and observer records was very narrow, from a low of .815 to a high of .980. The mean correlation across seven student-observer combinations is .942.

On negative contacts, the range of correlations is from .453 for one student-observer combination to 1.00 for two such combinations. These perfect correlations reflect the fact that students were often observed well into the experiment, during periods when negative contacts by teachers were few, often zero. Therefore, agreement between students and observers in the absence of negative contact for such periods is quite high. The average over the seven student-observer combinations is .957.

An interesting sidelight was that at the beginning, when procedures were piloted, the observer-aides consistently differed from the children in the number of positive comments made. Closer monitoring revealed that the aides were more accurate in recording, as often the special education children were unable to recognize conventional praise phrases as such. Therefore, they consistently underestimated the amount of praise that was given to them. Teachers were experimentally naive.

**Results**

Data were collected during a nine week period. With seven student-engineers, each with two teacher-clients, there were, in effect, fourteen replications to examine. An ABA design was employed: the first two weeks were considered baseline weeks, and were followed by five weeks of intervention. During the last two weeks, students were instructed to stop all reinforcements, thereby applying extinction.

**Table 1. Analysis of Variance for Positive Contacts in Student-Teacher Shaping as a Function of Weeks and Teacher Replication.**

| Source | df | ms | F |
|---|---|---|---|
| Subjects (S) | 6 | 113.83 | 4.84** |
| Weeks (A) | 8 | 975.88 | 41.49** |
| Teacher Rep. (B) | 1 | 6.00 | 1.50 |
| A × B | 8 | 6.00 | 1.68 |
| A × S | 48 | 23.52 | |
| B × S | 6 | 4.00 | |
| A × B × S | 48 | 3.58 | |

$**p < .01$

Data on positive contacts by each teacher-behavior engineering during the nine weeks were cast into a repeated-measures analysis of variance. One data point was used per student-teacher combination for each week (the average number of positive contacts during the week for that combination). The results of that ANOVA are summarized in Table 1.

The results are fairly straightforward. There is no significant interaction between Weeks and Teacher Replications, and no significant overall effect for Teachers. There is a very marked effect for Weeks (which we shall return to in our discussion briefly), and as might be expected, a significant effect for Subjects.

A similar analysis on negative teacher-as-client contacts is summarized in Table 2. In most respects, the effects here are similar to those for positive contacts. The exception is a significant effect for Teacher Replications which, though reliable, is quite small in magnitude.

Figure 1 shows a plot of average frequency of positive contact, and of negative contacts over the nine weeks of the experiment.

For positive contacts, there is a significant jump from Week 2 (a baseline week) to Week 3 (the first week of treatment). There is a general improvement in frequency of positive contacts throughout the next four weeks, all intervention weeks. With Week 8 (the first

**Table 2. Analysis of Variance for Negative Contacts in Student-Teacher Shaping as a Function of Weeks and Teacher Replication.**

| Source | df | ms | F |
|---|---|---|---|
| Subjects (S) | 6 | 211.50 | 7.06** |
| Weeks (A) | 8 | 562.75 | 18.80** |
| Teacher Rep. (B) | 1 | 8.00 | 9.64* |
| A × B | 8 | 1.25 | .48 |
| A × S | 48 | 29.94 | |
| B × S | 6 | .83 | |
| A × B × S | 48 | 2.60 | |

*p < .05
**p < .01

week of extinction), there is a marked and significant drop in positive contacts by teacher-clients. By Week 9, the frequency of positive contacts has fallen to below the base rates for Weeks 1 and 2, although this is not statistically significant.

The results on negative contacts are fairly analogous to those for positive contacts. Indeed, they appear to be mutually dependent, until we examine the extinction Weeks, 8 and 9. Here, although there is a significant increase in negative contact from the last week of treatment (Week 7) to the first week of extinction (Week 8), the frequency of negative contacts does not increase significantly between Weeks 8 and 9. Also, negative contacts during extinction are still significantly fewer than for Weeks 1 and 2, the baseline weeks. It can clearly be seen that children can modify teacher behavior, at least temporarily. However, the teacher-clients appear to be quite dependent on a maintained reinforcement schedule for positive contacts; this is less the case for negative contacts, at least as far as these data can show us. Of course, the frequency of negative contacts might have increased to base-rate levels, or even beyond in subsequent weeks, but these data are beyond the scope of the present analyses. Nevertheless, we might hazard a guess that teacher-clients did learn to be less punitive with training, and that this training held to some extent even when the reinforcements were withdrawn. It does appear however, that teachers, like most people, are backsliders and need a high level of reinforcement to maintain particular kinds of new behaviors.

A number of ethical questions are raised by this experiment, not the least of which is the surreptitious observation of teacher behavior by aides in order to establish a reliability coefficient. This was felt to be justified by the necessity for scientific validation of the pro-

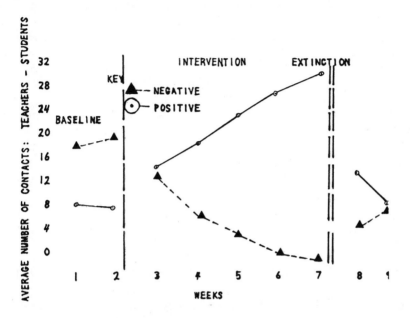

Fig. 1. Average number of positive and negative teacher contacts during baseline, intervention, and extinction.

cedure. The observations were in no way used as evaluation of teacher performance. These data will not affect teachers retaining jobs, getting increments, or contribute to any of the rewards or punishments established by the school system. Data concerning teachers and children are confidential; our interest is in exploring the consequences of particular management techniques, not in specifying or evaluating individuals.

The procedures used seemed to be effective within a very short period of time. The children's labor contributing to effective change was free; and it is certainly less costly to employ pupils, using reinforcements readily available in the classroom, than it is to pay clinical personnel within the traditional medical model, to change behavior.

## EXPERIMENT III:
## DEVIANT CHILDREN CHANGE NORMALS

The third experiment consisted of training special education children (officially designated as emotionally handicapped) to modify the behavior of "normal" children. This was again done using the rationale of the social deviancy model and the need the experimenters felt to change the interface between children who were clashing. We observed that often the "normal" children scapegoated the special education children, using derogatory terms such as "retards," "rejects from the funny farm" and "tardos." A popular game for the normal children was "Saluggi": bigger children would throw one child's cap around while the unfortunate owner ran around vainly trying to reclaim his property. Being teased, ignored and ridiculed were part of the social roles thrust upon the special education children.

### Method

Our work with the special education children consisted of individual counseling by two resource teachers. We explicitly explained and illustrated operant theory to the children. The counseling consisted of one thirty-minute session per week which lasted for a nine-week period. The special education children were asked to list those children who made school unpleasant for them. They specifically described the behavior of the children whose behavior they wanted to change, and those children they wished to spend more time with.

Among the things counted were the number of hostile physical contacts that took place on the playground with their "arch enemy" if that was the problem, or the number of snubs, or hostile remarks directed toward each child was recorded. Positive contacts with particular children were recorded and quantified if the special education child's goal was to increase such interactions. The data collection was done by the special education children and handed in each day to their counselors.

### Procedure

The behavioral engineers were taught the following method: (1) *Extinction,* or walking away from the chase the cap game, breaking eye contact with the provocative children, and ignoring negative remarks. (The children received primary reinforcers such as candy from the counselor for each instance in which they succeeded.) (2) *Reinforcement* or explicitly sharing toys or candy or giving compliments to those children who made positive contact with the behavior engineers. (3) *Reinforcing* incompatible responses, by first initiating and reinforcing the children participating in active ball games, etc. (4) *Setting contingencies* such as helping the children with homework, crafts, and school activities was also used.

*Reliability*

As with the student-to-teacher study, observers in the peer-to-peer experiment unobtrusively checked and recorded positive and negative comments by peer-clients. On positive contacts by peer-clients, the correlation between the six student trainers and their observers ranged from .570 to .984. The average correlation across student-observer combinations is .824, rather low as reliability coefficients should go, but given the inherent difficulties in making surreptitious observations in playgrounds and classrooms, the best we could get.

The reliability for negative comments are about the same as for positive comments, ranging from .435 to .957, for an average of .876. In the peer-to-peer study each of the six students as behavior engineers had three client-peers who entered treatment on a staggered baseline, as schematized in Fig. 3.

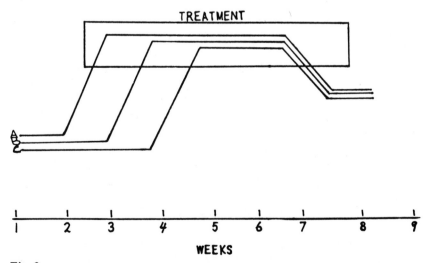

Fig. 3

Client A enters treatment after two baseline weeks; Client B after three weeks; Client C after four weeks. Reinforcements are subsequently withdrawn during two extinction weeks for all clients. Since there are six student-trainers, each line (A, B and C) applies to six different client-peer combinations.

## RESULTS

Data were cast into separate analyses of variance, one for each frequency of positive and negative contacts by client-peers. Table 4 shows a summary of ANOVA for positive contacts.

Table 4. Analysis of Variances for Positive Contacts in Peer-To-Peer Shaping as a Function of Weeks and Treatment-Entry Conditions.

| Source | df | ms | F |
|---|---|---|---|
| Subjects (S) | 5 | 81.00 | 5.08** |
| Weeks (A) | 8 | 571.75 | 35.89** |
| Entry Cond. (B) | 2 | 202.50 | 4.47* |
| A X B | 16 | 15.44 | 1.73+ |
| A X S | 40 | 15.93 | |
| B X S | 10 | 45.30 | |
| A X B X S | 80 | 8.95 | |

+p = .064
*p < .05
**p < .01

If the staggered baseline has a reliable impact, we would expect significance for the interaction between Weeks and Treatment-Entry Conditions, the A X B interaction term. The interaction is significant with a probability of .06 (which we take seriously enough).

Figure 4 shows a plot of positive contact frequencies over the nine weeks of the experiment for client-peers in the three different entry conditions.

Things turn out pretty well according to plan with the exception that the difference between Week 2 (the last baseline week) and Week 3, the first treatment week for A type clients, is not significant. The corresponding differences between the last week of baseline and

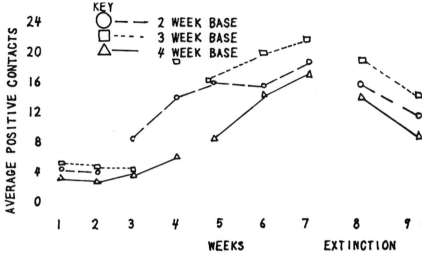

Fig. 4

the first week of treatment for B and C type clients are significant drops in positive contact frequencies. These drops are still well above the baseline rates for all three client groups. This can be contrasted to what happened to the teacher-clients who fell back to their base rates during extinction of positive contacts.

Table 5 shows the ANOVA for negative contacts in the peer-to-peer shaping.

Table 5. Analysis of Variance for Negative Contacts in Peer-to-Peer Shaping as a Function of Weeks and Treatment-Entry Conditions.

| Source | df | ms | F |
|---|---|---|---|
| Subjects (S) | 5 | 665.40 | 12.76** |
| Weeks (A) | 8 | 1321.88 | 25.36** |
| Entry Cond. (B) | 2 | 129.00 | 1.46 |
| A × B | 16 | 34.69 | 1.33 |
| A × S | 40 | 52.13 | |
| B × S | 10 | 88.50 | |
| A × B × S | 80 | 26.08 | |

**$p < .01$

Here, we must dismiss the Weeks by Entry Conditions interaction term as nonsignificant. There is, however, a clear effect for Weeks.

Figure 5 shows average positive and negative contact frequencies contrasted for all eighteen client-peers combined, ignoring the staggered baseline conditions.

Notice that negative contact rate shows a systematic drop with treatment beginning with Week 3, which actually reflects only a third of the client-peers in treatment. Extinction in Weeks 8 and 9 yields an increase in frequency of negative contacts, but once again, these averages are still different from any of those for baseline weeks.

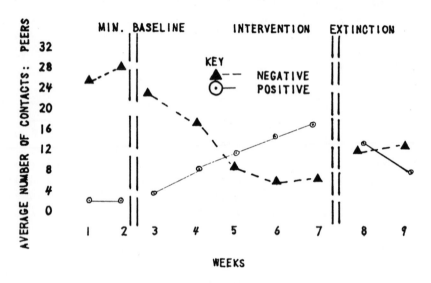

**Fig. 5**

We note that, at least with reference to positive contacts, the students — behavior engineers — are able to manage a fairly subtle posture, gradually bringing in a new client in successive weeks of treatment. They are doing about as well in exercising control over human behavior as many a graduate does in a Ph.D. thesis, or professionals who charge $50 an hour, for that matter.

Our conclusions from this data are that deviant children can change the behavior of "normal" children, and that hostile physical contacts, instances of teasing, etc., were considerably reduced. Moreover, approach behaviors, such as invitations to parties and invitations to play in ball games, etc., were considerably accelerated.

At no time did any teacher intervene with the normal children and encourage or limit their behavior.

Behavior modification appears to be a powerful tool which can give "deviant" children the social skills and power to change the behavior of others towards them. While the "deviant" children undoubtedly changed their own behavior, the important thing remains that they did dramatically change the behavior of others towards them.

## GENERAL SUMMARY AND CONCLUSION

The main implication of these two studies is that socially deviant groups can readily change the behavior of those groups who generally exercise the most control over them.

The program that was implemented in this school also shows that it is possible to diffuse power, even political power, in a way that is not usually available to those from minority groups. Currently, establishment groups, such as teachers, normals, and high-status children, retain control over the power structure within the schools. It has been demonstrated that this control may be neutralized by developing the capacity to change others' behavior in those groups usually regarded by society as being in need of change. This is particularly important, as several observers (e.g., Sloane, 1971; Madsen, 1970) have noted that when research or pilot programs are terminated, teachers tend to revert to normal or baseline conditions. Therefore, so crucial a variable as power, or the issue of behavior control, must be dealt with if the "deviant" is to be released from the not-too-tender mercies of power groups such as clinics, schools, and courts.

We feel confident that the lives of the individual children involved in these studies have been helped. We wonder in the long run what such diffusion of power might bring.

# REFERENCES

Benedict, R. *Patterns of culture.* Boston and New York: Houghton Mifflin Co., 1934.

Chekhov, A. *Ward six and other short novels.* New York: Signet Books, New American Library, 1965.

James, H. *Children in trouble: A national scandal.* New York: David McKay Co., Inc., 1969.

Madsen, C. Address delivered to Symposium on Behavior Analysis in Education. University of Kansas, 1970.

Rabkin, J., & Rabkin, R. Delinquency and the lateral boundary of the family. In P.S. Graubard (Ed.), *Children against schools: Education of the delinquent, disturbed, disruptive.* Chicago: Follett Educational Corp., 1969.

Rhodes, W.C. The disturbing child: A problem of ecological management. In P.S. Graubard (Ed.), *Children against schools: Education of the delinquent, disturbed, disruptive.* Chicago: Follett Educational Corp., 1969.

Sloane, H. Address delivered to Symposium on Behavior Analysis in Education. University of Kansas, 1971.

Szasz, T.S. *The manufacture of madness: The comparative study of the inquisition and the mental health movement.* New York: Harper and Row, 1970.

# Article 13
## A Remedial Reading Technique for Disabled Readers that Employs Students as Behavioral Engineers* †

JERRY W. WILLIS, BETTY MORRIS, and JEANE CROWDER

Failure to learn to read is a major stumbling block to further psychological, educational, and social development. In the traditional elementary school the child who does not learn to read faces educational hurdles that cannot be overcome unless reading skill already has been acquired. When this assumption is false, as it often is in many urban slum schools, the result is a school curriculum that is not relevant to the child, and one that is likely to produce behavior problems because it preordains failure.

This report describes an attempt to develop an effective and inexpensive approach to deal with reading problems in elementary-school children. It is based on a learning theory model that places the scheduling of rewards and stimulus material in a central role while it focuses on overt reading behavior as the primary intervention target. Previous investigators (Hewett, 1964; Staats, Minke, & Butts, 1970) have reported success with such approaches in spite of their relative disregard for specialized techniques to deal with presumed linguistic, perceptual-motor, visual-motor, and aural-oral deficits.

Learning theory based models of remedial reading often use tangible rewards to motivate students. However, few studies have made an attempt to study the effect of such rewards independent of other behavior modification techniques such as social rewards and

*Reprinted by permission from *Psychology in the Schools,* 1972, 9, 67-70.

†The authors wish to thank Miss Margaret Loranz of the Birmingham Board of Education for her support and assistance.

prescriptive academic material. Wolf, Giles, and Hall (1968), for example, described an extensive remedial education effort that included token reinforcement and demonstrated significant academic improvement with fifth and sixth-grade underachievers. However, no comparison was made with a control group that received similar remedial work but no tokens. A study by Walker, Mattson, and Buckley (1969) showed that although praise, teacher attention, and removal from the classroom where tokens were earned were effective to maintain attending behavior, token reinforcement *per se* was relatively ineffective with fourth to sixth graders enrolled in a special class for emotionally disturbed children.

A further problem in studies of tangible rewards has been the fact that in baseline-treatment designs the *E*s usually are aware that *S*s are not expected to do well during baseline. In the present study *E*s were given the impression that the initial condition, which used no tangible or back-up reinforcers, was the total program.

## METHOD

### Subjects

*S*s were 10 fourth-grade students referred to the counselor in a Birmingham, Alabama, school located in the inner city. All referrals were for serious reading problems. Ages ranged from 9 years, 8 months to 11 years, 8 months with a mean of 10.7 years. The mean pretest IQ on the Slossen Intelligence Test was 81,* with a range from 71 to 91. Mean pretest reading level on the Slossen Oral Reading Test was second grade, second month, with a range from 1.3 to 3.2.

### Procedures

The remedial program developed for the students had four major components.

1. Interesting reading material individually prescribed for each student was available. Every child had material that was both within his reading ability and interesting. Material used included the Know Your World and This Is Your World newspapers from American

*Only 7 of the 10 subjects were given intelligence tests.

Education Publications (Education Center, Columbus, Ohio), the Readers Digest reading series, and the Sullivan programmed reading series. However, there are many "high-interest, low-vocabulary" books that would have been equally appropriate.

2. The second component was a special remedial reading technique that emphasized immediate rewards for successful reading. Two basic approaches were used, both of which were carried out by eighth-grade students selected by the school counselor from a group of volunteers. The students were given two 1-hour training sessions in which modeling and role-playing techniques were the primary teaching tools. One method paired students of like ability and reading level. An eighth-grade student (Behavioral Engineer) then worked with the pair. As a student read, the behavioral engineer (BE) provided a green plastic chip for each sentence of five words or more read correctly. The BE also was taught to pair praise with the green chips and to show enthusiasm for successful reading behavior. When a student made an error the BE corrected the error and helped the student finish the sentence. Then he gave the student a red chip, and the other student was allowed to read and receive chips and praise until he made an error. The student began with the sentence in which the error was made thus reinforcing attending while the other student read.

Under the second approach the BE worked with only one student and provided the plastic chips and praise contingent on correct or incorrect sentence reading. Two students worked under this condition after charts of their daily work indicated poor performance under the more competitive condition.

For 45 days the students counted their red and green chips and helped record them at the end of the daily 30-minute sessions. For the final 30 days the chips were counted as usual, and, in addition, the students could turn in their accumulated points for prizes each Friday. Prizes included a variety of toys that ranged in value from 5¢ to $2.00.

3. The third component of the reading program was the daily collection of data. The number of sentences read correctly and incorrectly was recorded daily for each student, and charts of these behaviors were used as a guide to program changes. When the error rate dropped to zero the students were given more difficult reading material. In one case, when both members of a pair of boys began to do poorly, they were given individual tutors, and their rates went up again.

4. The final component was systematic reward and supervision

of the BE. A paraprofessional attended all the sessions and was a general supervisor of data collection. In addition, a counselor and/or consulting psychologist regularly visited the room in which the BEs worked and helped them correct any errors in the procedure. The BEs also were praised regularly for their work. After several weeks they were given distinctive gold pins that signified their successful work. The staff conveyed the idea that the BEs were doing an important job that might well make a long-range difference in the lives of their students.

## RESULTS

The results of this study are presented and evaluated according to the method set forth by Libaw, Berres, and Coleman (1965) to evaluate the effectiveness of treatment of learning difficulties. Measures of the reading levels of the children prior to treatment ranged from 1.3 years to 3.2 years with a mean of 2.2 years. Each child's rate of learning reading skills before the start of treatment was computed. For example, a child who had made 2 years' progress in reading in 4 years of schooling had a pretreatment learning rate of 0.5. Extrapolating on the basis of his rate, each child's achievement at the end of treatment was predicted. Predicted measures were compared with obtained measures at the end of treatment; a Sign Test was significant at the .001 level, which indicated that the $S$s made significantly more progress than predicted. Posttest reading levels ranged from 2.4 years to 4.8 years with a mean of 3.4 years. Thus a mean reading gain of 1.2 years was achieved by the students during the 75 days of treatment. All students exceeded their predicted rate of progress.

Although no control group was used, the fact that the mean IQ remained unchanged (Sign Text $x = 3$, Not Significant) lends further support to the hypothesis that the remedial program was indeed effective to improve reading behavior. Pretest IQs (Slossen Intelligence Test) ranged from 71 to 91 and posttest IQs from 76 to 89, each with a mean of 81.

During a period of 6 weeks prior to the institution of tangible rewards (toys and other small prizes), the students' median number of sentences read correctly each week was 167.5 In the 6 weeks after introduction of tangible rewards, the median was 272.5. A Sign Test ($x = 1$) was significant at the .01 level, which indicates that the tangible rewards were associated with increased reading rate. However, when the slopes of the graphs of individual students were considered, only 5 of the 10 students showed a substantial increase after the tangible rewards were begun. The other 5 continued to increase their rate at a pace comparable to that before the tangible rewards were instituted or actually showed a drop in rate.

## DISCUSSION

The reading test results indicate that the program was very effective and deserves wider use because of its simplicity and economy. Comments by teachers that indicated that the students were more active and interested in their work as well as better readers also offer support for the program. In addition, the school system in which the study was carried out was impressed favorably and has hired a full-time paraprofessional to carry out an expanded version of the program in the coming year. Since the Slossen test is not a comprehensive reading test, future studies should provide measures of a variety of skills including comprehension.

Perhaps the most sensitive measure of reading was the daily chart of correct and incorrect responses kept on each student. The charts were very helpful in making individual program changes and in quickly spotting developing difficulties.

The questionable effect of the tangible rewards with at least five subjects may indicate that, for these students, working with bright, enthusiastic, sincere eighth-grade students produced near maximum performance. The need for an individual prescription of motivating conditions as well as academic material is indicated. Competition may be a motivator for one child and the opposite for another.

The apparent success of this program must be contrasted with the 4 or more years of failure these children had experienced in regular classes. In addition, although the school had a remedial reading program, most of the students in this study were ineligible because their scores were so low it was felt the program would be ineffective. The results obtained through the work of eighth-grade students trained for 2 hours prior to the beginning of the program indicate that techniques are available that show promise to help these children.

# REFERENCES

Hewett, F. Teaching reading to an autistic boy through operant conditioning. *The Reading Teacher,* 1964, 17, 613-618.

Libaw, F., Berres, F., & Coleman, J.C. Evaluating the treatment of learning difficulties. N.J. Long, W.C. Morse, and R. Newman (Eds.), *Conflict in the classroom.* Belmont, Calif.: Wadsworth Publishing, 1965, pp. 505-508.

Staats, A., Minke, K., & Butts, P. A token reinforcement remedial reading program administered by black therapy-technicians to problem black children. *Behavior Therapy,* 1970, 1, 331-363.

# 6
# *Token Reinforcement Programs*

The use of reinforcers to influence academic and social behavior is certainly not new. According to Crossman (1975), in 610 A.D., a monk formed the ends of leftover bread dough into strips which he folded into a twisted loop to represent the folded arms of children in prayer. The baked treat, called a "pretiola" (Latin for "little reward"), was then offered to children as a reward for learning their prayers. Prizes, such as nuts, figs, and honey, were used to reward academic achievement in the 12th century during teaching of the Torah (O'Leary & Drabman, 1971), and in the 1830s, children in New York City schools were rewarded with praise, merit badges, and tickets which could be exchanged for toys (Ravich, 1974). In 1885, the Excelsior School System, a simple token reinforcement system with merits leading to certificates, was deemed so important that it was described in The Library of Congress (Ulman & Klem, 1975). Despite these and other isolated historical examples, token systems were not used routinely until the 1960s.

In the early 1960s, Staats initiated a token program for children with reading difficulties (This early program was discussed in a 1969 paper). About the same time Ayllon and Azrin started a token program for hospitalized psychiatric patients which was reported in 1968. Since then, token reinforcement programs have developed at a very rapid pace and can be found in Head Start centers, physical rehabilitation centers, alcoholic units, and in schools for the blind, retarded, and emotionally disturbed.

The basic ingredients of a token program usually include: (1) a set of instructions to the class about the behaviors that will be reinforced, (2) a means of making a potentially reinforcing stimulus—usually called a token—contingent upon behavior, and (3) a set of rules governing the exchange of tokens for back-up reinforcers, such as prizes or opportunities to engage in special activities. Generally when token programs are initiated, their primary purpose is to bring about rapid behavior change in people who for various reasons appear "unmotivated." The token program with its prizes or back-up reinforcers often serves as an effective "priming" device or means of dramatically increasing the probability of appropriate behaviors. Sometimes, when it is predicted that teacher praise, well-planned lessons, and frequent feedback will be ineffective in reducing classroom disruption and increasing academic achievement, the back-up reinforcers are prizes, such as candy, comics, or educational toys. These prizes are gradually withdrawn and replaced with reinforcers, such as stars and extra recess, that are available to any teacher. When possible, of course, it is recommended the teacher initially use back-up reinforcers, such as recess, special privileges, and free time, as these reinforcers need not be withdrawn. However, with severely disturbed children or adolescents in special classes or hospitals, more powerful reinforcers (e.g., edibles, comics, records, shaving cream) may be most advisable.

A frequent objection to token reinforcement programs is that rewards are sometimes seen as bribes. Unfortunately, the word "bribe" has several accepted meanings (Webster, 1967), and whether or not one considers a token system a form of bribery depends upon which meaning of "bribe" one uses. If a bribe is considered a method of influencing someone's behavior in a corrupt or dishonest manner, then the token programs exemplified in this book clearly do not deserve the term "bribery." On the other hand, if one accepts the secondary dictionary definition of a bribe—to dispense gifts for the purpose of influencing another's judgment or behavior—the token programs presented here clearly would be termed bribery systems. That is, token and back-up reinforcers are purposely made contingent upon appropriate behavior for the purpose of influencing the child's behavior. However, the use of such reinforcement procedures should not be deemed bribery in the sense that they are dishonest or immoral when they are used to establish behavior which is beneficial for the receiver of those reinforcement procedures. The only way one can legitimately regard such token reinforcement systems as methods of bribery is in recognition of the fact that reinforcement is a definite influencing process. A detailed discussion of the issue of bribery is provided by O'Leary, Poulos, and Devine (1971) dealing with both moral and methodological concerns related to tangible reinforcement. For those involved in the implementation of token programs, the consideration of a host of objections to tangible reinforcers by O'Leary et al. (1971) should be useful.

The Ayllon, Layman, and Burke (1972) study illustrated how disruptive classroom behavior can be reduced by reinforcing only academic behavior. To assure that the students understood the value of the tokens early in the program, the teacher gave the students problems which were easy for those students. The students received tokens for answering the questions correctly and *immediately* exchanged these tokens for back-up reinforcers. This study also provides suggestive evidence that systematic presentation of academic material alone (in the absence of token reinforcement) resulted in marked reduction in disruptive behavior (See Fig. 1 from Ayllon et al.).

Teachers might question the reading improvement of between two to four grades in less than 20 hours of reinforcement. This increase probably reflects performance and motivational differences from pre- to post-intervention, not the acquisition of two to four years' knowledge of reading skills in 20 hours. More specifically, these children may have known more than was reflected in their *pre*-treatment scores. Finally, most teachers who have used the SRA reading series know that when students advance from stories or books at SRA grade level 1 to SRA grade level 4, they probably would not show similar advancement on standardized achievement reading tests, such as the California or Metropolitan Reading Tests. Nonetheless, the improvement—even as reflected only in SRA reading level changes—is significant, and it illustrates how educable, mentally retarded children can be successfully motivated to improve academically.

An issue raised by the Ayllon et al. (1972) results is whether the focus of token reinforcement programs should be on academic or social behavior. While we do not advocate reinforcement of academic behavior to the exclusion of reinforcing social behavior, stronger emphasis should be placed on reinforcement of academic behavior, because when one directly reinforces academic behavior, some reduction in disruptive behavior almost always occurs. On the other hand, reinforcing social behavior alone does not always result in increases in academic behavior.

The Long and Williams (1973) article demonstrates the practical use of a group contingency used with junior high school students and compared a group contingency with an individual contingency. A group contingency is simply a contingency placed on a group rather than an individual. The reinforcer used was free time, something which can be regulated by any teacher. In this case, during free time the students could talk with friends, play games, read magazines and comics, use the tape recorder, play records, etc. While the behavior of eight highly disruptive students was observed daily, the group contingency was in effect for all 32 students. Thus, the behavior of any of the 32 students could result in a loss of points for the class (the observers simply watched eight students to obtain specific information on the effects of the group contingency on these eight highly disruptive students). Interestingly, well planned lesson activities and clear rules for classroom conduct did not increase appropriate student behavior, whereas contingent free time did result in increases in appropriate behavior. Of importance to any teacher was the authors' observation that the group contingency procedure was easier to implement than the individual contingency as the teacher did not have to give individual students feedback regarding their behavior. The teacher simply observed the class, and as an inappropriate behavior was displayed by any student, a point was lost. If increasing academic behavior (e.g., number of correctly completed problems) is the desired goal, evaluating the behavior of individual students is an absolute necessity. Therefore, a group contingency program is especially practical when the teacher's desire is to improve general classroom behavior rather than to shape individual children's academic skills. There is also some evidence, though, which suggests that a group contingency program results in greater increases in academic performance than an individual contingency program (Hamblin, Hathaway, & Wodarski, 1971). According to Hamblin et al., these increases in academic performance may have resulted from spontaneous peer tutoring of slow students. Finally, some evidence suggests that appropriate behavior is better maintained following a group reward when compared with an individual reward program (Rosenbaum, O'Leary, & Jacob, 1975), and this maintenance of appropriate behavior may have resulted from peer prompting of appropriate behavior even after a group reward program was removed.

Despite the above noted advantages of group contingency programs, on occasion there may be undue peer pressure evidenced by verbal threats (Axelrod, 1973). Further, one or two children might find it reinforcing to "subvert the program" or "beat the system."

Consequently, any use of a group contingency program must be very explicitly monitored to minimize or avoid such potential side effects (Krasner & Wilson, 1976). Martin (1975) went one step further and recommended that "the group contingency procedure be used only in situations where traditional methods fail and where the teacher makes special efforts to control the severity of the pressure." The present authors favor the recommendation by Krasner and Wilson (1976), i.e., that group contingency programs be carefully monitored although it may be premature to demand that all other alternatives be tried before implementing a group contingency procedure. As Bronfenbrenner (1970) has observed, the Russians have had some competition between rows, classes, and schools for years, but they have done so in a fashion that altruism and a group spirit are fostered. Competition flourishes there in a controlled sense with caring for one's peers held to be a supreme ideal. The altruism is seen not only as helping individuals but also in the sense of "group adoption" where one class takes on responsibility for the upbringing of a group of children at a lower level. An older class may "adopt" a younger class and help them in academic instruction, or one industrial plant may adopt one high school class in helping them prepare for later vocations. In brief, it appears that the general context in which competition occurs has a very significant bearing on the effects of any group contingency. As Long and Williams (1973) noted, choosing between group and individual contingency programs is partly a philosophical one. Especially in the absence of consistent differences between the two types of programs, a teacher's choice will be based on factors, such as whether s/he prefers to stress group efforts and cooperation or independent work and self-reliance.

Teachers often question whether a token reinforcement program can be used with a single student rather than with a whole class. In the individual contingency program of Long and Williams (1973) each child in the class received tokens and back-up reinforcers. In the next study to be presented, usually only one child in the class received token and back-up reinforcers. The study by O'Leary, Pelham, Rosenbaum, and Price (1976) illustrates how a home-based token reinforcement program for nine hyperactive children in eight different classes resulted in significant reductions in hyperactive behavior and specific problem behaviors at school. (The eight hyperactive children in the control group were from eight different classrooms; none of the treated children were in classes with the eight target control children.) Most importantly, the changes in the hyperactive children were comparable to those obtained with stimulant medication, and these changes were the result of a feedback and reinforcement system involving the parents. Although daily report systems have been successfully used by many investigators, they should be used with caution when parents are overly punitive. Negative feedback from the school could prompt aversive parent reactions. Secondly, to be effective, positive daily reports must be backed up by positive parent reactions. Because of this, frequent consultation and encouragement must be provided for the parents. When this consultation and encouragement can be provided, a daily report system can be a highly effective and practical means of motivating children. Some special advantages of the daily report are: (1) it can be used with only one child who needs special attention without developing a token reinforcement system for the whole class; (2) it prompts parental involvement in the child's schooling; (3) the teacher can more easily implement a daily report than a token reinforcement program where rewards or reinforcers are given in the class; (4) the back-up reinforcers are limited only by the ingenuity of the parents; and (5) the daily report system can be gradually faded to twice weekly, weekly, biweekly, monthly, and finally to the regular six to eight week evaluation used by the school.

# Article 14
# Disruptive Behavior and Reinforcement
# of Academic Performances* †

TEODORO AYLLON, DALE LAYMAN, and SANDRA BURKE

Abstract:   A study designed to strengthen academic performance in 4 highly disruptive, educable mentally retarded boys revealed that merely presenting academic material on a systematic basis virtually eliminated their disruptive behavior. When differential reinforcement was applied to math or reading, it resulted in maximal performance on that subject matter which was followed by token reinforcement. Further, within 19 hours of reinforcement contingent upon academic performance, reading comprehension improved from a pre-primer to a second-grade level for two children, and from first grade to fourth grade for the other two children. The data suggest it may be possible to reduce or eliminate disruptive behavior by arranging for systematic presentation of academic material.

The application of behavioral techniques in elementary classrooms has been the subject of several experimental studies. Most of these studies have dealt with increasing the frequency of topographical dimensions in the classroom. Included in these are eye contact with the teacher (Craig & Holland, 1970), out-of-seat behavior (Barrish, Saunders, & Wolf, 1969), and attending to task-oriented

*Reprinted by permission from *The Psychological Record,* 1972, 22, 315-323.

† A portion of this article was presented at the Second Annual Conference on Behavior Analysis in Education, 1971, Lawrence, Kansas. The authors wish to thank Jerry McCullen in the conduct of this study and Louise Berry, George O'Neill, and Michael D. Roberts for their help in the preparation of the manuscript.

behavior (Hall, Lund, & Jackson, 1968; Walker & Buckley, 1968). Only recently has rate of responding to academic stimuli been used as a dependent measure (Lovitt & Curtiss, 1968; McMichael & Corey, 1969; Sheppared & MacDermot, 1970; Glynn, 1970; Myers, 1970; Cristler, Cranston, & Tucker, 1970). Although schools evaluate academic progress through the use of achievement tests, only one study (Wolf, Giles, & Hall, 1968) used these measures to show academic gains through behavioral techniques.

Thus research with elementary school populations has focused solely on one of three major dimensions: (a) topographical behavior in the classroom, (b) behavioral analysis of academic performance, and (c) performance on standardized achievement tests. The present study was concerned with all three dimensions. The first objective was to define empirically a highly disruptive classroom for elementary school children through time-sampling observations; the second, to determine the relative effects of differential reinforcement on academic performance. The third objective was to provide some form of standardized measure to determine the children's academic achievement prior to and after the reinforcement procedures.

## METHOD

### Setting

The setting for this study was an educable mentally retarded classroom of an elementary public school. These children were regarded by the classroom teacher and resource teacher as the most unmotivated, undisciplined and troublesome in the school. The study was conducted in the fall of the regular school year and lasted a total of 23 days. Other than a stopwatch, kitchen timer, and tokens (2" squares of cardboard), no special facilities or equipment were used. Personnel consisted of the teacher and one observer-recorder.

### Subjects

Four students were chosen as $S$s out of a class of 13 children. These four were selected by the teacher as presenting the greatest problem in management; yelling, hitting, and throwing objects were frequently observed. All four were boys—two black and two white.

John and Leon were 13 years old; Wayne and Angelo were 12. I.Q.'s ranged from 72 to 80.

## Strategy

The major objective was to determine whether disruptive behavior could be influenced indirectly through manipulations performed on academic behavior alone. The initial tactic of the study, therefore, was to record disruptive behavior under usual classroom conditions (i.e., teacher was asked to conduct her class in her usual manner). Then, continuing with the recording of disruptive behavior, a procedure was to be added in order to assess academic performance systematically. After obtaining a stable baseline on academic performance, a series of manipulations was to be made and its effects noted not only on academic performance but on disruptive behavior as well.

## Definition of Disruptive Behavior

One $O$ recorded instances of disruptive behavior on a 10-second time-sample basis (see Becker, Madsen, Arnold, & Thomas, 1967). Intermittently, reliability checks were made by a second $O$. Reliability was always greater than 90%. Any occurrence of the following behaviors marked an interval as "disruptive": (a) gross motor (out of seat, walking or running around without purpose or permission, throwing objects), (b) verbalization (talking out loud to self or others, calling out to teacher or other pupils, ringing, whistling, or humming), (c) noise (tapping, pounding objects, feet or fingers, dropping objects, snapping fingers).

## Definition of Academic Performance

The behaviors selected for observation and recorded were those most relevant to academic performance, namely, reading and arithmetic. The focus of measurement was on evaluating $Ss$' academic progress through a medium that (a) required reading and writing of the children and (b) produced standard objective performance records for analysis and evaluation.

Reading was defined as comprehension; it was measured by using

SRA (Scientific Research Associates) programmed materials, Box 1. The level was selected by matching an SRA level with basal reading series level (Scott-Foresman).* The S was presented with a written story to be read silently in 2 minutes, followed by a written multiple choice test of five items, each with three choices, to be completed in 2 minutes. If a student reached 80 percent or more correct responses on two consecutive tests, he was presented the next higher level of SRA.

Arithmetic was defined as addition of whole numbers. Laidlow Series Workbooks 3, 4, and 5 were used to select increasingly difficult problems. The teacher used 5-minute periods for instruction, using the board for examples. At the end of this time she gave a written test of five problems to be correctly computed in 1½ minutes.

## Reinforcers

A large array of events and opportunities for behavior is particularly effective in generating and maintaining a wide range of behaviors (Ayllon & Azrin, 1968; Wolf, Giles, & Hall, 1968). An effort was made in this study to offer opportunities for the child to select an activity (or consumable) from a variety of reinforcers. Tokens (conditioned reinforcers) were used to provide immediate reinforcement which could be exchanged for back-up reinforcers later in the day. The back-up reinforcers included the following items: candy, opportunity for listening to records, playing with perceptual games, playing with puzzles, talking with a friend, access to self-chosen academic materials. The prices ranged from 1 to 5 tokens for each item or opportunity.

For the first 10 days of the experiment, tokens were exchanged for back-up reinforcers immediately after completion of the last test in both academic areas. For the last 9 days of the experiment, tokens were kept by each student until after the lunch break and exchanged for afternoon activities. All tokens had to be exchanged on the same day they were earned.

*The materials used in academic training are referenced below:

France, N., & Clark, B. 1971. *Spectrum.* River Forrest, Ill: Laidlow.

Parker, D.H., & Scannell, G. 1963. *SRA reading laboratory.* Chicago: Scientific Research Associates.

Robinson, H., Monroe, M., Huck, C., Jenkins, W., Aaron, A., Weintroub, S., & Greet, W. 1967. *Basic reading tests.* Glenview, Ill.: Scott Foresman.

## Procedure

For the first 2 days of baseline, the class was observed under regular classroom procedure. On the third day the class was structured (i.e., timed reading and math tests were given) in order to allow for assessment of academic performance.

Academic performance was measured (beginning with the third day) in two academic areas (reading and math) under three experimental conditions: (a) reading and math under extinction, (b) reading under extinction, and math under token reinforcement, (c) math under extinction, token reinforcement for reading.

The baseline procedure lasted for 3 class days. On the third day the class time was divided into 2 consecutive periods of 30 minutes each. During the first period the teacher instructed for 5 minutes and immediately presented a written test. Four of these teaching-testing sessions were presented each day. In the second period, material was distributed to be read by the students. After each 5 minutes a timed written test was given on the content of the material just read. Four of these reading-testing sessions were presented each day. At the end of each test (for both math and reading) the papers were collected, to be graded and returned later during the same day.

After baseline, a short priming procedure was enacted to make sure that all Ss were exposed to the reinforcement contingencies. The teacher wrote three math problems on the board, all below difficulty level of the students. The students were instructed to write the answers on paper before the bell (kitchen timer) rang. Immediately after this test, the teacher went to each student's desk and corrected the paper, giving one token for each right answer. The child was allowed to give back his tokens immediately for candy. The teacher then explained how the children could earn more tokens.

Following this priming period, systematic reinforcement of arithmetic was begun. Here the procedures were the same as under baseline, except that math tests were graded immediately and each correct answer earned one token. Reading was still under extinction. The reading test papers were collected immediately after each test, to be graded and returned later. This procedure lasted 4 days.

During the next 3-day period, reinforcement contingencies were reversed. The teacher explained to the students that math tests would continue to be given, but tokens could be earned only on reading tests. The same procedure of a 30-minute session of math and a 30-minute session of reading was maintained. Reading tests were graded immediately after they were taken, and tokens were given for correct answers. Math tests were collected after each test, to be graded and returned at a later date.

For the next 3 days tokens were again made contingent on the math alone. After this, for a period of 9 days, the contingencies were again reversed—reading was reinforced, math was under extinction. It was during this period that candy was gradually phased out as normal classroom activities were introduced as reinforcers.

## RESULTS

Figure 1 shows the average percentage of disruptive behavior for each phase of the study for all four $Ss$. During the first 2 days of baseline, disruptive behavior was recorded in 98 percent of the intervals. During this period the teacher made many attempts to instruct the children. While her teaching assignments were unsystematic, the very overwhelming discipline problems precluded addi-

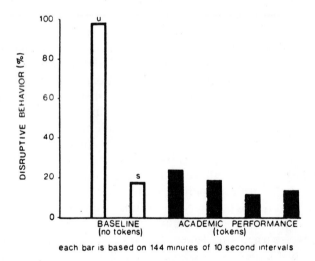

each bar is based on 144 minutes of 10 second intervals

Fig. 1. Percentage of disruptive behavior for four children. The first baseline bar designated with a U shows the level of disruptive behavior under unsystematic presentation of academic material. The second baseline bar designated with an S shows the level of disruptive behavior under systematic presentation of academic material. The remaining bars show the level of disruptive behavior during procedures of reinforcement for academic performance.

tional efforts. On the third day of baseline, when the teacher initiated a systematic set of procedures for presenting and collecting academic material within a fixed time interval, the high percentage of disruptive behavior was quickly and drastically reduced from 98 percent to 17 percent. Although no functional analysis was made, the data suggest that the introduction- of systematic assignments alone may have the effect of reducing disruptive behavior. However, as the measurement of academic performance was then available, the focus of the study shifted to an analysis of math and reading performance.

Figure 2 shows the academic performance for John. The initial 3 days of academic performance without reinforcement showed an average of 3 percent correct answers per test in math and an average of 25 percent correct answers per test in reading. When token reinforcement was made contingent upon math work (John's lowest performance), the percentage of correct responses increased from 3 percent to 75 percent, a gain of 72 percent per test. Reading, which was not reinforced, averaged 25 percent. When tokens were available for reading, the average percentage of reading responses increased from the initial level of 25 percent to 84 percent. Concurrently, under no tokens, the percentage of math responses decreased from 75 percent to 4 percent. When contingencies were again reversed, reinforced math responses increased 59 percent to 65 percent and non-reinforced reading responses decreased 34 percent to 50 percent. In the last period of reversal, the reinforced response, reading, increased from 50 percent to 94 percent. Math, unreinforced, dropped from 63 percent to 50 percent.

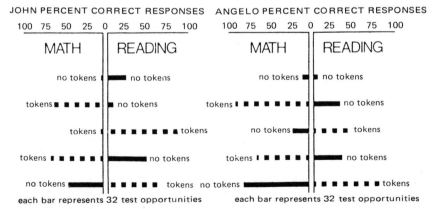

Fig. 2. John's academic performance in percentage. The token reinforcement procedure is preceded by a baseline period during which math and reading result in no tokens.

Fig. 3. Angelo's academic performance in percentage. The token reinforcement procedure is preceded by a baseline period during which math and reading result in no tokens.

Figures 3, 4, and 5 show the performance of each *S* on the same dimensions. The major feature in the individual performance is that they are consistently low prior to reinforcement procedures. John and Wayne were consistent throughout the experiment: The reinforced behavior was relatively high in each phase, and the behavior under extinction remained low in each phase. Angelo and Leon also responded well to the reinforcement procedure. However, during the final phase of the study, when reading was reinforced and math was under extinction, both Angelo and Leon responded to math at a relatively high level, although slightly lower than to reading.

During the conduct of this study, the level of complexity of the reading matter was adjusted upward. John and Leon began with SRA stories at the first-grade level, and in the last period both were reading fourth-grade-level stories. Wayne and Angelo increased in difficulty level from pre-primer to a second-grade level.

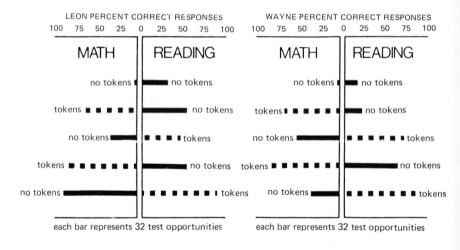

Fig. 4. Leon's academic performance in percentage. The token reinforcement procedure is preceded by a baseline period during which math and reading result in no tokens.

Fig. 5. Wayne's academic performance in percentage. The token reinforcement procedure is preceded by a baseline period during which math and reading result in no tokens.

## DISCUSSION

The reinforcement procedures were singularly effective in raising the academic performance of all four children. Within less than 20 hours of reinforcement procedures, two children improved in reading from pre-primer to second grade. The other two children improved from first to fourth grade. Further, in each case, after a series of exposures to differential reinforcement for a given subject matter, the child's final academic performance was significantly higher than his baseline, even when he did not receive token reinforcement for it. For example, John's math performance was virtually zero during the baseline when he received no tokens. At the conclusion of the study and again receiving no tokens, his math performance was 50 percent higher than his initial performance. The performance of the other three children parallels this finding. While reinforcement was critical in generating academic performance, it would seem that in time the children may begin working on academic material because of its intrinsic reinforcers.

This project has had a dramatic effect on each of the four target *S*s. Prior to this study, Angelo was very sullen, lazy, and hyperactive. He refused to do any work, and his behavior was almost completely out of hand, to the point that he was suspended from school for one week. Now Angelo completes all work and then asks for more. He takes more interest in class activities. He has volunteered to do outside projects and leads the class in singing.

At the beginning of the school term, Leon was most arrogant and lazy; it was on rare occasions that he finished his work. The slightest verbal rebuke from the teacher brought on a temper tantrum that resulted in cursing and throwing objects. Prior to this study, he too was suspended for one week. Leon is now a most conscientious student who never stops until all work is completed. He has not had a temper tantrum since the second week of the project. Leon, too, has volunteered for outside projects and leads the group in singing. He has also taken on the responsibility of teaching another student in the class his multiplication tables.

Prior to and throughout the project, Wayne was taking tranquilizers on doctor's orders. Before the behavioral intervention, Wayne would sleep the entire morning, and no matter how many times he was awakened by the teacher, he fell asleep again. By the afternoon Wayne became completely unmanageable. At present Wayne still sleeps some but not until all his work is completed and handed in. His temper tantrums have also decreased sharply.

According to baseline measures, John was the most disruptive of the four target children. At present, his classroom behavior has improved notably. Further, he now is enthusiastic about doing academic work and asks for math homework and outside science reports.

The impressive progress made by all four children suggests that the time has come for behavioral engineers to be satisfied with nothing less than academic objectives. If academic progress, such as that reported here, can be made with these so-called educable mentally retarded children, then it is time for the same procedure to be applied to assist in the education of the slow, the underachiever, and the undisciplined child. While disruptive behavior and discipline in the classroom are the major, and often the immediate, objectives of the classroom teacher, behavioral applications cannot in good conscience be exploited to foster classroom conformity. On the contrary, the classroom teacher must come to realize that behavioral techniques enable her to rededicate herself to her noble professional objective: the teaching of the young.

## REFERENCES

Ayllon, T., & Azrin, N.H. *The token economy: A motivational system for therapy and rehabilitation.* New York: Appleton-Century-Crofts, 1968.

Barrish, H.H., Saunders, M., & Wolf, M.M. Good behavior game: Effects of individual contingencies for group consequences on disruptive behavior in a classroom. *Journal of Applied Behavior Analysis,* 1969, 2, 119-124.

Becker, W.C., Madsen, C.H., Jr., Arnold, C.R., & Thomas, D.R. The contingent use of teacher attention and praise in reducing classroom behavior problems. *Journal of Special Education,* 1967, 1, 287-307.

Craig, H.B., & Holland, A.L. Reinforcement of visual attending in classrooms for deaf children. *Journal of Applied Behavior Analysis,* 1970. 3, 97-109.

Glynn, E.L. Classroom applications of self-determined reinforcement. *Journal of Applied Behavior Analysis,* 1970, 3, 123-132.

Hall, R.V., Cristler, C., Cranston, S.S., & Tucker, B. Teachers and parents as researchers using multiple baseline designs. *Journal of Applied Behavior Analysis,* 1970, 3, 247-255.

Hall, R.V., Lund, D., & Jackson, D. Effects of teacher attention on study behavior. *Journal of Applied Behavior Analysis,* 1968, 1, 1-12.

Lovitt, T.C., & Curtis, K.A. Academic response rate as a function of teacher- and self-imposed contingencies. *Journal of Applied Behavior Analysis,* 1969, 2, 49-53.

McMichael, J.S., & Corey, J.R. Contingency management in an introductory psychology course produces better learning. *Journal of Applied Behavior Analysis,* 1969, 2, 79-83.

Myers, W.A. Operant learning principles applied to teaching introductory statistics. *Journal of Applied Behavior Analysis,* 1970, 3, 191-197.

Sheppard, W.C., & MacDermot, H.G. Design and evaluation of a programmed course in introductory psychology. *Journal of Applied Behavior Analysis,* 1970, 3, 5-11.

Walker, H.M., & Buckley, N.K. The use of positive reinforcement in conditioning attending behavior. *Journal of Applied Behavior Analysis,* 1968, 1, 245-250.

Wolf, M.M., Giles, D.K., & Hall, R.V. Experiments with token reinforcement in a remedial classroom. *Behavior Research and Therapy,* 1968, 6, 51-64.

g

# Article 15
# The Comparative Effectiveness of Group and Individually Contingent Free Time with Inner-City Junior High School Students*

JAMES D. LONG and ROBERT L. WILLIAMS

Abstract: A major purpose of the study was to assess the relative effects of group *versus* individually contingent free time in modifying student behaviors. Other purposes were to determine the effectiveness of well-planned lesson activities and tokens without back-up reinforcers. Eight students in an inner-city seventh-grade class of 32 blacks served as subjects. Well-organized lesson activities and success feedback via tokens did not produce high levels of desirable behavior. In contrast, group and individually contingent free time produced substantially higher levels of appropriate behavior than did the baseline conditions. The group reinforcement procedure appeared to be slightly more effective than individual reinforcement.

Contingent free time is being used with increasing frequency as a backup reinforcer in classroom management systems (e.g., Anandam & Williams, 1971; Osborne, 1969; Packard, 1970; Williams & Anandam, in press; Williams, Long, & Yaokley, in press). As a backup reinforcer, free time may be contingent on either individual or group performance. Studies using individual contingencies (e.g., Osborne, 1969; Williams et al., in press) typically have involved groups of students rather than single subjects, but with access to desired consequences based upon individual performances. Under such conditions, reinforcement for a given student is dependent only

*Reprinted by permission from the *Journal of Applied Behavior Analysis,* Vol. 6, No. 3, 1973, 465-474. Copyright 1973 by the Society for the Experimental Analysis of Behavior, Inc.

upon his own behavior. In contrast, research studies employing group contingencies (e.g., Packard, 1970; Schmidt, & Ulrich, 1969; Sulzbacher, & Houser, 1968) have made reinforcement for any individual dependent upon the collective behavior of all members of the group.

The comparative effectiveness of group and individual contingencies remains an unresolved issue, largely because researchers have traditionally chosen to apply the two types of contingencies in separate studies and with different students. Only two previous studies have investigated the relative efficacy of group *versus* individually contingent reinforcement. One study (Hamblin, Hathaway, & Wodarski, 1971) revealed that group contingencies have some definite advantages (e.g., spontaneous peer tutoring of slow students) over individual contingencies in accelerating the academic performance of elementary students. The other study (Herman, & Tramontana, 1971) showed that group and individual contingencies were equally effective in reducing the inappropriate behavior of Head Start children. It should be pointed out that undesirable behavior dropped to zero for both conditions when instructions were added to clarify which behaviors were being reinforced. This cellar effect (lack of inappropriate behavior under either condition) in Herman, and Tramontana's research leaves only the Hamblin et al. (1971) study to provide answers regarding the efficacy of group *versus* individual contingencies. Since the latter study involved groupings of seven to nine students, generalization of its findings to regular classrooms of 30 to 40 students might be questionable. The present study attempted to establish the relative potency of group and individually contingent free time in the context of a total class of inner-city junior high school students. Other control and comparison conditions involved structured lesson materials and points without back-up reinforcements.

## METHOD

### Subjects and Setting

The study was conducted in an inner-city junior high school in a metropolitan area of Tennessee. Eight students (five males and three females) in a seventh-grade classroom of 32 blacks served as target subjects. The subjects were selected by the teacher as being the most disruptive students in regular attendance. All students in the classroom were 2 to 4 years behind in at least one subject area and had been grouped together because of low achievement. The treatments were applied in the students' math and geography classes.

The teacher (white, age 29) had received his B.S. in education the previous year and was in his first year of teaching. His classes were selected because he was experiencing major problems in managing classroom behaviors and wanted to participate in research on classroom control.

## Observer Training and Reliability Checks

Ten graduate and two advanced undergraduates served as target student observers. Observer training consisted of the observers and one experimenter simultaneously viewing a video-tape of a simulated classroom situation. The observers and the experimenter made independent judgments every 10 seconds as to the behavior being emitted by the selected target on tape. The records of the trainer and observers were compared interval by interval for agreements over 4 minute segments. An agreement occurred when the trainer and observer recorded the same behavior for the same interval. During the training and the subsequent reliability checks, the percentage of agreement was determined by dividing the number of agreements by the total number of agreements plus disagreements. In the training session, every observer achieved an agreement of 86 percent or better with the trainer on four 4-minute time segments. Subsequently, reliability was reassessed at the beginning of each treatment phase in both the math and geography classes. These classroom checks were conducted using an audible time signal on a cartridge tape recorder, equipped with a "Y" connector to which two ear plugs were connected, thus permitting the trainer and observer to make simultaneous but independent observations. The results of the classroom checks, each covering 32 minutes of observation, ranged from 0.88 to 0.97 (mean = 0.93).

## Recording Student Behaviors

A target student observer was present daily in math and geography for the duration of the study. The same eight students were observed in both classes. The observer began with Subject 1 and recorded the first identifiable response emitted by that subject at the beginning of each 10 second interval. Thus, only one behavior (i.e., the behavior occurring at the beginning of the interval) was logged for each interval. Subjects were observed one at a time for two consecutive minutes. The process was then repeated, beginning anew with Subject 1. Each subject, therefore, was observed for 4 minutes in each class or for a total of 8 minutes daily.

The subjects' behaviors were recorded in three major categories: appropriate behavior, time-off-task, and disruptive behavior. Appropriate behavior consisted of task-relevant responses and appropriate social interactions. Task-relevant behavior was defined as behavior consistent with ongoing lesson activity, e.g., answering or asking lesson-oriented questions, writing when directed to do so, looking at book when asked to do so, and hand raising to get the teacher's attention. Appropriate social interaction was recorded for responses such as laughing, talking, playing games, or just sitting at one's desk when these behaviors were not inconsistent with lesson activity and were not forbidden by the teacher. A behavior was considered as time-off-task when a student was not attending to less activity when instructed to do so. This category included behaviors such as just sitting at one's desk without appropriate materials, looking at non-lesson materials, and gazing out the window. Non-attending behavior was considered as time-off-task only if it was not distracting to other students. Disruptive behaviors were recorded for motor responses (e.g., getting out of seat without permission, standing up, walking around, rocking, squirming), noise making (e.g., tapping feet, tearing papers, or any nonverbal behavior not directly involved in task-relevant or appropriate social interaction), verbalizations (e.g., whistling, engaging in conversation by either talking or listening, and related behaviors not consistent with task-relevant or appropriate social interactions), and aggressions (e.g., hitting, pushing, slapping).

## Experimental Conditions

The overall procedure followed the standard intra-subject design where each subject acted as his own control (Sidman, 1969, pp. 317-340). Aspects of both reversal and multiple baselines were employed in the design, with data being recorded in math and geography during seven and eight experimental phases, respectively.

*I. Math—baseline, geography—baseline*
The students were together with the same teacher from 9:45 a.m. until 12:30 p.m., Monday through Friday. The classes selected for

observation were math (9:45 to 10:30) and geography (11:30 to 12:30). A lunch period separated the two classes. The corresponding baselines taken in math and geography reflected the frequency of specified student behaviors under usual classroom conditions.

## II. Math—structured lessons, geography—baseline

During the second phase, structured lessons were introduced in math but not in geography. In all the structured lesson phases, the teacher stood at the classroom door and provided a mimeographed handout of the day's lesson to each child as he entered. Additionally, rules of classroom conduct were made explicit during the structured-lessons phase. The teacher specified the rules and subsequently reviewed them sometime during each math period. The main rules were: (1) be in your seat and ready to start lesson by the time the second bell sounds; (2) bring paper and pencil to class every day; and, (3) work quietly, remain in your seat, and do not make unnecessary noise. No consequences were specified for adhering or not adhering to the rules. With the exception of implementing the experimental conditions (i.e., providing structured lessons, specifying rules), the teacher was free to respond in his usual manner. The basic reason for including this phase was to determine whether providing structured lessons and rules without implementing other changes (e.g., points for appropriate behavior, back-up consequences in the form of individually and group contingent free time) would produce effective behavioral changes.

## III. Math—group contingent free time, geography—structured lessons

In the third phase, group consequences were added to the structured lessons in math, whereas the structured lessons alone were implemented in the geography class. While group contingencies were in effect, a rotary-type file with 18 cards was mounted on the teacher's desk. The teacher gave the following instructions in introducing this treatment:

> For the next few days you will be able to earn certain privileges by helping to make a better classroom. By obeying the class rules, you can earn 18 minutes of free time each day. However, the free time can only be earned if every student cooperates. Each time any student violates a rule, I will flip *(demonstrates)* one of these cards, and the entire class will have one less minute of free time.
> We will stop the lesson activities near the end of regular

class time so that you may use the minutes of free time showing on the last card that has not been flipped. During your free time, you may engage in the following activities: talk with friends, play games, work on other assignments, read magazines and comics, play records, use the tape recorder, write on the chalk board, color, or spend your time in any activity that does not disturb others.

*IV. Math—structured lessons, geography—group contingent free time.*
During Phase IV, the group consequences were eliminated in math while being added to the previous condition in geography.

*V. Math—individually contingent free time, geography—structured lessons*
In this phase, individually contingent consequences were added in math at the same time group consequences were being withdrawn in geography. Individually contingent free time was implemented via a point system in which each student had to earn a minimum of 12 from a possible 16 points before being permitted to participate in free-time activities. Students earned two points for each preparatory behavior (i.e., being present, ready to start lessons at the sounding of the tardy bell, and bringing appropriate materials). Two additional points were awarded during each of three variable time intervals in which a student remained in his seat and worked quietly. A kitchen timer was used to signal the three time intervals, which ranged from 1 to 10 minutes. Four required points for engaging in free time were earned by completing the assignment. The behaviors for which students could earn points were intended to reflect the rules specified during structured lessons. For example, students in the group contingencies were penalized when observed not working quietly on their assignments. Similarly, during the individual contingencies, students lost points for a failure to work quietly during the variable time intervals.

Under the individually contingent free time, the teacher was asked to provide lessons that could be completed between 15 and 20 minutes before the end of class. How much free time a child earned, then, was a function of how quickly he completed assignments and how many points he earned for appropriate social behaviors. The students maintained their own point sheets, but these records were checked by the teacher before the student received free time. The teacher independently recorded any rule violations (i.e., failure to earn points) as a means of cross-checking the accuracy of the students' point sheets.

*VI. Math—structured lessons, geography—individually contingent free time*
During the sixth phase, the math class was returned to the structured lessons condition. Correspondingly, individual consequences were implemented in geography.

*VII. Math—points, geography—structured lessons*
Phase VII in math consisted of reimplementing the point system used in connection with the individually contingent free time. However, under the new condition, the points had no exchange value. The students maintained their own point sheets as they had done earlier. In the meantime, the geography class returned to the structured lessons condition.

*VIII. Geography—points*

## RESULTS

### Group Data

As can be seen from Fig. 1, the average percentages of appropriate behavior during the baseline periods were extremely low. The group means of appropriate behavior in math and geography were 31 percent and 29 percent, respectively. In Phase II, when the structured lessons condition was instituted in math, no noteworthy changes occurred. During the concomitant geography period, where baseline was still in effect, appropriate behavior continued at low levels.

Only the introduction of group and individually contingent free-time phases produced immediate and dramatic improvement in behavior. For example, when the group contingencies were first applied in the math class (Phase III), there was a sharp rise in appropriate behavior. The daily mean of appropriate behavior during the math group contingent free-time phase ranged from 65 percent to 98 percent (mean = 80%), while the daily rates of appropriate behavior during the corresponding structured lessons phase in geography ranged from 16 percent to 48 percent (mean = 31%).

During the fourth phase, when group consequences were withdrawn in math, rates of appropriate behavior declined to 50 percent. In the corresponding phase for geography, group contingent free time was introduced and the students' appropriate responses climbed

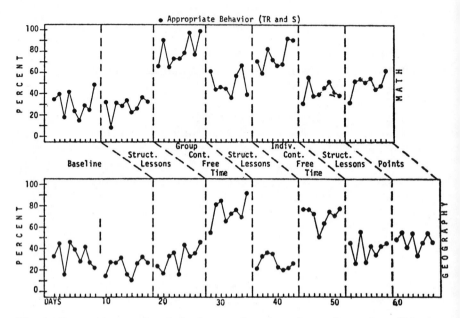

Fig. 1. Group: Appropriate behavior as a function of experimental conditions. TR = task relevant, S = appropriate social interactions.

to a daily average of 74 percent.

In the next phase, individually contingent free time was instituted in math. Concomitantly, the geography class returned to the structured-lessons condition. In this phase, the subjects yielded an average of 76 percent appropriate behavior during math and 26 percent during geography.

During the sixth treatment phase, individually contingent free time was simultaneously withdrawn in math and initiated in geography. At the outset of this phase, the match class was returned to the structured-lessons condition. Group levels of appropriate behavior in geography increased rapidly to a daily mean of 70 percent. Conversely, the group sharply reduced appropriate responses in math to a 43 percent average.

Progression to the final phase (points) in math increased the level of appropriate behavior approximately 7 percent above the preceding structured-lessons condition. Concurrently, the geography class returned to the structured lessons following the removal of the individually contingent free time. During this phase, the group reduced appropriate responding to 39 percent in the geography class. When the geography class advanced to the final points phase, the group produced a daily mean of 47 percent appropriate behavior. Although the group emitted far less appropriate behavior under the points phase than under the individual or group contingencies, the points phase was more effective than the structured lessons.

## Single Subject Data

With minor exceptions, the individual subject data corresponded to the previously delineated group trends (see Tables 1 and 2). For

**Table 1. Group and Individual Subjects' Mean Percentages of Appropriate Time-Off Task, and Disruptive Behavior for Each Phase in Math.**

|  | Baseline | Struct. Lessons | Group Cont. Free Time | Struct. Lessons | Indiv. Cont. Free Time | Struct. Lessons | Points |
|---|---|---|---|---|---|---|---|
| *Appropriate* | | | | | | | |
| Group Mean | 31 | 29 | 80 | 50 | 76 | 43 | 50 |
| Subject 1 | 12 | 23 | 74 | 36 | 58 | 23 | 35 |
| 2 | 38 | 24 | 72 | 58 | 71 | 38 | 27 |
| 3 | 29 | 29 | 84 | 61 | 82 | 58 | 70 |
| 4 | 42 | 42 | 87 | 63 | 86 | 58 | 69 |
| 5 | 38 | 20 | 91 | 46 | 87 | 55 | 57 |
| 6 | 33 | 38 | 85 | 58 | 86 | 48 | 50 |
| 7 | 23 | 32 | 71 | 46 | 72 | 30 | 33 |
| 8 | 30 | 23 | 77 | 28 | 68 | 33 | 61 |
| *Time-off-task* | | | | | | | |
| Group Mean | 33 | 34 | 14 | 31 | 14 | 32 | 20 |
| Subject 1 | 58 | 56 | 22 | 42 | 31 | 53 | 25 |
| 2 | 19 | 29 | 22 | 18 | 11 | 27 | 26 |
| 3 | 26 | 29 | 6 | 19 | 12 | 24 | 14 |
| 4 | 24 | 31 | 8 | 20 | 10 | 20 | 5 |
| 5 | 32 | 23 | 7 | 40 | 10 | 40 | 22 |
| 6 | 41 | 25 | 6 | 29 | 9 | 30 | 17 |
| 7 | 27 | 29 | 21 | 29 | 10 | 33 | 29 |
| 8 | 36 | 50 | 19 | 49 | 17 | 30 | 18 |
| *Disruptive* | | | | | | | |
| Group Mean | 36 | 37 | 6 | 20 | 10 | 25 | 30 |
| Subject 1 | 30 | 21 | 4 | 22 | 11 | 23 | 40 |
| 2 | 42 | 47 | 5 | 24 | 18 | 35 | 47 |
| 3 | 45 | 42 | 10 | 19 | 6 | 17 | 16 |
| 4 | 33 | 27 | 5 | 17 | 4 | 22 | 26 |
| 5 | 29 | 57 | 2 | 14 | 3 | 5 | 21 |
| 6 | 26 | 37 | 9 | 13 | 5 | 22 | 32 |
| 7 | 50 | 39 | 8 | 25 | 17 | 37 | 38 |
| 8 | 34 | 27 | 4 | 23 | 15 | 37 | 21 |

example, group means reveal that the group contingent consequences yielded higher rates of appropriate behavior in math and geography than did the individually contingent consequences. An examination of each subject's data showed that in math, six of the eight target students reached higher levels of desired behavior under group than under individual contingencies. Similarly, in geography, five of the subjects performed better during the group contingent free time. The group means also accurately reflect data obtained for single subjects

**Table 2. Group and Individual Subjects' Mean Percentages of Appropriate Time-Off Task, and Disruptive Behavior for Each Phase in Geography.**

|  | Baseline | Struct. Lessons | Group Cont. Free Time | Struct. Lessons | Indiv. Cont. Free Time | Struct. Lessons | Point |
|---|---|---|---|---|---|---|---|
| | | | Appropriate | | | | |
| Group Mean | 29 | 31 | 74 | 26 | 70 | 39 | 47 |
| Subject 1 | 13 | 12 | 76 | 14 | 62 | 8 | 19 |
| 2 | 28 | 23 | 65 | 7 | 64 | 33 | 61 |
| 3 | 33 | 35 | 76 | 49 | 74 | 49 | 64 |
| 4 | 41 | 43 | 80 | 35 | 81 | 46 | 58 |
| 5 | 30 | 41 | 78 | 24 | 82 | 63 | 48 |
| 6 | 37 | 35 | 84 | 22 | 71 | 48 | 66 |
| 7 | 25 | 33 | 70 | 38 | 73 | 36 | 35 |
| 8 | 26 | 30 | 65 | 19 | 54 | 30 | 26 |
| | | | Time-off-task | | | | |
| Group Mean | 39 | 37 | 12 | 38 | 17 | 27 | 28 |
| Subject 1 | 63 | 63 | 15 | 63 | 35 | 45 | 55 |
| 2 | 33 | 43 | 23 | 40 | 19 | 19 | 15 |
| 3 | 39 | 28 | 10 | 22 | 15 | 24 | 20 |
| 4 | 30 | 13 | 5 | 28 | 4 | 18 | 14 |
| 5 | 49 | 42 | 8 | 48 | 12 | 24 | 35 |
| 6 | 27 | 28 | 10 | 30 | 16 | 24 | 15 |
| 7 | 38 | 33 | 6 | 29 | 15 | 27 | 27 |
| 8 | 31 | 42 | 18 | 45 | 19 | 33 | 42 |
| | | | Disruptive | | | | |
| Group Mean | 32 | 32 | 14 | 36 | 13 | 34 | 25 |
| Subject 1 | 24 | 25 | 9 | 23 | 3 | 47 | 26 |
| 2 | 38 | 34 | 12 | 53 | 17 | 48 | 24 |
| 3 | 28 | 37 | 14 | 29 | 10 | 27 | 16 |
| 4 | 29 | 44 | 15 | 37 | 15 | 36 | 28 |
| 5 | 21 | 17 | 14 | 27 | 6 | 13 | 17 |
| 6 | 36 | 37 | 6 | 48 | 13 | 28 | 19 |
| 7 | 37 | 34 | 23 | 33 | 12 | 37 | 38 |
| 8 | 43 | 28 | 17 | 36 | 26 | 37 | 32 |

during other phases. Group averages of appropriate behavior, for example, demonstrate the superiority of individual contingencies over the points phase. All eight subjects achieved higher rates of appropriate behavior in math and geography under the individual contingencies than under the points phase. The primary difference between the group and individual subject data was the greater day-to-day variability evidenced by the individual subjects. Figure 2 shows behavioral changes for one of the more consistent subjects and Fig. 3 for one of the least consistent (see Figs. 2 and 3). Despite the variability they reveal, Figs. 2 and 3 show that overall treatment effects were essentially the same for individual subjects as for the group.

## DISCUSSION

Both the group and individually contingent free time proved to be highly efficient techniques for improving behavior in an inner-city classroom. Although differences between the two approaches were minimal for the majority of subjects (see Tables 1 and 2), the group approach did maintain slightly higher levels of appropriate behavior and greater day-to-day stability within and between subjects. Also, the group procedure made fewer demands on the teacher's time and seemed to be a simpler procedure to implement. Under the group contingent free time, for example, the teacher had merely to censor one student and the others behaved more appropriately.

The differences between the group and individual contingencies may, to some extent, have been a function of variation in procedures. Attempts were made to keep the two conditions similar except for the method by which students earned free time. The rules during the structured-lessons phase served as the basis for earning points during the individually contingent free time and constituted the source of penalties for the group condition. However, the amount of free time a student earned was not consistent across the conditions. Under the individually contingent free time, the teacher attempted to plan lessons to approximate the amount of free time students earned in the group contingent phase, but the actual time earned under the individual phase depended largely upon how quickly a student completed his assignment.

The selection of either group or individually contingent consequences as a classroom management technique, as the issue now stands, is to some degree a philosophical decision. Some teachers may

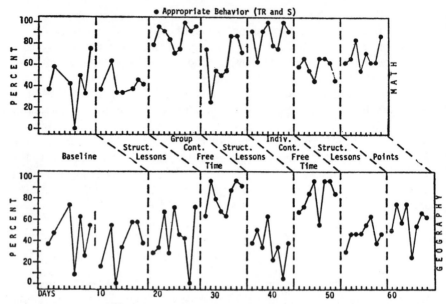

Fig. 2. Subject 4: Appropriate behavior as a function of experimental conditions. TR = task relevant, S = appropriate social interactions.

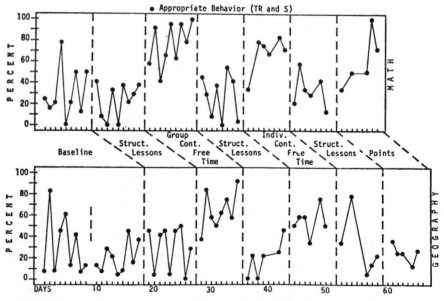

Fig. 3. Subject 8: Appropriate behavior as a function of experimental conditions. TR = task relevant, S = appropriate social interactions.

be opposed to penalizing or rewarding students on the basis of other students' behavior. If a teacher is convinced that the goals of education can best be served through independent accomplishments, he may be quite uncomfortable in using group contingencies. Conversely, others may regard group consequences as a method of achieving cooperation and commitment to common goals.

In attempting to compare individual and group contingencies, the authors had considered the possibility that type of organization (e.g., well-planned lesson activities and clearcut rules for classroom conduct) imposed on the environment, rather than back-up reinforcement, might be the real source of change produced by group and individual reinforcement programs. For these inner-city students, however, simply knowing what was expected of them was not enough to get them to perform better. The authors also considered the possibility that giving of tokens (e.g., points) *per se* could be the basis of desirable behavior changes. After all, tokens do provide immediate feedback as to whether a student is performing appropriately or inappropriately. Several previous studies (e.g., Jens & Shores, 1969; Jessee, unpublished; Sulzer, unpublished; Sulzer, Hunt, Ashby, Koniarski, & Krams, 1971) have indicated that points alone produce temporary improvements in behavior. However, with the highly disruptive students in the present study, tokens alone were not sufficiently potent to produce marked improvements. In contrast, group and individually contingent free time both produced generally acceptable frequencies (70 to 80%) of appropriate responses.

## REFERENCES

Anandam, K., & Williams, R.L. A model for consultation with classroom teachers on behavior management. *The School Counselor,* 1971, 4, 253-259.

Hamblin, R.T., Hathaway, C., & Wodarski, J. Group contingencies, peer tutoring and accelerating academic achievement. In E. Ramp and B.L. Hopkins (Eds.), *A new direction for education: Behavior analysis 1971.* Lawrence: The University of Kansas, 1971, Pp. 41-53.

Herman, S.H., & Tramontana, J. Instructions and group *versus* individual reinforcement in modifying disruptive group behavior. *Journal of Applied Behavior Analysis,* 1971, 4, 113-119.

Jens, K.G., & Shores, R.E. Educational materials: Behavior graphs as reinforcers for work behavior of mentally retarded adolescents. *Education and Training of the Mentally Retarded,* 1971, 4, 21-27.

Jessee, R.E. *The effects of points and backup reinforcers on appropriate classroom behavior.* Unpublished Master's thesis, University of Tennessee, 1971.

Osborne, J.G. Free-time as a reinforcer in the management of classroom behavior. *Journal of Applied Behavior Analysis,* 1969, 2, 113-118.

Packard, R.G. The control of "classroom attention": A group contingency for complex behavior. *Journal of Applied Behavior Analysis,* 1970, 3, 13-28.

Schmidt, G.W., & Ulrich, R.E. Effects of group contingent events upon classroom noise. *Journal of Applied Behavior Analysis,* 1969, 2, 171-179.

Sidman, M. *Tactics of scientific research.* New York: Basic Books, 1960.

Sulzbacher, S.I., & Houser, J.E. A tactic to eliminate disruptive behaviors in the classroom: Group contingent consequences. *American Journal of Mental Deficiency,* 1968, 73, 88-90.

Sulzer, B. *Matched to sample performance by normals and institutionalized retardates under different reinforcing conditions.* Unpublished Doctoral dissertation, University of Minnesota, 1966.

Sulzer, B., Hunt, S., Ashby, E., Koniarski, C., & Krams, M. Increasing rate and percentage correct in reading and spelling in a fifth grade public school class of slow readers by means of a token system. In E. Ramp & B.L. Hopkins (Eds.), *A new direction for education: Behavior analysis 1971.* Lawrence: The University of Kansas, 1971. Pp. 5-28.

Williams, R.L., & Anandam, K. The effect of behavior contracting on grades. *Journal of Educational Research* (in press).

Williams, R.L., Long, J.D., & Yaokley, R.W. The utility of behavior contracts and behavior proclamations with advantaged senior high school students. *Journal of School Psychology* (in press).

# Article 16
# Behavioral Treatment of Hyperkinetic Children:
# An Experimental Evaluation of its Usefulness*†

K. DANIEL O'LEARY, WILLIAM E. PELHAM,
ALAN ROSENBAUM, and GLORIA H. PRICE

Pharmacologic treatment of children diagnosed as hyperkinetic has been shown repeatedly to alter teacher ratings of hyperactivity and classroom disruption (Conners, 1971). However, physicians have expressed concern over side effects associated with stimulant medication, which is the preferred drug therapy for hyperkinesia. Suppression of growth, (Safer, & Allen, 1973) increased heart rate, or blood pressure elevations (Cohen, Douglas, & Morganstern, 1971; Knights, & Hinton, 1969; Rapoport, Quinn, Bradbard, Riddle, & Brooks, 1974) have been described with stimulant drugs. Moreover, in 30 to 50 percent of the cases, central stimulants are not effective even on a short-term basis (Wender, 1971; Fish, 1971). Consequently, it has become apparent that alternatives or supplements to pharmacologic treatment of hyperkinetic children are needed.

Several behavior therapy procedures have been shown effective in reducing excessive seat movements and disruption in special classrooms for retarded, hyperactive children (Patterson, Shaw, & Ebner, 1969; Christensen, & Sprague, 1973). The incidence of hyperkinesia is such that it is likely that there is one hyperkinetic child in almost every elementary school classroom (Dept of Health, Education &

*Reprinted by permission from *Clinical Pediatrics,* Vol. 15, No. 6, 1976, 510-515.

†This research was supported by Office of Education Grant OEG-0-71-28-72. The opinions expressed herein, however, do not necessarily reflect the position or policy of the U.S. Office of Education.

Welfare, 1971). We have carried out a controlled evaluation of a behavior treatment program for hyperkinetic children attending normal or nonremedial classes.

## GENERAL DESIGN AND MEASURES OF CHANGE

Teachers of children referred for hyperactivity were asked to use the Abbreviated Conners' Teacher Rating Scale (TRS), and children who received extreme scores ($\geq 15$) were taken into our study. The children thus referred were assigned randomly to the behavioral treatment group (N = 9), or a control group (N = 8). Those in the control group were not contacted until later.

The treatment given lasted for a ten-week period. Treatment effectiveness was assessed by the standardized TRS and by an individualized Problem Behavior Rating (PBR) established for each child. The TRS, shown to be sensitive to drug effects, has been widely used as a standardized measure of change in studies with hyperkinetic children (Sleator, & von Neumann, 1974). The PBR consisted of an eight-point target rating of the severity of four or five problem behaviors for each child (0 = no problem; 1, 2, 3 = mild or infrequent problem; 4, 5, 6 = serious or frequent problem; 7 = severe problem). All children referred for hyperkinesia were compared with randomly selected same-sex peers.

### Subject Selection

The children all came from the same large elementary school, grades 3-5, in a lower middle-class area. Teachers who referred children to us were told that our program would involve parents, and they were asked to refer parents who they thought might be cooperative and who had telephones. Actually, one parent of a treated child did not have a phone but was reached via ham-radio contact with a neighbor.

The children ranged in age from 8 years, 11 months to 10 years, 11 months; their average age was 10 years. As mentioned earlier, in order to be selected for the study: a child had to have a score $\geq 15$ on the TRS (Sleator, & von Neumann, 1974). The average score in the current sample of hyperkinetic children was 19.7, whereas a sample of randomly selected same-sex peers in the same rooms as our hyperkinetic children had an average score of 5.1 ($p < .001$).

In order to obtain some independent validation of the teacher ratings, observations of hyperactivity were made of the referred children (N = 17) and of randomly selected same-sex peers (N = 17) in the same classrooms. Each referred child and his randomly selected classmate were watched for simultaneous ten-minute classroom periods by trained observers who scored in 20-second intervals the presence of three behaviors symptomatic of hyperkinesis: locomotion, fidgeting, and not attending to task. (The observers had been trained to a reliability criterion of .85 before making these observations.) The children referred for hyperkinesia had significantly higher scores based on the average of these three behaviors than control subjects ($p < .025$).*

To allow normative comparison of our treated subjects with other previously published studies on hyperkinesia, the following assessments were made: Wechsler Intelligence Scale for Children, Wide Range Achievement Test (WRAT), NIMH Physical and Neurologic Examination for Soft Signs (PANESS), and the Werry-Weiss-Peters Activity Scale (Werry & Sprague, 1970).

All the children were of average intelligence, and seven of the nine were below average in achievement ($\geqslant$ 1 grade in math, spelling, or reading on WRAT). All of the children were above average on the activity scale completed by the parents (X = 20); this average is more than double the scores obtained from nine-year-old normal controls (Routh, Schroeder, & O'Tuama, 1974). On the PANESS, treated subjects had an average of 1.5 Soft Signs (range 0-4) as indicated by extreme scores on PANESS items. None of the children were receiving medication for hyperkinesia, although two of the treated children had been given Ritalin during the previous school year.

No behavior-control drugs were administered during any of these periods of experimental observation.

In sum, using standardization ratings, the children we selected for the program were deemed by both teachers and parents as being hyperkinetic. They were of average intelligence but lagged academically. When observed critically for hyperactivity, they were significantly different from randomly selected peer-classmates.

---

*Details about method of reliability calculation and methodologic issues concerning classroom observation can be obtained from the senior author.

## Management

The primary treatment consisted of a home-based reward program. This program had five components: (1) specification of each child's daily classroom goals; (2) praising the child for efforts to achieve those goals; (3) end-of-day evaluation of the child's behavior relevant to the specified goals; (4) sending the parents a daily report card on their child's daily progress; and (5) rewarding of the child by the parent for progress toward his goals.

The program began with a conference between the therapist and the parents. In this, the therapist obtained information about the child's behavior at home, and explained the parents' role in the program, including the selection of suitable rewards for the child. The therapist also met with the child's teacher for approximately one hour to choose the behavioral goals for the child. Throughout the program, the therapist maintained weekly contact with the parents by telephone and with the teachers through visits.

Selection of the child's school goals was a crucial aspect of the management program. Examples of the goals chosen were: completing assigned math, helping neighbor with class project, not fighting, bringing in homework. We did not reinforce the children directly for sitting still, attending, or not fidgeting. Instead, academic and prosocial goals were given priority as most salient behaviors to be changed.

During the program period, the teacher advised the parents on their child's progress by means of a daily report card (Table 1). At the end of each day, the teacher completed the daily report, to be taken home by the child to his parents. They, in turn, rewarded him every time he had met his goals for the day, as indicated by the teacher's report. When more than one goal was established, the teacher used his or her judgment in deciding whether a child should get a reward from his parents. This judgment was based on an impression of overall improvement or lack thereof.

Perhaps the most critical element of the program was the selection of appropriate rewards for the children. Care and ingenuity were exercised in selecting maximally motivating rewards. Several examples of frequently used rewards were: (1) 30 minutes extra television, (2) a special dessert, (3) spending time with either parent playing a game such as checkers, and (4) money to spend. In addition to those daily rewards, the children were given weekly rewards when four out of five daily report cards indicated improvement. Among the weekly rewards were a fishing trip with father, a dinner at a

**Table 1. Daily Report Card (Submitted Daily by Teacher to Parents).**

Name of Child _____

|  | Yes | No |
|---|---|---|
| 1. Finished math assignment | _____ | _____ |
| 2. 80 percent correct in spelling | _____ | _____ |
| 3. Cooperated with others | _____ | _____ |
|     Should get reward: | _____ | _____ |

Date: _____    Teacher's Signature: _____

favorite aunt's, and a family meal at a "fast-food" restaurant.

Only in two cases, where the parents did not consistently reward their children, was it necessary to establish an in-school reward program. These rewards consisted of a piece of candy per day for one child and "free time" in the school library for the other.

Just as no single drug or dose is appropriate for all hyperkinetic children, no single type of reward program can suffice for all cases. When one type of reward program fails to produce significant behavioral improvement, the therapist should consider modifying the program. The wide range of possible reward programs, limited only by environmental constraints and the ingenuity of the therapists, makes it likely that a behavioral program can be individually tailored for each child.

## Observations Made

The PBR and the TRS were the two primary measures utilized. These provided complementary information regarding behavior change—the PBR is individualized for each child, whereas the TRS is a standardized measure of a number of behaviors thought to be present in the hyperkinetic syndrome.

With the PBR, treatment and control groups did not differ significantly at the beginning of treatment, but they were significantly different by the end of treatment ($p < .012$) (Fig. 1). Both groups showed some decline, but only the change in the treatment group was significant ($p < .005$). Seven of the treated subjects improved $\geq 25$ percent on the PBR, whereas only two of the control

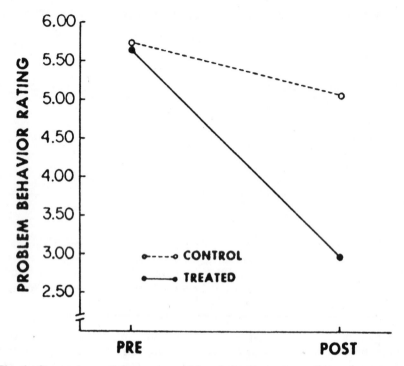

Fig. 1. Comparison of the mean problem behavior ratings of nine hyperkinetic children treated with behavior therapy, and of eight similar controls.

subjects evidenced such improvement.

With the TRS, also, both groups were essentially equivalent prior to treatment. (Fig. 2). During the treatment period, both groups improved significantly ($p < .005$), but at the end of the period the treated children's scores were significantly lower than the control ($p < .066$). Eight of the nine treated subjects showed improvement. In seven of these, the gains ($\geq 25\%$) with the TRS were quite substantial. Only one of the control subjects made gains of that magnitude. The changes on the TRS were generally comparable to the changes reported with stimulant drugs (Conners, 1972).

## Discussion

These results relate critically to the most commonly used treatment for hyperkinetic children, namely, stimulant drugs such as

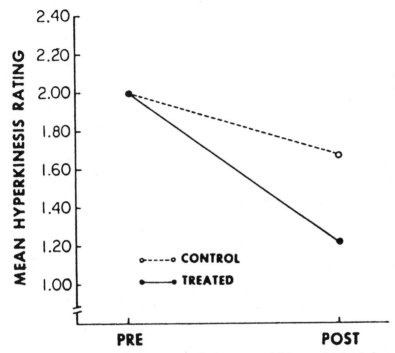

Fig. 2. Mean hyperkinesia ratings of the same children, obtained from the Teacher Rating Scale (TRS). The data reflect the mean item ratings (range 0.0-3.0) on the ten-item TRS.

methylphenidate (Ritalin) and dextroamphetamine.

First, stimulant therapy is quite effective with many hyperkinetic children (50 to 70% do respond), but not all will respond (Wender, 1971; Fish, 1971). When a pediatrician takes care of a child who fails to improve with medication, he should be aware of alternative modes of treatment. In our experience, behavior therapy can be an effective alternative for some hyperkinetic children.

Although early reports indicated that the adverse side effects of stimulant therapy were of limited duration, controllable by adjusting dosage, and thus of relatively small concern, different conclusions have been reached in recent studies. Safer and Allen (1973) reported suppression of growth in weight and height in some treated children. Other physiologic changes have been discovered which are attributed to the central effects of the drug while it is being administered (Cohen, Douglas, & Morganstern, 1971; Knights & Hinton, 1969; Rapoport, Quinn, Bradbard, Riddle, & Brooks, 1974). Obviously more research is needed, such as that of Sleator and von Neumann (1974), to assess the minimal dosages required for cognitive and social changes. It may be feasible to obtain desired results by combining lower and presumably safer dosages of stimulants with behavior therapy.

It is curious that, although stimulant drugs such as Ritalin are recommended "as adjunctive therapy to other remedial measures" in the treatment of hyperkinesis (Physicians Desk Reference, 1973), an all-too-common practice seems to be that of medicating these children to the exclusion of other remedial measures. Yet a number of recent reviews and discussions have stressed the importance of combining drug therapy with other forms of intervention for hyperkinesis (Eisenberg, 1972; Sroufe & Stewart, 1973; O'Malley & Eisenberg, 1973; Sroufe, 1975). Unfortunately, however, the effectiveness of other treatment and remedial measures has not been well documented, so that the pediatrician has the dilemma of not knowing which adjunctive therapy to utilize. On the basis of other controlled case studies and our own observations, behavior therapy appears to be an effective adjunct.

Drug therapy alone, may be helpful with hyperkinesia in the short term, but there is little evidence that drug therapy achieves any long-term change in the hyperkinetic child's social and academic behavior (Sroufe & Stewart, 1973). We have seen a number of children who, after having been on stimulant medication for a year or more, have reverted to their original behavior patterns immediately upon discontinuance of the medication. For, as Eisenberg (1972) has noted, drugs do not produce social or academic learning; they merely make it possible. Consequently, unless the calming effects of medication are associated with adjunctive, educational and psychologic management, any improvement in the child's behavior will not be lasting.

Finally, one other aspect of the effectiveness of drug treatment of hyperkinesia merits consideration. What effects do drugs have on a hyperkinetic child's problems at home? Therapy directed toward the home problems is as important as therapy directed toward school problems. Unfortunately, because of the anorexic and insomnious effects of the drugs, these often cannot be given in the late afternoon. As a consequence, their action may not continue into the evening. This is where adjunctive therapy dealing with home problems of hyperkinetic children becomes clearly desirable and often critical. Because of practical considerations we did not work with behavior in the home setting in this study, but we feel quite strongly, that because of its emphasis on parental involvement, behavior therapy is uniquely suited for use as adjunctive therapy in the home, during the evenings. In our every day clinical management of such children, we routinely and quite successfully utilize parent training as part of family therapy.

## Summary

Although drug therapy is helpful in the control of many children with hyperkinesia, alternative and adjunctive therapies are needed also, for a number of reasons: (1) not all of these children improve with medication; (2) the drugs may have adverse physiologic effects which at the least dictate caution in their use; (3) medication alone does not always return responding children to normal functioning; and (4) drug action cannot often be used to help with problems occurring in the children's home setting after school hours.

The data here presented suggest strongly that behavior therapy can be effective for hyperkinesia.

Since other therapeutic resources may be available in his community also, we urge the pediatrician to investigate and to make use of these resources as adjunctive or alternative approaches to the management of children diagnosed as being hyperkinetic.

## ACKNOWLEDGMENTS

Thanks are due Rolf Jacob, M.D., who consulted with us and who prompted us to begin research with hyperactive children (Jacob, O'Leary, & Price, unpublished manuscript, 1974, available from O'Leary). We are especially thankful to Carl Rosenblad, principal, Wm. Floyd Elementary School, for his cooperation.

# REFERENCES

Christensen, D.E., & Sprague, R.L. Reduction of hyperactive behaviors by conditioning procedures alone and combined with methylphenidate (Ritalin). *Beh. Res. Ther.* 11, 331, 1973.

Cohen, N., Douglas, V., & Morganstern, G. The effect of methylphenidate on attentive behavior and autonomic activity in hyperactive children. *Psychopharmacologia,* 22, 282, 1971.

Conners, C.K. Pharmacotherapy of psychopathology in children. In H.C. Quay and J.S. Werry (Eds.) *Psychopathological Disorders of Children.* New York, John Wiley, 1972, p. 316.

Conners, C.K. Psychological effects of stimulant drugs in children with minimal brain dysfunction. *Pediatrics,* 49, 702, 1972.

Department of Health, Education and Welfare, Office of Child Development, Report of the Conference on the Use of Stimulant Drugs in the Treatment of Behaviorally Disturbed Young School Children, Washington, D.C., U.S. Government Printing Office, January, 1971.

Eisenberg, L. Behavior modification by drugs. III. The clinical use of stimulant drugs in children. *Pediatrics,* 49, 709, 1972.

Fish, B. The "one child, one drug" myth of stimulants in hyperkinesis. *Arch. Gen. Psychiatr.* 25, 193, 1971.

Knights, R., & Hinton, G. The effects of methylphenidate (Ritalin) on motor skills and behavior of children with learning problems. *J. Nerv. Ment. Dis.* 148, 643, 1969.

O'Malley, J.E., & Eisenberg, L. The hyperkinetic syndrome. *Seminars Psychiatr.* 5, 95, 1973.

Patterson, G.R., Shaw, D.A., & Ebner, M.J. Teachers, peers, and parents as agents of change in the classroom. In F.A.M. Benson (Ed.) *Modifying Deviant Social Behaviors in Various Classroom Settings.* Eugene, Oregon, Department of Special Education Monographs, 1969, p. 13.

Physicians Desk Reference. Oradell, N.J., Medical Economics Company, 1973, p. 682.

Rapoport, J.L., Quinn, P.O., Bradbard, G., Riddle, D. & Brooks, E. Imipramine and Methylphenidate treatments of hyperactive boys. *Arch. Gen. Psychiatr.* 30, 789, 1974.

Routh, D.K., Schroeder, C.S., & O'Tuama, L.A. Development of activity level in children. *Dev. Psychol.* 10, 163, 1974.

Safer, D.J., & Allen, R.P. Factors influencing the suppressant effects of two stimulant drugs on the growth of hyperactive children. *Pediatrics,* 51, 660, 1973.

Sleator, E.K., & von Neumann, A.W. Methylphenidate in the treatment of hyperkinetic children. *Clin. Pediatr.* 13, 19, 1974.

Sroufe, L.A., & Stewart, M.A. Treating problem children with stimulant drugs. *N. Engl. J. Med.* 289, 407, 1973.

Sroufe, L.A. Drug treatment of children with behavior problems. In F. Horowitz (Ed.) *Review of Child Development Research,* 4, 347, 1975.

Wender, P.H. *Minimal Brain Dysfunction in Children.* New York, Wiley Interscience, 1971.

Werry, J.S., & Sprague, R.L. Hyperactivity. In C.G. Costello (Ed.) *Symptoms of Psychopathology.* New York, John Wiley, 1970, p. 397.

# 7
## *Self-Management*

"Control yourself!" "Count to 10!" "Hold your tongue!" "Think before you act!" "Look before you leap!" These are all admonitions given to children and adults in an attempt to help them to manage their own behavior. Though such admonitions are frequently given, one generally does not know whether they have any effect. Fortunately, since 1975, several articles appeared which showed practical ways in which self-control can be taught; these articles will be presented later with commentary about how the findings can best be used by teachers.

As has been shown throughout this book, behavior therapists have repeatedly demonstrated that changes in teacher behavior will influence children's behavior. Knowing how a teacher can influence a child is extremely useful, but the problems of *self*-management must be addressed if one is interested in long-term behavior change. It is true that no one's behavior is independent of the reactions from others, but to be effective change agents with children, part of our job is to decrease the amount of dependence a child has on adults. If children can be taught self-management skills, the regression often seen when adult approval or tangible reinforcers are withdrawn may be avoided. More importantly, a child with self-management skills will presumably be able to learn a great deal when the teacher or parent is completely absent.

Some believe that self-control is simply an illusion—that all of our behavior is ultimately determined by our biological, chemical, and social forces. Others maintain that an individual's choices and thoughts control his own behavior; further, they assert that these choices are made to some degree independent of any environmental forces acting upon him. They believe that each individual is free to choose certain courses of action. The crux of this argument hinges on an issue called "determinism"—a principle which holds that everything has a cause. Determinism is an issue that has been and will be debated for centuries (Sprague & Taylor, 1959). The present authors assert, however, that we all act as if we have some choice, and our social institutions (e.g., courts, school, and prisons) punish people *as if* they had *some* choice and control over their actions. Consistent with this assertion is the following view of self-control: Self-control refers to behavior that is relatively independent of external forces (Thoresen & Mahoney, 1974). As such, there is more or less self-control in any behavior; when an individual's behavior seems almost completely independent of external forces, we say he displays great self-control.

Generally, when one thinks of self-control, one recalls individuals with great persistence and ability to delay gratification, e.g., Odysseus, Gandhi, Dick Gregory, Helen Keller, Franklin Roosevelt. Self-control, however, involves not only the individual's ability to suppress desires and to delay gratification but also any manipulation by the individual designed to decrease *or* increase the frequency of his own behavior. In brief, self-control refers to behavior initiated by the individual where such behavior is relatively free from external constraints (Thoresen & Mahoney, 1974).

When children are very, very angry at someone or something, their ignoring the problem, counting to 10, or walking away is often not sufficient to allow them to effectively deal with their aggressive impulses. The Robin, Schneider, and Dolnick (1976) study shows teachers how to teach children to respond to their aggressive impulses. The "Turtle Technique" allows a child to have an immediate response and at the same time to delay any inappropriate action while the child ponders some possible solutions to the problem he faces. Delay, withdrawal into a turtle position, relaxation, and problem solving are the key ingredients in the Turtle Technique. The assumption of the turtle position, i.e., closing eyes, clenching fists, putting head on desk, is necessary only for a few days while the child is learning how to relax, to restrain his aggressive impulses, and to discover alternatives to aggression. Entire classrooms or individuals can be taught the Turtle Technique. If only one child in a regular-size class ($N = 25$) needs to be trained, teaching the child alone after school or during a class break when other children are not present is best. With a special class of children with social and behavioral problems, Schneider has found that the children especially enjoy learning to do the turtle and occasionally even teach their parents how to use the technique. In fact, in the beginning phases of teaching a class the Turtle Technique, children playfully tease and thus prompt others to use "The Turtle." As experience is gained in the technique, however, the emphasis is on social problem solving and discussion of prosocial ways to solve classroom problems.

The Bornstein and Quevillon (1976) program to teach self-instructional skills with pre-school boys is important for its is one of the first self-instruction programs which has shown practical effects in a classroom. As you will see, the program was associated with an increase in on-task behavior of approximately 65 percent from the baseline to post-treatment. More importantly, this increase was maintained more than a month later. Basically, the intent of the self-instructional package or program was to teach a child to talk to himself—initially aloud and later covertly. The child was taught to ask himself questions, to provide answers to those questions, and to evaluate and praise himself for appropriate behavior. For two hours the experimenter taught the child to use these skills in completing tasks that would require attention, concentration, and frustration tolerance. You should carefully note the modeling sequence used by the experimenter in which the whole task was demonstrated as were the self-instructions. When adults or children find tasks difficult, they sometimes begin to talk aloud to themselves (Meichenbaum, 1975), and this talking to themselves often facilitates task performance. Some impulsive children, however, do not know how to self-instruct, and they need to be taught how to do so (Meichenbaum & Goodman, 1971). Initially, the self-instructing may appear difficult and unnatural for a child, but almost all of us talk to ourselves—covertly, of course—and children can be helped by teaching them how to covertly self-instruct. The talking aloud to themselves is quickly faded to a whisper and finally to an inaudible self-instruction.

To facilitate transfer of effects from the training sessions outside the classroom to the classroom proper, the Bornstein and Quevillon training was done with the instruction that the classroom teacher wanted the child to do the tasks with the experimenter (e.g., the child was told that Mrs. E. wanted him to draw the picture, and then the child was asked to say to himself while doing the task, "Mrs. E. would want me to copy the letters this way."). The control condition in which the experimenters modeled appropriate reactions to the task *without teaching self-instruction* (described in the article) allows one to infer that the self-instructional training, not the modeling nor the experience with experimenter and the stimulus materials, was most important in bringing about change in the children's behavior. Perhaps the classroom teachers reacted positively to the children's behavior change when the children came into the class from the self-instructional sessions, and the changed teacher behavior helped maintain the children's appropriate behavior. In fact, it is likely that unless such teacher behavior occurred, the children's behavior change would have been only transitory. In sum, for young children, self-control is a means of bridging important gaps between the occurrence of a desired behavior and the occasions when parents and teachers praise and support that desired behavior.

The Turkewitz, O'Leary, and Ironsmith (1975) study demonstrates the utility of teaching self-evaluation skills to children in an after-school reading program, and it illustrates one method of withdrawing a token program. As you will see, before training, children's evaluations of their academic and social behavior did not influence their rates of disruptive behavior. In fact, initially the students consistently over-evaluated their behavior (Self-evaluation phase); only 14 percent of their ratings fell within one point of the teachers' ratings. However, as soon as the students were told that they would receive a bonus point for matching the teachers' ratings or that they would lose their points if their ratings were too discrepant from the teachers' ratings (greater than one point discrepancy), they immediately rated themselves quite accurately. Teachers generally want to know exactly on what basis the students and teachers in the study made their ratings. As stated in the Self-evaluation section of the article, the students were told to give themselves up to five points for academic behavior and up to five points for social behavior. They were further given general guidelines. Fives were to be given when they had near perfect academic work and when they had behaved in an exemplary fashion. They were also told that they were to give themselves threes when they had done average work (socially and academically). Finally, they were told that zeros were to be given to themselves when they had done no academic work and when they had been disruptive to the class (talked out of turn, ran around the room, cursed, hit a classmate). During the first 12 days of the token phase of the study, the children received continuous feedback, i.e., at the end of each 15-minute period, they received feedback regarding their social and academic behavior so that before the children were asked to match the teachers' ratings, the teachers had shown the children what rating they felt was deserved and had given reasons for such a rating. It should be stressed here that we have found that children between the ages of 9 and 14 can make such evaluations with a great deal of accuracy (Drabman, Spitalnik, & O'Leary, 1973; Santogrossi, O'Leary, Romanczyk, & Kaufman, 1973).

One must recognize the possibility that the teaching of self-evaluation may not have been the critical variable in producing generalization and maintenance. The gradual fading of reinforcers and the random selection of a control interval in which generalization was assessed may have been sufficient to produce the generalization and maintenance obtained. Nonetheless, the observation of comments during the last week of the program like: "I shouldn't do that; I'm going to lose a point," or "I shouldn't do that; it's against our rules," makes it seem plausible that the teaching of self-evaluative behavior was important in producing generalization and maintenance.

The different results in the Bornstein and Quevillon study and the Turkewitz et al. study pose an interesting problem, viz., why did Bornstein and Quevillon achieve generalization to the regular classroom with two hours of training when Turkewitz et al. did not in almost 50 days (hours) of training? First, the students in the Turkewitz et al. study were older and from classes for emotionally disturbed children, and their baseline rates of disruptive behavior, especially aggressive behavior, were almost the highest we have ever observed in children of this age (more than one disruptive behavior every 20 seconds). Second, the self-instructional training with the experimenter in the Bornstein and Quevillon study used the instruction that the *teacher* wanted the children to do certain tasks with the experimenter, whereas the teachers of the children in the Turkewitz et al. study did not discuss the children's behavior in their home class. Finally, it is very likely that the students in the Turkewitz et al. study were not reinforced by their regular class peers and/or teachers for good behavior, whereas the other children probably were. The children in the Turkewitz et al. study returned to a class of "emotionally disturbed" children where models for good behavior are few, and models for inappropriate behavior abound; presumably, such was not the case in the Head Start class of Bornstein and Quevillon.

# Article 17
# The Turtle Technique: An Extended
# Case Study of Self-Control
# in the Classroom*†

ARTHUR ROBIN, MARLENE SCHNEIDER, and MICHELLE DOLNICK

Abstract: A preliminary investigation of the Turtle Technique, a procedure for helping emotionally disturbed children control their own impulsive behavior, is described. The technique consists of four components: the "turtle response," relaxation, problem-solving, and peer support. Eleven children drawn from two classrooms were instructed in the use of the Turtle Technique for the self-control of aggression. The procedure was introduced according to a multiple-baseline design. Results revealed significant decrements in aggressive behavior in both classrooms. Implications for further research were considered.

In recent years behavior modifiers have developed many teacher-administered, externally controlled techniques for helping emotionally disturbed children control their impulses and overcome their behavioral deficits in classroom settings (O'Leary & O'Leary, 1972). While the effectiveness of these techniques has been demonstrated in a variety of classroom situations (O'Leary & O'Leary, 1972); some limitations have emerged, including the return of the behavior to nearly pre-treatment levels after the termination of treatment and

*The authors wish to acknowledge the advice of Dr. K.D. O'Leary in the formulation of this project and the comments of Dr. Ronald Kent on an earlier version of the present paper. The cooperation of Mr. Joseph Cullen, the three teachers, and the undergraduate observers is also gratefully acknowledged. This study was supported by Grant OE6-071-2872 from the U.S. Office of Education. The opinions expressed herein, however, do not necessarily reflect the position or policy of the U.S. Office of Education, and no official endorsement by the U.S. Office of Education should beinferred.

†Reprinted by permission from *Psychology in the Schools,* 1976.

the difficulties in the administration of such programs when applied over extended periods of time.

Self-control behavior modification procedures have been suggested as an alternative approach which might offer solutions to these problems (Thoreson & Mahoney, 1974). According to the self-control approach, children can be taught strategies to help them control their own inappropriate behavior with minimal teacher intervention. Recent evidence has suggested that self-control procedures are effective with both emotionally disturbed and normal children (Drabman, Spitalnik, & O'Leary, 1973; Felixbrod & O'Leary, 1973; Thoreson & Mahoney, 1974).

The present study is a preliminary evaluation of the Turtle Technique (Schneider, 1974), a promising procedure for helping children control their impulses towards aggressive behavior. The Turtle Technique makes use of the image of the turtle, which withdraws into its shell when provoked by its external environment. Young children are taught to react to impulses to aggress by (a) imagining that they are turtles withdrawing into their shells, pulling their arms close to their bodies, putting their heads down, and closing their eyes, (b) relaxing their muscles to cope with emotional tensions, and (c) using social problem solving to generate prosocial alternative responses. Peers are also instructed to support appropriate use of the technique. The Turtle Technique has been employed informally by the second author for the past two years. This study represents the first attempt to assess the effectiveness of the procedure with observational measures outside a laboratory school setting.

## METHOD

### Subjects

Eleven children from two primary classrooms in a school for emotionally disturbed children served as subjects. Six and five children from each class participated, respectively. The children were selected for participation in the study on the basis of teacher reports that they exhibited a high rate of aggressive behavior. Children had been grouped into these two classes by the school such that classroom A contained individuals with histories of severe aggressive behavior disturbances while classroom B contained individuals with histories of moderate disturbances. The regular classroom teachers implemented the program under the guidance of the authors.

## Procedure

Each class received instruction in the Turtle Technique in two settings: 15-minute daily planned practice periods and normal classroom periods. The technique was taught in phases corresponding to its sub-parts, the "turtle response," relaxation, and problem solving. Peer support was taught throughout all of the phases.

The goal of the first phase was to teach the children the turtle response of pulling their arms and legs in close to their body, putting their heads down on the desks, and imagining that they were turtles withdrawing into their shells. They were taught to adopt this response in four circumstances: (a) a child perceived that an aggressive interchange with a peer was about to occur; (b) a child became frustrated or angry at himself and was about to throw a tantrum; (c) the teacher called out "Turtle"; (d) a classmate called out "Turtle". The teacher introduced the turtle response through the use of the story paraphrased below:

> Little Turtle was a handsome young turtle very upset about going to school. He always got in trouble at school because he got into fights. Other kids would tease, bump, or hit him; he would get very angry and start big fights. The teacher would have to punish him. Then one day he met the big old tortoise, who told him that his shell was the secret answer to all his problems. The tortoise told Little Turtle to withdraw into his shell when he felt angry and rest until he was no longer angry. So he tried it the next day, and it worked. The teacher now smiled at him and he no longer got into big fights.

After relating the story, the teacher demonstrated the turtle response and asked the class to practice responding rapidly to the cue word "turtle" interspersed unexpectedly throughout her normal conversation. She then explained the four circumstances in which it was appropriate to adopt the turtle responses and had students role-play instances of incipient aggressive interchanges followed by correct turtle responses. Throughout regular classroom periods the teacher cued children by calling out "turtle" whenever she saw an incipient fight. In addition, reinforcement for correct responses was provided in the form of praise and candy. Finally, peer support was encouraged by cueing and reinforcing children for telling each other to "do turtle" at appropriate times.

The second phase of the Turtle Technique, muscle relaxation, was introduced in order to help children defuse the strong negative emotions aroused by the original aggressive situation. During group practice sessions children were taught to alternately tense and release the various muscle groups of their bodies according to the Jacobson (1938) relaxation induction. When the children had learned to release the tension in their muscles, they practiced relaxing while "doing turtle." In this manner the turtle response and relaxation were "chained" together.

The third phase, problem solving, consisted of role-playing and discussion aimed at teaching the children alternative strategies for coping with the problematic situations which initially caused them to emit the turtle response. Procedures developed by Goldfried and D'Zurilla (1971) and Shaftel and Shaftel (1967) were utilized. Children received instruction in (a) generating a number of alternative strategies for coping with aggressive-tantrum problems and (b) evaluating the consequences of each strategy; here the emphasis was on "choice"; it was repeatedly stressed that a child had choices other than to give into an initial impulse. Incomplete stores of typical problem situations were presented in group practice, and the class role-played alternative endings under the guidance of the teacher. During normal classroom periods the teacher reminded the children of their choices whenever they emitted a turtle response. Peer support was fostered by encouraging children to point out choices to each other.

Towards the end of phase three of training, the use of extrinsic rewards and teacher cues for correct application of the Turtle Technique were faded out. Intermittent prompts and reinforcement were maintained on a thin schedule.

A more detailed description of the Turtle Technique along with systematic instructions for its application is contained elsewhere (Schneider, 1974, Schneider & Robin, Note 1).*

The Turtle Technique was successfully introduced in each classroom according to a multiple-baseline design (Baer, Wolf, & Risley, 1968). In classroom A two weeks of baseline were followed by eight weeks of treatment; in classroom B seven weeks of baseline were followed by three weeks of treatment. The authors assisted the teachers in the initial introduction and returned intermittently to

---

*A copy of the *Turtle Manual* (Schneider, & Robin, 1973) can be obtained by writing the first author at the Point of Woods Laboratory School, Department of Psychology, SUNY at Stony Brook, N.Y. 11794. Send $1 to cover handling costs.

assist in the implementation of successive stages.

Observations of the children's aggressive behavior were taken as a measure of the effect of the Turtle Technique. Aggressive behavior was defined in accordance with the observational code devised by Tonick, Friehling, Kent, and Warhit (Note 2): an act constituted aggressive behavior when a child made a forceful movement directed either at another person or an inanimate object, including hitting, throwing objects, kicking, grabbing, tearing up his or another's materials, etc. Trained undergraduate observers sitting in the classroom recorded each child's aggressive behavior from 1 p.m. to 2 p.m. every Monday, Tuesday, Wednesday, and Friday. At each session the observer recorded the presence or absence of aggressive behavior during each 1-minute interval, and at the end of the session the total number of behaviors was divided by the total number of intervals and multiplied by 100 to yield a mean daily rate for the category. Reliability of observations was assessed by a checker who visited each classroom once a week and observed along with the primary observer. The number of behaviors on which the two observers agreed was divided by the number of agreements plus disagreements and multiplied by 100 to compute percent agreement. Percent agreement ranged from 64 percent to 100 percent with a mean of 81 percent.

## RESULTS

Mean weekly rates of aggressive behavior were computed for each group by averaging the mean daily rates of behavior of all children in that classroom. The following mean weekly rates were obtained in classroom A: 20, 21, 18, 12, 14, 15, 7, 10, 14, 6. An analysis by condition revealed that the rate of aggressive behavior decreased from a mean of 20.5 during baseline to a mean of 12.0 during treatment, a significant 41 percent decrement, $t(5) = 7.74, p < .001$. The following mean weekly rates were obtained in classroom B: 7, 4, 7, 5, 2, 5, 4, 4, 2, 2. The rate of aggressive behavior in classroom B decreased from a mean of 4.9 during baseline to a mean of 2.7 during treatment, a significant 45 percent decrement, $t(4) = 4.15, p < .01$.

For individual children percentage reductions ranging from 34 percent to 70 percent were obtained: (a) classroom A — 43%, 45%, 33%, 36%, 57%, 59%; (b) classroom B — 47%, 70%, 61%, 37%, 34%. Disruptive behavior decreased from baseline to treatment for every child. In classroom A, five children showed a reduction of over 40 percent while two showed a reduction of over 30 percent. In classroom B three children showed a reduction of over 40 percent while two showed a reduction of over 30 percent.

## DISCUSSION

The results of the present study suggest that young emotionally disturbed children can learn to control their own aggressive behavior. The significant decrement in aggression associated with the introduction of the Turtle Technique in each classroom indicates that the children's disruptive classroom behavior was successfully modified.

The results must be qualified in several respects. First, while the rate of aggression clearly decreased with the introduction of the Turtle Technique in each classroom, the extended baseline in classroom B showed a decreasing trend. This suggests that improvement resulting from the effects of time alone cannot be completely ruled out as a factor confounding the obtained results. Second, the Turtle technique consisted of three specific components as well as general social influence processes; without further analysis it is impossible to determine which elements of the treatment were the active ingredients. Third, the data were collected in a limited number of classrooms in a special school, making the results highly dependent upon the particular school and teachers involved. In addition, the difference in rates of aggression between classrooms was larger than the decrease within classrooms; this last fact was probably more a reflection of the concerted attempt of the school to group classes by degree of disruptiveness of the pupils than a function of the experimental treatment program. Taken together, these confounds render the results of the present study preliminary rather than definitive.

Nonetheless, the highly promising, novel nature of the Turtle Technique and the serious problems associated with externally based procedures underscore the importance of presenting even preliminary data concerning the effectiveness of this self-control procedure. While many previous applications of self-control in classroom settings have focused on academic responses within short, circumscribed periods of the school day (Felixbrod & O'Leary, 1973; Glynn, Thomas, & Shee, 1973), the present application focused on an extremely troublesome social behavior throughout a longer time period. Furthermore, the present procedure integrates contingency management, relaxation, and problem-solving into a unified treatment package with potential applicability in a variety of settings (Schneider & Robin, Note 3).

The decrements in aggressive behavior observed in the present study are comparable to the improvements noted throughout the two years of pilot work with the Turtle Technique at the Point of Woods Laboratory School. The present study has demonstrated that teachers in a special school can implement the Turtle Technique and produce reliable reductions in observed aggressive behavior. It remains for future investigations to complete large-scale, controlled outcome studies leading to definitive conclusions about the effects of the Turtle Technique on aggressive behavior.

## REFERENCE NOTES

Schneider, M., & Robin, A.L. *Turtle manual.* Unpublished manuscript, Point of Woods Laboratory School, State University of New York, Stony Brook, 1973.

Schneider, M., & Robin, A.L. The Turtle Technique: A method for the self-control of impulsive behavior. Unpublished manuscript, Point of Woods Laboratory School, State University of New York, Stony Brook, 1974.

Tonick, I., Friehling, J., Kent, R., & Warhit, J. Classroom observational code. Unpublished manuscript, Point of Woods Laboratory School, State University of New York, Stony Brook, 1973.

# REFERENCES

Baer, D.M., Wolf, M.M., & Risely, T.R. Some current dimensions of applied behavior analysis. *Journal of Applied Behavior Analysis,* 1968, 1, 91-97.

Drabman, R.S., Spitalnik, R., & O'Leary, K.D. Teaching self-control to disruptive children. *Journal of Abnormal Psychology,* 1973, 82, 10-16.

D'Zurilla, T.J., & Goldfried, M.R. Problem solving and behavior modification. *Journal of Abnormal Psychology,* 1971, 78, 107-126.

Felixbrod, J.J., & O'Leary, K.D. Effects of reinforcement on children's academic behavior as a function of self-determined and externally imposed contingencies. *Journal of Applied Behavior Analysis,* 1973, 6, 241-250.

Glynn, E.L., Thomas, J.O., & Shee, S.M. Behavioral self-control of on-task behavior in an elementary classroom. *Journal of Applied Behavior Analysis,* 1973, 6, 105-113.

Jacobson, E. *Progressive relaxation.* Chicago: University of Chicago Press, 1938.

O'Leary, K.D., & O'Leary, S.G. *Classroom management.* New York: Pergamon Press, 1972.

Schneider, M. Turtle Technique in the classroom. *Teaching Exceptional Children,* 1974, 7(1), 22-24.

Shaftel, F.R., & Shaftel, G.S. *Role playing for social values: Decision making in the social studies,* Englewood Cliffs, New Jersey: Prentice Hall, 1967.

Thoreson, C.E., & Mahoney, M.J. *Behavioral self-control.* New York: Holt, Rinehart and Winston, Inc., 1974.

# Article 18
## The Effects of a Self-Instructional
## Package on Overactive Preschool Boys*

PHILIP H. BORNSTEIN and RANDAL P. QUEVILLON

Abstract: The effects of a self-instructional package on three overactive preschool boys were investigated using a multiple-baseline design across subjects. Behavioral observations of the three target subjects indicated transfer of training effects from the experimental tasks to the classroom. On-task behaviors increased dramatically concomitant with the introduction of the self-instructional package, and treatment gains were maintained 22.5 weeks after baseline was initiated. In addition, the use of an observer-expectancy control condition gave further credibility to the demonstration of a causal relationship.

Descriptors: self-instruction, on-task behavior, overactive behavior, verbal mediation, massed practice, transfer of training, preschool children

The widespread use of behavioral principles with children has led to the development of several effective procedures for decreasing disruptive behavior and increasing attention in school settings. Aversive stimulation (Hall, Axelrod, Foundopoulos, Shellman, Campbell, & Cranston, 1971; Risley, 1968), response cost (Wolf, King,

*Reprinted by permission from the *Journal of Applied Behavior Analysis,* Vol. 9, No. 2, 1976 179-188. Copyright 1976 by the Society for the Experimental Analysis of Behavior, Inc. with the following abridgements:

Method: Observation and Recording—last paragraph

Results: Reliability—all *but* first two sentences

Discussion: Paragraph "The present study utilized several techniques . . . by means of constant overt reliability assessment." Corresponding references from this paragraph in References.

Lachowicz, & Giles, 1970), timeout (Carlson, Arnold, Becker, & Madsen, 1968; Kubany, Weiss, & Sloggett, 1971; Wahler, 1969), group contingencies (Barrish, Saunders, & Wolf, 1969; Harris & Sherman, 1973), and contingency management approaches (Hall, Lund, & Jackson, 1968; O'Leary & Drabman, 1971; Walker & Buckley, 1968) are among the procedures that have been shown to improve the behavior of "hyperactive" and disruptive children. However, these effects have been limited in two areas. First, some procedures have simply failed to affect significantly the behavior of a percentage of the subjects treated (Kazdin, 1973; Madsen, Becker, & Thomas, 1968). Second, lack of response maintenance at the cessation of intervention and failure to obtain transfer of training effects have been noted (Bornstein & Hamilton, 1975; Kazdin & Bootzin, 1972; O'Leary & Kent, 1973).

Kazdin (1975) has proposed training subjects in self-control (Bolstad & Johnson, 1972; Drabman, Spitalnik, & O'Leary, 1973; Meichenbaum, 1973) and the programming of generalization (Blanchard & Johnson, 1973; Walker & Buckley, 1972) as solutions to these problems. Within the former approach, verbally mediated self-control training would seem to have implication and utility in both problem areas defined above. That mediational processes exist in human learning has been amply demonstrated (Cole & Medin, 1973; Mahoney, 1974). In addition, the interaction between verbal and nonverbal behavior has received considerable attention (Luria, 1961; Vygotsky, 1962). Blackwood (1972) described speech as verbal chaining that produces discriminative stimuli and conditioned reinforcers. Self-produced verbalizations may therefore modify motor responses by mediating between stimulus situation and target behavior. The effects of verbal operants on motoric responses have been investigated (Bem, 1967; Lovaas, 1964; Meichenbaum & Goodman, 1969). Verbally mediated self-control training has been effective in eliminating lunchroom disruptions (MacPherson, Candee, & Hohman, 1974), and reducing rule-breaking behavior (Monahan & O'Leary, 1971), and the approach holds promise of reducing yet other forms of childrens' misbehavior (Blackwood, 1970). Additionally, since the individual is the source of behavioral control within the verbal mediation paradigm, response maintenance and transfer of training effects should be facilitated (Meichenbaum & Cameron, 1973).

One technique for training verbally mediated self-control is that of cognitive self-instruction (Meichenbaum & Cameron, 1974). This procedure consists of fading a set of prompts and instructions from an overt (spoken aloud), external (verbalized by a model) condition to a covert, self-produced target response. The effectiveness of the self-instructional package with school-age, "impulsive" children has been demonstrated (Meichenbaum & Goodman, 1971). Results have indicated that self-instructional guidance programs effectively modified the behavior of impulsive children relative to attentional and assessment control groups on several performance measures. Although improvement was maintained on a one-month follow-up assessment, no significant treatment effects were obtained on two indices of classroom behavior.

The present investigation sought to explore the functional utility of a self-instructional program for preschool, impulsive children and to demonstrate transfer of training effects from the experimental tasks to the actual classroom environment. Additionally, an observer-expectancy control condition was utilized such that treatment effects that arose were solely attributable to manipulations of the independent variable.

A multiple-baseline design was used in an attempt to demonstrate explicitly and reliably behavioral control within the self-instructional procedure. Thus, any ensuing behavioral changes within individual subjects were more readily apparent than in the more traditional group designs.

## METHOD

### Subjects and Setting

The three subjects were concurrently enrolled in one classroom of a preschool Head Start program. Children were systematically selected on the basis of teacher and aide reports of highly disruptive and undesirable classroom behavior. Accordingly, only these three children were chosen to participate in the present research. Their parents were of lower- to middle-class social standing and average yearly income did not exceed $5000.

Subject 1 (Scott) was a 4-year-old white male described as "a disciplinary problem because he is unable to follow directions for any extended length of time." He had been unable to complete standard tasks within the preschool classroom setting and often experienced violent outbursts of temper for no apparent reason. In addition, those working closely with him agreed that compliance and cooperation appeared to be minimal.

Subject 2 (Rod) was a 4-year-old white male described by teachers as "being out of control in the classroom." Major problems and behavioral deficits included short attention span, aggressiveness in response to other children, and a general overactivity.

Subject 3 (Tim) was a 4-year-old white male reported to be highly distractible both at home and in preschool. Anecdotal reports indicated that most of his classroom time was spent walking around the room, staring off into space, and/or not attending to task or instruction.

### Dependent Variable

The dependent variable was on-task behavior, defined as those subject behaviors directed toward the assigned tasks. During teacher instruction it was expected that the child would be attentive and silent. When asked to participate during a work period (e.g., figure drawing exercises, story reading, etc.), on-task behaviors included performing the prescribed and accepted classroom activity. Off-task behaviors included engaging in unassigned activity: movement about the room, playing with toys, shouting, fighting, kicking, and leaving the classroom without permission.

### Observation and Recording

Behaviors were observed and categorized as either on-task or off-task by two independent judges naive as to the design of the study. Judges had been trained for two weeks before baseline and had achieved interrater reliabilities exceeding 80 percent for four consecutive days.

During the study, rates of on-task and off-task behaviors were obtained for the selected children twice daily, four days per week. Thirty-minute observations were conducted in the morning and afternoon when class activities were more structured, to provide a clear indication of the presence or absence of appropriate behavior.

The measures of on-task performance were determined on a 10-second observe, 10-second record basis. That is, both observers would watch the first child on the list for 10 seconds, then take 10 seconds to record his behavior as "+" (on-task) or "0" (off-task). For the behavior to be coded as "+," the child had to be observed as on-task for the entire 10-second interval. Behavior was considered off-task if the subject did not meet the above requirements. Subjects were observed in a random order that varied daily.

Both observers sat in the rear of the room (although not within view of each other), avoided all forms of physical and/or verbal contact with the children, and remained relatively unobtrusive throughout the study.

### Reliability of observations
Since two observers were present during each phase of the investigation, continuous interobserver agreement data could be generated. The two records were, therefore, compared interval by interval for each child, and a measure of agreement obtained by calculating the number of observer agreements divided by the total number of agreements plus disagreements. Agreement was scored when both observers recorded the same behavior during the same 10-second observation interval. Disagreement was scored when one observer recorded a behavior code that the other had not.

## General Procedure

### Baseline
During the first eight days of the investigation, behavioral observations were made but there were no experimental manipulations.

### Self-instruction
Subjects were seen individually for a massed self-instruction session lasting two hours. The child worked with the experimenter for about 50 minutes, was given a 20-minute break, and then resumed work for another 50-minutes. The self-instructional training was similar to that described elsewhere (Meichenbaum & Goodman, 1971) and proceeded as follows: (1) the experimenter modeled the task while talking aloud to himself, (2) the subject performed the task while the experimenter instructed aloud, (3) the subject then performed the task talking aloud to himself while the experimenter whispered softly, (4) the subject performed the task whispering softly while the experimenter made lip movements but no sound, (5) the subject performed the task making lip movements without sound while the experimenter self-instructed covertly, and (6) the subject performed the task with covert self-instruction.

The verbalizations modeled were of four types: (a) questions about the task (e.g., "What does the teacher want me to do?"), (b) answers to questions in the form of cognitive rehearsal (e.g., "Oh, that's right, I'm supposed to copy that picture."), (c) self-instructions that guide through the task (e.g., "OK, first I draw a line here . . ."), and (d) self-reinforcement (e.g., "How about that; I really did that one well.").

It should also be noted that, in numerous tasks, the experimenter consciously erred and then corrected his error without hesitation. In addition, since initially the children did not seem motivated to work, the experimenter paired self-praise with material reward (M&M's) as a means of creating incentive. This reward was quickly leaned out as the children found they could complete the tasks successfully. Lastly, the entire training session was presented in a story-like manner. In each situation, the subject was told that the teacher (not the experimenter) had asked him to complete the task in question. When using self-instructions, then, the subject would respond as if he were in the classroom (e.g., "Mrs. B wants me to draw that picture over there. OK, how can I do that?").

More specifically, the self-instructional protocol consisted of the experimenter initially instructing the child " _____ (child's name), watch what I do and listen to what I say." Immediately, on gaining his attention, an M&M was placed in the child's mouth. When the first trial was completed, and if the child's attention had not shifted away from the experimental task, he was again given a candy reinforcer. The experimenter then said to the child, " ____(child's name), this time *you* do it while I say the words." Contingent on correct performance, the experimenter dispensed an M&M to the child paired with self-praise at the conclusion of this second trial. Candy reinforcers were then leaned out quite rapidly and given only at the close of a trial. No more than 10 reinforcers were given to any one child during a training session. Later in the training sequence, when the child was asked to verbalize on his own, acceptable responses were those that included correct performance and the four elements outlined above (i.e., questions about the task, answers, self-instructions, and self-reinforcement). If the child did not produce an acceptable response, the experimenter again modeled the task while talking aloud to himself. Following such demonstrations, the child was then returned to that part of the sequence where his error had been committed. If the child refused to comply, the experimenter merely reiterated his instructions and again modeled an appropriate response. When the child successfully completed a trial, he was given instructions for the next step in the training sequence. When all six steps in the sequence had been completed, the experimenter presented a new task and again modeled its performance while talking aloud to himself (i.e., step one).

A wide variety of tasks were employed in the 2-hour training sessions, with difficulty level increasing over time. These tasks varied from situations tapping simple sensory motor skills (e.g., copying of lines and figures) to more complex problem-solving situations (e.g., block design and conceptual grouping tasks). In all instances, subjects were required to verbalize the nature of the task and their problem-solving strategy. All tasks were modified slightly from those on the Stanford-Binet, Wechsler Intelligence Scale for Children or the McCarthy Scales of Children's Abilities.*

*Expectancy control*
In an attempt to control for any nonspecific effects of treatment (e.g., attention, interaction with stimulus materials, *etc.*) and observer-expectancy effects, all three children were given 2-hour training sessions with the experimenter on the day self-instruction was to be initiated. However, since treatment was sequentially administered in a multiple-baseline fashion across subjects, only one subject received the actual self-instruction training. The other two children were taken from the room in an identical manner and exposed to the same stimulus materials, but did not receive the self-instruction training at that time. Rather, in the expectancy-control condition, the experimenter modeled appropriate responses for the child without verbalization. More specifically, the experimenter initially instructed the child, "_____(child's name), watch what I do." Immediately, on gaining his attention, as in self-instructional training, an M&M was dispensed to the child. If the child remained attentive through the first trial, he was given a second candy reinforcer. The experimenter then said to the child, "_____(child's name), this time *you* do it while I watch." At the conclusion of this trial, reinforcement was again dispensed and then leaned out rapidly. No more than 10 reinforcers were given to any child during each expectancy-control condition. The procedure was then repeated a second time before presenting a new task. A second presentation was provided to equate across experimental and control conditions the amount of time spent with individual stimulus materials. The sequence in which the subjects were to be given the self-instruction

---

*A complete list of training tasks used is available from the senior author on request.

training was randomly determined, and observers were thus kept naive as to the nature of the treatment and the order in which it was to be presented to subjects.

## RESULTS

### Reliability

The levels of agreement between observers across experimental conditions for all subjects were: Subject A, 96%; Subject B, 92%; Subject C, 93%. Overall observer-observer reliability was 94% agreement.

### On-Task Behavior

Figure 1 represents the daily percent on-task behavior scores for each subject across experimental conditions. The mean rate of on-task behavior during the baseline condition for Scott, Rod, and Tim was 10.4%, 14.6%, and 10%, respectively. Following the 2-hour training in self-instruction, there was an immediate and dramatic increase in on-task behavior. Posttreatment means for the three experimental subjects were Scott, 82.3%, Rod, 70,8%; Tim, 77.8%. Postchecks were instituted on the sixtieth and ninetieth observation days after baseline was initiated, and results indicate that treatment gains were maintained. Percentage of postcheck on-task behaviors for the three subjects were: Scott, 70% and 77%; Rod, 64% and 67%; Tim, 70% and 68%. It should again be noted that observations occurred only four days per week. Thus, the final follow-up data collected (i.e., observation day 90) are a sample of classroom behavior 22.5 weeks after baseline was initiated.

## DISCUSSION

The present results demonstrate the utility of a self-instructional package as a means of increasing on-task behavior in preschool boys. Moreover, through the use of a multiple-baseline design across subjects and an observer-expectancy control manipulation, the results are made even more compelling. Specifically, the successive application of the self-instructional procedure and the corresponding increase in targeted subject's on-task behavior, as compared to nontargeted subject's baseline stability, unequivocally support the demonstration of a causal relationship. Since observers had no knowledge as to the

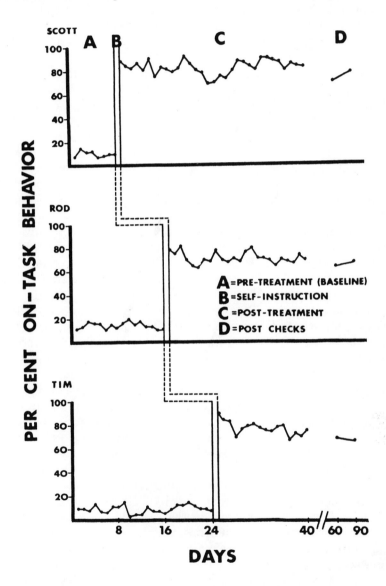

Fig. 1. Daily percent on-task behaviors for Scott, Rod, and Tim across experimental conditions.

timing of treatment effects, results cannot be attributed to expectation biases in the observational process. The present investigation was
intended not only to demonstrate the utility of a self-instructional
program for preschoolers, but also to extend treatment effects and
behavioral improvement beyond the experimental situation. Results
indicated that behavioral gains transferred to the classroom setting
and were maintained for a considerable period of time.

These findings are superior to those found in previous work with
verbal mediation and self-instructional training. For example, whereas Meichenbaum and Goodman (1969) obtained control of nonverbal
responding in first graders through self-instruction, minimal effects
were obtained with kindergarten subjects. The disparity between
these findings and the present results may be due to the fact
that Meichenbaum and Goodman (1969) used a minimal training,
self-instructional method, in which their subjects did not totally fade
verbal operants to the covert level. In addition, it is conceivable that
their target behavior (i.e., tapping speed) may have interacted with
developmental variables related to psychomotor skills. It thus seems
likely that self-instructional training may lend itself more readily to
the modification of certain classes of behavior rather than others.
More specifically, while qualitative task errors related to task
approach have been shown to be modifiable by self-direction,
performance related to task ability has not been similarly affected
(Palkes, Stewart, & Freedman, 1972). Using writing deficiencies as
target behavior, Robin, Armel, & O'Leary (1975) found self-
instruction superior to direct training following an extensive and
task-specific training package. The authors noted, however, that
while motor control deficiencies may have been affected by self-
instruction training, other abilities such as spatial-representation were
not. Therefore, it would appear that behaviors accompanied by
stable ability factors may not be as responsive to alterations in
self-control strategies. Moreover, behaviors not directly affected by
the demands of the task, such as resistance to temptation (Hartig, &
Kanfer, 1973), rule following (O'Leary, 1968), and on-task behavior
may, in turn, be more influenced by self-instructional training.
Certainly, further research is needed to explicate the classes of
behavior most amenable to modification via self-instruction.

Despite the obtained results indicating strength, durability, and
generalizability of treatment effects, one is unable to acknowledge
firmly the treatment components responsible for initial behavioral
change or transfer within the present therapeutic package. The
present self-instructional program involved a wide variety of pro-

cedures, including instruction, self-instruction, verbal modeling, prompts, reinforcement, and fading. Future investigations might therefore include a component analysis as a means of separating the effects of self-instruction from the full therapeutic package. With regard to the issue of transfer of behavioral improvement, Meichenbaum and Goodman (1971) reported a lack of generalization using a similar self-instructional program. Since the present research differed from the Meichenbaum and Goodman (1971) investigation in four major respects (i.e., preschool *versus* school-age children, massed *versus* spaced practice, brief use of material rewards, and "story-like" self-instructional training), isolation of individual procedural contributions becomes impossible. Any one of the above components, singly or in combination, may have been responsible for the observed effects. In terms of practical considerations, future studies should therefore also attempt to uncover the "active" agents of change responsible for generalization of treatment effects.

The maintenance of behavioral improvement following treatment intervention was quite remarkable. The authors suggest, however, that such dramatic transfer from the experimental setting to the classroom was a function of two factors: (1) The preschool environment has been described as a "behavioral trap" (Baer & Wolf, 1970) which, upon entry, shapes and maintains an ever-increasing repertoire of appropriate behaviors in children. As a result of such "trapping," changes in the boys' behavior may have produced changes in the teacher's behavior, leading to maintenance of treatment gains. (2) Children in the present investigation were asked to imagine, in the presence of the experimenter, that they were performing tasks assigned by their classroom teacher. The use of such specific covert rehearsal may thus facilitate development and maintenance of appropriate classroom behavior. Although these hypotheses remain to be tested, future investigators attempting to implement the self-instructional package should be forewarned that generalization may not occur without consideration of the above issues.

In conclusion, the positive results obtained in the present research indicate that further investigation of the treatment package is warranted. Future studies should attempt to demonstrate therapeutic effectiveness across a wide variety of situations, subjects, and behaviors. In addition, it appears that the role of self-instruction in the modification of children's behavior demands greater exploration. Behavior modifiers have for some time ignored the study of such "mediational" variables due to the problems they present in empirical investigation. The present research attempted to demonstrate, in part, that an experimental analysis of behavior can be equally applied to this topical domain with a comparable degree of confidence in the reliability of the findings.

## REFERENCES

Baer, D.M., & Wolf, M.M. The entry into natural communities of reinforcement. In R. Ulrich, T. Stachnik, & J. Mabry (Eds.), *Control of human behavior: From cure to prevention.* Glenview, Illinois: Scott, Foresman, 1970. Pp. 319-324.

Barrish, H.H., Saunders, M., & Wolf, M.M. Good behavior game: Effects of individual contingencies for group consequences on disruptive behavior in the classroom. *Journal of Applied Behavior Analysis,* 1969, 2, 119-124.

Bem, S. Verbal self-control: The establishment of effective self-instruction. *Journal of Experimental Psychology,* 1967, 74, 485-491.

Blackwood, R.O. The operant conditioning of verbally mediated self-control in the classroom. *Journal of School Psychology.* 1970, 8, 251-258.

Blackwood, R.O. *Mediated self-control: An operant model of rational behavior.* Akron, Ohio: Exordium Press, 1972.

Blanchard, E., & Johnson, R. Generalization of operant classroom control procedures. *Behavior Therapy,* 1973, 4, 219-229.

Bolstad, O., & Johnson, S. Self-regulation in the modification of disruptive classroom behavior. *Journal of Applied Behavior Analysis,* 1972, 5, 443-454.

Bornstein, P.H., & Hamilton, S.B. Token rewards and straw men. *American Psychologist,* 1975, 30, 780-781.

Carlson, C.S., Arnold, C.R., Becker, W.C., & Madsen, C.H. The elimination of tantrum behavior of a child in an elementary classroom. *Behavior Research and Therapy,* 1968, 6, 117-119.

Cole, M., & Medin, D. On the existence and occurence of mediation in discrimination transfer: A critical note. *Journal of Experimental Child Psychology,* 1973, 15, 352-355.

Drabman, R.S., Spitalnik, R.S., & O'Leary, K.D. Teaching self-control to disruptive children. *Journal of Abnormal Psychology,* 1973, 82, 10-16.

Hall, R.V., Axelrod, S., Foundopoulos, M., Shellman, J., Campbell, R., & Cranston, S. The effective use of punishment to modify behavior in the classroom. *Educational Technology,* 1971, 4, 24-26.

Hall, R.V., Lund, D., & Jackson, D. Effects of teacher attention on study behavior. *Journal of Applied Behavior Analysis,* 1968, 1, 1-12.

Harris, V.W., & Sherman, J.A. Use and analysis of the "good behavior game" to reduce disruptive classroom behavior. *Journal of Applied Behavior Analysis,* 1973, 6, 405-417.

Hartig, M., & Kanfer, F.H. The role of verbal self-instructions in children's resistance to temptation. *Journal of Personality and Social Psychology,* 1973, 25, 259-267.

Kazdin, A.E. The failure of some patients to respond to token programs. *Journal of Behavior Therapy and Experimental Psychiatry,* 1973, 4, 7-14.

Kazdin, A.E. *Behavior modification in applied settings.* Homewood, Illinois: Dorsey Press, 1975.

Kazdin, A.E., & Bootzin, R.R. The token economy: An evaluative review. *Journal of Applied Behavior Analysis,* 1972, 5, 343-372.

Kubany, E., Block, L., & Sloggett, B. The good behavior clock: Reinforcement/ timeout procedure for reducing disruptive classroom behavior. *Journal of Behavior Therapy and Experimental Psychiatry,* 1971, 2, 173-174.

Lovaas, O.I. Cue properties of words: the control of operant responding by rate and content of verbal operants. *Child Development,* 1964, 35, 245-256.

Luria, A.R. *The role of speech in the regulation of normal and abnormal behavior.* New York: Liveright, 1961.

MacPherson, E.M., Candee, B.L., & Hohman, R.J. A comparison of three methods for eliminating disruptive lunchroom behavior. *Journal of Applied Behavior Analysis,* 1974, 7, 287-297.

Madsen, C.H., Becker, W.C., & Thomas, D.R. Rules, praise, and ignoring: Elements of elementary classroom control. *Journal of Applied Behavior Analysis,* 1968, 1, 139-150.

Mahoney, M.J. *Cognition and behavior modification.* Cambridge, Massachusetts: Ballinger, 1974.

Meichenbaum, D.H. Cognitive factors in behavior modification: Modifying what clients say to themselves. In R.D. Rubin, J.P. Brady, and J.D. Henderson (Eds.), *Advances in behavior therapy,* Vol. 4. New York: Academic Press, 1973. Pp. 21-36.

Meichenbaum, D., & Cameron, R. Training schizophrenics to talk to themselves: A means of developing attentional controls. *Behavior Therapy,* 1973, 4, 515-534.

Meichenbaum, D., & Cameron, R. The clinical potential of modifying what clients say to themselves. In M.J. Mahoney and C.E. Thoresen (Eds.), *Self-control: Power to the person.* Belmont, California: Wadsworth, 1974. Pp. 263-290.

Meichenbaum, D., & Goodman, J. The developmental control of operant motor responding by verbal operants. *Journal of Experimental Child Psychology,* 1969, 7, 553-565.

Meichenbaum, D., & Goodman, J. Training impulsive children to talk to themselves: A means of developing self-control. *Journal of Abnormal Psychology,* 1971, 77, 115-126.

Monahan, J., & O'Leary, K.D. Effects of self-instruction on rule-breaking behavior. *Psychological Reports,* 1971, 29, 1059-1066.

O'Leary, K.D. The effects of self-instruction on immoral behavior. *Journal of Experimental Child Psychology,* 1968, 6, 297-301.

O'Leary, K.D., & Drabman, R. Token reinforcement programs in the classroom: A review. *Psychological Bulletin,* 1971, 75, 379-398.

O'Leary, K.D., & Kent, R. Behavior modification for social action: Research tactics and problems. In L. Hamerlynck, L. Handy, and E. Mash (Eds)., *Behavior change: Methodology, concepts, and practice.* Champaign, Illinois: Research Press, 1973. Pp. 69-96.

Palkes, H., Stewart, M., & Freedman, J. Improvement in maze performance of hyperactive boys as a function of verbal-training procedures. *Journal of Special Education,* 1972, 5, 337-343.

Risley, T.R. The effects and side effects of punishing the autistic behaviors of a deviant child. *Journal of Applied Behavior Analysis,* 1968, 1, 21-34.

Robin, A.L., Armel, S., & O'Leary, K.D. The effects of self-instruction on writing deficiencies. *Behavior Therapy,* 1975, 6, 178-187.

Vygotsky, L. *Thought and language.* New York: Wiley, 1962.

Wahler, R.G. Oppositional children: A quest for parental reinforcement control. *Journal of Applied Behavior Analysis,* 1969, 2, 159-170.

Walker, H.M., & Buckley, N.K. The use of positive reinforcement in conditioning attending behavior. *Journal of Applied Behavior Analysis,* 1968, 1, 245-250.

Walker, H.M., & Buckley, N.K. Programming generalization and maintenance of treatment effects across time and across settings. *Journal of Applied Behavior Analysis,* 1972, 5, 209-224.

Wolf, M.M., Hanley, E.L., King, L.A., Lachowicz, J., & Giles, D.K. The timer game: A variable interval contingency for the management of out-of-seat behavior. *Exceptional Children,* 1970, 37, 113-117.

# Article 19
## Generalization and Maintenance of Appropriate Behavior through Self-Control*†

HILLARY TURKEWITZ, K. DANIEL O'LEARY, and MARSHA IRONSMITH

Abstract: Eight disruptive children attended an after school reading tutorial program 1 hour a day for 72 days. After baseline, the children evaluated their academic and social behavior. A token program was instituted and then modified to include the following procedures: (a) points and backup reinforcers were made contingent upon accurate self-ratings; (b) the requirement of accurately matching teacher ratings was faded until the children had complete control over point distribution; and (c) backup reinforcers were also faded and eliminated. While there was a lack of generalization of appropriate social behavior to the regular classroom situation, generalization was demonstrated in the 15-minute control period of every class, and maintenance was demonstrated in the final week of the program after all backup reinforcers were withdrawn.

Many of the early classroom token programs demonstrated substantial reductions in inappropriate behavior, but when the token programs were withdrawn, this behavior change was not maintained

*From *Journal of Consulting and Clinical Psychology,* 1975, Vol. 43, No. 4, 577-583. Copyright 1975 by the American Psychological Association. Reprinted by permission.

†This study was supported by U.S. Office of Education Grant OEG-0-71-2872. The opinions expressed herein, however, do not necessarily reflect the postion or policy of the U.S. Office of Education, and no official endorsement by the U.S. Office of Education should be inferred. We are especially grateful to Warren Lowey and Thomas Stone and the teachers of the transitional adjustment classes of the Three Village Schools, Stony Brook, New York, for referring children to us. The authors wish to thank Dennis Dubey and Ron Prinz for their helpful suggestions.

(Birnbrauer, Wolf, Kidder, & Tague, 1965; Kuypers, Becker, & O'Leary, 1968; O'Leary, Becker, Evans, & Saudargas, 1969). Similarly, many studies have not found generalization effects of the token program to times of the day when the program was not in effect (Kuypers et al., 1968; Meichenbaum, Bowers, & Ross, 1968; O'Leary et al., 1969; Wolf, Giles, & Hall, 1968). Recently, however, there have been reports of maintenance or generalization. Bolstad and Johnson (1972) noted maintenance effects following removal of a token program, but since observers were responsible for token administration and checking of students' self-evaluative behavior, the continued observer presence during the token withdrawal phase may have had a suppressive effect on disruptive behavior (Surratt & Ulrich, 1969). Drabman (1973) had student captains or teachers evaluate student behavior following removal of the rewards associated with a token program and found that disruptive behavior remained relatively low during the reward withdrawal period. Walker and Buckley (1972) assessed various maintenance strategies following a special class token reinforcement program and found that if teachers continue to systematically apply variations of the special class behavioral interventions, the appropriate behavior is maintained at higher rates than if no maintenance intervention is used. O'Leary, Drabman, and Kass (1973) demonstrated maintenance of treatment effects in 8 weeks following withdrawal of a token program where no maintenance intervention was used. Finally, Drabman, Spitalnik, and O'Leary (1973) demonstrated very clear generalization effects of a token program to times of the day when the token program was not in effect. In sum, there is accumulating evidence of maintenance and generalization, although maintenance of appropriate behavior has not been unequivocally demonstrated in the absence of some maintenance strategy.

The present study was designed to produce both generalization and maintenance of a token reinforcement effect through the use of several procedures designed to increase the probability of successful self-management. As in the Drabman et al. (1973) study, the children were taught to evaluate their own behavior, and the teachers' control over point distribution was faded and eliminated. In addition, the backup reinforcers were gradually withdrawn. Thus, this study was a systematic replication and extension of Drabman et al. (1973).

## METHOD

### Children and Teachers

The experimental class consisted of eight children, five girls and three boys, between 7 and 11 years of age. The children, who were in "transitional adjustment" classes for students with academic and social problems, attended an after school token reinforcement reading program at the University laboratory school. Children were referred by their teachers for the program if they displayed high rates of disruptive classroom behavior and were at least a year below grade level in reading. Two female students, an undergraduate who had completed student teaching and a graduate student, served as teachers in this study. The class met five days a week from 4:00 to 5:00 p.m. Parents were asked to bring their children at least four times a week.

In addition to the eight children involved in the program, eight control children, who were matched for age and California Achievement Test reading scores and who were also in "transitional adjustment" classes, were observed in their home classes and given the same preachievement and postachievement tests as the children in the program.

### Procedure

This study lasted over a period of 4.5 months including 72 school days. Twelve different conditions were instituted at this time. The hour was divided into four 15-minute intervals, one of which was randomly chosen each day as a control period in which tokens were never given. The 12 conditions were as follows: (a) baseline, (b) goals, (c) self-evaluation, (d) tokens, (e) matching—100%, (f) matching—50%, (g) matching—33-1/3%, (h) no matching, (i) fading backups—50%, (j) fading backups—33-1/3%, (k) fading backups—12½%, and (l) no backups. These procedures are similar to those used by Drabman et al. (1973) with the exception of Phases i-l. The conditions involved the following procedures:

### Baseline

In this condition, the children were given Sullivan readers (Sullivan, 1969) and asked to work as far as they could. Every 15 minutes, they were stopped and their progress was noted in their book. Throughout the program, the two teachers were continually giving individual aid to the children at their desks and having them read out loud to develop their phonic skills. During this time teachers were asked to use any form of disciplinary control they thought was appropriate. This discipline primarily involved the use of praise and ignore techniques, although reprimands were used on occasion, and if a child was disrupting the entire class he or she was asked to leave the room and sit in the "principal's" office. This isolation procedure was used four times in the first three conditions of the program; it was never necessary after tokens were introduced. Baseline lasted 4 days.

*Goals*

In this phase, children were assigned goals that were written on a card taped to their desks at the beginning of each 15-minute interval. Goals continued to be assigned during all subsequent phases. Disruptive behavior was handled as in baseline. This condition lasted 6 days.

*Self-evaluation*

In this condition, children were asked to rate themselves on their goal cards at the end of every 15-minute interval. Children were instructed to give themselves up to 5 points for their academic work and up to 5 points for their behavior during the interval. Teachers also rated students during this phase; the students were given general feedback on their self-ratings but were not informed of the exact teachers' ratings. This condition was in effect for 5 days.

*Tokens*

During this phase the children were not asked to rate their own behavior. Instead it was explained that the teachers would be giving them points after three of the four intervals and that these points could be exchanged for candy, snacks, and small toys at the end of the hour. One randomly chosen interval served as a control period during which generalization was assessed. At the beginning of each control interval, the teachers announced that no points would be awarded during that 15-minute period. The control period during this and all subsequent phases was identical to the goal phase; i.e., children were assigned goals at the beginning of the period, but they were not asked to evaluate their behavior, and the teachers did not evaluate the children or give them rewards. During the three token intervals, the teachers were told to give the children up to 5 points for social behavior and up to 5 points for academic behavior. The teachers wrote the number of points on a card, gave the children feedback after each rating, and explained why such a rating was given. An additional contingency for cheating was instituted when it was discovered that the children were not working conscientiously on the Sullivan books but were looking at the answers beforehand. If the child was ever seen cheating during the interval, he lost all 5 academic points.

The number of points necessary to obtain any given reinforcer was determined by taking the retail price of the item and adding one-third. For example, a 15¢ candy bar could be obtained for 20 points. Teachers were advised to rate the children only on their behavior during the interval and not to be influenced by behavior during the control period. This condition lasted 12 days.

*Matching—100%*

In this condition, teachers again asked the children to rate their social and academic behavior. They were informed that if their ratings were within 1 point of the teachers' ratings, they would receive the number of points they had given themselves. If the two ratings matched exactly, they also received a bonus point. However, if there was more than a 1-point discrepancy between the ratings, they got no points for that interval. Teachers praised the students for accuracy in matching and gave feedback on inaccuracy. This phase lasted 8 days.

*Matching—50%*

In this phase, the children were informed that now only half of the children present would match their ratings with the teachers'. Names were chosen beforehand, so that in this phase each child would match an equal number of times. However, at the end of each interval, the names were put on pieces of paper and drawn out of a hat so that the children believed they were randomly chosen. Children who were not chosen to match received the number of points they gave themselves and could not receive a bonus point. Teachers rated all children but only reported their ratings to children who matched. However, they praised accuracy and gave feedback on inaccurate ratings to all children. This phase lasted 5 days.

*Matching—33-1/3%*

This phase was identical to the previous phase except that one third of the children present were chosen each day to match with the teachers'. This phase lasted 4 days.

334     Classroom Management

*No matching*

In this condition, children were informed that no one would match with the teacher and that they would all receive whatever points they gave themselves. Feedback was still given on the accuracy of the ratings. For the remainder of the study, the children were in complete control of the number of points they received. This phase lasted 5 days.

*Fading backups—50%*

In this condition, each child rated himself and did not match with the teacher. However, at the end of the hour, names of half of the children were chosen from a hat, and only those children were allowed to exchange their points for reinforcers that day. As before, the names were prechosen so that each child would be selected an equal number of times. Teachers' instructions to the children were as follows:

> We have been very happy with the way you have been working. We would like to help you learn how to work well without getting the candy and snacks. Most of the time you have been very accurate in your ratings; we think that you don't need rewards all the time to work well.
>
> What we are going to do at the end of each day is select some of your names—the same way we did when we matched. If your name is selected, you will exchange your points for that day. Each day we will select new names.

Feedback on accuracy of ratings was always given to each child. This phase lasted 5 days.

*Fading backups—33-1/3%*

In this phase, the procedures were the same as in Phase i, except that the names of one third of the children present were chosen each day to exchange their points. This phase lasted 5 days.

*Fading backups—12-1/2%*

This phase was identical to the previous two phases except that only one child was chosen each day to receive backups. This phase lasted 8 days.

*No backups*

In the final phase, a reinstitution of the self-evaluation condition, the children were informed that they had been doing good work and that we thought they could work without getting prizes. Therefore, they were told to continue to rate themselves during the three rating intervals but that they would no longer be able to trade their points for backups. Feedback on the accuracy of the children's rating was still given. This phase lasted 5 days.

## Dependent Measures

The primary dependent measure was the mean number of disruptive behaviors observed during a 20-second period. The observation code was that used by O'Leary, Kaufman, Kass, and Drabman (1970) for classroom assessment and included recordings of inappropriate verbalizations, aggression, not attending, and being out of their seats. Three trained undergraduates observed the children through a one-way mirror in the University laboratory school. Observations were made on a 20-second observe/10-second record basis. Each child was observed for one 15-minute interval each day. Reliability checks were made an average of 5.4 times per condition. Reliability was calculated by dividing the number of perfect agreements on the occurrences of disruptive behaviors by the total number of agreements plus disagreements. When a reliability check was taken, an average of the two observations was used for the data point. Reliabilities averaged across children for the various phases were as follows: baseline, .96; goals, .95; self-evaluation, .94; tokens, .91; matching—100%, .93; matching—50%, .86; matching—33-1/3%, .79; no matching, .91; fading backups—50%, .95; fading backups—33-1/3%, 1.00; fading backups—12½%, .97; no backups, .96.

Changes in reading skills were assessed in the experimental and control children through preadministrations and postadministrations of the California Achievement Test. In addition, two 15-minute class observations were made of each of the experimental and control children in their public school classrooms at the beginning and end of the tutorial program. Additional data available were teachers' ratings, the children's ratings, and the daily progress of the children on the Sullivan readers.

## RESULTS

The mean levels of disruptive behavior for the entire class across all conditions are presented graphically in Fig. 1. There were 4 days in which less than four children were present in the class. The data

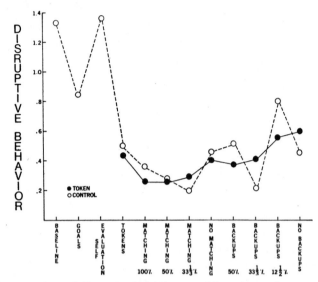

Fig. 1. Mean number of disruptive behaviors per 20-sec interval across all phases of the study.

gathered on these occasions are not included in the analysis. A repeated-measures analysis of variance revealed a significant treatment effect, $F(11) = 13.51$, $p < .01$. There was no significant difference between the level of disruptive behavior in the control intervals and the token periods, $t(8) = .1$, $p > .7$.

Baseline data indicate that the students were extremely disruptive, averaging 1.33 disruptive behaviors in every 20-second interval. The level of disruptive behavior dropped somewhat when the children were given academic goals every 15 minutes, but the effect of this procedure was only temporary. During the 5 days of self-evaluation, the level of disruptive behavior rose to just slightly above that during baseline. In addition, during self-evaluation the children's ratings of their own behavior were extremely inaccurate; only 14 percent of their ratings fell within 1 point of the teachers'. While the mean teacher rating for this phase was 2.83 points out of a possible 10, the mean self-rating was 8.99. The mean child and teacher ratings across conditions are presented in Table 1.

The disruptive behavior decreased dramatically with the introduction of the token program, both in the control and token intervals. The mean teacher rating rose to 7.94.

The disruptive behavior during token intervals dropped from .43 to .26 during the first matching condition. A similar decrease was evidenced in the control period, from .50 during the token phase to

**Table 1. Frequency of Disruptive Behavior, Academic Performance, and Student and Teacher Ratings.**

| Phase | Average no. disruptive behaviors per 20-sec interval | | Work output % goals met | Average ratings | | % self-ratings within 1 point of teachers' |
|---|---|---|---|---|---|---|
| | Token period | Control period | | Teacher | Student | |
| Baseline | | 1.33 | | | | |
| Goals | | .85 | 83.2 | | | |
| Self-evaluation | | 1.37 | 58.2 | 2.83 | 8.99 | 14 |
| Tokens | .43 | .50 | 69.0 | 7.94 | | |
| Matching – 100% | .26 | .34 | 85.9 | 8.05 | 8.89 | 84 |
| Matching – 50% | .26 | .27 | 80.4 | 8.60 | 9.45 | 81 |
| Matching – 33-1/3% | .29 | .19 | 93.3 | 8.73 | 9.88 | 81 |
| No matching | .40 | .46 | 86.9 | 8.28 | 9.80 | 61 |
| Backups 50% | .37 | .53 | 94.0 | 9.18 | 9.78 | 83 |
| Backups 33-1/3% | .40 | .26 | 86.4 | 9.01 | 9.71 | 81 |
| Backups – 12-1/2% | .56 | .81 | 86.2 | 7.75 | 9.88 | 63 |
| No backups | .60 | .46 | 82.8 | 7.95 | 9.57 | 60 |

.34 in the matching phase. The percentage of accurate matches (self-ratings within 1 point of teacher ratings) rose sharply to a mean of 84 percent. Forty-two percent of the self-ratings were in perfect agreement with the teacher ratings. The difference between the average teacher and student ratings was .8 points.

The low levels of disruptive behavior and the high degree of accuracy of self-ratings were maintained in the following two phases when the frequency of matching was faded to 50 percent and then to 33-1/3 percent of the time. During these phases the children reported that they wanted to be selected to match with the teacher since they had the opportunity to earn a bonus point for perfect matches. During the no-matching condition, the level of disruptive behavior rose slightly, and the percentage of accurate matches decreased to 61 percent.

During the first two days of the next phase, in which only 50 percent of the children received backup reinforcers, the level of disruptive behavior during the token periods was slightly lower than it was during the initial token phase—.39 disruptive behaviors per 20-second interval. Low levels of disruptive behavior continued throughout this phase. The children continued to rate their behavior accurately; 83 percent of the ratings were within 1 point of the teachers', and 60 percent of the ratings were perfect matches. Accurate self-evaluations and low levels of disruptive behavior were also maintained when one third of the children received backups.

During the phase in which one child received backups, the level of disruptive behavior rose to .56 during the token intervals and .81 during the control intervals, and the accuracy of the self-ratings dropped. The mean disruptive behavior in the last week of the program, when it was announced that all backup reinforcers were being withdrawn, was .60 during the intervals in which the students were self-evaluating and .46 during the control intervals.

Academic output, summarized in Table 1, is presented in terms of the percentage of intervals in which the student met the goal the teacher set for him. Although the Sullivan reader provides a precise measure of output, through the number of frames completed, this measure was confounded by the cheating the teachers found difficult to control in the early stages of the program. During the self-evaluation phase, the teachers deducted 5 points for cheating in 80 percent of their ratings; thus they saw a child cheating at least once in 80 percent of the 15-minute intervals. The children were working at a much faster rate than they would have been if they were actually reading the material instead of looking at the answers. When the token program was instituted and the children were informed of the penalty for this behavior, the frequency of cheating decreased drastically. The teachers deducted the 5 points only 20 percent of the time. This lower rate of cheating was maintained throughout the program, finally decreasing to 15 percent during the no-backup phase.

The children advanced an average of 2.5 grade levels in the Sullivan readers, with the gains ranging from 1.4 to 3.9 grades. However, only a 5-month gain in reading skills was demonstrated by the pretest and posttest scores on the California Achievement Test. There were no significant differences in the academic gains between the experimental and control children.

The observations of children in the public school revealed that there was no difference in the degree of behavior change between the experimental and control students. Both groups showed slight decreases in disruptive behavior from baseline to the end of the 4.5-month period of the after school program.


## DISCUSSION

This study clearly indicates that it is not necessary for a teacher to continually monitor a classroom token program, given appropriate shaping and fading procedures. In addition, the low levels of disruptive behavior in the control intervals demonstrate generalization of appropriate behavior, and the low levels of disruptive behavior following removal of the token program demonstrate maintenance of appropriate behavior.

One expectation of the investigators that was not confirmed was that the experimental subjects would demonstrate significantly greater reading gains than the control group. Throughout the token program, half of the points received were contingent upon academic output and accuracy. In fact, as evidenced by the work output data, the children were advancing steadily in their workbooks throughout the program. In addition, teachers were frequently giving individual tutoring at the children's desks. However, there are several possible reasons for the lack of differential gains: (a) the opportunity to cheat undermined the utility of the workbooks; (b) there appeared to be competition among the students to finish the books quickly; and (c) some of the children tended to "beat the system" by filling in the answers from cues in the preceding frames without reading the material. The teachers felt that it was difficult to motivate some of these children to learn academic skills. This lack of motivation plus the fact that the students reported that the workbooks were very boring may have contributed to the unproductive work habits cited previously and would clearly reduce the effectiveness of the Sullivan series. Drabman et al. (1973) reported that their subjects advanced 7.2 months in reading vocabulary during the 58 days of an after school token program, but this was the only subtest of the California Achievement Test they administered, and no treatment-control comparisons were made.

The observed generalization to the nontoken interval is a replication of the results of the Drabman et al. (1973) study. It was clear that the children were aware of the change in contingencies from the token to control intervals. The control intervals were always announced by the teacher, and the children often made statements to the effect that they could "be bad" because tokens were not being given. There are several possible reasons why they did not choose to do so. It may have been that the training in self-evaluation contributed to this effect, but one cannot conclude that this training was totally responsible for the generalization because in this study, as in the Drabman et al. (1973) investigation, the generalization to the control interval occurred before matching was instituted. It may be that either the random assignment of the control interval or the ratio of token to control time is the critical variable. However, these arguments cannot explain the maintenance effect that occurred when no backups were awarded. The rate of disruptive behavior during the no-backup phase was less than half of the baseline and self-evaluation conditions, and the mean disruptive behavior during the final 2 days of the last condition was lower than during the first 2.

The maintenance of low levels of disruptive behavior when backup reinforcers were withdrawn may have been due to the gradual fading of reinforcers, which actually began when the children lost points for inaccurate matches. Another possible explanation comes from the teachers' observation that the children made statements indicating that they were monitoring and evaluating their behavior, e.g., "I was out of my seat—I'm going to lose a point," and "I shouldn't do that or I'll lose a point." It is interesting that these statements were made during the 28 days when the children were in complete control of the points they were to receive, and even during the final week of the program when the children were evaluating themselves but the points were no longer exchangeable for back-ups.

One could argue that if accurate self-evaluations were a powerful change agent, then the disruptive behavior of the experimental subjects in their regular classrooms should have decreased. This negative finding underscores the difficulty of producing generalization to nontreatment settings. However, no attempt was made to prompt these children to self-evaluate in their home classes; this prompting, coupled with social reinforcement, may be necessary to produce generalized effects.

There are several important practical advantages of the treatment package presented. Less teacher time is involved in administration of the token program. The extrinsic reinforcers can be withdrawn completely without a return to baseline level of disruptive behavior. In addition, this procedure introduced self-evaluative skills that, with more extensive prompting and training, might be used by the child across various academic settings.

# REFERENCES

Birnbrauer, J.S., Wolf, M.M., Kidder, J.D., & Tague, C.E.    Classroom behavior of retarded pupils  with token reinforcement. *Joural of Experimental Child Psychology,* 1965, 2, 219-325.

Bolstad, O.D., & Johnson, S.M. Self-regulation in the modification of disruptive classroom behavior. *Journal of Applied Behavior Analysis,* 1972, 5, 443-454.

Drabman, R.S. Child- versus teacher-administered token programs in a psychiatric hospital school. *Journal of Abnormal Child Psychology,* 1973, 1, 68-87.

Drabman, R.S., Spitalnik, R., & O'Leary, K.D. Teaching self-control to disruptive children. *Journal of Abnormal Psychology,* 1973, 82, 10-16.

Kuypers, D.S., Becker, W.C., & O'Leary, K.D. How to make a token system fail. *Exceptional Children,* 1968, 35, 101-109.

Meichenbaum, D.H., Bowers, K.S., & Ross, R.R. Modification of classroom behavior of institutionalized female adolescent offenders. *Behavior Research and Therapy,* 1968, 6, 343-353.

O'Leary, K.D., Becker, W.C., Evans, M.B., & Saudargas, R.A.  A token reinforcement program in a public school: A replication and systematic analysis. *Journal of Applied Behavior Analysis,* 1969, 2, 3-13.

O'Leary, K.D., Drabman, R.S., & Kass, R.E. Maintenance of appropriate behavior in a token program. *Journal of Abnormal Child Psychology,* 1973, 1, 127-138.

O'Leary, K.D., Kaufman, K.F., Kass, R.E., & Drabman, R.S. The effects of loud and soft reprimands on the behavior of disruptive students. *Exceptional Children,* 1970, 37, 145-155.

Sullivan, M.W. *Reading.* Palo Alto, Calif.: Behavioral Research Laboratory, 1969.

Surratt, P.R., Ulrich, R.E., & Hawkins, R.P. An elementary student as a behavioral engineer. *Journal of Applied Behavior Analysis,* 1969, 2, 85-92.

Walker, H.M., & Buckley, N.K. Programming generalization and maintenance of treatment effects across time and across settings. *Journal of Applied Behavior Analysis,* 1972, 5, 209-224.

Wolf, M.M., Giles, D.K., & Hall, R.V. Experiments with token reinforcement in a remedial classroom. *Behaviour Research and Therapy,* 1968, 6, 51-64.

# 8
## *Environmental Assessment and Change*

During the past decade almost every profession has been influenced by ecological laws, concepts, and practice. In medicine, for example, it has now been determined that certain cancers are critically influenced by environmental factors. Only 10 years ago, however, the warnings of the famous biologist, Barry Steele Commoner (*Time,* 1975), that cancers were environmentally caused were deemed frivolous. Following some of his hypotheses, investigators have found that lung, liver, and bladder cancer are found in areas near chemical industries. Melanoma, a skin cancer, is more common in the South than in the North. In law, a new litigation specialization is developing which involves suits regarding the actual *and potential* environmental impact of myriad acts, e.g., pollution, building a dam for a hydroelectric plant. Fortunately, in teaching as well, there is an increased awareness of the impact of broad classroom environmental variables that influence children's behavior. This awareness is probably best exemplified in the research with open or informal classrooms and schools architecturally designed to facilitate certain social interaction patterns on the part of both students and teachers (Ruedi & West, 1973).

Ecological approaches to classrooms emphasize both the physical setting and the program, but more importantly, they stress what Gump (1975) referred to as a wide-angle analysis. He stated his case as follows:

When we stand back from the elements of a phenomenon and look, we may 'see better' [and] we see in a very different sense. For example, in the case of the trees and forest, the more distant perspective yields a perception of the boundaries. One can learn what other units are adjacent to the forest. Furthermore, within the forest it is possible to perceive the relation among the wooded areas which was not apparent when one inspected the individual trees. (p. 115)

Basically, his point is that close-up classroom observation yields only information about individual behaviors or certain relations between individuals. On the other hand, he feels that a more distant perspective can lead to equally, if not more, important information.

Some very interesting findings have emerged from this wide-angle analysis. Conant (1974) monitored the activities in 47 elementary school classes and found that only 30 percent of the teachers' time was directly related to academic instruction and learning. Clerical work and housekeeping occupied 40 percent of their time! Conant concluded that clerks should be assigned the latter duties and that teachers should be hired only to teach. Gump (1975) drew another, perhaps more reasoned conclusion, i.e., that activity management should be a central concern of educational research and that such findings should be communicated to teachers. Kounin (1970; 1975) was one of the first investigators to carefully delineate the behavioral effect of different classroom activities. In fact, his approach is aptly described as activity management, and the contrast with management via reinforcement will soon become apparent. Kounin analyzed videotapes of classrooms and ascertained which classroom activities and ways of arranging those activities were associated with the greatest amount of on-task behavior. He found that there was an average of 33 major changes in academic learning activities involving either the entire class or major subgroups of the class. In recitation settings, momentum or absence of slowdowns correlated with work involvement and freedom from deviancy. Examples of slowdowns were: dwelling too long on a subject as when a teacher reprimanded a student and then began to lecture the entire class, or similarly, dwelling on the props used in a lesson as when a teacher slowly passed out a mimeographed sheet to one child at a time. Smoothness or absence of jerkiness correlated with both work involvement and freedom from deviancy in recitation *and* seatwork settings. Smoothness referred to the absence of teacher actions that produced stops or jarring breaks in the activity flow. For example, a teacher might be walking down an aisle while explaining a history lesson. Seeing a note on the floor near a student the teacher would suddenly ask, "What is that piece of paper doing on the floor?" thus interrupting the even flow of the lesson.

The first experiment in the Krantz and Risley (1972) article demonstrates what may appear to some to be a patently obvious result, i.e., when children are seated very near one another, their attending decreases because of disruptions that occur between the children. The second study in that article, however, documents a result which should be noted by those who permit children to have an activity, such as playing soccer, hockey, or gymnastics, as a consequence in a reinforcement program. Classroom activities should be carefully sequenced so that they minimize disruption and most importantly, so that the behavior of one activity does not impede the activities in another.

The Bittle (1975) article is included in the Environmental Assessment and Change section because it reflects a novel way to increase communication between parents and teacher, i.e., a teacher telephone message system. As stated in the introduction to this section, the ecological approach focuses on a wide-angle analysis of classrooms. Going one step further, one may look at the determinants of classroom behavior outside the classroom. Parental influences have a very significant impact on scholastic achievement, particularly reading (Coleman, 1975), and thus, it is highly fitting that communication between schools and parents be encouraged and facilitated. In fact, given an average school day of five hours (300 minutes) of academic instruction (excluding recess and lunch), a teacher with 30 students has an average of 10 minutes that theoretically could be spent per student. Obviously, however, nonacademic pursuits occupy a significant portion of a teacher's time which decreases the potential time that can be devoted to each child. On the other hand, many parents can readily spend 10 minutes or more with their children per day in some academic endeavor. With a young child, a parent might listen while the student reads; with an older child, the parent might discuss a political event that is being covered in school the following day.

Although the particular Illinois sample may be unlike many metropolitan school districts, the Bittle article illustrates parental interest in a child's schooling. One may seriously question who was really calling the school (parent or child), but the behavioral effects of the communication system are strong enough to make one suspect that most parents were calling or asking their children to call and listen to the message. Finally, from a pragmatic standpoint, it should be remembered that the message was brief (2-3 minutes) and took only 10-15 minutes per day to prepare.

The cost of the service, $5/year/student, is obviously something to consider strongly. For example, in a school district of 10,000 elementary students, a $5 cost per student would be equivalent to $50,000 or possibly four special teachers (e.g., remedial reading specialists). Interestingly, one could empirically assess the comparative effects of the communication system and the remedial reading teachers' tutoring on the students' reading performance. On an a priori basis, it is unclear which would exact greater change in reading. Tutorial programs have long established reputations for helping children, but a comparison of the effects of tutoring with those of a communication system would be interesting. Perhaps the communication system would aid children with mild or no deficits but not help children with severe deficits. On the other hand, remedial tutors could not see each child or even 50 percent of the children in a district, although they might be best able to aid children with severe deficits.

The Trickett and Moos (1974) article exemplifies the type of research which can provide meaningful answers to teachers' questions regarding the impact of differing classroom environments. By surveying 36 high school classrooms and assessing student attitudes in those classes, they found that students report greatest learning in classrooms where: (1) students are highly involved (do extra work, put energy into what they do, enjoy the class); (2) there is high rule clarity (a clear set of rules; teacher makes a point of sticking to the rules s/he has made; teacher explains what will happen if a student breaks the rules); (3) there is competition (students try to get the best grade; some students try to see who can answer questions first; students have to work for a good grade). Satisfaction with the teacher is seen where there is student involvement, teacher support (teacher takes a personal interest in students; teacher is more like a friend than an authority; teacher goes out of way to help students), rule clarity, and teacher innovation (teacher encourages students to try new projects; variety in class work each day).

In interpreting Tables 1 and 2, only those correlations which were significant for both Samples 1 and 2 reflect important relationships that were obtained in both samples. Thus, only when you see an *a, b,* or *c* in both columns 1 and 2 for a CES subscale should you interpret the results with strong confidence. Those relationships are enclosed in boxes (as most of you probably recall, a correlation can range from -1.00 to +1.00). In Table 2, it is interesting to note that Rule Clarity is again important; students feel interested when there is high rule clarity and feel an *absence* of anger when there is order and organization in the classroom (assignments are clear, and activities are clearly and carefully planned).

Teacher praise has consistently been shown to result in less classroom disruption in elementary classes as evidenced by earlier articles. In these high school classes discussed by Trickett and Moos (1974), teacher support was consistently related to satisfaction with the teacher. While classroom disruption was not measured, one can presume that in classes with high teacher support, there was little disruption. Such is partly documented by the relationship between teacher support and students feeling interested. In sum, showing interest and being positive to students appear to be related ubiquitously to a classroom that is enjoyed and is without major disruptions.

# Article 20
# Behavioral Ecology in the Classroom* †

PATRICIA J. KRANTZ and TODD R. RISLEY

Abstract: Many investigators have been interested in the use of individual contingency management procedures to remediate undesirable classroom behavior, but far less attention has been paid to the impersonal variables or setting events that often engender inappropriate behavior in the classroom. The present studies explored the effects of two impersonal, ecological variables upon the behavior of black kindergarten children from a segregated, low-income neighborhood. Experiment I demonstrated that when children's seating arrangements were crowded, or when they were required to crowd around a teacher's demonstration, their visual attendance to the teacher and/or to the educational materials was markedly reduced. A second experiment showed that visual attendance to a teacher and/or to the books throughout a story period was markedly lower when this academic session had been preceded by a period of vigorous activity than when preceded by a rest period; and transition times were longer and more disruptive following vigorous activities. When individual contingency

*This is one in a series of studies conducted by the Living Environments Group at the University of Kansas under the direction of Todd R. Risely. The following members of that group participated in the design and conduct of the study: Francisco Montes and Lynn E. McClannahan. Special thanks are also due to Cordelia Murphy, teacher at Turner House Preschool. During the course of this work the first author was supported by a grant from the U.S. Office of Education, Educational and Professional Development Act, Traineeship for Training Teachers of Teachers. The research was supported by the National Institute of Child Health and Human Development Grant HD 03144 to the Bureau of Child Research at the University of Kansas. Reprints are available from Todd R. Risely, Department of Human Development, University of Kansas, Lawrence, Kansas 66045.

† Reprinted by permission.

management techniques were used, in both of these studies, to remediate the undesirable behaviors that occurred in the presence of unfavorable environmental conditions, the impersonal ecological arrangements were shown to be as effective and efficient in producing desired behavior change as these standard behavior modification procedures. These findings suggest that environmental arrangements may become as important a focus for applied behavior analysis as contingency management systems have been.

Within the areas of early childhood care and education, much has been written about the importance of creating physically attractive environments and general milieus that will result in social and intellectual growth for children. Many authors advance recommendations concerning the physical plant, daily program scheduling, and equipment and materials (e.g., Evans, Shub, & Weinstein, 1971; Leavitt, 1958; Leeper, Dales, Skipper, & Witherspoon, 1968), but often these recommendations are simply rooted in educational tradition and stand without empirical support.

Cruickshank and Quay (1970) point out that, on the surface, school planning and construction appear to be founded upon defined educational, architectural and construction goals, and indeed, design dimensions such as air circulation, cubic footage, lighting and building materials are usually carefully specified and researched, but not for questions of their effects upon child behavior. If educational outcomes are considered at all during planning and construction, input usually comes from anecdotal evidence supplied by teachers and school administrators, and not from any systematic observation that could establish empirical relationships between environmental arrangements and child behavior.

Sommer (1971) suggests that many aspects of classrooms and care settings are designed for ease of maintenance and efficiency of cleaning, with little cognizance of social functions. In addition, traditional physical arrangements often persist, although the rationales that led to their construction are no longer salient.

Even if educators and child care workers are aware of the richness and diversity of recent architectural innovations, their choices among these new design alternatives are usually a matter of guesswork, since there has been little empirical analysis of the types of physical facilities that support child care or educational goals (Barker & Gump, 1964; Doke, unpublished).

When writers in the area of early childhood education discuss the physical features of a classroom or day care setting, these are usually treated separately from desired program outcomes, with little or no consideration of the relationships between specific classroom designs or program characteristics and child behavior patterns. It is precisely at this interface between environmental components and behavioral outcomes that an ecological perspective becomes invaluable (Sells, 1969).

Recently, applied behavior analysts have become increasingly interested in explorations of the effects of impersonal, ecological variables upon behavior in natural settings (cf. Becker, Engelmann, & Thomas, 1971; Orme & Purnell, 1970; Tharp & Wetzel, 1969). Such ecological investigations employ the observational and experimental analysis of behavior in applied settings. For example, Cohen (1968), an architect-behavioral psychologist, uses behaviorally-based observation and time sampling procedures to examine the relationships between physical design and human behavior.

At the University of Kansas, the members of the Living Environments Group have also employed applied behavior analysis technology in exploring ecological variables pertaining to the design of living environments for dependent populations. Technologies have been developed for improving the quality of such environments as an infant day care center (Cataldo & Risley, 1974; LeLaurin, Cataldo, & Risely, in press; Twardosz, Cataldo, & Risley, 1974a, b); a toddler day care center (Twardosz, Cataldo, & Risley, 1974b, 1975); a preschool (Risley, 1971; Doke & Risely, 1972; Hart & Risely, 1974; Montes & Risely, in press; LeLaurin & Risley, 1972); a recreation program for disadvantaged children and adolescents (Pierce & Risely, 1974a, b; Quilitch & Risely, 1973); and a nursing home (McClannahan & Risely, 1973, 1974, 1975, in press). These studies use direct observation and measurement to obtain descriptive data on environmental dimensions and behavioral characteristics, and proceed from descriptive data to experimental manipulation of specific ecological variables within the living environments.

The studies presented in this paper are a part of this larger project; specifically, they are designed to show the relationships between classroom environmental variables and the preacademic or social behaviors of kindergarten children. Observations in many kindergartens, and interviews with kindergarten teachers were the basis for the choice of behaviors to be measured, as well as the selection of environmental variables to be manipulated.

During preliminary observations and interviews, it became apparent that in many kindergarten classrooms, there are particular activities and particular time periods during the day when the teachers consistently experience difficulties in implementing their program. It appeared that at these times, teachers arranged the environment in ineffective ways that, in fact, set the occasion for those behaviors that they least desired. The research presented below identified and manipulated some of the environmental variables that are associated with these disruptive occasions in the classroom.

## EXPERIMENT I:   EFFECTS OF SPATIAL DENSITY DURING TWO CLASSROOM ACTIVITIES

The physical environment often affects the manner in which persons arrange themselves in relation to one another, and these human arrangements may subsequently give rise to specific response patterns (Eastman & Harper, 1971; Hall, 1963). Ecological studies of the interactions between human arrangements and behavior often employ the concepts of social and spatial density. The term "social density" refers to the number of people per unit space, while "spatial density" refers to the amount of space per person.

Experimental studies of the behavioral effects of population densities on young children have most often measured aggression and group interaction. Although the results have not been totally consistent, in general they indicate that: (1) crowded conditions result in increased incidence of aggression (Jersild & Markey, 1935; Hutt & McGrew, 1967); and (2) high density situations produce decrements in close personal contacts among group members (Hutt & Vaisey, 1966; Loo, 1972; McGrew, 1970).

Most kindergarten teachers who were observed prior to the initiation of this study conducted story or lesson activities by asking children to come and sit cross-legged and in close physical proximity on the floor in front of their chairs. With a group of children crowded together and competing for limited space, the usual outcome was poking, shoving and failure to attend to the teacher and/or to the presented materials. It appeared that crowded conditions set the occasion for disruptive and inattentive behaviors that were incompatible with the acquisition of academic responses.

Similarly, observations in kindergarten classrooms indicated that project demonstrations were also occasions for crowding children together. Children were typically asked to gather around the teacher and visually attend to her and to the materials she was presenting. Again, children who were competing for limited space and visual access exhibited a variety of inattentive and disruptive behaviors.

These observations in the natural environment suggested that spatial arrangements and population densities might have important effects upon children's classroom behavior. Thus, the present study compared the effects of crowded versus uncrowded conditions on students' on-task behavior during two classroom activities, story periods and project demonstration sessions.

## Method

### Subject and Setting

The subjects for Experiment I were black children who had recently completed kindergarten in a segregated low-income neighborhood. The five boys and three girls who participated in these studies began to attend supplementary kindergarten sessions at Turner House Preschool immediately following the last day of the school year. Sessions were conducted for two and one-half hours per day, five days per week. The physical setting, as well as the daily routine, was designed to simulate a typical public school classroom. Each weekday, the children participated in both a story period and a demonstration session, during which spatial arrangements were manipulated.

### Story Periods

In order to test the effect of spatial density during story period, crowded and uncrowded seating arrangements were alternated daily, or every two days, in an equivalent time-samples design (Campbell & Stanley, 1963). During uncrowded conditions, the teacher asked the children to come to the rug in the story area and sit cross-legged on squares of masking tape placed two feet apart. During crowded conditions, a blanket was folded to 3 feet by 4 feet and placed on the rug, and the teacher instructed children to sit cross-legged on the blanket.

In order to insure that the spatial dimension was the only difference between conditions, the following variables were held constant across both crowded and uncrowded seating arrangements: (1) teacher, blanket and rug always occupied the same positions within the story area; (2) the children were not arranged in any specific seating sequence in either condition; (3) the teacher did not prompt or reinforce attentive behavior, nor did she respond to disruptive behavior in either condition; and (4) the same books and teacher were used during both conditions, to control for story content and possible teacher and story preferences.

On-task behavior during story period was defined as sitting cross-legged, visually attending to the teacher or to the materials presented, and not engaging in any disruptive behavior. Observations were made throughout the entire 15-minute story period, using a procedure of time sampling at a point in time. Observers located behind a one-way mirror observed the children every 30 seconds, and scored each child as being on-task or off-task at that point in time. Children were always observed in a predetermined sequence of left to right, and front row to back row.

Each session yielded the percent of time samples during which each of the eight children was scored as on-task. These percent figures were then averaged to obtain mean percent on-task behavior per day.

Measures of interobserver agreement were obtained during six story sessions; three during crowded and three during uncrowded conditions. Within each session, each pair of observations was scored as an agreement or as a disagreement, and interobserver agreement was computed according to the formula: total number of agreements divided by agreements plus disagreements, multiplied by 100. Interobserver agreement during story periods ranged from 86 percent to 97 percent with mean agreement of 94 percent.

*Project Demonstration Sessions*

During project demonstration sessions, the teacher showed the eight children how to use arts and crafts materials that were distributed to them immediately following her demonstration. In uncrowded project demonstration sessions, the teacher asked the children to sit in a semi-circle about one foot apart; in this arrangement, they were equidistant from each other and from the teacher, who sat in the center. In crowded project demonstrations, the teacher asked children to gather around behind her as she sat at a low table. The first three project demonstrations were done under uncrowded conditions; the next two under crowded conditions; subsequently, crowded and uncrowded conditions alternated daily, in an equivalent time-samples design.

The following variables were controlled during both uncrowded and crowded sessions: (1) the same teacher conducted all project demonstration sessions; (2) the same arts and crafts activities were demonstrated in both conditions; (3) children were always instructed to watch the teacher, so that they could do the project themselves following the demonstration; (4) children were not assigned positions in either condition; and (5) the teacher did not prompt or reinforce appropriate behavior, nor did she attend to disruptive behavior in either condition.

A child was defined as on-task during project demonstration sessions if his head was oriented in the direction of the teacher, if he was seated during the uncrowded demonstration and standing in the assigned area during the crowded demonstration, and if he was not engaging in any disruptive behavior. Observers stationed behind a one-way mirror recorded whether each subject was on-task or off-task; observations were made every 30 seconds throughout the project demonstration, using a procedure of time sampling at a point in time. Again, children were always observed in a predetermined sequence. Individual children's percentages of on-task behavior were averaged to obtain mean on-task behavior for each day.

Reliability estimates were obtained in four crowded and three uncrowded sessions and were calculated using the same formula used for story sessions. Interobserver agreement ranged from 90 percent to 100 percent, with mean agreement of 97 percent.

*Remediation of Off-Task Behavior under Crowded Conditions*

As indicated earlier, equivalent time-samples designs were employed both in story and project demonstration sessions, in order to assess the effects of crowded vs. uncrowded conditions upon children's on-task behavior. Subsequently, a multiple baseline design across activities was used to determine whether children's inappropriate classroom behavior under crowded conditions could be remediated, using standard contingency management procedures.

During this phase of the experiment, all procedures described earlier for story period and project demonstration sessions remained the same, with the exception that descriptive praise from the teacher and classroom privileges were delivered contingent upon children's on-task behavior during crowded conditions. Descriptive praise included compliments by the teacher to the effect that a child was "looking at the book," "sitting quietly," or "watching carefully." Immediately following story and project demonstration sessions those children who had been on-task were permitted classroom privileges which were paired with verbal contingency statements such as, "Johnny, since you always looked right at the teacher, you may [be first in line," or "feed the turtle," etc.].

Descriptive praise and classroom privileges were introduced first in project demonstrations and later in story periods. However, uncrowded conditions were used as probes on three days during project demonstrations and on one day during story period. On days when uncrowded conditions were implemented as probes, on-task behavior was not consequated with praise or privileges.

Interobserver agreement on measures obtained during remediation ranged from 91 percent to 97 percent, with mean interobserver agreement of 93 percent.

## Results

During both story periods and teacher demonstrations, children's levels of on-task behavior were found to be significantly higher under uncrowded conditions. While contingent teacher praise and classroom privileges successfully reduced off-task behavior under crowded conditions, these procedures were no more effective than the simple environmental tactic of separating children from one another.

### Crowded vs. Uncrowded Conditions

The lower graph of Fig. 1 shows the subjects' mean percent on-task behavior during story periods under both conditions. During days of uncrowded conditions, on-task behavior was always higher, averaging 88 percent across all days. The grand mean for on-task behavior during crowded conditions was 60 percent (T = 2.36, df = 26, p < .05).

Mean percent on-task behavior during project demonstrations under both conditions is shown in the upper graph of Fig. 1. Again, on-task behavior was always significantly higher under uncrowded conditions than under crowded conditions, averaging 50 percent (t = 6.38, df = 14, p < .01).

### Remediation of Off-Task Behavior under Crowded Conditions

The right-hand portions of Fig. 1 show the effects of introducing teacher praise and classroom privileges contingent upon on-task behavior under crowded conditions during both story periods and teacher demonstrations. During teacher demonstrations, such contingencies increased the level of on-task behavior from a grand mean of 50 percent during baseline to a grand mean of 88 percent during treatment. Similarly, during story periods the level of on-task behavior under crowded conditions rose from a grand mean of 60 percent during baseline to a grand mean of 92 percent when contingencies were applied.

During the treatment phase of the study, children were exposed to uncrowded conditions and no contingencies for three days of teacher demonstrations and one story period. The children's on-task behavior on these uncrowded probe days was consistently high, averaging 92 percent during teacher demonstrations and 95 percent during the story period, even though on-task behavior was not reinforced.

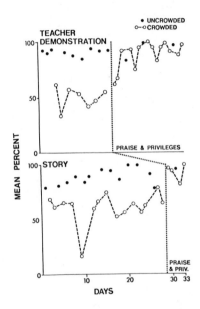

Fig. 1. Mean percent on-task behavior during teacher demonstration and story. During teacher demonstrations, on-task behavior was defined as being in the assigned area with head oriented toward the teacher and not engaged in disruptive behavior; and during story periods, on-task behavior was defined as sitting cross-legged, visually attending to the activity, and not engaged in disruptive behavior. In general, children remained on-task for a considerably greater percentage of the time when conditions were uncrowded (solid circles) than when they were crowded (open circles connected by dashed line). However, when descriptive praise and classroom privileges were introduced as consequences for on-task behavior, high levels of appropriate behavior were maintained even under crowded conditions.

## Discussion

In both story periods and teacher demonstrations significantly higher levels of on-task behavior were obtained during uncrowded than during crowded conditions. When descriptive praise from the teacher and the awarding of classroom privileges were used to reinforce on-task behavior during crowded conditions, differences in behavior during crowded and uncrowded conditions disappeared, indicating as expected that reinforcement procedures can be effective in remediating the inappropriate behaviors that occur when environmental arrangements are unfavorable. However, the data clearly show that simple ecological arrangements were as effective as individual contingency management procedures in producing appropriate classroom behavior.

## EXPERIMENT II:   EFFECTS OF ACTIVITY SEQUENCE ON CLASSROOM BEHAVIOR

Although much has been written about curriculum and content of activity periods, very little attention has been given to the possible effects of the sequence in which activities occur. The most frequently offered opinion is that children will be more attentive and less disruptive if the daily activity schedule is arranged so that active periods alternate with periods of quiet (Becker et. al., 1971; Hambilin, Mukerji, & Yonemura, 1967).

However, it might be hypothesized that alternating periods of gross motor activity and periods of quiet set the occasion for inappropriate behavior as children make the transition from one activity to another. For example, the child who is asked to come in from recess and take a nap must make rapid and radical adjustments in behavior in order to conform to classroom rules.

The present study examined these conflicting assumptions by manipulating classroom activity sequence.

## Method

*Subjects and Setting*

The subjects for Experiment II were the same eight children who participated in Experiment I, and the two and one-half hour kindergarten sessions, held at Turner House Preschool each weekday afternoon, were again designed to simulate those of a public school classroom.

In order to investigate the effects of different activity sequences, two activity schedules were used: (1) eight minutes of an active session (either dancing, musical chairs or outdoor play) followed by transition to story and a 15-minute story period; and (2) eight minutes of an inactive session (children resting with their heads on their desks) followed by transition to a story and a 15-minute story period. These two activity schedules were alternated every day, or every two or three days, in an equivalent time-samples design (Campbell & Stanley, 1963).

To assure that observed differences in child behavior could be attributed to activity sequencing, the following variables were held constant across both activity schedules: (1) the same teacher participated in all sessions; (2) the teacher prompted participation, and praised children for participating in the first activity of each sequence, whether that activity was active or inactive; (3) the teacher did not prompt or praise children for appropriate behavior during transitions or story periods, nor did she attend to disruptive behavior during transitions or story periods; (4) the teacher always began reading when all eight children were seated on the rug in the story area; and (5) the same stories were read in both activity schedules, in order to control for child preferences.

*Transition Period Measures*

Whether preceded by an active or an inactive session, transition period measures were always taken while children moved from the table area in the classroom to the rug in the story area. The teacher initiated transition periods by giving the instruction, "Everyone go and sit on the rug for story time now," and the transition measure ended when all eight children were seated on the rug in the story area.

Two child behaviors were measured during transition—transition time from table area to rug in story area, and disruptive behavior during transition. Observers stationed behind a one-way mirror started their stop-watches when the first child left the table area and stopped their watches when all children had been seated on the rug for five seconds. The same observers counted the frequency of disruptive behaviors during transition. Disruptive behaviors were defined as running, kicking, hitting, shoving, tripping, wrestling, standing on furniture and throwing objects.

Measures of interobserver agreement were obtained for seven

days: four days when transitions were preceded by an active session and three days when transitions were preceded by an inactive session. Interobserver agreement on time of transition was calculated by dividing the smaller number of seconds by the larger number of seconds and multiplying by 100. Percent agreement ranged from 90 to 98; the mean percent interobserver agreement was 94. Interobserver agreement on the occurrence of disruptive behavior was computed by dividing the smaller number of occurrences by the larger number of occurrences and multiplying by 100. The range of interobserver agreement on disruptive behavior was from 83 percent to 100 percent, with mean interobserver agreement of 94 percent.

*Story Period Measures*

After all eight children had been seated on the rug in the story area for five seconds, transition period ended and the teacher began reading a story. During the 15-minute story period, observers located behind a one-way mirror made observations of children's visual attendance, using a procedure of time sampling at a point in time. Every 30 seconds, the observers looked at the children in a predetermined sequence and scored each child as visually attending if his eyes were open and his head was oriented in the direction of the teacher and/or book.

Estimates of interobserver agreement were obtained on four days when the story period was preceded by an active session and on three days when the story period was preceded by an inactive session. For visual attendance, observers' data sheets were compared, and each pair of observations was scored as an agreement or a disagreement. Subsequently, percent interobserver agreement was obtained by dividing the total number of agreements by agreements plus disagreements, and multiplying by 100. Interobserver agreement on visual attendance ranged from 90 percent to 99 percent, with a mean interobserver agreement of 94 percent.

*Remediation of Undesirable Behaviors following Active Sessions*

In an effort to increase visual attendance during story periods and to reduce transition time and disruptive behavior following active play periods, contingent teacher praise and classroom privileges were introduced sequentially across story periods and transition times following active sessions in a multiple baseline design.

The consequences applied were identical to those employed in Experiment I. Children who made a rapid transition, did not engage in disruptive behavior, or visually attended to the teacher received behavior-specific praise from the teacher (e.g., "I like the way you are looking at the book," and "You walked very nicely to the story area when I asked you to") as well as classroom privileges such as helping the teacher and occupying positions of leadership. Observation procedures were the same as those described earlier. Interobserver agreement on visual attendance ranged from 93 to 99, with a mean of 96; on transition time ranged from 92 to 96, with a mean of 94; and on occurrence of disruptive behavior ranged from 97 to 100, with a mean of 98.

## Results

Children's behavior during transitions and story periods was found to vary significantly depending upon the preceding level of physical activity. In general, children's visual attendance to the story was significantly higher, the time needed for transition between activities and the level of disruptive behavior during transition significantly lower when preceded by a less active time. Contingencies were found to be effective in increasing acceptable behaviors following periods of high activity; however, such procedures are unnecessary if activities are sequenced so that active/play periods are not alternated with quiet periods.

### Effects of Activity Sequencing

The top graph of Fig. 2 shows the children's mean percent visual attendance to the teacher and/or the books during story periods following active play periods and inactive periods. Grand mean percent visual attendance was 86 following inactive periods and 63 following active periods ($t = 2.73$, df = 21, $p < .02$).

The length of time taken for transition from either an active play period or an inactive period to story time is shown in the middle graph on Fig. 2. Following active play periods, it took an average of 35 seconds for transition, whereas only 19 seconds were required following inactive periods ($t = 1.71$, df = 27, $p < .10$).

The rate of disruptive behaviors per minute following both active and inactive periods is shown in the bottom graph of Fig. 2. The mean rate of disruptions followings active periods was 11.8 per minute; following inactive periods the mean rate was 1.4 per minute ($t = 2.03$, df = 27, $p < .01$).

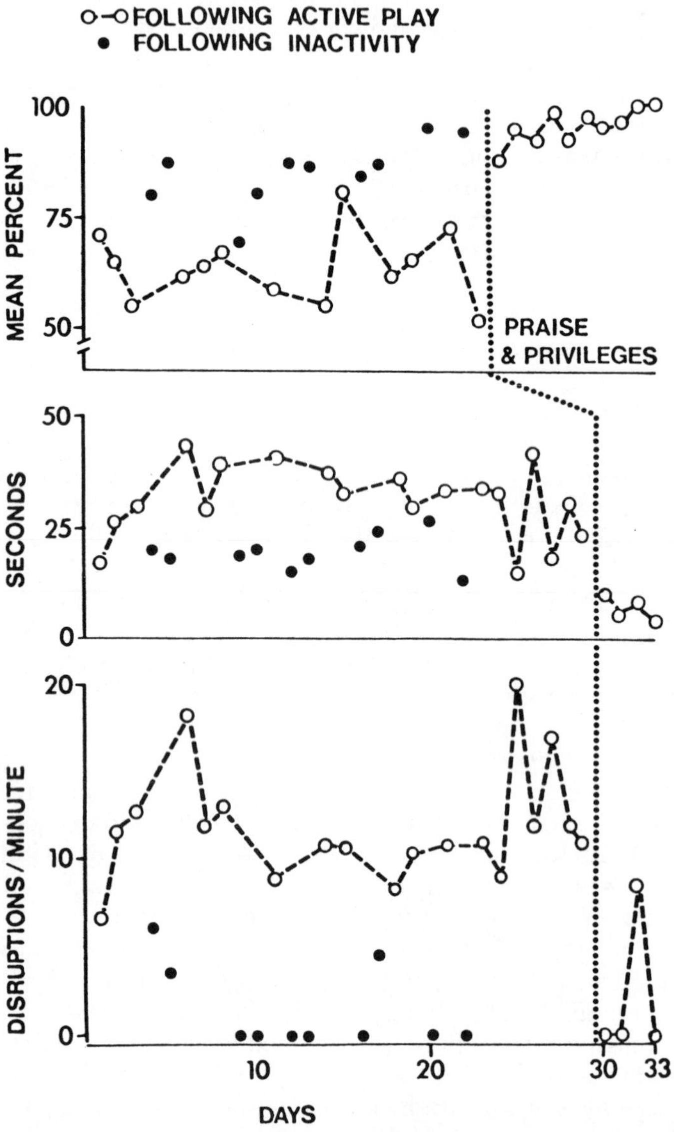

Fig. 2. The effects on children's behavior of scheduling a story period following both active play and sedentary activities: mean percent visual attendance to the story, time required for transition between activities, and level of disruptive behavior during transitions. Although the schedule which precedes the quiet story period with a sedentary activity was preferable in all cases, the provision of descriptive praise and classroom privileges for children whose behavior was appropriate was also effective.

*Remediation of Undesirable Behaviors following*
*Active Play Periods*

When behavior-specific praise and privileges were used to conse-
quate visual attendance, short transition times, and non-disruptive
behavior, children's performance improved despite unfavorable
activity sequencing, as can be seen in the right-hand portions of
Fig. 2. Visual attendance during story periods preceded by active
play periods, which averaged 63 percent during baseline, increased to
a grand mean of 95 percent when visual attendance was consequated
by the teacher. Similarly, time needed for transition decreased from
an average of 35 seconds during baseline to only seven seconds, and
the rate of disruptive behaviors decreased from a grand mean of 11.8
per minute during baseline to a grand mean of 2.1 per minute during
treatment.

## Discussion

Observations in the natural environment indicated that when
kindergarten teachers scheduled a very active session, such as recess,
immediately preceding a quiet period, such as story, they were more
likely to encounter inappropriate child behavior than when the quiet
period was preceded by a less active session.

The present study compared two activity sequences, active
session-transition-story period and inactive session-transition-story
period. When the former activity schedule was in effect, children's
transition times were longer, there was a higher rate of disruptive
behaviors during transitions, and visual attendance to the teacher
and/or the educational materials was lower during the story period.

These results suggest that an activity that prohibits children from
being physically mobile should not be immediately preceded by a
session that permits or encourages boisterousness or large motor
behavior. An optimally effective sequence of activities might
schedule gross motor activities to be succeeded by creative play or
seatwork sessions that allow freedom of movement and manipulation
of materials, followed finally by a quiet session requiring restricted
verbal and physical activity. Alternatively, a brief period of enforced
inactivity and rest might be interspersed between a period of
boisterous activity and a sedentary instructional session.

As in Experiment I, this study indicates that individual contingency management procedures can be used to obtain effective
classroom performances under less than optimal environment condi-

tions. Of even greater importance, however, is the demonstration that the desired behavioral results can be obtained at lower response cost to the teacher through the introduction of simple but effective ecological arrangements in the classroom.

## GENERAL DISCUSSION

The experiments presented here document the behavior change that can result from manipulation of ecological dimensions in the classroom. Because such behavior change strategies rely on alteration of impersonal variables, they do not require large expenditures of resources in the area of teacher training, nor do they result in the extra response cost to the teacher that may be associated with the use of individual contingency management procedures. Further, rearrangements of the classroom environment can often be achieved regardless of the educational models or theoretical orientations that are espoused by school personnel.

Manipulation of spatial density and activity sequencing produced effects comparable to those achieved with more traditional reinforcement procedures, thus obviating remedial measures that focus on consequent stimuli. These findings indicate that attention to setting events may result in the development of classroom environments that generate and maintain desired child behaviors.

## REFERENCES

Barker, R.G., & Gump, P. Big school, small school. Stanford: Stanford University Press, 1964.

Becker, W., Engelmann, S., & Thomas, D. Teaching: A course in applied psychology. Science Research Associates, 1971.

Campbell, D.T., & Stanley, J.C. Experimental and quasi-experimental designs for research. Rand McNally and Co., 1963.

Cataldo, M.F., & Risley, T.R. Infant day care. In R. Ulrich, T. Stachnik and J. Mabry (Eds.). Control of human behavior, Vol. III. Glenview, Ill.: Scott Foresman, 1974.

Cohen, H. Behavioral architecture in training professionals. In H.L. Cohen, I. Goldiamond, J. Filipezak, & R. Pooley. Procedures for the establishment of educational environments. Silver Springs: Institute for Behavioral Research, 1968.

Cruickshank, W.M., & Quay, H.C. Learning and physical environment: The necessity for research and research design. *Exceptional Children*, December, 1970.

Doke, L. Planning dimensions in group-care programs. Appendix to: The experimental analysis of group care: Activity schedules. University of Kansas, 1971, unpublished review paper.

Doke, L.A., & Risley, T.R. The organization of day care environments: Required vs. optional activities. *Journal of Applied Behavior Analysis*, 1972, 5, 405-420.

Eastman, C.M., & Harper, J. A study of proxemic behavior: Toward a predictive model. *Environment and Behavior*, 1971, 3.

Evans, Belle-E., Shub, B., & Weinstein, M. *Day care: How to plan, develop, and operate a day care center.* Beacon Press, 1971.

Hall, E.T. Proxemics—The study of man's spatial relations and boundaries. In I. Galdston (Ed.) *Man's image of medicine and anthropology.* New York: International Universities Press, 1963.

Hamblin, R., Mukerji, R., & Yonemura, M. *Schools for young disadvantaged children.* New York: Teachers College Press, 1967.

Hart, B.M., & Risely, T.R. Using preschool materials to modify the language of disadvantaged children. *Journal of Applied Behavior Analysis*, 1974, 7, 243-256.

Hutt, C., & McGrew, W.C. Effects of group density upon social behavior in humans. In: *Changes in behaviors with population density.* Symposium presented at meeting of the Association for the Study of Animal Behavior, Oxford, July 17-20, 1967.

Hutt, C., & Vaizey, M.J. Differential effects of group density on social behavior. *Nature*, 1966, 209, 1371-1372.

Jersild, A.T., & Markey, F.V. Conflicts between preschool children. *Child Development Mongraphs*, 1935, 21.

Leavitt, J.E. *Nursery-kindergarten education.* New York: McGraw-Hill Co., 1958.

Leeper, S.H., Dales, R.J., Skipper, D.S., & Witherspoon, R.L. *Good schools for young children,* New York: The Macmillan Co., 1968.

LeLaurin, K., Cataldo, M.F., & Risley, T.R. Improving individualized care by public display of individual schedules. *Journal of Applied Behavior Analysis,* in press.

LeLaurin, K., & Risley, T.R. The organization of day care environments: "Zone" versus "man to man" staff assignments, *Journal of Applied Behavior Analysis,* 1972, 5, 225-232.

Loo, C.M. The effects of spatial density on the social behavior of children. *Journal of Applied Social Psychology*, 1972, 2, 4, 372-381.

McClannahan, L.E., & Risley, T.R. A store for nursing home residents. *Nursing Homes,* June, 1973.

McClannahan, L.E., & Risely, T.R. Activities and materials for severely disabled geriatric patients. *Nursing Homes,* 1975, 24, 10-13.

McClannahan, L.E., & Risley, T.R. Design of living environment for nursing home residents: Increasing participation in recreation activities. *Journal of Applied Behavior Analysis,* in press.

McClannahan, L.E., & Risely, T.R. Design of living environments for nursing home residents: Recruiting attendance for activities, *The Gerontologist,* 1974, 14, 236-240.

McGrew, P.L., Social and spatial density effects on spacing behavior in preschool children. *Journal of Child Psychology and Psychiatry,* 1970, 11, 197-205.

Montes, F., & Risley, T.R. Evaluating traditional day care practices: An empirical approach. *Child Care Quarterly,* in press.

Orme, M.E.J., & Purnell, R.F. Behavior modification and transfer in an out-of-control classroom. In: G.A. Fargo, C. Behrns, & P. Nolen, *Behavior Modification in the Classroom,* Belmont: Wadsworth Publishing Co., 1970.

Pierce, C.H., & Risley, T.R. Improving job performance of neighborhood youth corps aides in an urban recreation program. *Journal of Applied Behavior Analysis,* 1974b, 7, 207-215.

Pierce, C.H., & Risley, T.R. Recreation as a reinforcer: Increasing membership and decreasing disruptions in an urban recreation center. *Journal of Applied Behavior Analysis,* 1974a, 7, 403-411.

Quilitch, H.R., & Risley, T.R. The effects of play materials on social play. *Journal of Applied Behavior Analysis,* 1973, 6, 573-578.

Risley, T.R. Spontaneous language and the preschool environment. In J.C. Stanley (Ed.), *Preschool programs for the disadvantaged: Five experimental approaches to early childhood education.* Baltimore: Johns Hopkins University Press, 1972.

Sells, S.B. Ecology and the science of psychology. In E.P. Willems & H.L. Raush (Eds.) *Naturalistic view points in psychological research,* New York: Holt, Rinehart and Winston, Inc., 1969.

Sommer, R. Small group ecology. In H. Hornstein, B.B. Bunk, W.W. Burke, M. Gindes & R.J. Lewicki *Social intervention: A behavioral science approach,* New York: The Free Press, Inc., 1971.

Tharp, R.G., & Wetzel, R.J. *Behavior modification in the natural environment,* New York: Academic Press, Inc., 1969.

Twardosz, D., Cataldo, M.F., & Risley, T.R. Infants' use of crib toys. *Young Children,* 1974a, 29, 271-276.

Twardosz, S., Cataldo, M.F., & Risley, T.R. Menus for toddler day care: Food preference and spoon use. *Young Children,* 1975, 30, 129-144.

Twardosz, S., Cataldo, M.F., & Risley, T.R. Open environment design for infant and toddler day care. *Journal of Applied Behavior Analysis,* 1974b, 7, 529-546.

# Article 21
## Improving Parent-Teacher Communication through Recorded Telephone Messages* †

RONALD G. BITTLE

**Abstract**: This study assessed the effects of a teacher-parent communication system which used a daily recorded telephone message as a communications link between parents and their children's teacher. A class of 21 first grade students in a rural southern Illinois community served as Ss. A three-part experiment was conducted to determine: (1) if the parents would use such a system; (2) if the use of such a system would have any beneficial effects on learning; and (3) if the inclusion of non-academic information would be of value. The results of the experiment were that (1) the system was used extensively; (2) the inclusion of academic information in the daily message resulted in improved academic performance by every student in the class; and (3) families complied with recorded teacher instructions of a non-academic nature at a much higher rate than they did when these instructions were sent home with the child in memo form alone.

In the typical educational system in our society, parent-teacher communication is relegated to a minor role. Educators, of course, are concerned about the problem of communication with and reporting to parents. However, despite the interest among educators concerning these problems, few experimental studies have investigated the problem of parent-teacher communication. Many studies concerned

*Reprinted by permission from the *Journal of Educational Research*, Nov. 1975, 69, 87-95.

†This study was based on a doctoral dissertation submitted by the author to Southern Illinois University.

with the general area have appeared, but the great majority of these studies are concerned with the traditional methods of reporting to parents, reflect personal or professional opinion, and are not data based (17). These traditional methods of communication include the report card (3, 7, 14, 16, 17, 26), the parent-teacher conference (5, 6, 8, 21, 25), failure reports (31), informal letters (25), personal contacts between parents and teachers (18, 28, 29), and newsletters (10). Most of the research reported concerns minor variations from these standard procedures. Such things as changes in grading symbols (23), comparisons between formal and informal reporting systems (1, 20), addition of anecdotal information to regular grade report cards (23, 25), and comparison of normative versus individualized information (2, 11, 13, 30) constitute the type of problems with which the literature in this area has generally been concerned.

With regard to communications in general, one of the most common methods used in today's society is the telephone. The telephone represents a technological development of such tremendous importance and our society utilizes it in so many situations, that its utility is taken for granted. Almost every home, business, and other location where people are likely to congregate has a telephone. However, in spite of its commonality, it seems to be used sparingly as an educational communications tool. Why such an important communications tool is excluded from our classrooms is a question which should be asked of today's educators. Such answers as (1) it would be too expensive, (2) it would be too disruptive, (3) teachers would not want to use it for its intended purpose, and (4) parents really don't care enough to call, would surely be given. The real reason is probably none of the above, but rather the simple fact that it is not a traditional way of communication in today's schools.

It is true that schools have telephones and that parents and teachers occasionally communicate via this method. There is, however, evidence in the literature of systematic attempts to utilize this extremely common form of communication to assist in the attainment of school objectives. For example, the Educational Telephone Network of the University of Wisconsin—Extension, adopted in 1965, has served nearly 20,000 students registered for course work via the telephone (22). Another similar telephone instructional unit is reported by Rookey, Gill and Gill (24). In the above cases, the use of the telephone was for large-group instruction and required the student to be at a listening station in order to hear and communicate with instructors. Another report (4) demonstrated that school attendance could be improved by a method in which the school principal called the students' parents on the telephone and praised them for their children's attendance at school. In the same study the authors demonstrated that social praise was an important aspect of the telephone procedure. Although telephone calls without social reinforcement did increase attendance, they did not increase it to the level that occurred when the calls included praise for the parents. A similar phone-call procedure is reported by Hunt (15). In this study, daily phone calls were made to parents of retarded children enrolled in a special class, thanking and praising them for returning their children's homework assignments. Although other feedback variables were being used simultaneously with the phone calls, the feedback procedure in which phone calls were a part resulted in maintaining high levels of parental performance. Another way the telephone has been used effectively for many years has been the school-to-home services provided to handicapped students (24).

Since the present methods of parent-teacher communication appear to be inadequate, new methods need to be considered. One way would seem to be to encourage more use of the telephone. Upon considering alternative methods, concern should be given to the essential characteristics of an effective parent-teacher communications system. First, it should allow for a continuous flow of information between the two parties. Secondly, the information provided should be meaningful and useful, and third, the system should be economically feasible in terms of cost and time.

In order to evaluate a parent-teacher communication system which incorporated these characteristics, a three-part experiment was conducted.

## METHOD

The experiment involved providing a daily recorded telephone message which reported each day's activities, homework assignments, and announcements of future events. Parents could obtain this information by dialing a special telephone number used only for this purpose any time, day or night, except between 3 and 3:30 p.m. Throughout the school day as the teacher progressed through her routine, she recorded on a clipboard kept especially for this purpose any item of information which occurred to her as being useful for her daily message. At the end of the school day, the teacher recorded a summary of this information on a telephone answering service device. The duration of the message varied from two to three and one-half minutes, depending on the amount of information to be given on any particular day. The maximum time available for a message was three and one-half minutes. The specific academic information provided by the teacher in the daily messages was applicable to all students. Specific mention of the assignment or behavior of any particular child did not occur. Information related directly to academic activities occurring in the classroom was given first on the message. General information, such as lunch menu and schedule of future school activities, was provided at the end of each tape.

By including academic information first and general nonacademic information second on the message, the procedure insured that those calling for general information were exposed to the academic information.

The teacher spent approximately 10 to 15 minutes per day summarizing her information and recording and checking her message. The answering service device was equipped with a counter which permitted recording of the number of calls received by the service daily. It was also equipped with a timer which signaled the teacher in sufficient time to permit her to conclude her daily message in a smooth and orderly fashion before the tape time expired.

The device used was a Model ATS2 Automatic Telephone Secretary purchased for about $400 from General Telecommunications, Chicago, Illinois. This recorder contained several features not essential to the present experiment, which accounted for the high cost. Similar devices capable of performing the functions of the experiment are available commercially for less than $100. The cost of the telephone service, excluding the one-time installation fee of $20, was about $13 per month.

Part I of the experiment was designed to determine if the availability of a recorded telephone message containing information about class activities, homework assignments and other general information would affect the rate of parent initiated parent-teacher contacts. Part II, which was conducted concurrently with Part I, was an attempt to determine if parent exposure to the message would have an effect on academic performance of the students in the class. Part III was conducted during the final week of the experiment and was designed to determine the effects of the inclusion of non-academic instructions on the recorded message on the rate of parent compliance with non-academic instructions.

# PART I

## Subjects and Setting

The study was conducted in a first grade class in a small rural town in southern Illinois. The class enrollment totaled 21 students, nine girls and 12 boys. Assignment to the class was made on a random basis at the end of the kindergarten year. The students were all Caucasian and were primarily from low to middle class socio-economic backgrounds. The parents of two of the students were college trained.

## Procedure

A 30-week baseline period was conducted during which time the teacher kept a written record of the number of times (dependent variable) she was contacted by parents by phone, letter or in person concerning any aspect of their child's school behavior. Contacts between the teacher and parents at regular school functions such as PTA meetings were not included in the baseline data. On the 31st week of school, a private telephone and an automatic answering device were installed in the classroom.

Parents were informed of the availability of this message service by a letter which explained the service to them. This answering service represented the independent variable and the effects of its availability were determined by comparing the rate of parent-initiated communications with the teacher during the baseline period with the rate of parent-initiated communications with the teacher following the introduction of the answering service. The telephone number to call to obtain the information provided by the teacher was made available only to the parents of the children involved. The answering service could be used by the parents at any time, day or night, with the exception of a period at the end of the school day when the teacher recorded her message concerning the day's activities and assignments for the following day.

## Results

The number of parent-initiated contacts with the teacher are presented in Figure 1. During the baseline period (first 30 weeks) a

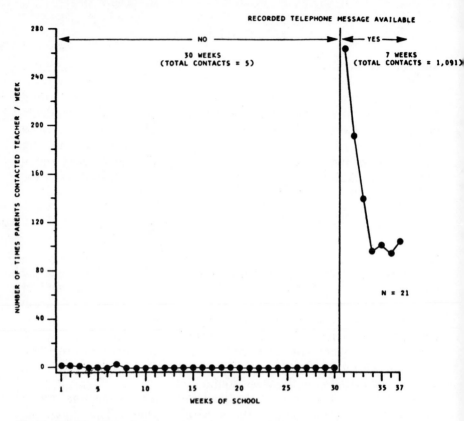

Fig. 1. Weekly plot of the number of parent-initiated contacts with the teacher for the entire school year.

total of five contacts were made, including one each during weeks 1, 2, and 3, and two during week 7. When the daily recorded message was made available during week 31, the number of parent-initiated contacts increased to 267 per week. During the second and third weeks this number decreased to 193 and 140 contacts per week, respectively. By week 34 the number of parent-initiated contacts reached a level of approximately 100 per week, where it remained for the final four weeks of the experiment. The number of contacts during the final four weeks averaged 20.5 per day. Since there were 21 students in the class, this represents approximately one call per student per day.

## Discussion

The results clearly demonstrate that parents will seek out information about their children's school activities when it is convenient for them to do so. The answering service provided an impersonal method whereby parents could, at their convenience, find out what their children had been doing at school and whether or not they had homework for any particular day. Parents could also find out information about things of general interest such as the lunch menu for the following day and the details of future special activities their children would be participating in.

The initial introduction of the answering service produced a dramatic increase in the number of parent-initiated contacts. The novelty effect lasted for about three weeks, during which time the number of daily calls far exceeded the number of students in the class. Although the large number of calls can probably be attributed to the novelty of the procedure, it can also be assumed to have contributed to the continued use of the procedure, since it permitted those calling to sample the information contained in the daily messages. This sampling behavior demonstrated the usefulness of the service, thereby increasing the probability of its future use by those whose children were enrolled in the class.

The results obtained were probably due to one or more of the following reasons:

1) The parents were able to contact the school at any time, day or night, concerning information about their child's school activities. 2) The parents were able to contact the school on days that their child was absent and find out what the child needed to do in order to keep abreast of his class activities. 3) The parents were able to contact the teacher without direct personal involvement with the teacher. 4) The parents did not have to rely on the children for information about school activities. 5) The teacher was able to provide much more information to the parent than would be possible if she had to provide it all in written form. 6) The parents were aware of the fact that the information was available on a daily basis, but that access to it was contingent upon their initiative in seeking it out. As a result, the parents became active participants in the educational process, instead of passive recipients of occasional written information. 8) Parents who were reluctant to contact their child's teacher because of their concern for the teacher's privacy had no inhibitions about calling the answering service. And 9) general information such as lunch menu, etc., was available at all times.

The extent to which parents used the present communications system offers clear evidence that the parents were concerned about their children's school activities. This evidence should be useful in changing teachers' opinions concerning parental interest, which according to Goldman is that "Most teachers believe that many parents do not care about their children's school progress." (12:521).

From the teacher's point of view, the daily recorded message afforded an opportunity to advise parents of ways in which they might be helpful in the education of their children. Once parents were advised of the fact that information was available, the teacher could no longer be considered negligent in keeping parents informed. The burden was therefore shifted to the parents, and those who might otherwise have been inclined to blame the teacher for their child's educational inadequacies found themselves in a position in which they would at least have to share this responsibility. Since most parents seemed to seek out ways of helping their children, as evidenced by the large number of calls, it is logical to conclude that the availability of such an informational procedure was beneficial to both parents and teachers. The parents were able to secure information they needed in order to be helpful to their children. The job of the teacher can be expected to be less demanding, because the parents could use the information to assist with the instruction of their children, thereby reducing the work load of the teacher.

The fact that the number of parent-initiated contacts increased dramatically following the availability of the answering service indicated that parent interest was high. It did not, however, in and of itself, give an indication of any academic benefits which might be derived from such a system. In order to determine if there were any beneficial academic effects of this increased communication, Part II of the experiment was conducted to study the effects of academic information included on the daily message on the student's performance in a specific academic area. The academic area chosen was spelling and the results of the experiment follow.

## PART II

### Subjects

The subjects were the same 21 students who served as subjects in Part I.

## Procedures

An ABAB experimental design was used to compare the effect of two different conditions on daily spelling test scores. Condition A (baseline) was in effect for the first 11 days. In condition A the children were required to list four spelling words on which they would be tested the following day. At the close of each day the teacher checked each child's list to insure that it contained all four words spelled correctly, and reminded the children to take the list to the parents. On day 12 condition B was started, and remained in effect for 11 days. In condition B, the procedure used in condition A was continued, and, in addition, the teacher included the list of spelling words on a daily recorded telephone message. A reversal of conditions from condition B back to baseline (condition A) was started on day 23, and remained in effect for 7 days at which time, day 30, another reversal back to Condition B was started. Condition B remained in effect for the final six days of the experiment.

## Results

Figure 2 shows a daily plot of the average percentage of spelling errors for the entire class across all four conditions of the ABAB experimental design. In the initial baseline period when the word list was used alone, the overall average of spelling errors was about 35 percent. This percentage of errors was based on the average daily percentage of errors for days 1 through 11, which ranged from 18 to 59 percent. When condition B was introduced and the spelling words were included with the daily recorded telephone message, the overall average of spelling errors decreased to six percent, a drop of 28.5 percent. During this period from day 12 to day 22, the average daily percentage of errors ranged from 1.2 to 13 percent. On day 23 a seven-day reversal from condition B back to condition A (baseline) was initiated. During this period the overall average of spelling errors increased to 22.6 percent. Although the overall mean did not return to the 34.5 percent level of the initial baseline period, it did approximate the stable level seen during the final four days (7, 8, 9 and 10) of that baseline period. On day 30, condition B was reinstated. On the first day of this condition, the percentage of spelling errors dropped to zero. The overall average of errors for the six-day period was 5.3 percent, or approximately the same level seen previously under the first B condition.

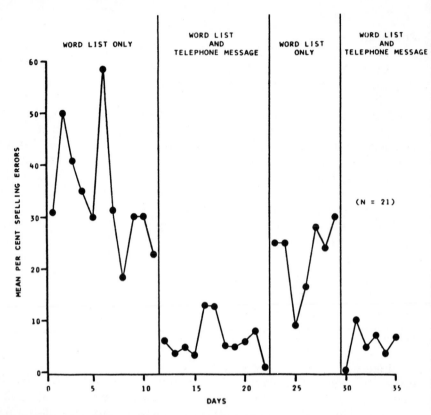

Fig. 2. Daily plot of the mean percentage of spelling errors for the entire group during the ABAB conditions of Part II of the experiment.

Figure 3 shows the percentage of students completing the daily spelling quiz without errors for each of the four conditions in Part II. During condition A (baseline), when only the word list was sent to parents, the average percentage of students scoring 100 percent was 39 percent. On days 12 through 22 (condition B), when the recorded telephone message included the daily spelling words, the average increased to 80 percent. This represents an increase in students scoring perfectly on daily tests of about 103 percent. On days 23 through 29, when again only the spelling word list was sent to parents, the average percentage of students performing perfectly dropped to 53 percent. On days 30 through 35 (second B condition), the spelling words were again listed on the daily recorded telephone message. The average percentage of students performing perfectly rose to 86 percent. Included within this average is one day (30) on

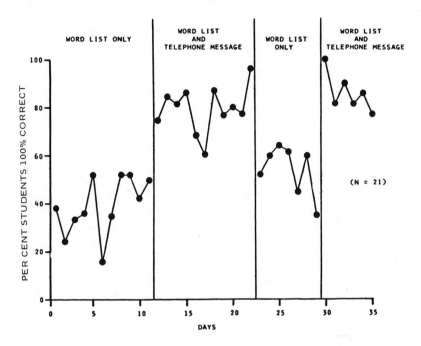

**Fig. 3.** Daily plot of the percentage of students scoring perfectly on daily spelling tests during the ABAB conditions of Part II of the experiment.

which all 21 students in the class performed perfectly.

The average percentage of spelling errors for each student in the class across all four conditions of Part II is presented in Figure 4. The open bars represent performance during baseline conditions, the dotted bars, performance during the experimental condition. Examination of this figure reveals that the initial inclusion of the spelling words on the recorded telephone message (first dotted bar) resulted in a reduction of spelling errors for all subjects with the single exception of Subject 20, who had made no errors previously, therefore making reduction of errors impossible. Subject 20 made one error during the initial 11 day period of condition B which resulted in the slight increase in percentage of errors for this subject. When the spelling words were again omitted from the daily recorded message (second open bar), the percentage of errors increased from the level seen in condition B (first dotted bar) for 17 of the 21 subjects, remained the same for two subjects, and decreased for two subjects. During the final condition B (second dotted bar) when the spelling words were again included in the daily recorded telephone message, errors decreased for 18 of the 21 subjects. The other three subjects made no errors during the preceding condition, therefore their error rate could not decrease. All three of these subjects continued to score perfectly throughout the final condition.

## Discussion

The results of Part II of the experiment demonstrate the influence of the procedure on student academic achievement. With regard to the improved spelling performance the results of this study compare favorably with other studies designed to improve spelling performance (9, 19, 27). These studies involved the manipulation of contingencies within the classroom and therefore required considerable class time. The present study produced comparable results without using class time and without the necessity of planning and implementing a contingency program. The simple listing of spelling

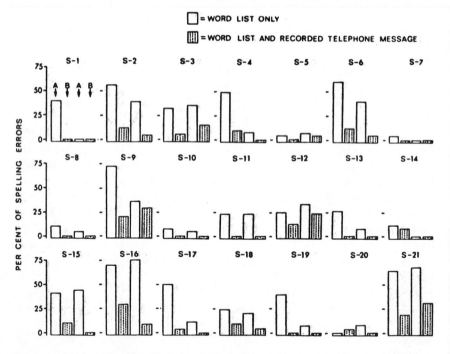

Fig. 4. Percentage of spelling errors for each of the 21 students during each of the experimental conditions of Part II of the experiment.

words on the daily message was a sufficient condition to produce improvement in spelling by all of the students in the class. The students showing the greatest improvement were those whose performance was the weakest during the baseline conditions. These results indicate that the information provided is most beneficial to the students most in need of assistance. Students who were doing well during the baseline condition also benefitted from the information and several of them performed at a perfect or near perfect level during the experimental conditions. The differences in performance levels in conditions A and B serve to point up the problem of reliance upon students for communication between parents and teachers, since the spelling word list was continuously being sent home to the parents. The lower performance in the absence of the telephone message information suggests that either parents do not attend to written information sent home to them with the children, or the children are not reliable in getting the information to the parents. Another point of view suggests that the parents are likely to be more helpful when their role in the process is an active rather than a passive one. For example, when the procedure required the parents' active involvement in seeking information, their children performed better than when the parents were passive recipients of written information.

During the course of the experiment, the teacher noticed that students were complying with requests of a nonacademic nature included on the daily message at a higher rate than had been customary in the absence of the recorded telephone message. For example, when the teacher requested on one daily message that the students bring some type of kitchen utensil for use in an art project, 18 of the 21 students complied. The teacher estimated that previous verbal or written requests of this type generally resulted in less than 50 percent compliance. Since the message appeared to produce a greater degree of compliance with instructions of a nonacademic nature, a systematic effort was made to determine if this was true. The discussion of Part III of the experiment reports the findings.

## PART III

### Subjects

Part III included an experimental group consisting of the 21 members of the first grade class who served as subjects in Part I and

II of the experiment and a control group consisting of 20 students from another first grade in the same school. The control group members were from essentially the same socio-economic background as the members of the experimental group and were also assigned to their class on a random basis at the end of their kindergarten year.

## Procedure

The purpose of this experiment was to evaluate the extent to which students complied with teacher instructions as a function of whether or not the instructions were included on the daily recorded message. More specifically, notices were sent home with the children on a Friday, advising the parents of a year-end school picnic to be held the following Wednesday. The notice requested that the parents sign and return a consent form the following Monday. It also required that the parents send 15 cents to cover the cost of refreshments at the picnic. Identical notices were sent home with each class member of the experimental and control groups. In addition, the teacher of the experimental group included the same instructions in her daily recorded message.

## Results

Figure 5 shows the percentage of students complying with the instructions. It can be seen that the students in the experimental group were in 100 percent compliance with the instructions to return the consent form and to bring a specified amount of money. In the control group, on the other hand, only 30 percent of the students complied with the instructions to bring a specified amount of money and 60 percent complied with the instruction to return the consent form.

## Discussion

The rate of compliance with the nonacademic instructions by the students in the experimental group provides evidence of the value of a daily communications system in assuring compliance with teacher requests. This findings is of major importance when viewed in the context of classroom efficiency and time-saving potential. The

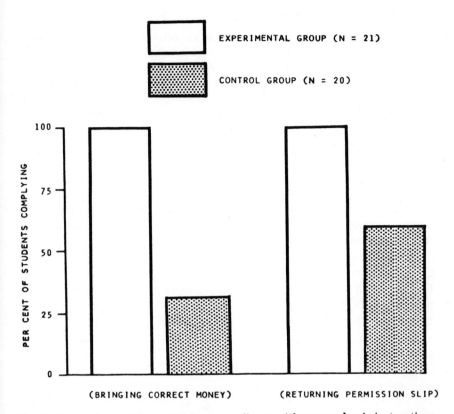

EXPERIMENTAL GROUP (N = 21)

CONTROL GROUP (N = 20)

Fig. 5. Comparison of the percentage compliance with nonacademic instructions between experimental and control group students in Part III of the experiment.

case mentioned previously involving the art project illustrates how classroom efficiency is affected. Since most of the students brought the requested materials, the teacher did not have to spend much time obtaining and distributing materials required for the activity. The experiment in Part III illustrates the time-saving potential. The teacher of the experimental group was able to complete the book-keeping and planning duties associated with the task quickly. The teacher of the control group, on the other hand, had to devote time to this task on subsequent days. The time saved by the experimental group could be used for more important educational activities. In the course of a school year, the numerous nonacademic record keeping requirements deprive students of many valuable hours of instruction. Any system which reduces this time requirement should prove to be beneficial to the educational process. Another beneficial aspect of the inclusion of instructions of this type on the daily message is the opportunity it affords the teacher to determine whether or not the service is being used by the parent. When all or nearly all of the students comply with the requests included on the message, the teacher has a good indication that parents are using the service. This convenient method enables the teacher to determine parent interest indirectly without embarrassing the parents.

## Conclusions

The communication procedure used in this experiment proved to be an effective parent-teacher communications system. It provided a continuous daily flow of information from the teacher to the parents. The information provided was easy to understand and useful to the parents. The system was economical in terms of cost and time. The cost of the system would have amounted to six cents per day per student for 21 students based on a 180-day school year and a recording instrument costing $100. Since the purchase of the instrument and installation cost are one-time expenditures, the second year cost per student for the same class would drop to about three cents per day per student, or a total of about $5 per student for the entire school year.

The system required very little teacher time (less than 15 minutes daily) in message preparation and no more than three minutes per day of parent time. The time required by the teacher was probably more than offset by the reduction in record-keeping tasks resulting from a higher level of compliance with her instructions. Most important of all, the system resulted in improved academic performance for every student in the class. Although the present experiment systematically investigated only the academic area of spelling, information concerning other academic areas such as reading and arithmetic was included in the daily message. It seems likely that the inclusion of this information resulted in improvement in these areas. This suggests many future research possibilities. These possibilities include 1) systematic manipulation of information concerning any particular academic area in the same or in a similar manner, as was done with spelling in this experiment; 2) evaluation of parent use of such a system as a function of grade level; 3) evaluation of the nature of the content of the message. Systematic variations in the nature of verbal communications could be studied with the present system.

The effects of parental application of contingencies for classroom behaviors could be systematically evaluated by prescribing contingencies in the daily message for either rewarding or punishing classroom behaviors. With the present system this could be accomplished on a group contingency basis only, since it does not provide for information of an individual nature. However, development of a future system which includes provisions for individual information without sacrificing confidentiality would allow for contingency prescriptions to individual parents.

The availability of a daily message might tend to reduce the existing level of direct parent-teacher contact, since the parents may feel that the teacher, having provided the recorded message, may not want further communication. To overcome this, attempts to increase personal contacts between parents and teachers could be programmed into the daily message. Specific prompting suggestions could be given to generate more direct personal contact. Once personal contacts are established, the effects of systematic variation of social variables such as praise and expressions of appreciation could be studied to determine their effect on the maintenance of continued personal contact.

Parents using such a system can obtain considerable information about their children's school activities. This raises the question of whether the availability of this information results in a decrease in parent-child communication. Although this alternative source of information may produce such a decrease, it may also serve as a catalyst to increase parent-child communication, since many topics for discussion can be presented in the daily message. Studies should be conducted to determine the effects of such a system on parent-child communication, and to develop methods which insure that beneficial parent-child communication is maintained.

The rate of absenteeism is a major problem at higher levels of education which could possibly be studied with the present system. The inclusion of a list of absentees in the daily message might be a sufficient condition to lower absenteeism, especially in those cases where the parents are unaware of its occurrence.

The present system did not provide feedback to the parents in the form of grades or subjective evaluations. The system simply provided information regarding past and future class activities. The information could be considered feedback, since it helped keep the parents informed of the activities of their child's class. Fortunately, at the first grade level and most elementary levels the parents are capable of evaluating their child's performance if they know what is expected. The teacher is likely, therefore, to be much more objective in her ratings of students when she knows that the parents have been continuously aware of her expectations and have been able to evaluate their children's performance relative to these expectations.

One of the advantages of the communication system used in the present study was the focusing on preparation of students for future school activities rather than solely summarizing past performance, as is done with most reporting systems presently used. A system of this type avoids the negative aspects of most communications systems which evaluate performance and assign grades. Parents desiring to use this system can do so without the apprehensions they are likely to have when receiving periodic report cards. This consideration is especially important for parents of children who have difficulty in school, for their communication with the teacher in a system such as the one used concerns itself with matters of a positive nature, rather than the negative reports of failure or inadequacy they are accustomed to receiving.

A final point of discussion concerns the human reactions to the system. When the system was first proposed, the school principal expressed a rather negative or at most neutral outlook toward it. Once it was operative, he became an enthusiastic supporter. Several of the teachers in the school expressed an interest in the system and a desire to use it in their own classrooms. Parents of the students and others in the community who became aware of the procedure expressed enthusiasm for and support of the system. In view of this it is likely that little difficulty would be encountered in initiating similar systems in other communities. The resistance to innovation which customarily exists may not be so great a problem when the innovation involves the mere application of a technological tool as common to the entire population as the telephone.

The present system provided an inexpensive, time-saving way of providing information to parents. The resulting improved academic performance and increased level of compliance with nonacademic instructions indicated that the extensive use of the system served a useful purpose. The results suggest a way for educators to close the communications gap which has existed for so long between parents and teachers.

# REFERENCES

1. Austin, M.C. Report cards and parents, *The Reading Teacher*, 660-662, 1965.
2. Brooks, H.B. What can be done about comparative marks and formal report cards? *California Journal of Secondary Education*, 10: 101-106, 1935.
3. Chansky, N.M. Elementary school teachers rate report cards, *Journal of Educational Research*, 56: 523-528, 1963.
4. Copeland, R.E., Brown, R.E., Axelrod, S., Hall, V.R. Effects of a school principal praising parents for student attendance, *Educational Technology*, 56-59, 1972.
5. Coulter, K.C. Parent teacher conferences, *Elementary School Journal*, 47: 385-390, 1947.
6. Cutright, P.B. Planning for child growth through parent-teacher conferences, *Childhood Education*, 24: 266-269, 1948.
7. DePencier, I.B. Trends in reporting pupil progress in the elementary grades, *Elementary School Journal*, 2: 519-523, 1951.
8. Driscoll, G.P. Parent-teacher conference, *Teacher's College Record*, 40: 463-470, 1944.
9. Evans, G.W., Oswalt, G.L. Acceleration of academic progress through the manipulation of peer influence, *Behaviour Research and Therapy*, 6: 189-195, 1968.
10. Fedderson, J., Jr. Establishing an effective parent-teacher communication system, *Childhood Education*, 75-79, 1972.
11. Frenkel, H. Individualized report cards, *Instructor*, 75: 38, 1965.
12. Goldman, R. Cross-cultural adaptation of a program to involve parents in their children's learning, *Child Welfare*, 52: 521-531, 1973.
13. Halliwell, J.W. The relationship of certain factors to marking practices in individualized reporting programs, *Journal of Educational Research*, 54: 76-78, 1960.
14. Hockstad, P. Report cards—helpful or harmful? *Education*, 84: 174-175, 1963.
15. Hunt, S.K. The effects of feedback on parent consistency in running homework sessions with their children, unpublished doctoral dissertation, Southern Illinois University, 1972.
16. Jones, J.A. Grading, marking and reporting in the modern elementary school, *Educational Forum* 19: 45-54, 1954.
17. Kingston, A.J., Walsh, J.A., Jr. Research on reporting systems, *The National Elementary Principal*, 65: 36-40, 1966.
18. Lawrence, M. Helping parents help their children—informal discussion groups, *Instruction*, 82: 63, 1972.
19. Lovitt, T.T., Guppy, T.E., Blattner, J.E. The use of a free time contingency

with fourth graders to increase spelling accuracy, *Behaviour Research and Therapy,* 7: 151-157, 1969.

20. Mann, L., O'dell, C., Parsons, L.J., & Walbert, W.W. A comparison of formal and informal reporting systems in a first grade population, *The Journal of Educational Research,* 60: 75-79, 1966.

21. McCowen, E., & Bryan, R.C. Reporting to parents on pupil progress, *The Elementary School Journal,* 56: 332-334, 1955.

22. Parker, L.A. Educational telephone network and subsidiary communications authorization: Educational media for continuing education in Wisconsin, *Educational Technology,* 34-36, 1974.

23. Phillips, B.N. Characteristics of elementary report cards, *Educational Administration and Supervision,* 42: 385-397, 1956.

24. Rookey, E.J., Gill, L.W., & Gill, F.J. An educational telephone network, *Educational Technology,* 37-39, 1971.

25. Ruby, J.E. Reporting pupil progress, *Pennsylvania School Journal,* 300, 1962.

26. Simon, S.B. Grades must go, *Pennsylvania Education,* 3: 19-21, 1972.

27. Sulzer, B., Hunt, S., Ashby, E., Koniarski, D., & Krum, M. Increasing rate and percentage correct in reading and spelling in a fifth grade public school class of slow readers by a token system, in E.A. Ramp and B.L. Hopkins (eds.), *A New Direction for Education: Behavior Analysis,* Department of Human Development, Kansas: 1971, p. 5-28.

28. Taylor, J. School and community-partners in education, *Instructor,* 82: 53-54, 1972.

29. Wall, K. Parents can be private tutors, *Instructor,* 82:55, 1972.

30. Williams, R.L. On school marks, *The Elementary School Journal,* 1-4, 1968.

31. Wooden, V.C., & Gardner, M.E. Are failure notices effective? *The Clearing House,* 399-400, 1964.

# Article 22
# Personal Correlates of Contrasting Environments:
# Student Satisfactions in High School Classrooms* †

EDISON J. TRICKETT and RUDOLF H. MOOS

**Abstract**: The relationship of perceived environment of the high school classroom to students' satisfactions and moods was assessed in two matched samples of 18 classrooms each. A number of significant and replicated relationships were found between the perceived environment and various satisfactions and moods. The strongest relationships with student satisfactions and positive student mood involved those classrooms emphasizing personal relationship dimensions and clarity of rules. The study was conceptualized and discussed in the context of two central aspects of community psychology: the assessment of environments and the implications of such assessments for planning and change.

One of the central conceptual and empirical problems of community psychology involves the assessment of environments and the impact of environments on people. The underlying assumption is that environments exercise meaningful coercive power over their members; like psychological experiments, they have certain "demand

*Reprinted by permission from the *American Journal of Community Psychology*. Vol. 2, No. 1, 1974, 1-12.

†The authors wish to thank Paul Schaffner, David Erichsen, Leslie Sapir, Robert Shelton, Penny Smail, and Bernie Van Dort for their work in data collection and analysis. This research was supported at Yale University by the Center for the Study of Education, Institution for Social and Policy Studies, and at Stanford University School of Medicine by NIMH Grant MH 16026.

characteristics" (Orne, 1962) which influence the participants in those environments. The task for the community psychologist is to develop a framework to view these environments, (work settings, school settings, or rehabilitative settings such as correctional institutions) and to assess the impact of these environments on their members. Implications for this general approach are aimed both at the structure and functions of settings and at the process and probable consequences of change in a setting (Trickett, Kelly, & Todd, 1972).

Various approaches to the conceptualization and assessment of environments have been reported from diverse disciplines (Moos, 1972). Within psychology, the work of Roger Barker and his colleagues on the definition and description of behavior settings represents one line of empirical inquiry (Barker, 1968). His work clearly demonstrates the coercive power of the setting and suggests the predictve importance of the setting in which the behavior occurs. It is demonstrably valid from Barker's work that "When someone is in church, he behaves 'church'; when in a drugstore, he behaves 'drugstore.' " From another conception of human ecology, Kelly and his colleagues have articulated a series of principles drawn from field biology which have led to both conceptual and empirical work on the structure and functions of diverse environments (Kelly, 1967, 1970; Trickett, Kelly, & Todd, 1972; Trickett & Todd, 1972). Kelly has taken a particular ecological variable, turnover rate or rate of population exchange in contrasting high schools, and drawn implications for the nature of student experiences and the socialization process at these schools. A third approach to environmental assessment uses the concept of "perceived environment," in which the environment of a particular setting is defined by the shared perceptions of members of that setting along a number of environmental "dimensions." The extensive early work of Stern (1970) and Pace (1970) assessed the social atmospheres of college environments. Later work by Moos and his colleagues extended this general logic to such settings as psychiatric wards (Moos, 1973), living units at correctional institutions (Moos, 1970), and high school and junior high school classrooms (Trickett & Moos, 1973).

These same investigators have not only demonstrated differing ways of assessing environments; they have shown that different environments have clearly different consequences for their inhabitants. Barker and Gump (1964), for example, demonstrated that the ecological variable of size affects student experience in high school. In large schools, behavior settings are more likely to be "overmanned," with fewer students actively participating in core roles, thus creating more "bystanders." In small schools, however, behavior settings are more likely to be "undermanned," with each member of the culture given more personal responsibility and consequently feeling more "crucial." Kelly (1967), in his study of the effects of turnover rates in high schools, found that the probability of being perceived as deviant depended on the interaction of person and setting. Thus, students high in exploration as a personal coping style were more likely to be nominated as deviant in a constant or low-turnover environment than in a fluid or high-turnover school. Moos (1970) found that living units in correctional institutions which differed in social climate also differed on variables related to general reactions of residents on the units and on the initiatives which residents perceived themselves as taking.

The present study attempts to extend this general logic into one particular environment: the high school classroom. Its purpose is to assess the psychosocial environment of the classroom and the relationship of different kinds of classroom environments to student reactions in the class. Early supportive evidence of general relationships comes from the work of Lewin, Lippitt, and White (1939) in a study of democratically led versus authoritarian led boys' groups. The setting was not a classroom, and methodological criticisms suggest further possible limitations of the findings (Sechrest, 1964); however, Lewin, Lippitt, and White did report that different group climates affected group spontaneity and amount of aggressive behavior. Withall (1951) and, more recently, Walberg (1968, 1969) also suggest that different classroom environments have differential effects on students. Walberg (1968) found that classes which students perceived as more difficult gained more on physics achievement and science understanding than classes perceived as less difficult.

The instrument used in the present study to assess the classroom environment is the Classroom Environment Scale (CES), developed by the authors and reported in greater detail elsewhere (Trickett & Moos, 1973). It measures nine dimensions of the classroom environment which fall under three general conceptual categories: (1) interpersonal relationship dimensions, including affective aspects of teacher-student relationships; (2) goal orientation or personal growth dimensions, such as academic competition among students; and (3) system maintenance and system change dimensions, such as the degree of order and organization. Students were asked to respond "True" or "False" to statements about the classroom; each statement was an indicant of one of the nine dimensions. Their individual perceptions were then pooled to arrive at what Murray (1938) called the "beta press," a consensual or shared definition of reality.

The dependent variable of primary interest was satisfaction with the class. Thus, the general question was "What kind of classrooms do students find satisfying?" Interestingly, we found no prior research in classrooms utilizing student satisfaction as a relevant *dependent* variable, though Walberg's Learning Environment Inventory assesses it as an environmental dimension (Walberg & Anderson, 1967). Consistent with prior work (e.g., Trickett & Moos, 1972), satisfaction was not defined solely as a global concept, but was differentiated into a number of different areas, such as satisfaction with the teacher and satisfaction with the amount of material learned. A secondary set of dependent variables were "mood" items – i.e., asking whether or not a particular class made students feel "anxious" or "secure."

The general hypothesis was that differences in classroom environment would be systematically related to differential student satisfactions and moods. Thus, different kinds of satisfactions would correlate with differing environments. Further, it was expected that these patterns of satisfactions would mirror the general conceptual rationale underlying the scale. For example, general satisfaction with the teacher and the class was predicted to correlate with a classroom emphasizing high Teacher Support and high Student Involvement. In like vein, satisfaction with the amount of material learned was expected to be high in classrooms emphasizing "getting the job done." No specific hypotheses were made concerning the relation of student mood to classroom environment, nor were any predictions made about the relationship of classroom "rules and regulations" to student satisfaction.

## SUBJECTS AND METHOD

As part of a larger data collection culminating in a normative sample for the CES of 315 classrooms, students were asked to fill out three sets of questions. The first was the Classroom Environment Scale (Trickett & Moos, 1973), which yields classroom scores on each of nine dimensions. The nine dimensions are: Student Involvement, Affiliation, Teacher Support, Task Orientation, Competition, Order and Organization, Rule Clarity, Teacher Control, and Teacher Innovation. Their specifics are described in greater detail in Trickett and Moos, 1973. (See Webb, Campbell, Schwartz, & Sechrest, [1966] for multiple method nonreactive approaches to studying naturalistic behavior).

The second and third sets of questions dealt with student reactions to various aspects of the classroom and the school. The first set of questions involved student satisfaction. It included: (a) "In general, how satisfied are you with this school?"; (b) "In general, how satisfied are you with this class?", (c) "How much do you like the other students in this class?"; (d) "In general, how satisfied are you with the teacher in this class?"; (e) "How much *actual material* do you feel you're learning in this class?"; and (f) "In general, how satisfied are you with *the way* this class is taught?" The third set of questions asked students to rate their feelings or mood in the class. They followed the same format as the questions in set one: "How happy (angry, anxious, secure, interested) do you generally feel in this class?" Thus, the CES asked students to report on their perception of the classroom environment, and the other sets of questions asked for their personal reactions to the classroom. The entire questionnaire was administered to each class during a single class period, and virtually all students successfully completed all sections of the questionnaire.

The classrooms used for analysis in the present study consisted of two matched samples of 18 classrooms drawn from the larger normative sample. These matched samples included one classroom each from 18 high schools, which were selected in the following manner: Within each school, classes with identical titles were paired (e.g., English II). If no exact match existed, classes belonging to the same subject area were paired. In both samples of 18, the proportion of classes in each subject area was equal to the proportion of classes in that same subject area in the total normative sample. (For example, since 16% of the classes in the normative sample were social studies classes, 16% or three of the classes in each of the two matched samples were social studies classes.) Thus the two matched samples were not only comparable in class content, they mirrored the content composition of the normative sample from which they were drawn. In terms of content, each of the final samples included one foreign language class, three English classes, four science classes, three math classes, four business and technical classes, and three social studies classes.

An additional criterion was employed to determine the compatability of the two matched samples with the overall sample of classrooms. Three CES dimensions — Student Involvement, Teacher

Support, and Teacher Innovation—were selected and standard scores for these dimensions were tallied for the intervals of one standard deviation, two standard deviations, or more than two standard deviations from the mean. The assumption was that if the samples were representative of the population of classrooms from which they were taken, then we would expect 68% of the scores to fall within one SD of the mean, 95% within two SDs and 5% outside two SDs. A comparison of the mean number observed in each interval for each sample with the expected number per interval indicated that the samples are highly representative.

Finally, the number of students per class was ascertained as an index of comparability between the two samples. The 18 classrooms in Sample 1 ranged from 9 to 28 students, with a mean of 16.1 and a standard deviation of 5.0. Classroom size in Sample 2 ranged from 9 to 30, with a mean of 17.7 and a standard deviation of 5.75. Taken together, these three indices of comparability suggested that the two matched samples were comparable to each other and were representative of the normative sample from which they were drawn.

## RESULTS

A total of 608 students in the two samples completed the entire questionnaire. The following scores were then derived for each student: (1) nine subscale scores for the nine dimensions of the CES; (2) six satisfaction scores for the six items assessing satisfaction with different aspects of the classroom and the school; and (3) five "mood" scores for the five items asking about students' feelings in the class. After the 20 individual scores were computed for each student, classroom scores for each of the 20 variables were computed by averaging the individual scores of students in each classroom. Classrooms were then separated into the two matched samples described above, with the second sample serving as a replication for the first.

First, using classroom scores on each of the 20 variables, an intercorrelation matrix was generated for each sample. On the basis of these intercorrelations, selected satisfaction and mood items were dropped from the final analyses because of their extremely high intercorrelations ($r > .8$). For example, three of the six satisfaction items clustered together with average intercorrelations in both samples of around .85. Empirically, "satisfaction with the class," "satisfaction with the teacher," and "satisfaction with the way the class is taught" are essentially redundant. Consequently only "satisfaction with the teacher" was preserved for the final analysis. A similar situation was found among the mood items. Consequently, only three mood items ("angry," "secure," "interested") were retained.

Table 1 presents the Pearson product-moment correlations of the nine CES dimensions with the remaining "satisfaction" items for the two samples.

These results indicate essentially no relationship between the classroom environment of a particular class and general satisfaction with the school. There are, however, a number of significant, replicated relationships between "in-class" satisfactions and the perceived environment of the classroom, using as a criterion the .05 level in both samples.

The general hypothesis that classrooms emphasizing positive interpersonal relationships would be perceived as satisfying receives strong support. Consistent and replicated relationships are found between Satisfaction with the Teacher and Teacher Support (of students as people), Innovation (in teaching approaches), and Student Involvement in the class. An additional aspect of the classroom environment which relates positively to Student Satisfaction with the Class is the Clarity of Rules in the class.

A somewhat more differentiated picture is presented by the results dealing with the environmental correlates of the other satisfactions. There exists a significant relationship between satisfaction with fellow classmates and high student-student Affiliation in the class. No other aspect of the classroom relates to satisfaction with classmates. Student perception of the amount of material

**Table 1. Correlations over Classrooms (N=18 per sample) between CES Subscales and Satisfactions for Sample 1 and Sample 2.**

| CES Subscale | Satisfaction With School 1 | 2 | Like Other Students 1 | 2 | Satisfaction With Teacher 1 | 2 | Actual Material Learned 1 | 2 |
|---|---|---|---|---|---|---|---|---|
| Involvement | .13 | .41 | .06 | .38 | .79c | .69c | .73c | .79c |
| Affiliation | .15 | .23 | .46a | .72c | .41 | .38 | .30 | .55a |
| Teacher Support | .33 | -.31 | -.20 | .02 | .70b | .82c | .40 | .39 |
| Task Orientation | -51a | -.02 | -.20 | .09 | -.14 | .06 | .36 | .26 |
| Competition | -51a | -.21 | .16 | -.18 | .28 | .06 | .55a | .62b |
| Order Organization | -.02 | -.07 | .28 | .02 | .17 | .54a | .42 | .35 |
| Rule Clarity | -.20 | -.59b | .25 | -.07 | .59b | .47a | .83c | .47a |
| Teacher Control | -.23 | -.37 | -.50a | .23 | -.04 | -.06 | .26 | .26 |
| Teacher Innovation | .21 | -.14 | .01 | -.33 | .70c | .46a | .47a | .28 |

ap < .05 = .46          bp < .01 = .58          cp < .001 = .69

learned, however, relates positively to several aspects of the classroom environment, including Competition, Student Involvement, and the clarity of rules governing classroom behavior. In addition, a consistent trend ($p < .10$) is found for Teacher Support in both samples.

Table 2 presents the correlation between the nine CES dimensions and the three mood items. Again, only findings replicated at the .05 level are considered.

With respect to student anger, the only replicated finding suggests that students feel angrier in classes which are low in Order and Organization. Feelings of security relate positively to Teacher Support and Student Involvement, while feelings of interest relate positively to classes high in Involvement, Teacher Support, and Rule Clarity.

The sum of this data indictes strong support for the general hypothesis that differences in classroom environments are systematically related to different student satisfactions and moods, i.e., that the properties of the psychosocial environment of a locale have systematic bearing on the psychological state of those in that locale. In addition, the data from both the satisfaction and mood items demonstrate the importance of relationship dimensions of the class-

**Table 2. Correlations over Classrooms (N=18 per sample) between CES Subscales and Moods for Sample 1 and Sample 2.**

| CES Subscale | Feel Angry 1 | Feel Angry 2 | Feel Secure 1 | Feel Secure 2 | Feel Interested 1 | Feel Interested 2 |
|---|---|---|---|---|---|---|
| Student Involvement | -1.2 | -.55a | .66b | .55a | .84c | .73c |
| Affiliation | -.28 | -.22 | .34 | .55a | .30 | .55a |
| Teacher Support | -.37 | -.55a | .40 | .62b | .56a | .70c |
| Task Orientation | -.12 | -.29 | -.13 | -.32 | -.12 | -.03 |
| Competition | .22 | -.07 | .27 | .03 | .40 | .21 |
| Order and Organization | -.47a | -.71c | .15 | .22 | .13 | .14 |
| Rule Clarity | .11 | -.23 | .29 | .28 | .54a | .55a |
| Teacher Control | .48a | .07 | .06 | .03 | .05 | .04 |
| Teacher Innovation | -.12 | -.16 | .28 | .17 | .66b | .30 |

a $p < .05 = .46$     b $p < .01 = .58$     v $p < .0001 = .69$

room environment in relating to such noncognitive variables as satisfactions and moods. Student Involvement and Teacher Support showed consistent relationship to satisfaction with the teacher, amount of material learned, and feelings of interest and security on the part of students. The finding is stronger for Student Involvement, in that Teacher Support indicates only a replicated trend with respect to amount of material learned. Finally, those aspects of the classroom relating to teacher authority functions and task variables, with the singular exception of Rule Clarity, bear little relationship to the satisfaction and mood items.

## DISCUSSION

The most general rationale behind the present study was to highlight a central conceptual problem in community psychology, that of environmental assessment, and to provide data relevant to the proposition that different environments are systematically related to different psychological states of participants. The high school classroom was chosen to demonstrate not only this more global concern but to do so in a way which specifies that certain dimensions of the environment have correlates in terms of the satisfactions and moods of classroom participants. Results of the study are supportive of this contention.

With reference to the "in-class" data on student *satisfactions,* it is clear that a general set of classroom characteristics exist which relate to student satisfaction with the class and the teacher. These include a personal student-teacher relationship, high student involvement, innovative teaching efforts, and clarity of rules governing classroom behavior. While the first three of these four dimensions cluster around positive interpersonal relationships and an openness to "experimentation," the strong relationship between Rule Clarity and student satisfaction attests to the importance of structure around rules and predictability of the environment for students. (See Wilkinson, & Reppucci, 1973, for a similar finding in a study of token economy cottages in a correctional institution.)

In addition to this general picture of the "satisfying" classroom, another area of interest involved a pivotal academic function of learning actual material. Because this is seen as such a primary function of the classroom, the kind of classroom environment which relates to this educational goal has important implications. The present data suggests that the classroom where students perceive that much material is learned is both similar to and different from the "satisfying" class. It shares with the "satisfying" class the emphasis on Student Involvement and Rule Clarity and shows a trend (.10 in both samples) toward high Teacher Support. Unlike the generally satisfying class, however, an emphasis is placed on Competition. Thus, the emergent picture of the classroom where students report a great deal of content learning combines an affective concern with students as people with an emphasis on students working hard for academic rewards in a coherent, organized context.

These findings about the environmental correlates of student satisfaction and material learned are generally congruent with Walberg's (1969) conclusion that while environments must be intellectually challenging to encourage growth in achievement and understanding, they must be cohesive and satisfying in order to encourage "noncognitive" growth. However, findings from the present study suggest that certain "noncognitive" aspects of the environment (e.g., Teacher Support) may relate to cognitive outcomes. They also show that some environmental characteristics which one might expect would relate to cognitive outcomes (e.g., amount of material learned) fail to do so. Task Orientation and Teacher Control, for example, are often rationalized on the basis that students will learn more in such an atmosphere. That this relationship was not found may suggest limitations on the education ideology underlying it.

Finally, satisfaction with the other students in the class did not emerge as a very pervasive correlate of classroom environment. Indeed, such satisfaction was correlated only with classrooms emphasizing student-student interaction and working together.

The data on the relationship of classroom environment to student *mood* also has implications for educational theory and practice. For example, feelings of security and interest relate positively to the interpersonal dimensions of Involvement and Teacher Support, suggesting that such classrooms involve a kind of nonanxious enthusiasm on the part of students. It might be hypothesized that such circumstances promote personal risk taking, an educational goal congruent with the ideology of many "alternative" schools. In addition, the relationship of student feelings of anger to low Order and Organization in the classroom suggests the negative implications of classroom disruption and lack of teacher preparedness for the class. A classroom which is "out of control" is presumably not a pleasant experience for either teachers or students.

One last point bears mentioning. There was essentially no relationship between the perceived environment of the classroom and satisfaction with the school in general. This is to be expected, since any particular class does not generally encompass a large part of a student's total school experience. It does, however, raise the interesting and important question of the relation of classroom experience in general to satisfaction with school. Because of numerous extra-classroom influences on adolescents in schools (e.g., peer group ties, extracurricular activities), determining what aspects of school bear most heavily on student satisfaction is a salient research concern.

The patterns of satisfactions and their relationships to aspects of the perceived environment suggest some more general comments about both the assessment of environments *and* their effects on persons. For example, while satisfaction may be seen as a global or general variable, more specific information about the satisfaction correlates of environments may be gleaned by assessing specific as well as general satisfactions (see Trickett, & Moos, 1972). In the present study, general satisfaction with the teacher (and the class) relates to several aspects of the classroom environment. When the dependent variable becomes the amount of material learned, this also relates to several aspects of the environment, but with only moderate overlap in terms of specific dimensions with satisfaction with the teacher. Most specifically, satisfaction with classmates relates *only* to that aspect of the environment involving student-student relationships. By pinpointing multiple areas of satisfaction varying in both degree of specificity and content area, a more differentiated picture of student reactions in classrooms emerges.

A similar logic is applicable in conceptualizing environments as multidimensional phenomenological fields. For example, in the present study some aspects of the environment were related to both satisfaction with the teacher and amount of material learned (e.g., Rule Clarity), some to only one of these dependent variables (e.g., Competition), and one (Affiliation) was not related to either of them but was related to a third variable, i.e., satisfaction with classmates. By assessing environments in multidimensional fashion and by conceptualizing such dependent variables as satisfaction in both general and specific terms, one can derive both a global *and* a differential picture of the effects of environments on their inhabitants.

Such differentiated portraits of people in context have, in addition to the conceptual relevance mentioned above, important implications for another central concern of community psychology: the area of social planning and change. If one can specify, for example, the desired "outcomes" of a particular environment such as a classroom, one can then gather relevant information on what kind of classroom environments are likely to relate to those outcomes. The data from the present study suggests that one would attempt to create a somewhat different classroom environment if student perception of "amount of material learned" was seen as a primary goal than if "satisfaction with the teacher" was seen as primary. The CES itself can also be used to assess possible discrepancies between the current environment and the desired environment in terms of specific "outcome" criteria. Such discrepancies can also be used to trigger discussion of possible changes in the environment, a logic similar to reported attempts at environmental alteration in psychiatric wards (Pierce, Trickett, & Moos, 1972) and adolescent residential centers (Moos, & Otto, 1972). Both of these potential uses for measures of the perceived environment are more fully discussed elsewhere (Barrett, & Trickett, 1972; Moos, 1974).

The pattern of relationships among satisfaction indices, mood indices, and dimensions of the perceived environment suggests something further about approaches to change which involve such tools, namely, that one can assess the differential costs and benefits of change toward a particular goal if one develops multiple outcome criteria such as the different aspects of satisfaction and mood described in the present study. For example, with respect to the satisfaction data in the present study, one might hypothesize that as a classroom moves toward an environment stressing the learning of material, one might sacrifice some of the interpersonal satisfactions gained through supportive student-student relationships. In any case, multivariate dependent measures are one approach to assessing the differential effects of change strategies on diverse aspects of the environment.

In sum, the perceived psychological environment of high school classrooms is seen as having significant relationships to the satisfactions and moods of students. In addition, while some dimensions of the classroom environment relate to a number of different student satisfactions in the classroom, some specificity exists in the relation between specific dimensions of the environment and specific satisfactions. These results were discussed in the context of two central aspects of community psychology; the assessment of environments and the implications of such assessments for planning and change.

# REFERENCES

Barker, R.G. *Ecological psychology*. Stanford, Calif.: Stanford University Press, 1968.

Barker, R.G., & Gump, P.V. *Big school, small school*. Stanford, Calif.: Stanford University Press, 1964.

Barrett, D.M., & Trickett, E.J. Climate, consultation, and change: Alternative assumptions and strategies. In S. Insel (Chm.), The perceived psychosocial environment of diverse situations: Measurements, underlying commonalities, utilization for social change. Symposium presented at the Convention of the American Psychological Association, 1972.

Kelly, J.G. Naturalistic observation and theory confirmation: An example, *Human Development*, 1967, 101, 212-222.

Kelly, J.G. The quest for valid preventive interventions. In C.D. Spielberger (Ed.), *Current topics in clinical and community psychology*. Vol. 2. New York: Academic Press, 1970.

Lewin, K., Lippitt, R., & White, R.K. Patterns of aggressive behavior in experimentally created "social climates." *Journal of Social Psychology*, 1939, 10, 271-299.

Moos, R.H. The assessment of the social climates of correctional institutions. *Journal of Research in Crime and Delinquency*, 1970, 7, 71-82.

Moos, R.H. Systems for the assessment and classification of human environments: An overview. In R. Moos and P. Insel (Eds.), *Issues in social ecology: Human milieus*. Palo Alto, Calif.: National Press, 1973.

Moos, R.H. *Evaluating treatment environments: A social ecological approach*. New York: Wiley, 1974, in press.

Moos, R.H., & Otto, J. The community-oriented programs environment scale: A methodology for the facilitation and evaluation of social change. *Community Mental Health Journal*, 1972, 8, 28-37.

Murray, H. *Explorations in personality*. New York: Oxford University Press, 1938.

Orne, M.T. On the social psychology of the psychological experiment: With particular reference to demand characteristics and their implications. *American Psychologist*, 1962, 17, 776-783.

Pace, R. Differences in campus atmosphere. In M. Miles and W. Charters (Eds.) *Learning in social settings*. Boston: Allyn & Bacon, 1970.

Pierce, W.D., Trickett, E.J., & Moos, R.H. Changing ward atmosphere through staff discussion of the ward environment. *Archives of General Psychiatry*, 1972, 26, 35-41.

Sechrest, L. Studies of classroom atmosphere. *Psychology in the Schools*. 1964, 1, 103-118.

Stern, G. *People in context: Measuring person-environment congruence in education and industry*. New York: Wiley, 1970.

Trickett, E.J., Kelly, J.G., & Todd, D.M. The social environment of the high school: Guidelines for individual change and organization development. In S. Golann and C. Eisdoefer (Eds.). *Handbook of community mental health.* New York: Appleton-Century-Crofts, 1972.

Trickett, E.J., & Moos, R.H. Satisfaction with the correctional institution environment: An instance of perceived self-environment similarity. *Journal of Personality,* 1972, 40, 75-87.

Trickett, E.J., & Moos, R.H. The social environment of junior high and high school classrooms. *Journal of Educational Psychology,* 1973, 65, 93-102.

Trickett, E.J., & Todd, D.M. The assessment of the high school culture: An ecological perspective. *Theory into Practice,* 1972, 11, 28-37.

Walberg, H.J. Structural and affective aspects of classroom climate. *Psychology in the Schools,* 1968, 5, 247-253.

Walberg, H.J. Social environment as a mediator of classroom learning. *Journal of Educational Psychology.* 1969, 60, 443-448.

Walberg, H.J., & Anderson, G.J. *Learning environment inventory.* Cambridge, Mass.: Harvard University, 1967, mimeo.

Webb, E.J., Campbell, D.T., Schwartz, R.D., & Sechrest, L. *Unobtrusive measures: Nonreactive research in the social sciences.* Chicago: Rand McNally, 1966.

Wilkinson, L., & Reppucci, N.D. Perception of social climate among participants in token economy cottages in a juvenile correctional institution. *American Journal of Community Psychology.* 1973, 1, (1), 36-43.

Withall, J. The development of a climate index. *Journal of Educational Research.* 1951, 45, 93-99.

# 9
## *Implementation*


## ASSESSMENT

The previous chapters presented an introduction to behavioral principles and several demonstrations of how these principles have been applied in the classroom. This chapter discusses the practical issues faced by teachers who wish to implement behavioral procedures in their classes. Typically, decision-making has the following sequence: the teacher first identifies the problem child, consults other teachers and professional staff members who are familiar with the child, and then makes decisions regarding the possible referral of the child to a consultant or agency. If she decides to deal with the problem child herself, she becomes concerned with making a more detailed assessment of the problem situation, with implementing procedures to alleviate the problem, and with relating her approach to parents and other school personnel. Let us consider each of these decision areas in more detail.


### Identification of Problem Children

For a number of reasons children are often not identified as problem children until they reach school age. Behaviors which are tolerated at home may not be tolerated in the classroom. Problems which go unnoticed or ignored in the preschool years may become more obvious when the child is in school. Finally, the school situation may exacerbate or produce difficulties in relatively problem-free children. Early detection of problem children is clearly advantageous. Many problem behaviors become more difficult to change the longer they are left untreated, and more and more areas of a child's life are affected if a problem is allowed to continue. For example, if a child has poor vision, the parents may not be aware of the problem before the child enters school partly because the preschool child isn't usually presented with situations which require normal visual acuity, e.g., reading small print or copying from the board. Once he is in school, his reading will be affected. If his vision is not corrected, he will experience a considerable amount of failure and may become disruptive since he receives little approval for academic success but can gain attention by disrupting the class. Fortunately, most vision and hearing problems are detected by the school's health personnel who routinely examine all children.

However, many problems are not so easily and routinely detected by student service personnel. The responsibility of identifying existing or potential social and academic problems rests with the teacher because she has a unique opportunity to observe the child in many diverse situations. The teacher observes the child's reactions to peers and other adults, to success and failure, to both academic and social demands, and in both structured and unstructured settings. In essence, the teacher often knows the child better than anyone else — certainly better than the psychologist and occasionally even better than his parents know him. In fact, long-term studies of children referred to child guidance clinics indicate that the teachers may be right in their greater concern for the disruptive child than for the withdrawn child. Robbins (1966) found that the disruptive or "acting-out" child was referred for psychiatric aid in his adult life more frequently than was the withdrawn or nervous child. While it may be true that the excessively withdrawn child is less likely to be a problem when he grows up than is the "acting-out" child, there are some special difficulties in identifying the withdrawn child who is a problem in elementary school. The withdrawn child whose academic work is adequate does not usually disrupt either the teacher or the rest of the class. As a consequence, the teacher may not realize that such a child is deficient in social skills or is unhappy. Even when aware of these problems the teacher may ignore them perhaps feeling that the disruptive children in the class must be dealt with first.

Granting that early detection is desirable and that the teacher is in a particularly good position to identify problems, what are the types of problems that the teacher may expect to encounter? First, there are problems which occur infrequently and which are usually identified in the preschool years but which sometimes go unnoticed or untreated until the child is in school. Included in this group are autism, mental retardation, childhood schizophrenia, enuresis (bed wetting), physical handicaps (severe hearing or vision loss), speech difficulties (stuttering or stammering), and epilepsy. Autism occurs in a very small percentage of the population and is characterized by behaviors such as extreme aloneness, speech disturbances (mutism or parrot-like speech), obsession for sameness, idiosyncratic eating patterns, and purposeless and repetitive activity. Retardation is often noticed when a child who enters nursery school, kindergarten, or first grade is particularly slow in language development or self-help skills. Approximately 2.5% of all children have IQ's below 70 and are called retarded. Thus, a retarded child of 10 years may be expected to behave more like a seven-year-old child. Childhood schizophrenia is identified with behaviors such as little interest in daily activities, hyper- or hypo-activity, extreme fear reactions, and peculiar thinking or verbal behavior. Epilepsy occurs in seven out of every 100,000 children of school age (Bakwin & Bakwin, 1967). The epileptic seizure or attack varies from often unnoticed petit mal attacks to violent grand mal seizures. Enuresis (day or night wetting or both) occurs in about 15% of all four-year-old children, in 10% of all six-year-olds, and in 4% of all 12-year-olds (Lovibond, 1964).

A regular classroom teacher may rarely be faced with children who fit into any of the problem areas above but should certainly be aware of their existence. However, we can say with certainty that a teacher will frequently encounter problems like those discussed in the previous chapters of this book. Briefly, this group of problem behaviors includes hyperactivity, destructive behaviors, aggression, isolation, disobedience, short attention span, fears, lying, frequent physical complaints, unhappiness, and truancy.

Given the broad range of behaviors which are at least potential problems and the varying degree to which any particular child will display problem behaviors, the teacher needs some guidelines by which to make an initial evaluation of a child's problem. One can be fairly certain that the child requires some special attention (1) if his social behavior interferes significantly with his academic work, (2) if he interferes with the other children's academic work or social behavior, (3) if he interferes with the teacher's ability to operate effectively, or (4) if the child is unusually withdrawn.

At this point we offer a word of caution. There is a general

tendency to label problem children as emotionally disturbed, retarded, brain damaged, learning disabled, or hyperactive. Almost any
experienced educator will attest to the fact that once a child is
labeled "abnormal," he will have considerably more difficulty
regaining a "normal" label than he had in acquiring the "abnormal"
label. We can see no advantage in hastily applied labels. The
assumption, "if we can classify or label the problem child, then we
know how to treat him," is unjustly optimistic considering the state
of our knowledge regarding the relationship between diagnosis and
treatment. Premature labeling not only allows us to fool ourselves
into thinking that the problem is nearly solved but also may have the
effect of *creating* a child who lives up to his label. Teachers, parents,
and other children convey to the "emotionally disturbed" child their
expectations of how an "emotionally disturbed" child should
behave, e.g., unpredictably, disruptively, or incompetently. Believing
that this is how he should behave, the problem child often is
surprisingly adept at fulfilling our expectations. Children do respond
differently to various teachers, and since a teacher who reads that a
child was a "problem child" might respond to him as such, a good
practice for the teacher would be to avoid reading case records or
reports about pupils until the teacher has formed his own opinions of
the children.


### Referral Decisions

Since teachers are not expected to deal with all types of
children's problems entirely on their own, most school systems hire a
number of professional personnel who provide special services to the
teachers and children. While the particular service personnel vary
from school to school, a full complement would include school
counselors, school psychologists, school social workers, nurses,
doctors, reading specialists, speech therapists, and people trained to
diagnose hearing and vision problems. A new teacher should quickly
(1) become acquainted with the school's general referral policies and
procedures, (2) locate the service personnel in the school, and (3)
determine the responsibilities, capabilities, and limitations of these
individuals. In addition to the services provided by the school, there
are often a number of community agencies to which a child may be
referred, e.g., child guidance clinics, speech and hearing centers,
tutoring services, community or university psychological clinics,
medical clinics, and specialists in private practice.

The functions normally performed by school service personnel vary considerably from school to school and from individual to individual. However, a brief general description of the typical activities of the school psychologist, counselor, and social worker is useful for emphasizing the responsibility of the teacher in assessing and treating problem children. Traditionally, the school psychologist administers intelligence and personality tests which are used as the basis for a report to the teacher. The report is likely to contain the psychologist's general reaction to the child, a description of the child's intellectual abilities relative to those of other children of his age, and a judgment regarding the personality factors which may be relevant to the child's problem. It has been our experience that teachers find an intellectual and achievement assessment useful, especially when the child is young or new to the school. Unfortunately, many school psychologists have not been trained to provide teachers with specific suggestions for achieving changes in classroom behavior. Therefore, the school psychologist usually does not take an active part in treating the child but may make referral suggestions.

In contrast to the diagnostically oriented traditional psychologist, the school counselor typically takes an active part in treatment. At the junior or senior high school level the emphasis is likely to be on educational and vocational guidance. Both elementary and secondary counselors may offer individual or group counseling regarding emotional or behavioral problems. It is generally assumed that sessions in the counselor's office will lead to changes in the child's personality which will be evident not only in the counselor's office but also at home or in the classroom. This assumption has questionable validity, particularly with respect to elementary school children who have considerable difficulty translating the counselor's suggestions into improved classroom behavior.

The school social worker is subject to the difficulties of situation-specific behavior and typically assumes, often rightly, that the source of school behavior problems is in the home. However, the social worker also assumes that by focusing attention on changes in the family situation changes will be effected in the child's school behavior. Just as they may behave differently in different school situations, children may be a problem at school without being a problem at home. In fact, it is likely that a large number of school problems develop as a result of factors which are unique to the school environments, e.g., competition with other children for the teacher's attention or difficulty with academic material. However, one should not overlook the fact that parent cooperation in a treatment program being conducted in the classroom can greatly facilitate its success, and by working in conjunction with the classroom teacher, the school social worker can encourage such parent cooperation and involvement. A social worker can probably be of most help by assuring the school or a family that they are getting all the social services that are due them under current law. For example, a social worker can acquaint the parent with available medical care, nursing care, food allowances, and home-based tutorial programs and should help the parent in acquiring such services. A social worker also may make home visits to insure that children are receiving proper food, clothing, and living facilities and to determine whether there is any evidence of physical or psychological neglect or abuse of a child.

Let us assume that the teacher has a good understanding of the referral sources which are available and has identified a problem situation. The next decision should be whether to deal with the problem personally or to involve the referral sources and if so, to what degree. A decision-making process which clearly prescribes the best solution for every problem is difficult to outline. However, in cases where physical or medical factors are suspected of being major contributors to the problem, as in the case of hearing and vision problems and epilepsy, referral to the appropriate persons is always advisable. Similarly, referrals to the school psychologist and/or the family doctor should be made routinely in cases of extremely bizarre behavior of the kind generally associated with autism, and childhood schizophrenia, and in cases of possible retardation. As mentioned earlier, the teacher should consider seeking consultation if the child's behavior is interfering with his or others' academic and social progress or if the child is unusually withdrawn. The extent to which a teacher will use referral sources for these cases will vary according to the teacher's competence and limitations, the nature of the particular problem, and the skill of available referral personnel.

If you are beginning to suspect that we believe the teacher can be competent enough to handle a significant number of classroom problems almost entirely on his or her own, you are correct. This is certainly not to say that we would advise against consultation. A discussion with service personnel or with another particularly skillful teacher can be extremely useful. However, teachers often over-estimate the success and skills of service personnel while under-estimating the importance and often the necessity of treating the problem within the classroom situation. The teacher should be aware of his or her own limitations but should be willing to take some responsibility for social behavior problems just as he or she takes responsibility for the students' academic progress.

We have already discussed the approach generally adopted by some of the traditional service personnel. If seeking help from a behaviorally-oriented psychologist, the teacher should be prepared for a slightly different approach. A behavioral consultant is likely to begin by observing the problem child in the classroom on several occasions. He may then ask the teacher to assist in the assessment of the problem by recording certain aspects of the child's behavior and perhaps the behavior of his peers or the teacher's own behavior. He may decide to see the child on his own for a short time and gradually introduce his behavior change procedures into the classroom. Alternately, he may suggest that the teacher implement a procedure in the classroom directly, often asking the teacher to take responsibility for the implementation with more and more intermittent consulting on his part.

If the teacher decides to seek help from professionals, there are several ways to facilitate the treatment process. The problem should be specifically and objectively described. If the problem behavior is discrete and easily observable, e.g., hitting other children, the teacher can count the number of times the behavior occurs over a 4-5 day period, noting the situation at the time the behavior occurs and the teacher's reaction to it (*see* the discussion of more detailed assessment procedures below). The teacher can also provide the professional source with a synopsis of the child's school history and the opinions of other teachers the child has had. If the onset of the problem was sudden, any information the teacher can provide regarding changes in the classroom routine or the child's social and family environment would be useful. After the referral has been made, the teacher should continue to provide any information which he or she considers relevant regarding the problem behavior. Active and voluntary participation on the teacher's part will give the service personnel useful feedback concerning their effectiveness and will probably encourage direct and more effective treatment.

## Assessment Measures

When the teacher elects to deal with the problem or to collaborate with a behavioral consultant, a detailed assessment of the problem situation is indispensable, not only prior to any treatment decisions but also during treatment and periodically following treatment. Relevant information should be sought from other school personnel who deal with the child, e.g., the lunchroom aide, school nurse, principal. Parental involvement can also be very useful. A variety of assessment techniques have been used in the classroom, and they are designed to serve any of several purposes: (1) to clearly and objectively describe the problem, (2) to clarify factors influencing the problem, (3) to aid in making decisions concerning treatment, (4) to evaluate the effects of treatment, (5) to provide information regarding the possible reappearance or increase in the severity of the problem following treatment, and (6) to provide information for teachers the child may have in the future. We will describe four types of assessment devices which teachers can easily implement. The anecdotal record (*see* Table 1) consists of a short paragraph in which the teacher notes her general evaluation of the problem situation and any factors she feels may be relevant. An anecdotal record is useful in the initial stages of assessment because it focuses the teacher's attention on the specific behaviors which constitute the problem and some of the variables which may be contributing to the problem. From her sample anecdotal record we know that Sam's problem behaviors include fighting, inappropriate

**Table 1. Anecdotal Record.**

---

Sam has become increasingly difficult to handle in my first grade class. He picks fights almost every day. Although he has no real friends, he is interested in the other children. This concern about what everyone else is doing often leads to general disruption in the class. Sam ignores all pleas to return to his seat and work, but is constantly seeking my attention.

---

concern for the other children's activities, and attention seeking. There is the implication that he lacks adequate skills to make friends. Unfortunately, the anecdotal record yields only a general description of the problem behaviors and is unlikely to reflect gradual changes over time. For example, if the teacher implements a program to decrease Sam's fighting, the anecdotal record will not reflect a change from four fights to three—which would indicate that the treatment was effective. Knowing that Sam "has no real friends" does not suggest what he could do to establish better peer relations. As the record is the teacher's subjective reaction to the situation, personal biases, emotions, and attitudes can easily influence the objectivity of the record and make it improbable that another observer would produce an equivalent evaluation of the situation. To the extent that the record is subjective, the usefulness of the record for reflecting treatment changes and aiding consultants or other teachers is limited.

A second classroom assessment tool is the checklist (*see* Table 2) which consists of a list of adjectives (Scarr, 1966) or, as exemplified here, descriptions of children's behaviors—usually problem behaviors. The teacher simply checks the behaviors which apply to the child in question. The checklist is potentially more objective than the anecdotal record if the items are well defined and cover a wide range of behaviors. The teacher's own biases have less influence on the checklist than on the anecdotal record and agreement between observers is easier to achieve. Since the checklist makes reliable observations of children's behavior possible, one can investigate the relation between the pattern of behaviors checked and such variables as treatment effectiveness and prognosis. Gross changes in the child's behavior over time may be reflected on the checklist. An additional advantage of the checklist is that it may alert the teacher to important behaviors which had not been focused on previously. Some of the major disadvantages of the checklist are that (1) it provides little information on the frequency of the problem behaviors; (2) it is not sensitive to gradual changes over time: (3) it does

**Table 2. Checklist.**

| Child: | Sam | Date: | 11/9/76 | Teacher: | Mrs. A. |
|--------|-----|-------|---------|----------|---------|

| | | |
|------|------|----------------------------------------------|
| —— | 1. | bites nails |
| X | 2. | hits other children |
| X | 3. | talks out of turn |
| —— | 4. | prefers to play by himself |
| —— | 5. | fails to complete assignments |
| X | 6. | gives orders to other children |
| X | 7. | is restless |
| —— | 8. | is jealous of attention paid to other children |
| X | 9. | has feelings of inferiority |
| X | 10. | lacks interest—is bored |

not indicate in any way factors which may be influencing the problem behaviors, and (4) it gives no information on the relative importance of the behaviors checked. It should be noted that there are significant differences among checklists with respect to the specificity of the adjectives or behavior descriptions. The more specific and less global the items are, the more useful and meaningful the checklist will be.

The behavior rating scale is an adaptation of the checklist (*see* Table 3). In addition to checking the behaviors the problem child displays, the teacher notes the degree to which each behavior applies

Table 3. Rating Scale.

Child:    Sam                 Date: 11/9/76   Teacher: Mrs. A.

| | | | | |
|---|---|---|---|---|
| ⓪ | 1 | 2 | 1. | bites nails |
| 0 | ① | 2 | 2. | hits other children |
| 0 | 1 | ② | 3. | talks out of turn |
| 0 | ① | 2 | 4. | prefers to play by himself |
| 0 | ① | 2 | 5. | fails to complete assignments |
| 0 | ① | 2 | 6. | gives orders to other children |
| 0 | 1 | ② | 7. | is restless |
| 0 | 1 | ② | 8. | is jealous of attention paid to other children |
| ⓪ | 1 | 2 | 9. | has feelings of inferiority |
| 0 | 1 | ② | 10. | lacks interest—is bored |

Note:    0 = no problem, 1 = mild problem, 2 = severe problem

to the child (Peterson, 1961). Like the checklist, the rating scale is relatively objective, allows for reliability checks between two or more raters, and can be used as an indicator of behavior change. Its primary advantage over the checklist is that the rating scale provides some information, albeit crude, regarding the frequency and relative importance of the child's behavior. The rating scale is also very convenient for teachers and may be used on either a daily or weekly basis.

The last assessment technique we shall discuss is the one used by the majority of investigators represented in this book—the assessment of target behaviors (Iwata & Bailey, 1974; Madsen, Becker, & Thomas, 1968; O'Leary, Kaufman, Kass, & Drabman, 1970;

Solomon & Wahler, 1973). As will become apparent in the following discussion, target assessment has many of the advantages of the anecdotal record, checklist, and rating scale but few of their disadvantages. Target assessment can very objectively describe problem behaviors, can suggest and evaluate factors influencing the problem situation, has implications for treatment, can be used to evaluate both short- and long-term effects of treatment, and is clearly meaningful to other people interested in the child's problem. After completing an anecdotal record and perhaps a checklist or behavior rating scale, the teacher has fairly well identified the behaviors which require modification, that is, the target behaviors.

The first step in proceeding with a target assessment is the careful specification of the target behaviors (*see* Table 4). A good guideline for writing behavior descriptions is to make the descriptions as complete and unambiguous as possible so that another person could use the descriptions to produce observations of the child's behavior that would agree very closely with the teacher's ratings. In Sam's

Table 4. Descriptions of Contact, Verbalization, and Gross Motor Behaviors (Madsen, Becker, & Thomas, 1968).

| Symbol | Title | Description |
|---|---|---|
| A. | Gross Motor | Getting out of seat, standing up, running, hopping, skipping, jumping, walking around, moving chair, etc. |
| D. | Contact (high and low intensity) | Hitting, kicking, shoving, pinching, slapping, striking with object, throwing object which hits another person, poking with object, biting, pulling hair, touching, patting, etc. Any physical contact is rated. |
| E. | Verbalization | Carrying on conversations with other children when it is not permitted. Answers teacher without raising hand or without being called on; making comments or calling out remarks when no questions have been asked; calling teacher's name to get her attention; crying, coughing, or blowing loudly. These responses may be directed to teacher or children. |

case, the teacher might decide to focus on hitting other children, restlessness, and attention-seeking. Although Sam's boredom seems to be an important behavior, it is very difficult to specify the behaviors from which the teacher makes the conclusion that Sam is bored. One obvious factor related to boredom which can easily be assessed by the teacher is the level of Sam's academic performance. There are two possibilities. Sam may be doing poorly and is bored because he doesn't understand the assignments, or he may be doing well and is bored because he is not challenged. While this chapter focuses on social behavior problems, the teacher should be aware of the influence academic problems can have on social behaviors and take appropriate action with respect to academic problems as quickly as possible either by seeing that the child receives extra help or by providing him with more stimulating material.

As mentioned above, Sam's teacher had decided to focus on hitting, restlessness, and attention-seeking. In writing the behavioral descriptions, exactly what is meant by hitting, restlessness, and attention-seeking must be determined. Thus, descriptions like those in Table 4 are developed. Because intent is difficult to establish when observing aggression (physical contact), the teacher may decide to rate all contact. By restlessness, the teacher may mean any number of things. For the purposes of our example, let us assume that Sam's most disruptive restless behavior seems to involve getting out of his seat (gross motor behavior). Attention-seeking may include coming to the teacher's desk frequently and talking out of turn. Since coming to the teacher's desk is included under gross motor behavior, no new category is required. Talking out of turn can be described as verbalization. Note that by focusing on physical contact, gross motor behavior, and verbalization, the teacher is directing her attention to only a few of Sam's behaviors, and no attempt is made to achieve a comprehensive record of the entire range of his behaviors.

Once the teacher has written descriptions of the disruptive behavior of concern, these codes will be used to record the frequency of the behaviors. There are several procedures for recording behaviors. If teacher aides or volunteers are available, they can observe the behaviors. More frequently, the teacher will need to make the observations. As making continuous observations may be difficult for the classroom teacher, two other options are suggested: event recording and time sampling. Event recording (Table 5) is appropriate if the behavior occurs infrequently (e.g., 0 to 5 times per day) or is of particularly short duration (e.g., talking out). The teacher can simply make a tally on a sheet of paper every time the behavior

**Table 5. Event Recording: Number of Events/Day.**

|  | Monday | Tuesday | Wednesday | Thursday | Friday | Weekly Average |
|---|---|---|---|---|---|---|
| Contact | /// <br> 3 | 卌 <br> 5 | 卌 / <br> 6 | 卌 <br> 4 | 卌 <br> 4 | 4.4 |
| Verbalization | 卌 /// <br> 8 | 卌 卌 <br> 10 | 卌 / <br> 6 | 卌 卌 // <br> 12 | 卌 卌/ <br> 11 | 9.4 |

occurs. If duration is an important aspect of behavior (e.g., temper tantrums), the duration of each behavioral event should be recorded. The frequency or average duration of each behavior should be calculated each day. For more frequently occurring behaviors, a time sampling procedure (Table 6) is useful. The teacher might select two

**Table 6. Time Sampling.**

Monday 10:00 - 10:30—Independent seat work

|  | Minutes | | | | | | | | | |
|---|---|---|---|---|---|---|---|---|---|---|
|  | 3 | 6 | 9 | 12 | 15 | 18 | 21 | 24 | 27 | 30 |
| **Gross Motor Behavior** | | | | | | | | | | |
| Behavior | | | | | | | | | | |
| Teacher | X | - | - | X | X | X | X | X | - | X |
| Reliability Checker | X | - | - | - | - | X | X | X | X | X |

% Out of Seat = 7 (x)/10 (intervals) = 70% (Use Teacher ratings).
% Reliability = Agreements/Agreements + Disagreements

$$= \frac{5}{5+3} = \frac{5}{8} = 62\%$$

or three 15- to 30-minute intervals during the day when the target behaviors will be recorded. The interval selected, e.g., 30 min., should be divided into smaller segments, e.g., ten 3-min. segments. Every 3 minutes the teacher should look at the child and note whether the behavior is occurring (see Table 6). It is advisable to make observations in a variety of situations initially, e.g., small reading groups, lectures to the entire class, independent seat work, recess, or the first half-hour of the day, because some behaviors may occur in one or two situations but not in others. The situations in which the behavior occurs with the highest frequency should be selected for continued observation. At the end of each day, the teacher should calculate the average frequency of each behavior observed (Table 6). Plotting these daily averages on a graph provides a good visual description of the child's behavior changes.

Although target assessment is potentially the most objective assessment tool available to teachers, the attitudes and expectations of the teacher-observer can bias the observations. Consequently, the teacher may want to ask someone else to make simultaneous observations on a periodic basis. The procedure for calculating the reliability or agreement between two observers is illustrated in Table 6. Note that only those intervals in which at least one observer recorded an occurrence of the behavior are used in determining reliability. If the reliability is high (e.g., over 70%), the teacher can be confident that the observations accurately reflect the child's behavior.

There are several other kinds of observations which the teacher will find especially useful in the assessment of children's problem behaviors. By systematically observing behaviors such as the frequency with which other children in the class are out of their seats, the teacher may be better able to judge the severity of Sam's behavior. Sometimes a child's disruptive behavior, e.g., punching other children, is maintained by the way his peers respond. It is possible that the only attention some children receive from their peers occurs during or immediately after a fight. When the teacher suspects that peer attention to the target behavior is important, peer reactions to the target behaviors should be systematically observed. Similarly, the teacher may inadvertently be attending to or reinforcing disruptive behavior by failing to provide sufficient rewards for appropriate behaviors, or by unduly criticizing or harshly reprimanding the child. By systematically recording subjective reactions to the disruptive child—or by having someone else observe his or her behavior—the teacher can make better judgments regarding treatment and can be made more directly aware of the influence he or she has over the child.

To summarize the important elements of target assessment mentioned above, the teacher should:

1. Select one to four behaviors on which to focus attention.

2. Write a detailed behavior description which is as complete and unambiguous as possible.

3. Decide which type of recording system to use. If the teacher can have someone else do the observing, continuous recording is preferred. If the teacher is making the observations, choose either event recording or time sampling.

4. Record the behaviors in as many situations as possible as frequently as possible (1/2 hr./day minimum for time sampling).

5. Arrange for regular reliability checks (at least once a week).

6. Obtain similar observations of his or her own behaviors and possibly of some other children in the class.

7. Make daily summaries of observations and record them graphically.

As you have seen from the articles in this book, target assessment is integrally tied to behavioral treatment procedures. The choice of the term "assessment" is not accidental. Rather than providing a "diagnosis" of the child before treatment, target assessment provides not only ongoing evaluation of the child's behavior but also an evaluation of other important aspects of the problem situation including the teacher's behaviors and the effects of treatment. Target assessment is objective when the reliability of the observations is high; it provides detailed information on the frequency and relative importance of the behaviors observed; it provides unambiguous information to consultants, parents, and other teachers; and it has direct implications for treatment.

When teachers and students are presented with a description of target assessment, the usual reaction is that they see the advantages and understand the rationale but question the feasibility of making regular observations, checking the reliability of their observations, and continuing their assessment through treatment and follow-up. Most of the research in this book was conducted by the teacher with rather constant supervision by the experimenter, who usually provided observers and reliability checkers. However, Hall, Fox, Willard, Goldsmith, Emerson, Owen, Davis, and Porcia (1971) presented six excellent responses to the question of feasibility. Six teachers who were taking a course in classroom management employed target assessment and primarily praise and ignore procedures to modify talking-out-of-turn behaviors in their respective classes. In each case, the teacher systematically recorded the relevant behaviors, arranged for reliability checks, conducted a treatment procedure, and evaluated the effectiveness of the treatment by temporarily withdrawing the treatment procedure. Methods used to record the behaviors included paper and pencil tallies, mechanical counters similar to those used in keeping golf scores, and tape recorders. Similarly, the teachers were able to obtain reliability checks by using existing school resources, e.g., a pupil, a teacher aide, a tape recorder, and a fellow teacher. The generality of their success is exemplified by the wide variety of classes and children dealt with: a 15-year-old boy in a class of 15 junior high school educable mentally retarded, a 10-year-old boy in a class for educable mentally retarded, a 13-year-old boy in a class of six junior high school emotionally disturbed children, a boy in a regular class of 27 third graders, 30 children in a poverty area regular first-grade class, and 27 children in a poverty area regular second-grade class.

So the answer to the question of feasibility is "yes," when the teacher has the kind of background outlined in this book. We might add that it is not uncommon for a teacher to feel under less pressure and to spend less time dealing with a problem when she uses target assessment and actively initiates a solution to the problem than when she worries extensively about what to do and is unsuccessful in receiving help from an outside source.

## IMPLEMENTATION

It would be difficult to find a substitute for good common sense when it comes to putting into practice the behavioral principles and procedures described in this book, but we can offer a few general guidelines which should be useful. To reiterate a point, a good, thoughtful teacher with a bit of courage should be able to implement a number of the behavioral techniques independently. Among those procedures which all teachers should make a part of their natural interactions with their children are: praising desirable behavior, ignoring minor disruptions, making classroom rules clear to all children, modeling desirable behaviors, shaping both academic and social behaviors, praising and shaping behavior incompatible with disruptive behavior, and using soft reprimands. With consultation or after some supervised experience with the procedures, a teacher should be able to use simple punishment techniques, self-instruction, self-reinforcement, and peers and other paraprofessionals as behavior modifiers. Token programs and time-out procedures require careful planning and continued evaluation. When properly implemented, they can produce dramatic changes; however, misuse of powerful programs can have detrimental affects on the children and even on the school district.

In selecting a procedure to employ with a problem child, the teacher should first decide whether he wants to increase and/or decrease the frequency of certain behaviors. If he wants to decrease the frequency of some behavior, he must simultaneously develop another behavior to take its place. Children are always behaving, and if the frequency of a disruptive behavior is decreased (e.g., aggression), the child will do something else on the occasions that he was aggressive. It behooves the teacher to develop appropriate social behavior to replace aggressive behavior since a child left to his own devices will replace aggression with other behaviors already in his repertoire and these may not always be the most desirable (e.g., swearing).

As another general rule, we would advise a teacher to implement the simplest and most natural procedures first, e.g., praising appropriate behaviors and ignoring minor disruptions. Only if these procedures are not sufficiently effective should more complex programs be considered. Regular observations of the child's and the teacher's behavior will be the best indicator of when to try another procedure, and any procedure adopted should be in effect for at least one week before the teacher can make a judgment regarding its efficacy.

Finally, some special comments should be made concerning what is the most basic and, on the surface, the simplest procedure discussed in this book—the contingent use of teacher's praise and attention. It is our experience that there is a wide range of individual differences regarding the ease and spontaneity with which teachers are physically affectionate and verbally encouraging toward their students. On occasion, even the most naturally rewarding and affectionate teacher will find it difficult to maintain her spontaneity. This seems to be especially true when teachers are implementing behavioral techniques for the first time and when they are faced with a particularly obstreperous child. There are several reasons why some teachers may feel unnatural or mechanical when they first use behavioral procedures. If the teacher is systematically observing his own behavior, he will be aware to a much greater degree than usual of exactly what he is doing. In deciding to praise a child more frequently, the teacher will be continuously noticing when and how often he praises or is affectionate toward the child. Thus, closely observing one's own behavior may lead to feelings of artificiality and a lack of spontaneity—although the behavior may look completely natural to an outside observer.

There are occasions when a teacher will not only feel unnatural but will, in fact, look uncomfortable, forced, or stilted in her attempts to praise a child. Even the most experienced teacher may have difficulty in reacting positively when she is faced with a child who is a great deal of trouble, who seems to respond adversely to her attention, or who may even present a real threat to her. Some teachers—like many other people—find it difficult to be affectionate in public. Such a teacher might function very well with older children but would be handicapped in dealing with first or second graders.

Unfortunately, simply instructing a teacher to be more positive does not always work, but we can make some suggestions which a consultant or the teacher might find useful. All the suggestions we will make are based on the principle of shaping. That is, the teacher should not expect to become instantly and appropriately positive to all children—she must teach herself to be affectionate and to praise as gradually and systematically as she would teach a child to read.

In general, a teacher should begin with a child whom she likes and gradually change her behavior toward more difficult children. It will be easier to concentrate first on verbal praise and then to focus on physical affection. Give praise or affection as soon as possible following an appropriate behavior. *Smile* when you praise a child. Vary the volume and intensity of your voice. Become excited when appropriate. The use of stars may be helpful since the occasion for attention is specified and since the child will usually respond positively to the tokens even if he would not respond to teacher-attention by itself. Remember, the teacher's behavior must be rewarded, and a positive response from a child is a very effective reinforcer. A positive response from a child is more likely if the teacher mentions the child's name when praising him or plans other activities which will make the teacher and the school more positive in the child's eyes, e.g., individual tutoring sessions, compliments on the child's appearance, active interest in something the child likes, or special projects with the child.

The teacher may ask someone to observe her either in individual sessions or in the classroom and to give her immediate feedback regarding how and when she used her attention to children more effectively. It would be useful for the teacher to observe a teacher or consultant who skillfully uses praise and affection. The teacher may also make use of tape recorders, videotape recorders, and role-playing sessions to change her behavior. A teacher might list a variety of praise comments, decide to praise a child a certain number of times a day, and monitor her own behavior by making a tally each time she praises a child. In addition, she could make notes to herself in her instructional material to remind her to praise more frequently and to be affectionate.

Since it is difficult for some teachers to develop examples of praise and affection, we include the following list:

Johnny, that's the *right* answer!
The class is so quiet, I can hear myself think.
Mary, you're working very well today.
Tom, that's a good looking shirt.
Your handwriting is much better today, Judy.
Bill, thank you very much for helping Joe.
You read that whole paragraph perfectly, John.
Look at how well Carol is paying attention.
Touch the child's hand when he comes to your desk.
Hug the child when he is standing close to you on the playground.
Put your hand on his back when you're at his desk.
Pat a well-behaved child on the back as you pass him.

With practice, the teacher will gradually find herself feeling more spontaneous and natural, and her children will respond accordingly.

## Consultation

In addition to the referral issues discussed earlier in this chapter, a number of factors should be noted about the necessity of consultation in various instances.

Consultation usually should be sought:

1. When a token reinforcement program utilizing extrinsic back-up reinforcers is being considered because of the unusual types of prizes, because of the frequent failures in implementations of token programs by inexperienced personnel, and because such token programs are *not* necessary in many instances although they are occasionally seen as the only answer by teachers, principals, and hospital directors.

2. When there is a systematic use of frequent reprimanding or timeout from reinforcement. Again, such procedures are often not indicated, and because of their possible negative side-effects, they generally should be avoided. Furthermore, as evidenced earlier in this book, some forms of reprimands actually may lead to increases in inappropriate behavior. Timeout from reinforcement in the form of placing a child at the side or back of the room is a procedure occasionally used by a number of teachers. On the other hand, the use of a small room (Timeout Booth) should probably be reserved for hospitals and classrooms for emotionally disturbed children—*after* other more positive methods of behavior change have been tried.

3. When precise evaluation of a procedure for research purposes is sought. A teacher obviously cannot record the host of critical factors which are simultaneously operating in a classroom; and even if she could, because of her own opinions, her data might be biased.

4. When a teacher is attempting to implement a large scale behavior modification program for the *first* time—e.g., a token program.

5. When it is unclear whether the particular program being implemented will be powerful enough to change the child's problem behavior.

6. When it is thought that problems or hardships in the home are impeding the progress of a program (e.g., frequent fighting among family members, death of a parent, absence of adequate food or clothing), or when there may be some physical impediment which would hamper progress of the program (e.g., epilepsy or brain damage).

7. When it is unclear whether the teacher should place her major emphasis on academic or social behavior.

## Evaluating the Success of Treatment

As has been emphasized repeatedly in this book, objective evaluations of treatment should always be made. While a teacher need not engage in evaluations which are as extensive as those of the researcher some evaluation is necessary if she wants to know whether her methods are effective. Such evaluations have the advantage of:

1. Making the teacher more attuned to her own behavior and its effects or lack of effects on her class.

2. Providing the teacher with objective evaluations of procedures

that were tried with a child to aid in any referral process.

3. Providing the teacher with some indication of gradual changes in a child that would be difficult to detect by simple anecdotal records or retrospective reports of what the child is like.

4. Providing the teacher with critical information concerning the necessity for changing certain aspects of a particular program.

5. Prompting teachers to become critical consumers of research since after engaging in evaluations themselves, they will be in a better position to evaluate how other research is done.

It should now be evident to the reader that objective observations alone are not enough to assess whether a treatment is successful. To clearly demonstrate that the treatment employed led to the observed behavior change, there must be some *manipulation* of the treatment procedure; it must be withdrawn, intensified, or diminished (identified as an ABAB design, see Drabman & Lahey, 1974). Alternatively, the treatment procedure might be applied in a sequential fashion to different behaviors; it could be applied to one behavior during a particular period but not applied in another period (multiple baseline, see Long & Williams, 1973). A third possibility is to use a control group, e.g., implement a procedure with a few children in the class while observing the behavior of several children (see O'Leary, Pelham, Rosenbaum, & Price, 1976). Because the withdrawal of successful procedures is sometimes difficult for a teacher to implement and may be detrimental to the children, let us re-examine the use of the multiple baseline and control group as they are applied in the classroom. Assume that the teacher (1) has particular difficulty with children talking out of turn during reading and arithmetic classes and (2) wants to examine the effectiveness of increasing her praise to a child when he raises his hand. She or an observer would record the frequency of talking out of turn during both classes. Using a multiple baseline approach, she would then increase the number of praise comments during one of the classes, e.g., reading, while continuing to respond in her usual manner during arithmetic. Later she would increase the number of praise comments during both classes. If a decline in the frequency of talking out of turn during each class period was observed when the use of praise was increased during that class period, the teacher could probably feel confident in saying that her praise reduced the frequency of talking out of turn. If a control group procedure were to be used, the teacher would observe all children who were talking out of turn, for example, six. Next, she would increase her praise comments to three of the children when they raised their hands. If talking out decreased for these children but remained at a high rate for those children whom she did not praise, then she could have some confidence that praise was an effective procedure and could apply the procedure to all children.

## Follow-Through

As mentioned in Chapter 1, the term Follow-Through has been used recently by the Office of Education and the Department of Health Education and Welfare in Washington to designate the continuation of special teaching or special programs which follow a child's Head Start Program. The government rightly recognized that a child could be taught certain skills in Head Start but that such skills often were not maintained several years later. By the time they reached third grade, children who were in Head Start were not distinguishable from those children who did not have a Head Start experience. Similarly, because psychologists are recognizing the clear relation between a child's ever changing environment and thus ever changing behavior, there is a greater focus on the child's environment following particular treatment programs. As evidenced in this book by ABAB experimental designs, when different classroom treatment programs were withdrawn or dramatically changed, the behavior of the children usually deteriorated. Let us again restate that when a child's behavior is not reinforced, it will extinguish or decrease in frequency. Thus, when one withdraws a particular program which helped prompt and maintain or reinforce a child's behavior, one must make sure that there are different reinforcers that can be scheduled less frequently than those used in the special program but which will maintain the child's behavior. In short, someone must see that there is some follow-through! In a few instances, when a new skill is taught, its mastery will be reinforcing enough to maintain a child's behavior when the special program is withdrawn. However, for the large majority of children with social problems, the new mastery or new competence will not be sufficiently reinforcing to maintain the appropriate behavior, and one must insure that the new skill is prompted and reinforced in whatever new environments the child enters. This is especially true in the case of social behavior since the natural school environment does not provide regular and immediate feedback regarding social behavior as it does for academic behavior.

## Generalization

Intimately related to the problem of follow-through is the issue of generalization. Generalization refers to the extent to which a particular program will have long range or far-reaching effects. That is, if a treatment focuses on a particular behavior or group of behaviors, will the treatment influence other groups of behaviors? In addition, people wish to know how long the effects of a program will last, or how long the good behavior will be maintained when the treatment program is stopped. People also want to know whether a treatment program will influence a child in situations where the treatment has not been instituted. Actually, a teacher might be interested in several variations of the types of generalization discussed above, but in every case the question hinges around the issue of producing a behavior change which will not be limited to the treatment situation. That is, to be maximally effective, one must teach behavior which will have wide-ranging effects. When one teaches a mute child to speak by using food or token reinforcement, such reinforcement can later be withdrawn, and the child will continue to speak in a variety of times and places. He probably will start saying things that were not taught to him in his special speech program. However, speech is a very special behavior in that it will always be reinforced by one's natural environment. On the other hand, teaching a ghetto child mathematics will not have such naturally occurring positive consequences. For example, a ghetto child's gang, his parents, and sometimes even his teachers will do little to reinforce any newly acquired mathematics skill. Similarly, one may teach a hospitalized adolescent child a number of social skills which most adults would call appropriate, polite behavior; however, when such polite behavior is displayed on the ward, it may not be reinforced by the child's peers or even by the attendants, and his behavior would thus decline. Because of this problem of maintaining, behavior, Ayllon and Azrin (1968) have developed the following general rule or guideline for use in developing goals of programs in hospital settings which we feel has relevance for any training program: "Teach only those behaviors that will continue to be reinforced after training." The implications of such a rule are clear for a teacher. She should try to teach skills which will be rewarded by the child's natural environments, and if she doubts that such rewards will be forthcoming, she should talk to the parents of the child, the child's new teacher, or the child's other teachers and specifically enlist their cooperation in reinforcing the newly acquired skill.

Because of the apparent situation-specificity of many of the behaviors that have been discussed in this book, we hope that research during the next decade will concentrate on teaching children skills in a manner that will diminish the problem of the rapid extinction of such skills. Until such research is completed, however, there are a number of behavioral principles which can be followed to maximize such generalization. Let us assume that being polite is a behavior or group of behaviors which one would like to increase. First, one can teach general rules of conduct which specify what polite behaviors a child should exhibit in a wide variety of situations. For example, one should usually teach a child to be polite with everyone, not just with a particular teacher or a particular parent. A number of people should be asked to reinforce the skill being taught, e.g., parents, teachers (Wahler, 1969), and peers (a teacher can prompt a single child or several children to respond positively to polite behaviors of a particular peer). The teacher should also describe to the child the *various* kinds of behaviors which are considered polite, e.g., saying "please," thanking, asking for a toy instead of grabbing it, sharing toys, etc. That is, if we wish to see some generalization across different kinds of behaviors, the child must know what sorts of different behaviors to display. If such behaviors cannot be easily practiced in the classroom where a child or adult can reinforce them, the teacher might role-play a number of interactions with the child to practice behaving politely in a *variety* of ways. The teacher may also take advantage of other children's polite behaviors and reinforce them so that such behavior can serve as a positive model for a child who is being taught to be polite. Similarly, a teacher should monitor her own behavior and see that she does, in fact, display polite behavior toward the children in her own class lest she be a victim of the adage, "Children do as you do, not as you say."

## PUBLIC RELATIONS ISSUES

### Behavior Modification Programs to be Discussed with the Public

Whenever a teacher is considering the implementation of a program which might be viewed negatively by other teachers, parents, or community members, both the principal and the parents should be alerted to the program, and their approval should be obtained before such a program is instituted. For example, if a child is being considered for a program where extrinsic reinforcers are to be used, or where a high school or older elementary school child will be used as a tutor, the parents should be consulted. If explained carefully, the use of either extrinsic reinforcers or peer tutoring can be easily justified to parents of very disruptive children. An explanation of any procedures which are not ordinarily part of a teacher's routine and which might be viewed negatively by parents will not only aid in the execution of such procedures, it may also prevent a great deal of misunderstanding. In this endeavor, as in many others, "An ounce of prevention is worth a pound of cure."

## Problems of Dealing with Powerful Procedures

Very frequently, when a behavior modification approach is initiated in a hospital or school setting, one hears comments such as, "You are manipulating the lives of children," or "You are controlling a child instead of allowing him to develop freely." Whether we wish to admit it or not, we are all being controlled and exerting control in various ways in our daily lives. However, the application of behavior modification principles makes this control very apparent. When one can see behavior change dramatically before his very eyes, the issues of control and its various ramifications cannot be ignored. An important consequence of dealing with a powerful procedure is that one must consider whether it is really advisable to change a behavior. That is, one can easily be duped into maintaining a poor educational system when, in fact, he ought to be revamping the system. In short, the application of any principles of behavior cannot be divorced from social values. The classrooms and the goals of education in the year 2000 may be very unlike the classrooms and goals of 1976, but the *principles* of behavior modification described in this book will still apply to changing children's behaviors. The behavior modification approach provides a set of rather well-defined procedures to change behavior, but the procedures do not spell out the goals or the behaviors which *ought* to be taught or changed. It is always the duty of every educator, scientist, and citizen to evaluate the aims of our educational systems. Whether the goals of education in the year 2000 involve a structured class or an unstructured class, a class which emphasizes affective or cognitive development, it is our opinion that the types of principles and procedures described in this book will be helpful in reaching whatever goals our educational systems choose.

# REFERENCES

Alexander, J.F., & Parsons, B.V. Short-term behavioral intervention with delinquent families: Impact on family process and recidivism. *Journal of Abnormal Psychology,* 1973, 81, 219-225.

Allerhand, M.E. Effectiveness of parents of Head Start children as administrators of psychological tests. *Journal of Consulting Psychology,* 1967, 31, 286-290.

Atkinson, R.C. Computerized instruction and the learning process. *American Psychologist,* 1968, 23, 225-239.

Axelrod, S. Comparison of individual and group contingencies in two special classes. *Behavior Therapy,* 1973, 4, 83-90.

Ayllon, T., & Azrin, N.H. *A motivating environment for therapy and rehabilitation.* New York: Appleton-Century-Crofts, 1968.

Ayllon, T., Layman, D., & Burke, S. Disruptive behavior and reinforcement of academic performance. *Psychological Record,* 1972, 22, 315-323.

Ayllon, T., Smith, D., & Rogers, M. Behavioral management of school phobia. *Journal of Behavior Therapy and Experimental Psychiatry,* 1970, 1, 125-128.

Azrin, N.H., & Foxx, R.M. A rapid method of toilet training the institutionalized retarded. *Journal of Applied Behavior Analysis,* 1971, 4, 89-99.

Azrin, N.H., & Lindsley, O.R. The reinforcement of cooperation between children. *Journal of Abnormal and Social Psychology,* 1956, 52, 100-102.

Azrin, N.H., Sneed, T.J., & Foxx, R.M. Dry-bed training: Rapid elimination of childhood eneuresis. *Behavior Research and Therapy,* 1974, 12, 147-156.

Baer, D.M. The consultation process model as an irrational state of affairs. *Psychology in the Schools,* 1970, 7, 341-344.

Baer, D.M., Peterson, R.F., & Sherman, J.A. The development of imitation by reinforcing behavioral similarity to a model. *Journal of the Experimental Analysis of Behavior,* 1967, 10, 405-416.

Bakwin, H., & Bakwin, R.M. *Clinical management of behavior disorders in children.* New York: Saunders, 1967.

Baller, W.R. *Bed-wetting: Origins and treatment.* New York: Pergamon, 1975.

Bandura, A. *Modeling approaches to the modification of phobic disorders.* Paper presented to Ciba Foundation Symposium, London, 1968.

Bandura, A. *Principles of behavior modification.* New York: Holt, Rinehart & Winston, 1969.

Bandura, A., Grusec, J.E., & Menlove, F.L. Vicarious extinction of avoidance behavior. *Journal of Personality and Social Psychology,* 1967, 5, 16-23.

Bandura, A., & Kupers, C.J. Transmission of patterns of self-reinforcement through modeling. *Journal of Abnormal and Social Psychology,* 1964, 69, 1-9.

Bandura, A., & Perloff, B. Relative efficacy of self-monitored and externally imposed reinforcement systems. *Journal of Personality and Social Psychology,* 1967, 7, 111-116.

Bandura, A., Ross, D., & Ross, S.A. Imitation of film-mediated aggressive models. *Journal of Abnormal and Social Psychology,* 1963, 66, 3-11.

Bandura, A., & Walters, R.H. *Social learning and personality development.* New York: Holt, Rinehart & Winston, 1963.

Becker, W.C. *Some necessary conditions for the controlled study of achievement and aptitude.* Paper presented to CTB/McGraw-Hill Invitational Conference on the Aptitude-Achievement Distinction. Carmel, California, February 1973.

Becker, W.C., Madsen, C.H., Arnold, C.R., & Thomas, D.R. The contingent use of teacher attention and praise in reducing classroom behavior problems. *Journal of Special Education,* 1967, 1, 287-307.

*Behavior Today,* 3, # 46: 1972.

Bem, S.L. Verbal self-control: The establishment of effective self-instruction. *Journal of Experimental Psychology,* 1967, 74, 485-491.

Berkowitz, H. A preliminary assessment of the extent of interaction between child psychiatric clinics and public schools. *Psychology in the Schools,* 1968, 5, 291-295.

Bijou, S.W. Experimental studies of child behavior, normal and deviant. In L. Krasner & L.P. Ullmann (Eds.), *Research in behavior modification.* New York: Holt, Rinehart & Winston, 1965.

Birnbrauer, J.S., Wolf, M.M., Kidder, J.D., & Tague, C.E. Classroom behavior of retarded pupils with token reinforcement. *Journal of Experimental Child Psychology,* 1965, 2, 219-235.

Bittle, R.G. Improving parent-teacher communication through recorded telephone messages. *The Journal of Educational Research,* 1975, 69, 87-95.

Bornstein, P.H., & Quevillon, R.P. The effects of a self-instructional package with overactive pre-school boys. *Journal of Applied Behavior Analysis,* 1976, 9, 179-188.

Bregman, E.O. An attempt to modify the emotional attitudes of infants by the conditioned response technique. *Journal of Genetic Psychology,* 1934, 45, 169-198.

Broden, M., Bruce, C., Mitchell, M.A., Carter, V., & Hall, R.V. Effects of teacher attention on attending behavior of two boys at adjacent desks. *Journal of Applied Behavior Analysis,* 1970, 3, 199-203.

Broden, M., Hall, R.V., & Mitts, B. The effect of self-recording on the classroom behavior of two eighth grade students. *Journal of Applied Behavior Analysis,* 1971, 4, 191-200.

Bronfenbrenner, U. *Two worlds of childhood: U.S. and U.S.S.R.* New York: Russell Sage Foundation, 1970.

Brown, D., Reschly, D., & Wasserman, H. Effects of surreptitious modeling upon teacher classroom behaviors. *Psychology in the Schools,* 1974, 11, 366-369.

Brown, P., & Elliot, R. Control of aggression in a nursery school class. *Journal of Experimental Child Psychology,* 1965, 2, 103-107.

Bryan, J.H., & Walbek, N.H. Preaching and practicing generosity: Children's actions and reactions. *Child Development,* 1970, 41, 329-353.

Bushell, D., Wrobel, P.A., & Michaelis, M.L. Applying "group" contingencies to the classroom study behavior of preschool children. *Journal of Applied Behavior Analysis,* 1968, 1, 55-61.

Carlson, C.S., Arnold, C.R., Becker, W.C., & Madsen, C.H. The elimination of tantrum behavior of a child in an elementary classroom. *Behaviour Research and Therapy,* 1968, 6, 117-119.

Circirelli, V., Cooper, W., & Granger, R. *The impact of Head Start: An evaluation of the effects of Head Start and children's cognitive and affective development.* Westinghouse Learning Corporation, June 12, 1969.

Coleman, J.S. Methods and results in the IEA studies of effects of school on learning. *Review of Educational Research,* 1975, 45, 335-386.

Conant, E. What do teachers do all day? *Saturday Review World,* June 1, 1974, p. 55.

Conners, C.K. A teacher rating scale for use in drug studies with children. *American Journal of Psychiatry,* 1969, 126, 152-156.

Conners, C.K., Eisenberg, L., & Barcai, A. Effect of dextroamphetamine on children. *Archives of General Psychiatry,* 1967, 17, 478-485.

Crossman, E. Communication. *Journal of Applied Behavior Analysis,* 1975, 8, 348.

Despert, J.L. *The emotionally disturbed child—then and now.* New York: Vantage, 1965.

Drabman, R.S. Child- versus teacher-administered token programs in a psychiatric hospital school. *Journal of Abnormal Child Psychology,* 1973, 1, 68-87.

Drabman, R.S., & Lahey, B.B. Feedback in classroom behavior modification: Effects on the target and her classmates. *Journal of Applied Behavior Analysis,* 1974, 7, 591-598.

Drabman, R.S., & Spitalnik, R. Social isolation as a punishment procedure: A controlled study. *Journal of Experimental Child Psychology,* 1973, 16, 236-249.

Drabman, R.S., Spitalnik, R., & O'Leary, K.D. Teaching self-control to disruptive children. *Journal of Abnormal Psychology,* 1973, 82, 10-16.

Early, H.G. Ten thousand children battered and starved. In J.E. Levitt (Ed.), *The battered child.* Morristown, N.J.: General Learning Corp., 1974.

English, H.B. Three cases of the "conditioned fear response." *Journal of Abnormal and Social Psychology,* 1929, 24, 221-225.

Evans, G.W., & Oswalt, G.L. Acceleration of academic progress through the manipulation of peer influence. *Behaviour Research and Therapy,* 1968, 6, 189-195.

Felixbrod, J.J., & O'Leary, K.D. Effects of reinforcement on children's academic behavior as a function of self-determined and externally imposed contingencies. *Journal of Applied Behavior Analysis,* 1973, 6, 241-250.

Felixbrod, J.J., & O'Leary, K.D. Self-determination of academic standards by children: Toward freedom from external control. *Journal of Educational Psychology*, 1974, 66, 845-850.

Ferster, C.B., & DeMyer, M.K. A method for the experimental analysis of the behavior of autistic children. *American Journal of Orthopsychiatry*, 1962, 32, 89-98.

Freud, A. *The psychoanalytical treatment of children.* New York: Schocken, 1964.

Friedrich, L.K., & Stein, A.H. Aggressive and prosocial television programs and the natural behavior of preschool children. *Monographs of the Society for Research in Child Development*, 1973, 38, # 4.

Gewirtz, J.L., & Baer, D.M. Deprivation and satiation of social reinforcers as drive conditioners. *Journal of Abnormal and Social Psychology*, 1958, 57, 165-172.

Graubard, P.S., Rosenberg, H., & Miller, M.B. Student applications of behavior modification to teachers and environments or ecological approaches to social deviancy. In E.A. Ramp & B.L. Hopkins (Eds.), *A new direction for education: Behavior analysis,* 1971 (Vol. 1). The University of Kansas: Support and Development Center for Follow Through, Department of Human Development, Lawrence, Kansas, 1971.

Gump, P.V. Education as an environmental enterprise. In R.A. Weinberg & F.H. Wood (Eds.), *Observation of pupils and teachers in mainstream and special education settings: Alternative strategies.* Minneapolis, Minn.: Leadership Training Institute, 1975, 109-122.

Hall, G.S. The contents of children's minds. *Princeton Review*, 1883, 249-272.

Hall, R.V., Axelrod, S., Foundopoulos, M., Shellman, J., Campbell, R.A., & Cranston, S. The effective use of punishment to modify behavior in the classroom. *Educational Technology*, April, 1971, 24-26.

Hall, R.V., Fox, R., Willard, D., Goldsmith, L., Emerson, M., Owen, M., Davis, F., & Porcia, E. The teacher as observer and experimenter in the modification of disputing and talking-out behaviors. *Journal of Applied Behavior Analysis*, 1971, 4, 141-149.

Hamblin, R.E., Hathaway, C., & Wodarski, J. Group contingencies, peer tutoring, and accelerating academic achievement. In E.A. Ramp & B.L. Hopkins (Eds.), *A new direction for education: Behavior analysis* 1971 (Vol. 1). The University of Kansas: Support and Development Center for Follow Through, Department of Human Development, Lawrence, Kansas, 1971.

Harris, F.R., Johnston, M.K., Kelley, C.S., & Wolf, M.M. Effects of positive social reinforcement on regressed crawling of a nursery school child. *Journal of Educational Psychology,* 1964, 55, 35-41.

Henderson, R.W., Swanson, R., & Zimmerman, B.J. Inquiry response induction in preschool children through televised modeling. *Developmental Psychology,* 1975, 11, 523-524.

Hobbs, N. (Ed.), *Issues in the classification of children.* San Francisco, CA: Jossey-Bass, 1975.

Holland, J.G., & Skinner, B.F. *The analysis of behavior.* New York: McGraw-Hill, 1961.

Homme, L.E. Perspectives in psychology: XXIV. Control of coverants, the operants of the mind. *Psychological Record,* 1965, 15, 501-511.

Homme, L.E., DeBaca, P.C., Devine, J.V., Steinhorst, R., & Rickert, E.J. Use of the Premack principle in controlling the behavior of nursery school children. *Journal of Experimental Analysis of Behavior,* 1963, 6, 544.

Iwata, B.A., & Bailey, J.S. Reward versus cost token systems: An analysis of the effects on students and teacher. *Journal of Applied Behavior Analysis,* 1974, 7, 567-576.

Jacobsen, E. *Progressive relaxation.* Chicago: University of Chicago Press, 1938.

Jones, E. *The life and work of Sigmund Freud.* New York: Basic Books, 1955.

Jones, F.H., & Miller, W.H. The effective use of negative attention for reducing group disruption in special elementary school classrooms. *The Psychological Record,* 1974, 24, 435-448.

Jones, M.C. The elimination of children's fear. *Journal of Experimental Psychology,* 1924, 7, 383-390.

Kaufman, K.F., & O'Leary, K.D. Reward, cost, and self-evaluation procedures for disruptive adolescents in a psychiatric hospital school. *Journal of Applied Behavior Analysis,* 1972, 5, 293-310.

Kent, R.N., & O'Leary, K.D. A controlled evaluation of behavior modification with conduct problem children. *Journal of Consulting and Clincial Psychology,* 1976, **44**, 586-596.

Kirby, F.D., & Shields, F. Modification of arithmetic response rate and attending behavior in a seventh-grade student. *Journal of Applied Behavior Analysis,* 1972, 5, 79-84.

Kounin, J.S. *Discipline and group management in classrooms.* New York: Holt, 1970.

Kounin, J.S. An ecological approach to classroom activity settings: Some methods and findings. In R.A. Weinberg & F.H. Wood

(Eds.), *Observation of pupils and teachers in mainstream and special education settings: Alternative strategies.* Minneapolis, Minn.: Leadership Training Institute, 1975, 149-158.

Krantz, P.J., & Risley, T.R. *Behavioral ecology in the classroom.* Unpublished manuscript, from paper presented at American Psychological Association, Honolulu, 1972.

Krasner, L., & Wilson, G.T. *Ethical issues regarding behavior modification in the schools.* A.P.A. Committee on Ethics in Behavior Modification. Unpublished manuscript, Rutgers University, New Brunswick, N.J., June 1976.

Krumboltz, J.D., & Thoresen, C.E. The effect of behavioral counseling in group and individual settings on information-seeking behavior. *Journal of Counseling Psychology,* 1964, 11, 324-333.

Lahey, B.B., McNees, M.P., & McNees, M.C. Control of an obscene "verbal tic" through time-out in an elementary school classroom. *Journal of Applied Behavior Analysis,* 1973, 6, 101-104.

Lawler, E.E., & Hackman, J.R. Impact of employee participation in the development of pay incentive plans: A field experiment. *Journal of Applied Psychology,* 1969, 53, 467-471.

Lazarus, A.A., Davison, G.C., & Polefka, D.A. Classical and operant factors in the treatment of a school phobia. *Journal of Abnormal and Social Psychology,* 1965, 70, 225-229.

Lazarus, A.A., & Rachman, S. The use of systematic desensitization in psychotherapy. *South African Medical Journal,* 1967, 31, 934-937.

Levitt, E. The results of psychotherapy with children: An evaluation. *Journal of Consulting Psychology,* 1957, 21, 189-196.

Levitt, E. Psychotherapy with children: A further evaluation. *Behaviour Research and Therapy,* 1963, 1, 45-51.

Liebert, R.M., Neale, J.M., & Davidson, E. *The early window: Effects of television on children and youth.* New York: Pergamon, 1973.

Long, J.D., & Williams, R.L. The comparative effectiveness of group and individually contingent free time with inner-city junior high school students. *Journal of Applied Behavior Analysis,* 1973, 6, 465-474.

Lovaas, O.I. A behavior therapy approach to the treatment of childhood schizophrenia. In J.P. Hill (Ed.), *Minnesota Symposium on Child Psychology.* Minneapolis, Minn.: University of Minnesota Press, 1967, pp. 108-159.

Lovaas, O.I., Koegel, R., Simmons, J.Q., & Long, J.S. Some generalization and follow-up measures on autistic children in behavior therapy. *Journal of Applied Behavior Analysis,* 1973, 6, 131-166.

Lovibond, S.H. *Conditioning and enuresis.* Oxford: Pergamon, 1964.

Lovitt, T.C., & Curtiss, K.A. Academic response rate as a function of teacher and self-imposed contingencies. *Journal of Applied Behavior Analysis,* 1969, 2, 49-53.

Luria, A.R. Psychological studies of mental deficiency in the Soviet Union, In N.R. Ellis (Ed.), *Handbook on mental deficiency.* New York: McGraw-Hill, 1963, pp. 353-387.

Madsen, C.H., Becker, W.C., & Thomas, D.R. Rules, praise, and ignoring: Elements of elementary classroom control. *Journal of Applied Behavior Analysis,* 1968, 1, 139-150.

Madsen, C.H., Becker, W.C., Thomas, D.R., Koser, L., & Plager, E. An analysis of the reinforcing function of "sit down" commands. In R.K. Parker (Ed.), *Readings in educational psychology.* Boston: Allyn & Bacon, 1968.

Mann, J. Vicarious desensitization of test anxiety through observation of videotaped treatment. *Journal of Counseling Psychology,* 1972, 19, 1-7.

Mann, J., & Rosenthal, T.L. Vicarious and direct counterconditioning of test anxiety through individual and group desensitization. *Behaviour Research and Therapy,* 1969, 7, 354-367.

Martin, R. Ethical and legal implications of behavior modification in the classroom. In G.R. Gredler (Ed.), *Ethical and legal factors in the practice of school psychology.* Harrisburg, Pa.: State Dept. of Education, 1975.

Masserman, J.H. *Behavior and neurosis.* Chicago: University of Chicago Press, 1943.

McAllister, L.W., Stachowiak, J.G., Baer, D.M., & Conderman, L. The application of operant conditioning techniques in a secondary school classroom. *Journal of Applied Behavior Analysis,* 1969, 2, 277-285.

McIntire, R.W., Jensen, J., & Davis, G. *Control of disruptive behavior with a token economy.* Paper presented to Eastern Psychological Association, Philadelphia, 1968.

McKenzie, H.S., Clark, M., Wolf, M.M., Kothera, R., & Benson, C. Behavior modification of children with learning disabilities using grades as tokens and allowances as back up reinforcers. *Exceptional Children,* 1968, 34, 745-752.

Meichenbaum, D. *Toward a cognitive theory of self-control.* Research Report No. 48, Department of Psychology, University of Waterloo, Ontario, Canada, January 24, 1975.

Meichenbaum, D.H., Bowers, K.S., & Ross, R.R. A behavioral analysis of teacher expectancy effect. *Journal of Personality and Social Psychology,* 1969, 13, 306-316.

Meichenbaum, D., & Goodman, J. The developmental control of operant motor responding by verbal operants. *Child Development,* 1969, 40, 785-798.

Meichenbaum, D., & Goodman, J. Training impulsive children to talk to themselves: A means of developing self-control. *Journal of Abnormal Psychology,* 1971, 77, 115-126.

Melamed, B.G., & Siegel, L.J. Reduction of anxiety in children facing hospitalization and surgery by use of filmed modeling. *Journal of Consulting and Clinical Psychology,* 1975, 43, 511-521.

Meyer, A. The role of mental factors in psychiatry. *American Journal of Insanity,* 1908, 65, 39-56.

Miller, N.E. Learning of visceral and glandular responses. *Science,* 1969, 163, 434-445.

Monahan, J., & O'Leary, K.D. Effects of self-instruction on rule-breaking behavior, *Psychological Reports,* 1971, 29, 1059-1066.

Morrill, C.S. Teaching machines: A review. *Psychological Bulletin,* 1961, 58, 363-375.

Mowrer, O.H., & Mowrer, W.A. Enuresis: A method for its study and treatment. *American Journal of Orthopsychiatry,* 1938, 8, 436-447.

Obler, M., & Terwilliger, R.F. Pilot study of the effectiveness of systematic desensitization with neurologically impaired children with phobic disorders. *Journal of Consulting and Clinical Psychology,* 1970, 34, 314-318.

O'Connor, R.D. Modification of social withdrawal through symbolic modeling. *Journal of Applied Behavior Analysis,* 1969, 2, 15-22.

O'Connor, R.D. Relative efficacy of modeling, shaping, and the combined procedures for modification of social withdrawal. *Journal of Abnormal Psychology,* 1972, 79, 327-334.

O'Leary, K.D. *Establishing token programs in schools: Issues and problems.* Paper presented to American Psychological Association, Washington, D.C., August, 1969.

O'Leary, K.D. Behavior modification in the classroom: A rejoinder to Winett and Winkler. *Journal of Applied Behavior Analysis,* 1972, 5, 505-510.

O'Leary, K.D. Token reinforcement programs in the classroom. In T. Brigham & C. Catania (Eds.), *The analysis of behavior: Social and educational processes,* Irving-Nailbert/Wiley, 1977.

O'Leary, K.D., & Becker, W.C. Behavior modification of an adjustment class: Token reinforcement program. *Exceptional Children,* 1967, 33, 637-642.

O'Leary, K.D., & Drabman, R.S. Token reinforcement programs in the classroom: A review. *Psychological Bulletin,* 1971, 75, 379-398.

O'Leary, K.D., & Becker, W.C. The effects of the intensity of a teacher's reprimands on children's behavior. *Journal of School Psychology,* 1968, 7, 8-11.

O'Leary, K.D., Becker, W.C., Evans, M.B., & Saudargas, R.A. A token reinforcement program in a public school: A replication and systematic analysis. *Journal of Applied Behavior Analysis,* 1969, 2, 3-13.

O'Leary, K.D., Kaufman, K.F., Kass, R.E., & Drabman, R.S. The effects of loud and soft reprimands on the behavior of disruptive students. *Exceptional Children,* 1970, 37, 145-155.

O'Leary, K.D., Pelham, W.E., Rosenbaum, A., & Price, G.H. Behavioral treatment of hyperkinetic children: An experimental evaluation of its usefulness. *Clinical Pediatrics,* 1976, 15, 274-279.

O'Leary, K.D., Poulos, R.W., & Devine, V.T. Tangible reinforcers: Bonuses or bribes. *Journal of Consulting and Clinical Psychology,* 1972, 38, 1-8.

Osborne, J.G. Free-time as a reinforcer in the management of classroom behavior. *Journal of Applied Behavior Analysis,* 1969, 2, 113-118.

Patterson, G.R. An application of conditioning techniques to the control of a hyperactive child. In L.P. Ullmann & L. Krasner (Eds.), *Case studies in behavior modification.* New York: Holt, Rinehart & Winston, 1965. Pp. 370-375.

Paul, G.L. *Insight versus desensitization in psychotherapy.* Stanford, CA: Stanford University Press, 1966.

Pelham, W. Withdrawal of a stimulant drug (methylphenidate) and the implementation of behavioral psychotherapy in the treatment of a hyperactive child. *Behavior Therapy,* in press.

Pendergrass, V. *Children and behavior modification: Time-out from positive reinforcement as a punishment procedure.* Paper read at Florida Psychological Association, Miami, Florida, May 1, 1970.

Peterson, D.R. Behavior problems of middle childhood. *Journal of Consulting Psychology,* 1961, 25, 205-209.

Phillips, E.L., Wolf, M.M., & Fixsen, D.L. Achievement Place: Development of an elected manager system. *Journal of Applied Behavior Analysis,* 1973, 6, 541-561.

Poser, E.G. The effect of therapist's training on group therapeutic outcome. *Journal of Consulting Psychology,* 1966, 30, 283-289.

Ravitch, D. *The great school wars: New York City, 1805-1973.* New York: Basic Books, Inc., 1974.

Reese, H.W., & Parnes, S.J. Programming creative behavior. *Child Development,* 1970, 41, 413-423.

Reisman, J.M. *The development of clinical psychology.* New York: Appleton-Century-Crofts, 1966.

Rioch, M.J., Elkes, E., Flint, A.A., Usdansky, B.C., Newman, R.G., & Silber, E. National Institute of Mental Health pilot study in training mental health counselors. *American Journal of Orthopsychiatry,* 1963, 33, 678-689.

Robbins, L.N. *Deviant children grown up.* Baltimore, Md.: Williams & Wilkins, 1966.

Robin, A., Armel, S., & O'Leary, K.D. The effects of self-instruction on writing deficiencies. *Behavior Therapy,* 1975, 6, 178-187.

Robin, A., Schneider, M., & Dolnick, M. The Turtle Technique: An extended case study of self-control in the classroom. *Psychology in the Schools,* in press.

Rosenbaum, A., O'Leary, K.D., & Jacob, R.G. Behavioral intervention with hyperactive children: Group consequences as a supplement to individual contingencies. *Behavior Therapy,* 1975, 6, 315-323.

Rosenthal, R., & Jacobsen, L. Teachers' expectancies: Determinants of pupils' IQ gains. *Psychological Reports,* 1966, 19, 115-118.

Ruedi, J., & West, C.K. Pupil self-concept in an "open" school and in a "traditional" school. *Psychology in the Schools,* 1973, 10, 48-53.

Ryback, D., & Staats, A.W. Parents as behavior therapy-technicians in treating reading deficits (dyslexia). *Journal of Behavior Therapy and Experimental Psychiatry,* 1970, 1, 109-119.

Santogrossi, D.A., O'Leary, K.D., Romanczyk, R.G., & Kaufman, K.F. Self-evaluation by adolescents in a psychiatric hospital school token program. *Journal of Applied Behavior Analysis,* 1973, 6, 277-288.

Scarr, S. The adjective check list as a personality assessment technique with children: Validity of the scales. *Journal of Consulting Psychology,* 1966, 30, 122-128.

Schrag, P., & Divoky, D. *The myth of the hyperactive child.* New York: Pantheon, 1975.

Schwitzgebel, R. *Street corner research: An experimental approach to the juvenile delinquent.* Cambridge, Mass: Harvard University Press, 1964.

Shapiro, A.K., & Shapiro, E. Treatment of Gilles de la Tourette's syndrome with haloperidol. *British Journal of Psychiatry,* 1968, 114, 345-358.

Silberman, C.E. *Crisis in the classroom.* New York: Random House, 1970.

Skinner, B.F. *Science and human behavior.* New York: Macmillan, 1953.

Skinner, B.F. Reflections on a decade of teaching machines. *Teacher's College Record,* 1963, 65, 168-177.

Skinner, B.F. *The technology of teaching.* New York: Appleton-Century-Crofts, 1968.

Snow, R.E. Unfinished Pygmalion. *Contemporary Psychology,* 1969, 14, 197-199.

Solomon, R.L. Punishment. *American Psychologist,* 1964, 19, 239-253.

Solomon, R.W., & Wahler, R.G. Peer reinforcement control of classroom problem behavior. *Journal of Applied Behavior Analysis,* 1973, 6, 49-56.

Spradlin, J.E., & Girardeau, F.L. The behavior of moderately and severely retarded persons. In N.R. Ellis (Ed.), *International review of research in mental retardation* (Vol. 1). New York: Academic Press, 1966, pp. 257-298.

Sprague, E., & Taylor, P.W. (Eds.), *Knowledge and value.* New York: Harcourt, Brace & Co., 1959.

Staats, A. *Development, use, and social extensions of reinforcer systems in the solution of human problems.* Paper presented at a conference on behavior modification. January, 1969, Honolulu, Hawaii.

Subotnik, L. Spontaneous remission: Fact or artifact? *Psychological Bulletin,* 1972, 77, 32-48.

Surratt, P.R., Ulrich, R.E., & Hawkins, R.P. An elementary student as a behavioral engineer. *Journal of Applied Behavior Analysis,* 1969, 2, 85-92.

Thomas, D.A., Becker, W.C., & Armstrong, M. Production and elimination of disruptive classroom behavior by systematically varying teacher's attention. *Journal of Applied Behavior Analysis,* 1968, 1, 35-45.

Thomas, D.A., Nielsen, L.J., Kuypers, D.S., & Becker, W.C. Social reinforcement and remedial instruction in the elimination of a classroom behavior problem. *The Journal of Special Education,* 1968, 2, 291-305.

Thoresen, C.E., & Mahoney, M.J. *Behavioral self-control.* New York: Holt, Rinehart & Winston, 1974.

Thorndike, R.L. Pygmalion in the classroom: A review. *Teacher's College Record,* 1969, 70, 805-807.

*Time.* Commoner cancer screen; mutagenic screening test for carcino-genicity, 106, Aug. 11, 1975, pp. 45+.

Trickett, E.J., & Moss, R.H. Personal correlates of contrasting environments: Student satisfactions in high school classrooms. *American Journal of Community Psychology,* 1974, 2, 1-12.

Trotter, R.J. Behavior modification: Here, there, and everywhere. *Science News,* 1973, 103(16), 260-263.

Tunney, J.V. How smart do you want your child to be? *McCalls,* October, 1970.

Turkewitz, H., O'Leary, K.D., & Ironsmith, M. Generalization and maintenance of appropriate behavior through self-control. *Journal of Consulting and Clinical Psychology,* 1975, 43, 577-583.

Ulett, G.A., & Goodrich, D.W. *A synopsis of contemporary psychiatry.* St. Louis: C.V. Mosby, 1969.

Ullmann, L.P., & Krasner, L. *Case studies in behavior modification.* New York: Holt, Rinehart, & Winston, 1965.

Ullmann, L.P., & Krasner, L. *A psychological approach to abnormal behavior.* Englewood Cliffs: N.J.: Prentice-Hall, 1969.

Ullmann, L.P., & Krasner, L. *A psychological approach to abnormal behavior.* Second Edition. Englewood Cliffs, N.J.: Prentice-Hall, 1975.

Ulman, J.D., & Klem, J.L. The Excelsior School System (1885 Congressional Entry). Reprinted in *Journal of Applied Behavior Analysis,* 1975, 8, 210.

Ulrich, R., Wallace, F., & Dulaney, S. *Pyramidal instruction: The use of elementary students as teachers of infants.* Unpublished manuscript. Western Michigan University, 1970.

Wahler, R.G. Setting generality: Some specific and general effects of child behavior therapy. *Journal of Applied Behavior Analysis,* 1969, 2, 239-246.

Walters, R.H., Parke, R.D., & Cane, V.A. Timing of punishment and the observation of consequences to others as determinants of response inhibition. *Journal of Experimental Child Psychology,* 1965, 2, 10-30.

Ward, M.H., & Baker, B.L. Reinforcement therapy in the classroom. *Journal of Applied Behavior Analysis,* 1968, 1, 323-328.

Watson, J.B. Psychology as a behaviorist views it. *Psychological Review,* 1913, 20, 158-177.

Watson, J.B., & Rayner, R. Conditioned emotional reactions. *Journal of Experimental Psychology,* 1920, 3, 1-14.

*Webster's Third New International Dictionary* (unabridged). Springfield, Mass.: G. & C. Merriam Company, 1967.

Williams, C.D. The elimination of tantrum behavior by extinction procedures: Case report. *Journal of Abnormal and Social Psychology,* 1959, 59, 269.

Williams, C.F., Gilmore, A.S., & Malpass, L.F. Programmed instruction for culturally deprived slow-learning children. *The Journal of Special Education,* 1968, 2, 421-427.

Willis, J.W., Morris, B., & Crowder, J. A remedial reading technique for disabled readers that employs students as behavioral engineers. *Psychology in the Schools,* 1972, 9, 67-70.

Winett, R.A., Richards, C.S., Krasner, L., & Krasner, M. Child monitored token reading program. *Psychology in the Schools,* 1971, 8, 259-262.

Winett, R.A., & Winkler, R.C. Current behavior modification in the classroom: Be still, be quiet, be docile. *Journal of Applied Behavior Analysis,* 1972, 5, 499-504.

Witmer, H. *Psychiatric interviews with children.* Cambridge, Mass.: Harvard University Press, 1946.

Witmer, L. *The special class for backward children.* Philadelphia: The Psychological Clinic Press, 1911.

Wolf, M.M., Birnbrauer, J.S., Williams, T., & Lawler, J. A note on apparent extinction of vomiting behavior of a retarded child. In L.P. Ullmann & L. Krasner (Eds.), *Case studies in behavior modification.* New York: Holt, Rinehart & Winston, 1965.

Wolpe, J. *Psychotherapy by reciprocal inhibition.* Stanford: Stanford University Press, 1958.

Wolpe, J., & Rachman, S. Psychoanalytic "evidence": A critique based on Freud's case of Little Hans. *Journal of Nervous and Mental Diseases,* 1960, 130, 135-148.

Yates, A.J. *Behavior therapy.* New York: Wiley, 1970.

Yates, A.J. *Theory and practice in behavior therapy.* New York: Wiley, 1975.

Zimmerman, B.J., & Pike, E.O. Effects of modeling and reinforcement on the acquisition and generalization of question-asking behavior. *Child Development,* 1972, 43, 892-907.

Zimmerman, E.H., & Zimmerman, J. The alteration of behavior in a special classroom situation. *Journal of the Experimental Analysis of Behavior,* 1962, 5, 59-60.

# Index

# TITLES IN THE PERGAMON GENERAL PSYCHOLOGY SERIES (Continued)